The *Niʿmatnāma* Manuscript of the Sultans of Mandu

The *Niʿmatnāma* is a late fifteenth-century book of the recipes of the eccentric Sultan of Mandu (Madhya Pradesh), Ghiyath Shahi, collected and added to by his son and successor, Nasir Shah. It contains recipes for cooking a variety of delicacies and epicurean delights, as well as providing remedies and aphrodisiacs for the Sultan and his court. It also includes important sections on the preparation of betel leaves as well as advice on the logistics of hunting expeditions and warfare. The text provides a unique and tantalising account of rarified courtly life in a fifteenth-century Indian Sultanate region.

There is only one known copy of the Sultan's Book of Delights in existence and it is held in the Oriental and India Office Collections of the British Library (BL. Persian 149). The manuscript is illustrated with fifty elegant miniature paintings, most of which show the Sultan, Ghiyath Shahi, observing the women of his court as they prepare and serve him various dishes. The book is fascinating in that the text documents a remarkable stage in the history of Indian cookery whilst the miniatures demonstrate the influence of imported Persian artists on the style of the Indian artists employed in Ghiyath Shahi's academy.

The first few miniatures are painted in a distinctive Shiraz (Southern Iranian) style but, increasingly, the later illustrations show the indigenous styles of book painting found in Central and Western India. They are important as the earliest known example of miniature painting in an Islamic Deccani style. In addition, the text itself is a very early example of written Urdu. For the first time a facsimile of the original text is reproduced for a scholarly audience. Norah M. Titley, the British Library's retired curator of illustrated Persian manuscripts, has translated this exquisite book.

Norah M. Titley is one of the scholars in Britain specialising in the study of Persian language manuscripts and miniature paintings. She began her career in the British Museum's Department of Oriental Manuscripts in 1950 and retired as the British Library's curator of illustrated Persian manuscripts in 1983. Since retiring, she has worked intensively on translating the *Niʿmatnāma*.

RoutledgeCurzon Studies in South Asia
Editor: Michael Willis
The British Museum

RoutledgeCurzon publishes a monograph series in association with *The Society for South Asian Studies*, London.

Boats of South Asia
Seán McGrail

Muslim Architecture of South India
Mehrdad Shokoohy

The Partition of Bengal and Assam
Contour of Freedom
Bidyut Chakrabarty

The *Niʿmatnāma* Manuscript of the Sultans of Mandu
The Sultan's Book of Delights
Translated by Norah M. Titley

The *Niʿmatnāma* Manuscript of the Sultans of Mandu

The Sultan's Book of Delights

Translated by Norah M. Titley

LONDON AND NEW YORK

First published 2005
by Routledge
2 Park Square, Milton Park, Abingdon, Oxon OX14 4RN

Simultaneously published in the USA and Canada
by Routledge
711 Third Ave, New York, NY 10017

First issued in paperback 2012
Routledge is an imprint of the Taylor & Francis Group

Typeset in Times by RefineCatch Ltd, Bungay, Suffolk

British Library Cataloguing in Publication Data
A catalogue record for this book is available from the British Library

Library of Congress Cataloging in Publication Data
A catalog record for this book has been requested

ISBN13: 978-0-415-65046-5 (PBK)

ISBN13: 978-0-415-35059-4 (HBK)

Contents

Preface vii
Introduction ix
Description of the miniatures xv

The Book of Delights 1

Glossary 95
Bibliography 111
Index 113

The miniatures

Facsimile of the manuscript
(reads from right to left, from the back of the book)

Preface

The *Niʿmatnāma*, or Book of Delights of Sultan Ghiyath Shahi, who reigned at Mandu in Malwa (Central India) from AD 1469 to 1500, is a most unusual work from several different aspects. The unique manuscript is in the India Office Collections in the British Library. Although there is a long history of the editing or publishing of manuscripts on medieval Indo-Muslim politics, war, political organisation and, more recently, social history, there is very little on the domestic arts and the life of households, even of the ruling classes, nor does the *Niʿmatnāma* appear to have been used as source material by authors on Indian cookery. In addition to the contents, interest lies in the date of compilation (*c.* AD 1500), the language (one of the earliest manuscripts to include written Urdu), the illustrations (showing strong Persian influence in the early miniatures, becoming more Indianised in the later ones) and the renowned eccentricity of Ghiyath Shahi, which all add up to a fascinating work.

Robert Skelton first drew attention to the *Niʿmatnāma* in an article published in 1959 in which he deals in depth with the background history of both text and miniatures. It was this article that inspired a wish in the present translator to find out what went into the recipes, whether they were for food, drink, medicine, perfume, betel chews or aphrodisiacs, as well as the nature of the necessities so vital to a successful hunting expedition or on the battlefield.

My thanks are due to Mr J. P. Losty for his patient and meticulous editing, to Dr B. Brend for photographs of Mandu, to Dr H. Ginsburg for practical help, to Dr Peter Hardy for timely assistance, to Dr M. I. Waley and to Dr J. Seyller for help in reading the opening and closing inscriptions, and to Mr R. Skelton whose pioneering work provided the inspiration.

Mr G. Shaw, Director of the Library's Oriental and African Collections, generously agreed to fund the scanning of the complete manuscript for publication. Without additional support by the Society for South Asian Studies, publication would not have been possible, and gratitude is due to both bodies that this unique manuscript can now reach a wider readership via this translation and facsimile of the text.

Norah M. Titley
Angmering, 2004

Introduction

After the sack of Delhi by Timur (Tamerlane), in AD 1398, which heralded the collapse of centralised Muslim rule in India, Malwa in Central India became one of the independent states with its own rulers and its capital at Mandu. Ghiyath Shahi succeeded his father, Mahmud Shah, as ruler of Malwa in 1469 and immediately 'put out the hand of liberality and lavishness from the sleeve of generosity and made all sections of the people satisfied and grateful'. An eccentric and a bon viveur, his method of enjoying the pleasures of life is amply demonstrated by the contents and illustrations of the *Niʿmatnāma* or Book of Delights. The manuscript (*IO Isl. Ms. 149*) of this work has long been one of the treasures of the India Office Library (now included in the Oriental and India Office Collections of the British Library), since its discovery and publication by Robert Skelton in 1959.[1] Datable to 1495–1505, it appears to have covered the period before Ghiyath Shahi's death in 1500 and the early years of the reign of his son and successor, Nasir Shah, who probably added a supplement. It now bears the title *Niʿmatnāma-i Nāṣir al-Dīn Shāhī.*

The work consists of recipes for food and drink, for the preparation and distillation of perfumes and essences and also for aphrodisiacs and remedies for illnesses. There is a fairly long section, with illustrations, on the preparation and benefits of betel chewing as well as advice on what to take into battle and instructions concerning hunting expeditions. Ingredients for recipes and remedies are varied and numerous, and include gum, resin, fruit, leaves, bark, stems, roots, tubers, juice, nectar, pollen, kernels, and nuts from plants and trees as well as exotica such as bamboo manna and the crushed perfumed shell of a freshwater mollusc. Recipes for perfumes also include aromatic pastes, powders and pellets. Essences and flavours are also dealt with. There are stern warnings regarding the danger of eating certain fish or of chewing betel when suffering from specific illnesses, and there is a long list of foods not to be eaten with milk. However, the greater majority of the recipes are of positive benefit, to the extent that they sometimes end with

1 Skelton 1959.

comments such as 'this is delicious!' or 'this is a favourite of Ghiyath Shahi.' It is remarkable how many of the cooking recipes are still in use today, nearly five hundred years later.

In his accession speech, Ghiyath Shahi announced that, having supported his father, Mahmud Shah, for thirty-four years, he had decided not to extend his kingdom nor spend his time on the cares of state in general. He proposed to give himself up to seeking pleasure and enjoyment in the hope that his subjects would share it with him. He made his son, Nasir Shah, his heir and left him virtually to run the kingdom while he amused himself and filled his palace with musicians, beautiful female slaves and the daughters of rajas and high officials. Each girl was taught an art or profession, according to ability, including dancing, singing, reading, recitation, flute playing and, for a few, the art of wrestling. The city of Mandu was not for nothing known at this time as Shadiyabad (City of Joy). Besides the girls who entertained him, Ghiyath Shahi set up a female army of five hundred Abyssinian slaves who were clad in armour and armed with swords and shields. Some of the most intelligent of the slave girls were trained in various kinds of learning and would join Ghiyath Shahi at his meals every day. Others were trained in administration or to run factories or to act as accountants. It is recorded (and exaggeration must be allowed for) that, all in all, he had sixteen thousand slave girls.

Most of the fifty miniatures in the Book of Delights include a few of Ghiyath Shahi's companions, slaves, attendants and cooks while he, himself, is usually shown taking a keen interest in the activities, whether it is cooking or the preparation of betel or perfumes or else leading the way on horseback out hunting. His interest and benevolence extended to the palace livestock, food being placed near the holes of rats and mice at his command, whilst the tame pigeons and parrots were also generously catered for.

Following the tradition of many Muslim rulers, Ghiyath Shahi maintained a studio of artists and those concerned with book production. The few surviving illustrated manuscripts that were produced at Mandu during this period demonstrate the influence of Persian artists working there. After Robert Skelton's article appeared in 1959, another illustrated manuscript from Malwa of the same period and written in the same bold *naskh* was discovered in the British Library (*Or. 3299*).[2] A glossary of rare words found in ancient Persian poetry (*Miftaḥ al-fuẓāla*), it was compiled in 1468–9 by Muhammad ibn Da'ud ibn Muhammad ibn Mahmud Shadiyabadi, the latter part of his name indicating he worked at Mandu (or Shadiyabad). The manuscript of this work, datable to about 1490–1500, appears to pre-date the *Niʿmatnāma* or Book of Delights, as the 187 small miniatures are strongly influenced by the Shiraz 'Turkman' style of the second half of the fifteenth century. One of the illustrations in the glossary (*folio 146b, Plate 53*) illustrating royal golden shoes, appears to be of Ghiyath Shahi accepting

2 See Titley 1964–5.

them, because the king is shown with the impressive moustache that is evident in all the *Niʿmatnāma* miniatures featuring him. In the latter manuscript he is also wearing his golden shoes (*folio 189b, Plate 51*).

The British Library is most fortunate to include these two manuscripts in the collections as they belong to such a small group of known Indian Sultanate works extant. They were joined more recently by a third, a manuscript (*Or. 13718*) of the *ʿAjāʾīb aṣ-ṣanāʾī*, a Persian translation from Arabic of *Kitāb fī maʾrifat al-ḥiyal al-handasiyya* (Book of Knowledge of Ingenious Mechanical Devices) by Ibn ar-Razzaz al-Jazari. The translator was Muhammad ibn Da'ud Shadiyabadi, the author of the *Miftaḥ al-fuẓāla* above, and the manuscript which is dated 1509 is the fair copy. It has approximately 175 illustrations of the automata beloved by various medieval Muslim rulers, but in a fairly crude style.[3] Only one other royal illustrated manuscript from Mandu is known, a copy dated 1502–3 of the Persian classic text the *Būstān* of Saʿdi, which is now in the National Museum, New Delhi (*Ms. 48.6/4*). This highly finished manuscript has forty-three miniatures, in a style which shows dependence not on Shiraz but on Herat, but this time without much obvious Indian stylistic influence.[4]

In the fifty *Niʿmatnāma* illustrations, the Persian 'Turkman' influence from Shiraz is still apparent in the miniatures, particularly in those at the beginning of the manuscript, but they become more and more Indianised, especially in respect of costume, architecture and the drawing of faces in profile (as opposed to the usual half-profile seen in Persian styles of painting). The *Niʿmatnāma* is very important in the study of miniature painting as the illustrations demonstrate one of the earliest and most complete mingling of Indian and Persian styles.

In some instances, especially in the first few miniatures, a minute word has been written in a cursive hand above or by the side of the miniature, possibly as a guide to the artist, indicating the particular activity to be illustrated, e.g. the word *sanbūsa* is written alongside the miniature illustrating the preparation of samosas. Sometimes specific subjects mentioned in the text are portrayed, whilst others appear to be general scenes in which Ghiyath Shahi is supervising the cooks. In his article in *Marg*, which first published the manuscript in 1959, Robert Skelton identified two different artists.

Also of great interest is the fact that it is written in a mixture of Urdu and Farsi (Persian), a very early example of written Urdu in which all the words are written in the Persian form without the four dots that much later were used to distinguish purely Urdu characters. There is no distinction made between the characters for 'k' and 'g', whilst 'r' and 'l' are interchangeable, as are 'b' and 'p'. Like the glossary mentioned above, it is written in the bold *naskh* hand so characteristic of Mandu calligraphy.

3 Described in Losty 1982, no. 43.

4 Published by R. Ettinghausen in 1959. See also Losty 1982, no. 42.

New recipes in the text are indicated in two ways: the leading words are written in red and the character *ba* appears in the margin. There is little order in the way the recipes follow each other, and there is a great amount of repetition: for instance, recipes for sherbet may unexpectedly be interspersed with those for soup as if the thought of liquid had jogged the compiler's memory. The manuscript refers to Ghiyath Shahi's favourite recipes in a way that suggests he was still alive when compilation began. His son, Nasir Shah, appears to have had the work continued as the illuminated heading on folio 162b gives the title 'The Book of the *Niʿmatnāma* of Nasir Shah'. The text following refers to Nasir Shah's own favourite recipes as well as those of his father Ghiyath Shahi and his grandfather Mahmud Shah.

The manuscript has three different foliation systems, viz. (i) a modern foliation system written in the East India Company's library (India Office Library), (ii) Farsi numerals, (iii) written out words in Farsi. The modern system runs straight through from 1 to 196. The Farsi numbers and words (1 to 207) correspond with each other, and their absence indicates where most gaps occur. These gaps are confirmed by the catchwords in the lower margin of the verso not tallying with the first word of the following recto. They amount to eleven missing in all, as follows: between 16b and 17a (1 missing); 17b–18a (1); 19b–20a (1); 37b–38a (2); 46b–47a (1); 56b–57a (1); 60b–61a (1); 67b–68a (1); 151b–152a (2). In addition, in four further instances, although the Farsi foliation is uninterrupted, the catchword does not correspond to the first word of the next (recto) page, as follows: 79b–80a; 85b–86a; 126b–127a; 131b–132a. These four folios must have been extracted before the manuscript entered the royal library where it was foliated and had not been noticed by the foliator. The other eleven folios were extracted after it had left the library, but before it entered the East India Company's library. Additionally, the catchword between folios 5b and 6a is *slightly* suspect. One or more miniatures must be missing, especially between folios 47a–56b and 61a–67b. Folio 153a has no Farsi foliation numbers. A note on folio 162a in Farsi reads: 'The assembled *Niʿmatnāma* 207 pages'. There are fifty surviving miniatures, which are discussed below.

There are several inscriptions and seals. On folio 1a:

1 'The book describing the cooking of Ghiyath Shahi's samosas.'
2 'O King of the cockroaches!' (*yā kabīkaj*, in a bold *naskh*). The same inscription is repeated on folio 196a in a similarly bold hand just at the end of the text.[5]
3 In a good, possibly Mughal, hand: 'On medicine, in *naskh* writing [and] in a crimson binding. [It] entered into the Royal Library from the

5 According to Steingass (1957) this is frequently inscribed on the first page of books in India (and elsewhere) under the superstitious belief that, out of respect for the name of their king, the cockroaches will spare the book and leave it undamaged. Here they are playing safe by putting it at the end of the text as well.

possession of Malik Almās on the 24th day of the month of *Rabīʿ al-avval*, AH 1044 (24th July 1634).'

4 A faded inscription stating that this is the *Niʿmatnāma* of Nasir Shahi dealing with the methods for cooking food and aphrodisiacs (*hashvār*) and the preparation of rosewater (*gulāb*), spirits (*ʿaraq*) and perfumes (*aṭṭārī'āt*).

5 The red seal of the 'E. I. Comp.'s Library'.

At the end of the manuscript, on the final folio (folio 196b), is a short inscription in a cursive hand, of which only the date can be discerned: 24th of the month of *Shaʿbān*, AH 978 (*c*. 29th June 1570), together with another 'E. I. Comp.'s Library' seal. On the flyleaf recto (unfoliated) appear the following:

1 'Tippoo MS' (in pencil) and '149' (in red), written by the East India Company's librarian.

2 A repeat of the inscription on f.1a, more crudely written, referring to the *Niʿmatnāma* 'on the art of medicine', but with the date of being taken into the Royal Library given as the 30th day of the month of *Rabīʿ al-avval*, AH 1044 (30th July 1634), six days later than the inscription on folio 1a. It is followed by the letters of the Arabic alphabet, crudely written, leaving out the characters for 'p', 'ch', 'ḥ' and 'g' (which are found in Persian but not Arabic manuscripts, being substituted here by 'b', 'j', 'h' and 'k'). In a big bold hand is written the title of the work, with *duvum* ('second') above it. Above are two round seals, which as yet defy interpretation. One of them is a Mughal period seventeenth-century seal, the other is almost certainly from its appearance (circular, with a decorative rim) a Sultanate period seal.[6]

The manuscript may have been taken from Mandu in AD 1562 when the Mughal Emperor Akbar defeated the last independent Sultan of Mandu, Baz Bahadur. There is some evidence that the manuscript was taken into the Mughal library – an inscription on folio 1a refers to the manuscript entering the Royal Library (presumably the Mughal one) in AD 1634. Later it appears to have travelled south, since a note on the flyleaf records it as a 'Tippoo MS', i.e. as having been in the library of Tipu Sultan of Mysore when his capital of Seringapatam was captured by the British in 1799. It is not, however, included in the catalogue of that collection published by Charles Stewart in 1809, and its precise route into the East India Company's library is mysterious.

6 John Seyller writes in a personal communication: 'All in all, the only indication that I see for a Mughal provenance is the use of "duwum", a word used in an elaborate system of qualitative classification that I have seen nowhere else. Conversely, the Mughals did not normally use "amirat" (royal) to indicate their library, but I do not know who else would have claimed to have one at this point. Manuscripts in Deccani collections normally had seals impressed near their inscriptions.'

Apart from the fact that folios had been removed, there had been some damage to the pages also before the manuscript came to London, particularly towards the end. Damp and other calamities had caused smudging, obliteration of words and, worst of all, holes in the paper. Restoration has been very skilfully carried out by the British Library's Conservation Department, but even they could not restore words lost by holing or by complete obliteration.

The text itself is also difficult to understand at times, is often abbreviated (where the author assumes knowledge now lost on the part of his reader), and uses many now obscure terms. It rarely gives quantities, but sometimes gets them wrong. The reader who wants to try out these recipes must be prepared to experiment, but the translator takes no responsibility for the results. Despite the difficulties, this text offers the sorts of insights into medieval Indian life given by few other works of the period.

Description of the miniatures

Plates 1 and 2 Mandu

Folio 4b Section on the use of milk in *kashk*, pottage, and the feeding of cows. The high horizon, heavy vegetation are features of the Persian Shiraz Turkman style of the late fifteenth century. The small cursive inscription *gāv u shīr* (cow and milk) above the top margin are probably instructions to the artist. (Plate 3)

Folio 5a The small inscription is *kās*, cup, bowl, or *kāsa*, a royal meal. This section concerns the preparation of samosas and *lās*, meat stew. Ghiyath Shahi is enthroned, wearing a crown and attended by four servants. (Plate 4)

Folio 6b The small inscription just below the throne is simply *ʿalaf*, food or provender. The section is concerned with the cooking of rice or pulses with milk. Ghiyath Shahi barefooted has seven attendants and is watching the cook in the foreground with his cooking pots. (Plate 5)

Folio 8b The small inscription appears to be *ṭalīb*, teaching or instruction. Ghiyath Shahi is pointing towards the cook who is handing a dish of food to one attendant, while four others are standing near the throne, holding dishes and watching procedures. Ghiyath Shahi, crowned and barefooted, is in a blue-domed pavilion, which has a circular pool in the foreground. The section is explaining the ingredients needed for *baṛa*, pulse balls fried in oil, dried in the sun and used for flavouring. (Plate 6)

Folio 11a The small inscription appears to be *mādab*, feast or entertainment. Again a garden pavilion with typical Mandu architecture of a tower topped by a small dome. Ghiyath Shahi is wearing informal clothes, seated on cushions with the usual attendants holding dishes. A female cook kneels by the stove in the foreground, to the left of a large pool or cascade. The section is concerned with bread making. (Plate 7)

Folio 14a No small inscription. Ghiyath Shahi is seated in a tiled garden pavilion with trees in the background and a round pool in the centre. A male cook attends to the stove, on which he is stirring and fanning a cooking pot.

Ghiyath Shahi is gesturing towards the cook. There are eight attendants. The section concerns methods for cooking meat. (Plate 8)

Folio 18a The small inscription appears to be *randhān*, the preparation of food. Again Ghiyath Shahi is seated in a garden pavilion, gesturing towards the two male cooks kneeling by their stove. Pink tiled courtyard in the foreground with a stream running through it. One of the cooks is chopping meat. The section is concerned with soup and skewered meat (*sīkh*). (Plate 9)

Folio 23a The small inscription is *taghḍiya*, food, nourishment. Ghiyath Shahi is seated in a garden pavilion which has a large blue dome. Two cooks are near the stove in the foreground, one is chopping meat, the other has his hand on the pot lid. The meat, *lās*, hashed meat broth, or *yakhnī*, soup, section. (Plate 10)

Folio 25b The small inscription is obscure, possibly *mādab*, feast or entertainment. Ghiyath Shahi is seated on a divan in a garden, near a small white-domed pavilion which has an inscription 'The Sultan, the Just' over the door. Ghiyath Shahi appears to be giving instructions. His dark cook is pouring (probably) oil into a pan on the stove. A stream and ducks are in the foreground. Section of rice recipes. (Plate 11)

Folio 29a Two small inscriptions (i) *ṭarā*, fresh vegetables, and (ii) *shamaṭ*, potherbs. Ghiyath Shahi is seated in a tiled courtyard, with two cooks with the stove and pots in the foreground. Stream with ducks. Recipe below the miniature is for rustic (vegetarian) food. (Plate 12)

Folio 32a Small inscription *gāgar*, water pot. Ghiyath Shahi is in a courtyard in front of a blue-domed garden pavilion. Cook has two pots on tripods and is chopping ingredients. This section for rice or pulse water, *pīchha*. (Plate 13)

Folio 35b Small inscription is *lanvās*, i.e. *lās*, stew or meaty broth. Ghiyath Shahi in a white-domed pavilion courtyard. The cook who is holding a soup ladle has two pots on tripods. Male and female attendants. The section deals with ingredients for soup. (Plate 14)

Folio 40b No small inscription. Ghiyath Shahi seated in a garden pavilion, being offered dishes by female attendants. Section for congee recipes. (Plate 15)

Folio 44b No small inscription. Ghiyath Shahi is seated on a throne under a canopy in a garden, the cook and stove are in the foreground. This appears to be by a different artist who has placed Ghiyath Shahi's attendants in a row, unlike the other compositions in which they are depicted in groups or singly. The method of drawing the attendants' heads in a strict row is also to be seen in *Or. 1403*, a copy of the *Shāhnāma* in the British Library, dated 1438 and influenced by an earlier Shiraz style. No provenance is given for *Or. 1403* but it was undoubtedly produced in India, as details such as lotus flowers, the distinctive yellow pigment and faces in profile all point to its origin. This section gives recipes for *bhāt*, boiled rice. (Plate 16)

Folio 51a No small inscription. Ghiyath Shahi is seated on a stool, one of his woman companions next to him. A garden scene with a stream with lotus plants in the foreground. Male cook holding a ladle kneels by his stove. The section deals with *kaṛhī*, chickpea pulse, sour milk and spices recipe. (Plate 17)

Folio 54a No small inscription. Ghiyath Shahi seated on a stool watching his cooks at work out of doors. The pot on top of a blazing stove is being stirred. The miniature appears in the section concerned with buttermilk recipes. (Plate 18)

Folio 66a No small inscription. Ghiyath Shahi seated on a stool under a tree out of doors at night, watching his two cooks. A section on sherbet. (Plate 19)

Folio 71b Small inscription: *raṣā*, soup or gravy. Ghiyath Shahi in a garden pavilion watching his two cooks preparing meat, one is cutting a haunch with his knife, the other is chopping meat. Both men have Persian features whereas the two women with Ghiyath Shahi have Indian features and dress, and large earrings. The section concerns *qīma*, minced meat. (Plate 20)

Folio 76a Small inscription ?*manzar var* (unclear) below the left-hand cooking pot. Ghiyath Shahi being offered a cup. Two female cooks, one ladling food from the cooking pot onto a plate, the other cook supervising the stove. Unusual plain white landscape. Section on sherbet and soft food. (Plate 21)

Folio 79b No small inscription. Ghiyath Shahi on a stool under red awning in a garden at night supervising his cooks, one of whom, a dark girl, is blowing up the fire with a hollow tube. The other cook has greens or potherbs. The recipes here are for greens and potherbs. (Plate 22)

Folio 83b Small inscription *sanbūsa*, samosa. Ghiyath Shahi seated on a stool in a garden is being offered a dish, possibly of samosas. A cook is frying them over a stove, while another is placing them on a round dish. Section on recipes for *baṛa* and samosas. (Plate 23)

Folio 88b No small inscription. Ghiyath Shahi standing in a doorway pointing towards his cook who is stirring a pot. A gold and blue metal plate on the (damaged) tiled floor. The section is on medicinal food. (Plate 24)

Folio 91b No small inscription. Ghiyath Shahi out of doors, in white (night?) clothes, reclining on a divan, being fanned and massaged. There is a night sky and a background of heavy vegetation. The section is on instructions for a healthy way of life. (Plate 25)

Folio 94a No small inscription. Ghiyath Shahi out of doors apparently in discussion with three of his attendants. In the foreground a flask is being

is concerned with the preparation of scented oils. Two men working in the foreground, one blowing the stove fire. (Plate 44)

Folio 171b (slightly damaged) Ghiyath Shahi seated on a stool under an awning out of doors at night. The section is concerned with method of distilling camphor and also of distilling rosewater and other flower perfumes. Ten glass distillery flasks in the foreground. (Plate 45)

Folio 174b (damaged) No small inscription. Ghiyath Shahi seated in a tent. The method for distilling perfumes and frankincense is described. The servant is removing the clay pot of frankincense from the stove with tongs as described in the text. Other attendants are offering a gold dish and a flask. A sword bearer stands on the left. (Plate 46)

Folio 177b (damaged) No small inscription. Ghiyath Shahi riding towards a group of people followed by his mounted parasol bearer. People in the group are offering him cups, possibly of sherbet, with which this section is concerned. Cook kneeling by a stove is taking the lid off a large metal cooking pot. (Plate 47)

Folio 180b (damaged) No small inscription. Ghiyath Shahi sitting on a carpet in a walled garden with nine gold and ceramic dishes of food before him. Other dishes are carried by four attendants. A servant in the foreground is dishing up more food. The section is for ways of cooking meat. (Plate 48)

Folio 183b (damaged) No small inscription. Ghiyath Shahi enthroned beneath a canopy out of doors. Usual dishes and flasks in the foreground. A section on *pūrī* bread stuffed with minced meat. (Plate 49)

Folio 186b (damaged) No small inscription. Ghiyath Shahi seated on a stool in conversation with dark female companion. Stove and cooking pots in the foreground. Scene out of doors. Recipes for *kūfta*, minced meat balls. (Plate 50)

Folio 189b (damaged) No small inscription. Ghiyath Shahi standing under a canopy out of doors, his dark female companion has her arm round his shoulder. The recipes are for *khīs*, flummery. A cook in the foreground is rolling or crushing something on a board. Attendants include a sword bearer. Ghiyath Shahi is wearing gold shoes, which are seen being presented to him in the *Miftaḥ al-fuẓāla* (*Or. 3299, f.146b*). (Plates 51 and 53)

Folio 192b (damaged) No small inscription. Ghiyath Shahi fishing, seated on a stool holding a fishing rod. He is turning round to his dark female companion who is offering him what appears to be a betel chew. Small rectangular pool with three fish. An attendant is removing a fish from the fishing line and another servant is kneeling in the foreground holding a fish. Water cooler being fanned in left foreground. (Plate 52)

The Book of Delights

(*f.1b*) Take a cooking pot, either gold or silver or brass and put it into another cooking pot of copper or iron. Put in water and add *'alaf*[1] so that the water comes over the *'alaf*. Put a lid on it and seal it firmly. Take fresh cow's milk that is not mixed with water, cook it by the method of fanning with a piece of pure cloth on a stick. Take the milk up in that cloth and knead it on a plate, hour by hour, by the same method as in kneading bread, until the milk on the plate thickens. Remove it and, using an iron utensil, pick up the milk. Prepare the samosas and fill (*f.2a*) them with that which has been described.

Another kind of Ghiyath Shahi's samosas: take five *sīrs* of good grains of pure wheat, put one *sīr* of sweet-smelling ghee (*rūghan*) into it and grind it by hand and pound it with a wooden pestle. When it is well-mixed, prepare slices of *māhīcha* paste the thickness of a finger and fry them in ghee. Put the fried paste amongst roses so that it acquires a sweet smell, then knead it by hand and crush it so that it becomes fragmented. Add potherbs, musk, camphor, cardamoms and cloves and mix them all together. Stuff the samosas, filling them very full and pick them up by the hand.[2] They are very delicious and (*f.2b*) good.

Another kind of Ghiyath Shahi's samosas: take well-cooked mince with the same amount of minced onion and flavour it with dried ginger (*zanjabīl*). Having ground a quarter of that with half a *tūlcha* of garlic, mix them all together. Grind three *tūlchas* of saffron in rosewater and mix it with the mince. Remove the pulp from aubergines and, having mixed it with the mince, stuff the samosas and fry them in ghee. They can be either of thin dry bread or of fine flour bread or of uncooked dough. Cook each of the three kinds of samosas, they are delicious and good.

Another kind of Ghiyath Shahi's samosas: take finely minced deer meat and flavour ghee (*f.3a*) with fenugreek and, having mixed the mince with saffron, put it in the ghee. Roast salt and cumin together. Having added cumin, cloves, coriander and a quarter of a *rattī* of musk to the mince, cook it well. Put half the minced onion and a quarter of the minced dried ginger into the meat. When it has become well-cooked, put in rosewater. Take it off and stuff the samosas. Make a hole in the samosa with a stick and fry it in sweet-smelling ghee and serve it (*when*) tender. By the same method samosas of any kind of meat that is desired, can be made.

The method for samosas of tender meat of mountain sheep (*parbatī*) or of deer: mince (*the meat*) finely (*f.3b*) and add turmeric, cumin, fenugreek, coriander, cardamom and cloves and mix them together. Flavour sweet-smelling ghee with asafoetida. When the ghee has become well-flavoured,

1 Obscure; according to Steingass, *'alaf* is provender or food.
2 i.e. eat them with the fingers.

put the mince in it and leave it so that it becomes well-cooked. Add lime juice and pepper and then put in a quarter of a *sīr* of dried ginger (*zanjabīl*) and one *sīr* of chopped onion and remove it. Add one *rattī* of camphor and one *rattī* of musk. Prepare a few large samosas and a few small ones the size of one mouthful. Having stuffed them with the mince, fry them in sweet-smelling ghee and, when they are to be eaten, sprinkle them with vinegar or lime juice. Serve them and eat them.

(*f.4a*) Another method: buy a yellow cow or a black cow, feed it on sugarcane, green grass, cotton seeds and date sugar and also coconut, nutmeg, cinnamon, pulses, partridge eggs and bamboo leaves, or else use a sheep or a cow buffalo. Take the milk from it, boil it and skim off the cream that rises to the top. Drink the milk lukewarm. Strain the cream in a cloth and, having added wheat flour to it, prepare *kashk*.[3] Fry it in ghee and add a quantity of camphor, cardamoms, cloves, date sugar and round peppers. It is very tasty.[4]

(*f.4b, with a miniature*) Another of Ghiyath Shahi's samosas: mix together well-cooked mince with the same amount of minced onion and chopped dried ginger, a quarter of those, and half a *tūlcha* of ground garlic and, having ground three *tūlchas* of saffron in rosewater, mix it with the mince together with aubergine pulp (*f.5a, with a miniature*). Stuff the samosas and fry (*them*) in ghee. Whether made from thin coarse flour bread or from fine flour bread or from uncooked dough, any of the three (*can be used*) for cooking samosas, they are delicious.

Also a stew (*lanvās, i.e. lās*) of Ghiyath Shahi: take thin pieces of meat and flavour them with the essence of asafoetida and fenugreek. Mix the meat with some turmeric (*f.5b*) and cook it until it is very tender. Put plenty of sweet-smelling ghee on it and, having added some cardamoms and cloves and a little camphor and rice flour, cook it. When it is well-cooked add very large pieces of onion and big pieces of dried ginger and scatter dry ground pepper on it and sprinkle it with lime juice. It is delicious.

Another plain rice of Ghiyath Shahi: heat palm sugar sherbet and when it comes to the boil, add the rice. When it is well-cooked, take it off and put cardamoms, camphor and cloves into the water which has been strained from the rice . . . (*missing folio(s)*)[5] . . . (*f.6a*) . . . having stitched together those leaves, cool the milk. It is delicious.

Again, in the making of *baṛa*[6] with milk: having soaked rice in water, grind it finely. When the milk has become hot in the cooking pot, put the rice flour

3 A thick pottage made of milk and flour, here obviously so thick as to be almost solid.

4 Note in the top margin: 'viands, victuals.'

5 The catchword on f.5b is slightly suspect, and partly obliterated.

6 *Baṛa* or *baṛī* is normally a cake made of ground pulse, allowed to ferment, and then deep fried in ghee – the modern *wāda*. Here rice flour is used instead.

into it. If there are five *sīrs* of milk, then put in four *sīrs* of flour and leave it so that it becomes well-cooked. Take it off and add one handful of fine white flour to it and, having prepared the *baṛa*, cook it in ghee. Put potherbs, camphor, musk, cardamoms and cloves on the pulse and also add perfume prepared from the scent of flowers.

Again the method for milk rice: boil the milk well and add well-washed rice to it (*f.6b, with a miniature*) or put in those kernels of wheat that are very white or put in *sarūla* flour[7] or put in finely cut *māhīcha* paste and add camphor, musk, rosewater and a small amount of white ambergris. When it is well-cooked, take it off. It must not be too thick, nor equally, too thin, when cooked.

(*f.7a*) Another kind of milk rice: well-boil five *sīrs* of milk. Grind half a *sīr* of washed rice with milk, strain it through a cloth and put it into that milk. Add some potherbs that are not too sweet and, when cooked, do not shrink. Add sour-orange *taranj* pulp which has been de-pipped. If the orange is not sweet and produces acid, then wash the sour-orange pulp in water so that the acidity runs out. Put the pulp into the milk and, having added rosewater, camphor and musk, take it off and cool it. It is delicious.

Another kind of *baṛa* with *māst* (sour coagulated milk). Tie the *māst* in a cloth (*f.7b*) and shake it well so that it thickens, then add one handful of fine white flour. Having prepared the *baṛa* and cooked it in sweet-smelling ghee, fry it. Put cardamoms, camphor, musk, potherbs and cloves on the *baṛa* as well as perfume prepared from sweet-smelling flowers.

(*f.7b, marginal note:*) Another kind of *baṛa* from bean pulse (*māsh*): having soaked the pulse in water, throw away the liquid. Then having dried it (*the pulse*), grind it. Make the dough gradually, by degrees, so that the flour grains are well-kneaded. Then in the usual way, having mixed it with potherbs, cook it in well-flavoured ghee.[8]

Again *kasīrū*[9] *baṛa* cake: wash five *sīrs* of pulse (*dāl māsh*) well and grind it finely. Then having ground fifty *kasīrū* tubers, mix them (*with the pulse*) and put five *sīrs* of fresh butter into it and knead it by hand, then rub in some asafoetida and salt with the palm of the hand. Cook it in sweet-smelling ghee. Put camphor, musk, potherbs, cardamoms and cloves on the *baṛa* as well as perfume prepared from the scent of flowers.

(*f.8a*) Keep some pieces of this *baṛa* which have not been sweetened. Prepare

7 *Sarūla* are small balls of paste made from a confection of flour mixed with sugar, ghee, poppy seed, dates and almonds and then boiled in milk. Perhaps here meaning flour suitable for making *sarūla*?

8 End of marginal note.

9 *Kasīrū*: *Cyperus tuberosus* root which is either ground or else eaten as a fruit.

good *kaṛhi*[10] either with *dūgh*[11] sprinkled on it or perfumed *kānjī* (congee) and put this same *baṛa* into it. After the *baṛa* has been put into the *kaṛhi* or *dūgh* or congee, eat it immediately before it dissolves. Again, for yam[12] *baṛa*: grind the yams well and add one handful of fine white flour to them. Fry the *baṛa* in sweet-smelling ghee and add potherbs, camphor, musk, cardamoms, pepper and ground cloves. By the same method make red yam *baṛa* and, also by the same method make jackfruit (*kathal*) *baṛa* and also by the same method mango *baṛa*.[13]

Also for a better method of preparing pulse (*māsh*) *baṛa* (*f.8b, with a miniature*), make sour milk (*qatagh*) with tamarind and add potherbs, rose-water, camphor, musk, cardamoms and cloves and flavour it with the scent of oil of aloes. Put the *baṛa* into very hot water, then take it out and put it into the *qatagh*. By the same method prepare *mūng baṛa*. Another recipe for *māsh baṛa* and milk: (*f.9a*) wash the pulse thoroughly, grind it finely and mix it with asafoetida, onion, dried ginger, cumin and fenugreek and prepare the *baṛa*. Make another *baṛa* with fresh butter and put butter on it, prepare another *baṛa* from pulse and put fresh butter on it and thus place pieces of *baṛa*, layer by layer – one layer with butter and one layer with pulse, one on top of the other and then fry it in ghee. Heat up the milk and put potherbs, camphor, musk and rosewater into it. Keep some of the milk unsweetened but in both recipes use very hot milk. Put fermented *dūgh* on the milk, (*f.9b*) thus creating a layer of *māst* and a layer of that *baṛa*. It is delicious.

Another kind of *kaṛhi baṛa*: take sour *dūgh* and having washed (*some*) rice well, grind it and put it into the *dūgh*. Roast fresh coriander, cumin and fenugreek and put that in. Add ground cardamoms, onions, cloves and fresh ginger. Boil the *kaṛhi* well and add salt and pepper. When it has boiled, take it off and heat two earthenware pots. Put asafoetida, cumin, fenugreek, cardamoms, cloves and sesame into one and place it on top of the second pot. Cover both of them with a cooking pot. When it has become well-flavoured, put the *kaṛhi* into the cooking pot, add the *baṛa* (*f.10a*) and make it very hot.

Another method, for *phīnī* (a sweetmeat): take five *sīrs* of pure wheat grains and a quarter of a *sīr* of ghee. When the grain has been pounded, add the ghee so that it becomes sweet-smelling and pure. Mix in washed rice that has been ground and prepare slices of flour paste (*māhīcha āradī*), knead it and roll it out. Rub fresh butter on it and cut it with a knife. Fry the prepared *phīnī* in sweet-smelling ghee. If at any time another variety is required, then wrap red paste on one and white paste on one so that it forms leaves (*i.e. sheets of paste*) of each kind and the *phīnī* becomes coloured.

10 *Kaṛhi*: chickpea pulse dressed with spices and sour milk.
11 Churned sour milk, still thin and runny.
12 *Panḍālū*, yam.
13 Note in the left margin: '*kaṭhal* namely *phanas*', both meaning 'jackfruit'.

Another kind of *khājā* (sweetmeat): put five grains (*ruḥ*) into one *sīr* of ghee and knead it with the palm of the hand. (*f.10b*) Then pound it well and put ghee into it, drop by drop. Roll it out with a rolling-pin and use the bread making method to make it. Rub fresh butter into rice flour and knead it and fold the dough and take the *khājā* piece by piece with an equivalent amount of the dough and roll them out and make the *khājā* thin and, either with tweezers (*manqāsh*) or with a nail, draw a picture on it and fry it in ghee. Having made a pure syrup, put it on and flavour it with the perfume of flowers.

Another *phīnī* of pulse: having washed *mūng* pulse, grind it finely and soak it in hot water. Roll it out and allow it to rise and put into it . . . (*damaged*) and cut it with a knife as for the method for *phīnī* and . . . (*damaged*). Another method for *phīnī* (*f.11a, with a miniature*): having made the *phīnī*, fry it in ghee and put pure syrup on it and, by the same method, make chickpea pulse *phīnī* and, by the same method, prepare several that are also delicious.

Another method, for thin bread (*nān-i-tang*) of all kinds. Grind potherbs well in ghee. Add camphor, musk, cardamoms and cloves. Make dough of white grains for thin bread (*f.11b*) by the same method. Take enough grains to make enough pieces for thin bread and make the equivalent number of pieces of dough. Having added the potherbs, cook the thin bread.

Another recipe for thin bread: having put water and potherbs into *mūng* pulse or into chickpea pulse, cook it well. Just as dough is made from the flour of stoneground grains for *pūrī* (balloon) bread, so having made the dough in the same way, divide it into small portions and cook it. Another kind of thin bread made from pure white grains: knead camphor, musk, cardamoms, potherbs and ghee together, fold the dough and fry it in ghee and flavour it with the scent of roses. This is called sweetened *nān-i-tang*.

(*f.12a*) Another recipe for *nān-i-tang* is made from *kalt*.[14] Soak fresh *kalt* pulse in water and grind it finely. Mix it with water and strain it through a thin cloth. Heat it up in a frying pan, having greased the pan with ghee. Wrap *pālūda*[15] in a clean cloth and pound that cloth over the frying pan.

Another method, for soup (*shūrbā*): take water that rice has been cooked in and save it. Having mixed together turmeric, saffron, cardamoms, cloves, pepper, cumin and cooked meat, cook them again. Take them out, add asafoetida and salt and put in ghee and also lime juice. Another method for soup: having put in pounded wheat, meat and whole potherbs, (*f.12b*) cook the soup. Another recipe for soup: add cooked meat to *kaṛhī* and boil it. Put in cassia, cinnamon, cardamoms, camphor, dried ginger juice, lime juice and salt and put it (*all*) into a cooking pot. It is delicious.

14 *Sic*, probably *kalthī*, a kind of horse gram pulse (*Dolichos uniflorus*).
15 A mixture of water, flour and honey.

Another recipe, for *zarat* (millet)[16] flour soup: put in *dūgh*, cumin, salt and onions and cook it. Add lime juice, cardamoms and cloves and take it off. When it is cool, flavour it with asafoetida and sesame. Another recipe for soup: grind rice flour or *zarat* flour or the rough parched wheat called *thūlī* (*sic*).[17] Put either one of them, or else washed *zarat* or washed *mūng* pulse, into milk. Boil it and put in an equivalent amount of palm sugar. Sprinkle mace and camphor on it.

Another (*f.13a*) method for a drink: mix *zarat*, wheat, barley, lentils and roasted chickpeas in rice water and cook them. Add salt and two *dirams* of ghee and drain off the liquid. Flavour the liquid with ghee or with sesame and then make it either sweet or sour or sweet-smelling or sharp or put in lime juice and garlic. These are all varieties. Put sesame seeds in sweetened and sweet-smelling water and this (*also*) is a variety. Another recipe for a method for a dry bread drink: soak the dry bread in water, knead it by hand, drain off the water and add flavours and sweeteners.

Again, the recipe for boiled grain: (*f.13b*) steam the rice (*until it is*) soft as for *baṛī* and, after it has been taken off, put in roasted chickpea flour or roasted *kaṛharī*[18] or roasted almonds or roasted water lily seeds or roasted jackfruit kernels or roasted mango kernels or roasted *jāman* kernels. Having added them (*to the rice*) cook it.

Another recipe, for *chaklī* (a kind of cake): having cleaned *zarat*, pound it and having put cumin into *dūgh*, cook it. Cool it with *māst*, cumin and salt. It is called *maṭṭhā*. Eat it.

Another recipe, for meat (*with*) potherbs: put a round spoonful of sweet-smelling *rūghan* ghee into a cooking pot and when it has become hot, flavour it with cumin, onions and fenugreek. When it has become well-flavoured, put in dry ground turmeric, when (*f.14a, with a miniature*) the turmeric has turned red, put the meat into the cooking pot. When the meat is well-roasted, add water, *sūnf*, coriander, cumin, fenugreek, and potherbs. When they are well-soaked, squeeze out the water and throw it away. Put the potherbs with the meat and add salt. When it has become well-cooked, put in large pieces of dried ginger and the juice of ginger and lime with a little salt, then serve it.

Another recipe, for *pūrī* (balloon bread): (*f.14b*) prepare the *pūrī* and, having mixed together roasted and peeled sesame seeds, potherbs, camphor, musk, cardamoms and cloves, put them in (*to the pūrī*). Make the edges of the *pūrī* strong and fry it in ghee and flavour it with the perfume of roses.

16 *Zarat* means 'maize' according to Steingass (1957) and Platts (1965), but given the date of the text, it possibly refers here and elsewhere to a kind of millet (Arabic *zarat*).

17 *Thūrī* (parched grain) must be meant.

18 *Kaṛharī*: the black nut of a fruit of which the kernel is white and much esteemed in tonics and aphrodisiacs.

Another recipe, for *laḍḍū* (a sweetmeat): add five *sīrs* of white grains to a quarter of a *sīr* of ghee and one *diram* of salt. Make a good dough and pound it in a mortar. While pounding, gradually add one *sīr* of ghee and make balls or slices of dough (*mahīchā*). Having fried them in ghee and marinated them in pure syrup, make the *laḍḍū* and flavour it with the scent of roses. Another kind of *laḍḍū* is made from *mahīchā*: put together one *sīr* of grain, one *tūlcha* of ghee[19] and one *māsa* of salt. Make the dough (*f.15a*) and when it is well-moistened, pound it in a mortar. Then, as in preparing *pāpaṛ*,[20] cut it by hand, as in the method for *pāra-yi ārd*,[21] and similarly prepare the *mahīchā* (*so that it is*) thin like hairs, and put them in a thin cloth and fry them in ghee. Put half of the *mahīchā* above and half below and, in between the layers of paste put potherbs, camphor and musk and flavour it with the perfume of roses.

Another recipe for *mūng laḍḍū*: wash *mūng dāl* well and boil it slightly and add potherbs, camphor and musk. Fold the *laḍḍū*, mix fine white flour in water and mix them together. Fry them in ghee and flavour with the scent of roses. Another recipe for *laḍḍū* (*to satisfy*) hunger: soak five *sīrs* of white flour grains well (*f.15b*) and pound it in a mortar by hand with a wooden pestle. Flavour it with one and a half *sīrs* of ghee. Prepare a number of pieces of *mahīchā* the thickness of a finger and fry them in ghee. Make perfume from roses and sprinkle it on the *mahīchā*. Then, having mixed together two *sīrs* of ground peeled almonds and two *sīrs* of grated coconut with potherbs, camphor, musk, cardamoms, and cloves, fold them into the *laḍḍū*.

Another recipe for the method for different meats: put together five *sīrs* of meat, a quarter of a *sīr* of turmeric, half a *tūlcha* of cloves, one *tūlcha* of cardamoms and a quarter of a *tūlcha* each of roasted cumin and roasted fenugreek and a quarter of a *tūlcha* of coriander. Put sweet-smelling ghee into a cooking pot and put it on top (*of the fire*). When it has become hot, put asafoetida, cardamoms, cloves and fresh coriander in water and flavour it. (*f.16a*) When the water has become well-flavoured put the meat into it. When the meat has become well-stewed, add water and two *tūlchas* of salt. When it has become well-cooked, add one *rattī* of camphor and one *rattī* of musk. Put in a quarter of a *tūlcha* of pepper and the juice of two limes or put in greens or whatever is to hand.

Another method for mince: mix together five *sīrs* of mince, three *tūlchas* of turmeric, one *tūlcha* of cardamoms, half a *tūlcha* of cloves, a quarter of a *tūlcha* of coriander, one *tūlcha* of fenugreek, a quarter of a *tūlcha* of roast cumin, fresh coriander and a quarter of a *tūlcha* each of chopped fresh ginger and onions. Put two *sīrs* of ghee into a cooking pot and place it on top of the

19 This seems a wrong measurement.

20 Wafers of *dāl* dough, i.e. pappadum.

21 Peasant's gruel.

fire. When (*f.16b*) it has become hot, flavour it first with asafoetida and then add fenugreek. When the fenugreek has turned red, add the minced meat and a small cupful of asafoetida. Put together two *rattīs* of camphor, one *rattī* of musk and the juice of two limes. Cook them and add two *sīrs* of minced onion, four *tūlchas* of minced dried ginger (*zanjabīl*) and a quarter of a *tūlcha* of long pepper and serve it.

The method for meat *lanvās*:[22] put together four *sīrs* of meat and four *tūlchas* of turmeric and other suitable potherbs and, having cooked it by the same method (*as above*), take it off. Having taken it off, grind one *tūlcha* of lovage by hand and put it in and also put in very large pieces of onion and fresh ginger (*adrak*).

Another recipe for meat: cut the meat up finely, so that it is minced. Cook it . . . (*missing folio(s)*)[23] (*f.17a*) and flavour it with asafoetida and fenugreek. Put the meat and the above-mentioned potherbs into a cooking pot and, when it has become well-cooked, remove the broth and throw away the meat. Flavour the broth with cumin, fenugreek, asafoetida, cardamoms and cloves.

Another recipe for meat without ghee: put the meat with the above-mentioned herbs into water and put it on top of the fire. When it is cooked take it off and remove the soup. Strain it and throw away the meat and flavour the soup with fenugreek and asafoetida. Another recipe: the mince must be ground in advance, then cook it by the same method. Mix together mustard (*rā'ī*) seeds, *māst*, turmeric, salt and lime juice. Put sweet sesame into a cooking pot and place it on the fire. When it has become well-heated, (*f.17b*) flavour it with asafoetida. After mixing the meat with the mustard seeds and *māst*, put it into the cooking pot. When it is cooked, serve it.

Another recipe for *baṛa* made from meat and pulse (*māsh*): mince the *baṛa* finely and, having mixed turmeric, cumin, fenugreek, cardamom, cloves, camphor, musk, fresh coriander, asafoetida, salt, pepper, lime juice, fresh ginger and chopped onion with a little ghee, put them into the *baṛa*. Keep some minced onion and fresh ginger separate, and mix them with dried coriander, *sūnf*, cardamoms, cloves, camphor, musk, lime juice and salt separately. Make two loaves from the minced meat and put the stuffing between those loaves and strengthen the sides. By the same recipe make a number of other loaves and put a cooking pot on top so that . . . (*missing folio(s)*)[24] . . . (*f.18a, with a miniature*) flavour it. Remove it from the fire and,

22 i.e. *lās*, a stew or meaty broth.

23 The catchword on f.16b is *dūgh* but f.17a starts *va bakhār*. The Farsi foliation indicates one folio is missing.

24 Catchword on f.17b is *kīyāh* but f.18a begins *ṭa'ām khūrdan*. The Farsi foliation indicates one missing folio.

having put it on a dish, serve it. Make rabbit soup (*yakhnī*) by the same recipe and use the same recipe for any *yakhnī* that is required.

Another recipe is for skewered meat (*sīkh*) for use where fires are available, either for *ṭaghrān* (game birds) or sheep meat. First of all cut the meat very finely, wash it with turmeric and (*f.18b*) good water and boil it. Add salt, asafoetida and chopped potherbs and boil it. If it has become well-cooked, tie it with a thread and marinate it with all kinds of potherbs mixed with lime juice. Leave it in one place for several hours (*to marinate*) and then roast it. When the potherbs in the meat turn red and become absorbed, then put musk, camphor and rosewater into ghee and rub it on the meat and roast it once more. When it has become well-cooked, and it is time to eat, throw away the thread.

Another recipe for clay oven (*darkā*) meat: make a ditch two *gaz* deep and one and a half *gaz* wide. Rub flowers on the inside of the ditch, line it with clay and put sticks into it. Light a fire and make the clay oven very hot (*f.19a*) and make the stones lining it hot. Either the flesh of cows or of sheep or of game birds may be used. Wrap the meat in banana leaves and put stones in the ditch oven and put banana leaves on the stones. Put the meat wrapped in banana leaves on top of the stones and, again, put banana leaves over the meat. Once more put in hot stones and on those stones put banana leaves. Place meat on those leaves and once more put banana leaves on the meat. In this way put layers of whatever quantity is required, whether sheep, chicken or pigeon (*f.19b*) and (*finally*) put a lot of banana leaves on the ditch oven and top it up with flowers. Seal it so that nothing runs out of it. This recipe is for one or two cows but put in whatever quantity is required and leave it for a whole night so that it cooks. Burn two or three bundles of firewood on the oven and when it is time to eat the meat, take it out and eat it.

Another recipe for the method for fish: take the bones out of the fish and wash it with *dūgh*, turmeric and asafoetida. Burn pure asafoetida in oil and grind it and, having mixed together cumin, roast fenugreek, turmeric, pepper, coriander and roast sesame seeds, rub them into the fish. Add onion and ground fresh ginger and the oil in which the asafoetida . . . (*missing folio(s)*)[25] . . . (*f.20a*) First, having pounded the cooked fish in ghee (*and*) similarly, having put ghee on (*damaged*) cook it, and take a plate made of stitched orange leaves (*paṭṭal*) and put the mince on it and tie it with thread. Flavour it with small white cardamoms and add water so that it becomes well-flavoured and put the orange leaf plates into a cooking pot. Directly it comes to the boil take it off and serve it. By the same recipe, having placed a quantity of mince on screw pine (*kīyūra*) leaves, cook it and by the same recipe spread it on

25 Catchword on f.19b is *hing* but f.20a begins *avval pukhtan*. The Farsi foliation indicates one missing folio.

banana leaves or the leaves of red roses or white China roses (*sīvatī*). Place the mince on them as stuffing and fasten them up. Prepare meat by the same recipe, partridge, quail, rabbit, deer, whichever kind is required.

(*f.20b*) Another recipe for a method for skewered (*sīkh*) fish: just as, previously, we cooked mince in ghee, cook fish by the same method and mix it with coarsely ground roasted coriander and roasted fennel seeds. Having mixed the mince with potherbs, a good method is to add some ebony fruit (*tīndū*), and wrap it in cotton and fasten it to a skewer. Mix camphor, musk and rosewater with ghee and rub the ghee on to the skewered mince every hour. When it has become thoroughly red, serve it.

Another recipe for rustic (*rūstā*) fish *kabāb*, namely *ganvārī*:[26] having placed one sweet-scented earthenware pot on top of another, make them both hot. Stuff the boned fish with *dūgh* and asafoetida and wash it with water. Rub salt, asafoetida, pepper, cardamoms and dried ground cloves on it and also rub lime juice on the fish and roast it in the earthenware, namely clay, cooking pot. (*f.21a*) When it has become well-roasted, flavour it with pure asafoetida. By the same recipe make *kabābs* of partridges, quails, kid, chicken and pigeon and also, by the same recipe, make rabbit *kabābs*.

Another recipe for fish *yakhnī*: prepare fish, as explained previously, by the same recipe and use the same flavours, or else flavour it with orange leaves and spread a cloth over it. Rub the fish with lime juice and salt, put it in and place a lid on the cooking pot. When it is cooked, take it off and squeeze the water out and throw the fish away and make the *yakhnī* by the method of bean *yakhnī*. Mix cardamoms, cloves, pepper, lime juice, salt, ginger and finely cut onions all together and flavour them with pure asafoetida. Sew two sour-orange (*taranj*) leaf plates, (*f.21b*) place them, one over and one under, in the *yakhnī*. Take them out at meal time and serve the *yakhnī*. By the same recipe make *yakhnī* of any meat that is liked.

Another recipe for the meat of mountain sheep: take it complete with bones and wash it well and, having added asafoetida, onions, fresh ginger, salt, fresh greens and fresh coriander, cook it. Put in plenty of water. Add some pepper and lime juice and, when it is well-cooked, take it off and either eat it as it is or else flavour it with asafoetida essence.

Another recipe for the method of frying fish: wash the fish as explained previously and mix it with chopped potherbs and fry it either in *sarsūn* (rape) seed oil or in mustard (*rā'ī*) seed oil (*f.22a*) and flavour it with asafoetida.

Another recipe for the method of saffron meat: wash the meat well and, having put sweet-smelling ghee into a cooking pot, put the meat into it. When

26 Also meaning 'rustic'.

the ghee is hot, flavour it with saffron, rosewater and camphor. Mix the meat with the saffron to flavour it and when it has become well-marinated, add a quantity of water. Chop cardamoms, cloves, coriander, fennel, cinnamon, cassia, cumin and fenugreek, tie them up in muslin and put them with the meat. Cook almonds, pine kernels, pistachios, and raisins in tamarind syrup and add them to the meat. Put in rosewater, camphor, musk and ambergris and serve it. By the same method cook partridge, quail, (*f.22b*) chicken and pigeon.

Another recipe: wash the meat well. Flavour ghee with asafoetida and, having mixed the meat with saffron, put it into the ghee. When it has become well-marinated, add hot water, salt, cardamoms, cloves, *sūnf*, coriander, cumin and fenugreek. When it is well-cooked, put in lime juice and pepper. Take it off and add whole sour-orange (*taranj*) leaves or sweet-orange (*nārang*) peel. Another recipe: cook the meat as previously explained and put leaves into a number of cooking pots. Put mangoes into some and put unripe mangoes (*kīrī*) into some. Another recipe: heat some ghee and flavour it with ambergris, rosewater and musk. Put the meat in and when it is flavoured, mix it with rosewater or saffron. When (*f.23a, with miniature*) it has become well-marinated, put in hot water and cook it well. When it has become well-cooked put in fresh ginger, onions and the juice of sour-oranges. Take it off and put onions into some of it and also put in cucumber.

Another recipe: take hashed meat broth (*yazdā'ī yakhnī*) either of sheep meat or partridge or beef or rabbit, whichever *yakhnī* is required. Make it and having kneaded the meat in it, cook the meat broth and add turmeric, salt and all kinds of potherbs. (*f.23b*) Flavour it with ghee, add water and make the soup. Put in plenty of onion and the soup becomes very good. Add pepper and lime juice and serve it. Another recipe is for Mongol *yakhnī*: having stuffed meat very well with onions, fresh ginger, potherbs and salt, boil it. Either cut the meat very finely or, if it is so desired, have it uncut and, if it is required in soup, put it in soup. Another recipe for Mongol *yakhnī*: take pieces of meat complete with bones and boil it with onions, fresh ginger, salt and all kinds of potherbs. When it is well-cooked, add either lime juice or ghee.

Another recipe, for meat: wash the meat well and put it in vinegar, (*f.24a*) keep it and marinate it in ghee flavoured with asafoetida. Mix the meat with potherbs of all kinds and put it into a cooking pot. When it is well-cooked, add lime juice, pepper and fresh ginger and serve it. Another recipe for meat: boil very large pieces of meat, take them out and cut them very finely as for bean *yakhnī*. Add onions, fresh ginger and sliced radishes and flavour it well with asafoetida. Another recipe, for *yakhnī*: cut fresh ginger and onions finely and mix in salt. Cut up the stewed meat finely and mix it in, add lime juice and flavour it with ghee. Another recipe, for meat: cut the meat up and tie one portion of meat and one portion of onion with thread. Prepare several portions by this method and marinate them in flavoured ghee. Add water, (*f.24b*) cook them well and add cardamoms, cloves, salt, cumin, turmeric and coriander. When it is well-cooked, put in pepper and lime juice and take it off and, according to inclination, eat it as a stew or a soup.

Another recipe, for rice without ghee: mix together half water and half congee and put it on to boil. When it comes to the boil put the washed rice and ground saffron into the cooking pot. When it is well-cooked, strain off the surplus liquid and keep it separate and put into it half a *sīr* of rice and a quantity of sweet-smelling ghee and add rosewater and camphor. Another recipe, for plain rice: soak tamarind in water and when it has become soaked, knead it and strain off the water. Keep the water and throw the tamarind away. (*f.25a*) Flavour the water with *marhaṭṭī* aloes[27] and perfume it with the scent of roses and boil the water. Wash the rice well and soak it in water and, when the cooking pot has come to the boil, put the rice into it. Cook the rice and strain off the water and throw it away. Put rosewater into the rice and take it off. Make *kaṛhī* with the strained water or, having put in potherbs, make sherbet. By the same recipe cook parched grain and by the same recipe, having added sour-orange or sour pomegranate juice, cook it.

Another recipe for plain rice: boil water thoroughly and put the rice in. When it is cooked, strain it and add rosewater to it. Put in white China rose and camphor and take it off. Another recipe for plain rice (*f.25b, with a miniature*): take two parts of water and one part of milk and put them into a cooking pot and set it to boil. When it comes to the boil, add the rice. When it is cooked, strain off the surplus water and remove the steamed rice. Another recipe for plain rice: put saffron into water and set it to boil. When it comes to the boil, add the rice. When it is cooked, strain it and throw away the water. Mix saffron, ambergris, rosewater, camphor and musk (*f.26a*) together and put them into the rice and having kneaded it by hand with sweet-smelling ghee, mix the rice, flavour it and serve it.

Another recipe for plain rice decorated with gold: set the water to boil and, when it comes to the boil, add the rice. When the rice is cooked, take it off and cool it. Spread the rice on a large plate and press it, so that it becomes fused, and decorate it with gold leaf. Another recipe for plain rice: having put potherbs into tamarind juice, set it to boil. When it comes to the boil, add the rice. When it is cooked, strain it and prepare cold sherbet with the water, and put camphor, musk and rosewater on to the rice. When it becomes runny, put pepper on it.

A recipe for rice with ghee: put good ghee into a cooking pot. (*f.26b*) When it becomes hot, flavour it with camphor, rosewater and white ambergris.

27 *Marhaṭṭī* meaning 'related to the Marathas', but the connection with aloes is obscure.

Then, having mixed rice with saffron and salt, put it in the ghee and fry it well. Then add water, pine kernels, pistachio nuts, peeled almonds, cardamoms, cloves and shelled white coconut. Break them into pieces, do not mince them. Mix them all together and put them into a cooking pot and cook them well. Then having added leaves of sweet basil (*raiḥān*) and sacred basil (*tulsī*) or sour-orange, serve it.

Another recipe, for *qalīya* rice:[28] put ghee into a cooking pot and when it has become hot, flavour it with asafoetida and garlic. When it has become well-flavoured, put the meat, mixed with chopped potherbs, into the ghee. (*f.27a*) When it has become marinated, add water and add, to an equal amount, one *sīr* of cow's milk. When it has come to the boil, add the washed rice. When it is well-cooked, take it off. Cook other rice by the same recipe and, likewise, do not make it with cow's milk but put in four *sīrs* of garlic and whole peppers, and serve it.

Another recipe, for the method for parched grain: when sweet-smelling ghee has become hot in the cooking pot, flavour it with cumin or fenugreek or asafoetida or onions, then put the parched grain into it and fry it well. Put in enough water to cook it and then serve it. Another recipe for parched grain: when the sweet-smelling ghee has become hot, flavour it (*f.27b*) with sacred basil and camphor. Mix parched grain with saffron, put it in a cooking pot and fry it well. Add water and salt and, when it has become well-cooked, put some rosewater on it and serve it.

Another recipe, for *zarat bhāt*:[29] having made the *zarat* very white, pound it. Throw away the husks, take that which remains whole and put it into buffalo cow's milk and put fermented *dūgh* on to it. The second day, take the *māst* and remove the layer of *zarat* which is under it. Separate the buttermilk and keep the separated fresh butter. Wash the *zarat* well (*f.28a*) and quickly take the pure water which remains on top of the *dūgh* and keep it. Set half the water to boil, put the *zarat* in it. When it has become well-cooked, strain off the water and throw it (*the water*) away. Take the cooked *zarat* and cool some of it and put it into *dūgh* that has been flavoured with asafoetida and put fresh lime leaves on top of it.

Another recipe, for the method of kedgeree (*khichrī*): put three parts of *mūng dāl* and one part of rice into sweet-smelling ghee which has been flavoured with fenugreek, and fry it well. Add water and salt, cook it well and serve it. Another recipe for *kaṛharī*[30] *khichrī*: (*f.28b*) set water to boil and when it comes to the boil, put in *kaṛharī dāl*. When it is cooked, add washed rice and salt. When it has become well-cooked, add sweet-smelling ghee and serve it.

28 *Qalīya* is a kind of fricassee of meat.

29 *Bhāt* is a dish of cooked rice or *zarat*.

30 *Kaṛharī* is a nut used in cooking and medicine – perhaps ground up to make the kedgeree?

Another recipe, for the method for fish: take the flesh of the fish and throw away all the bones. Then burn asafoetida in sweet oil or in rape seed oil and chop it. Mix fresh lime leaves, cardamoms, cloves, cumin, fenugreek, salt and lime juice with the flesh and oil and leave them overnight. The next day prepare a small loaf from that flesh and dry it in the sun. Then place it in a large pan (*māt*), and whenever it is required, (*f.29a, with a miniature*) fry some in ghee. Eat it dry or else fry it over the fire and eat it. By the same recipe, prepare the flesh of partridges and deer and quails and ground sesame seeds, whichever is required, prepare it.

Another recipe, for rural or vegetarian food: take root vegetables and boil them well, then take them off and fry them in ghee flavoured with sesame and asafoetida. (*f.29b*) Add lime juice, salt and burned vegetable oil and mix it as explained above. Take some of it, flavour it and cook it. By the same recipe cook the seeds of the radish which is called the siliqua (*sīngrī*) and by the same method cook all kinds of potherbs.

Another recipe is for the method for corinda (*karūnda*):[31] having put mustard, salt and lime juice in *māst*, mix them together. Slightly boil the corinda and put it in the *māst*. Put sweet sesame seeds into a cooking pot, put it on and add essence of pure asafoetida. When it is well-fried, add the *māst* and corinda. It can be eaten when parboiled. Serve it.[32]

Another recipe, for the method for swollen pulse: (*f.30a*) soak *mūng dāl* thoroughly in water, grind it finely and cook it in water until soft. Then rub a plate with oil flavoured with asafoetida and put the pulse, that has been soft-cooked, on that plate and allow it to swell. When it has thickened, mix together pepper, lime juice and vegetable oil that has been flavoured with asafoetida. Take some in the palm of the hand and knead the pulse. Cut it with a knife and remove it from the plate and put it into another receptacle.

Another recipe is for the method of *kaṛhī*: take fresh *dūgh* and [*put?*] either rice flour or chickpea flour into it, then add turmeric, asafoetida and salt and boil it. When it is cooked, take it off. Flavour vegetable oil with asafoetida, cumin, fenugreek and cardamoms. (*f.30b*) Then prepare *baṛī* from *mūng* flour or chickpea flour, fry it in ghee or vegetable oil and put it in the *kaṛhī*. Another recipe, for white *kaṛhī*: take some *dūgh* and put into it asafoetida and coriander, either fresh or dried, and add salt and boil it. When it is parboiled, add cardamoms, cloves, fresh ginger, onions and pepper and take it off and, in the same way as previously explained, flavour this recipe. By the same recipe prepare *kaṛhī* from woodapple (*kītha*) and myrobalan (*āmla*) and *mūng* pulse and mint and garlic, whichever is desired.

Another recipe, for the method for *kaṛhī* made with cow's *dūgh* flavoured with

31 Corinda (*Carissa carandas*), a small acid fruit.

32 Note in the right margin: '*karūnda*'.

fresh ginger. Cook it and add turmeric and salt (*f.31a*) and put in the amount that will not burn the mouth. Add some rice flour and boil it. Another recipe for the method for *kaṛhī*. Put myrobalan, rice pulse, fried *shāl*,[33] cassia, cinnamon, cardamoms, cloves and salt into cow's *dūgh* and boil it and serve it.

Another recipe, for the method for *kaṛhī*: mix together almond flour, *dūgh*, white sugar, cardamoms and cloves and put it on and boil it. When it is cooked, serve it. Another recipe for *kaṛhī*: put chopped lime leaves into *dūgh* and sprinkle it with lime juice and also the peel of limes. Then, having added salt, cardamoms and cloves, boil it. When it is cooked, serve it. (*f.31b*) Another recipe for *kaṛhī* made from dark green pumpkin (*ḍangrī*): knead the pumpkin by hand and strain off the juice and keep it. Boil the pulp and also keep its juice. Then, having put in palm sugar, cardamoms and cloves, boil it. When it is cooked serve it.

Another recipe, for the method for *pīchha*, namely the surplus water that is removed from the cooking pot after cooking rice and separating it. Put *mūng* pulse into the water and boil it. Chop fresh sandal and take its juice. Put myrobalan and cardamoms into it and cook it. Put in salt. When it is cooked, add some mint leaves and serve it. Another recipe (*f.32a, with a miniature*) for rice water: take the water of cooked rice, put in plenty of grape-sugar and add cardamoms, camphor, cloves and rosewater. When it is well-cooked, serve it. Another recipe for the method for *pīchha* made from chickpeas. Boil chickpeas, take the water and, having added salt, cumin, asafoetida, cardamoms, cloves, pepper and sour-orange juice, boil it. When it is cooked, serve it. Another recipe for *pīchha*: (*f.32b*) fry *mūng* in ghee and flavour it with dried ginger juice, salt and asafoetida.

Another recipe, for split pulse: flavour ghee with asafoetida, add *mūng* pulse to it and fry it and then add salt and water. When it is cooked, put in either fried sesame seed flour or fried chickpea flour. Add some sweet-smelling ghee and serve it. Another recipe, for split chickpea pulse flavoured with *sūn*[34] that is, the *sūn* pulse of Ghiyath Shahi: pound chickpea pulse and *zarat* grains finely with a clean pestle, put them in a cloth, strain them and keep the water. Chop very fresh saffron (*f.33a*), add it and mix it all together and then cook it for the amount of time it takes for the pulse and the liquid to become as one and for the colours to be blended. Add salt, lime juice and dried ginger juice. Put in the peel of sweet-oranges (*narangī*) and sour-oranges (*taranj*) and take it off. Then take a lapis lazuli plate or a turquoise plate. Put cooked rice (*bhāt*) on one and place the *dāl* by the side of the rice. Having put sweet-smelling ghee on a separate plate in advance, flavour the *sūn dāl* of Ghiyath Shahi with sweet-scented perfumes. The perfumes are as follows: make perfume from

33 i.e. *shālī*, wild rice.

34 A kind of red sugarcane, *Bignonia indica*.

champa flowers and yellow *sūn* flowers. Put *sūn* and screw pine (*kītkī*)[35] (*f.33b*) into the cooked chickpea pulse and wrap it up in cotton. Flavour it a little and put red roses and white China roses and rosewater or the flowers of orange, either *taranj, nāranj* or *narangī*, and, if it is so desired, cook some of these varieties quite separately.

Another recipe for split *mūng*: having cooked whole *mūng*, tie it in a butter cloth.[36] Pound flowers of every kind in another cloth[37] and place it on the buttered pulse. Fasten the flower cloth on to the butter (cloth). Put water into a cooking pot with the butter and place a lid on the pot. When the scent of the flowers has permeated the split *mūng*, then take it out, add (*f.34a*) rosewater and camphor and eat it.

Another recipe, for the method for vegetables: put green vegetables into a cooking pot, add asafoetida, salt and ghee, and cook them. When they are cooked, put in sacred basil leaves, sweet basil leaves, fresh leaves of the mango tree, fresh lime leaves, fresh sour-orange leaves and mint, each of which has been tied separately into a bunch. Place the bunches on the vegetables. Put the bunches and the vegetables on a dish, and dish them up. Throw away the bunches and eat the vegetables.

Another recipe, for the method for curds (*maṭṭhā*): take and mix together, strained *māst*, potherbs, palm sugar, sugar, cardamoms, cloves, cassia, cinnamon, nutmeg, date sugar, pepper, *sūnf*, camphor and musk. (*f.34b*) This becomes good *maṭṭha*.

Another recipe, for the method for *pīchha*: bake *mūng* in an earthenware pot, then put it into a cooking pot and add water, salt, fresh ginger juice and sour-orange juice. When it is well-cooked, take it off and flavour it with the essence of asafoetida. Another recipe for *pīchha*: bake rice (*biryān*)[38] and then put it into plenty of water and boil it. Add salt and loaf sugar and also put in three or four myrobalans (*cherry plums*). When it is well-cooked, flavour it with asafoetida and fenugreek. Another recipe for *pīchha:* having baked wild rice (*shāl*), grind it finely and put it into sour *dūgh* (*f.35a*) water[39] and add salt and loaf sugar. When it is well-cooked, put in chopped baked cumin. Cook one lot in this way and cook another lot in sweet water.

Another recipe, for the method for soup. It may be made of rabbit or partridge or quail. Put the meat into pure water, add asafoetida, cumin, coriander and salt and cook it. When it is cooked put in sour-orange juice,

35 *Kītkī* and *kīyūra* are both *Pandanus odaratissimus* (screw pine), *kītkī* being smaller than *kīyūra*.

36 i.e. a butter muslin cloth.

37 i.e. one of the perfumed cloths described previously.

38 *Biryān*: literally, baked food.

39 i.e. whey.

take it off and flavour it with asafoetida. Another recipe for soup: having put in meat, turmeric, cumin, fenugreek, cardamoms, cloves, salt and asafoetida, boil it and cook it. When it is well-cooked, strain the soup and keep it. Then having mixed cardamoms, cloves, asafoetida, cumin, (*f.35b, with a miniature*) fenugreek and salt together, flavour it. Another recipe for soup: having mixed meat with saffron, put it into flavoured ghee, add cardamoms, cloves, coriander, *sūnf* and salt and cook it. When it is well-cooked, put in some pepper and sour-orange juice, scatter rosewater on it and serve it.

Another recipe (*f.36a*) for the method for boiling meat: put a lot of water into a cooking pot and flavour it with sour-orange leaves or mango leaves and put in some kind of meat, chicken or pigeon or partridge or quail, put into it whatever kind of meat that is desired. Mix together asafoetida, cumin, fenugreek, cloves, turmeric, cardamoms and salt, crush them and put them on top of onions. Wrap up the lid of the cooking pot and seal it with flour dough so that the flavour does not escape. When it is well-cooked, take it off and, having strained the crushed potherbs, throw them away. Then mix together saffron, rosewater, white aloes, one *rattī* of camphor, one *rattī* of musk (*f.36b*) and rub them into that meat. Return it to the cooking pot, cook it while watching it carefully. When serving it at meal time, rub in some sweet-smelling ghee and serve it and [*also*] serve some without ghee.

Another recipe, for the method for samosas: take finely minced venison and flavour some ghee with asafoetida and fenugreek. Mix the minced meat with saffron and put it in the ghee. Then bake asafoetida, salt, cumin and fenugreek. Put cardamoms, cloves, coriander, one *rattī* of camphor and one *rattī* of musk into the mince and cook it well, and add a half quantity of (*f.37a*) finely minced onions and a quarter of minced dried ginger into the meat. When it has become well-cooked, sprinkle it with rosewater and take it off and stuff the samosas. Make a hole in the samosas with a stick and fry them in sweet-smelling ghee until they are tender. By the same recipe, samosas can be made from any kind of meat that is desired.

Another recipe for meat after that manner: take very finely ground mince and mix saffron or turmeric together with cardamoms, cloves, coriander, pepper, salt, lime juice, camphor, musk, onions and fresh ginger. Heat some ghee and flavour it with asafoetida (*f.37b*) and put the mince with it. Make it tasty with white ambergris and rosewater and take it off. Having made flour dough, make two loaves and put the mince between them. Cook the loaf, making it firm and well-cooked, and then remove it. Put camphor, musk and rosewater into sweet-smelling ghee and, having made the loaves in the above-mentioned way, put the ghee on them.

Another recipe, for the method for *khīs* or *anbal*:[40] wash rice well and grind it

40 i.e. flummery.

on a grinding-board. Sift the flour in a cloth. Having made *biryān* of *dūgh*, salt and finely chopped ginger . . . (*missing folio(s)*)[41] . . . (*f.38a*) they call this *anbal*. It is either eaten with milk or with water. Another recipe for making flummery (*khīs*): cook fine rice flour, either with water, juice or congee, and with potherbs of the amount that does not make it too sweet. When it is cooked, take it off. Another recipe for *khīs* with tamarind: cook rice flour in tamarind juice, take it off. Another recipe for *khīs*: put together rice flour, potherbs and tamarind juice and cook them. When they are cooked, take them off and put in camphor and rosewater. Another recipe for *khīs*: puff some grain and scrape it well (*f.38b*) and cut very finely. Dry it in the sun and grind it finely. Take the ground part and the flour. Take two parts of congee, or, if there is no congee, use *dūgh*, add a few potherbs and the puffed grain flour and cook the *khīs*. When it is cooked, remove it and cool it. Eat it either with cold milk or cold *dūgh*. Also, having dried some puffed grain, fry it in ghee and eat it.

Another recipe, for the method for *dūgh*: put salt into sour *dūgh*, add asafoetida, cardamoms, cloves, cumin, fenugreek and vegetable oil. Mix it all together and heat two earthenware pans. Put some of the same potherbs on to one of the earthenware (*f.39a*) baking pans and place the second pan on top of it and then put a cooking pot on top of both of them. Make the cooking pot aromatic, flavouring it five or six times, and put the *dūgh* into it. This *dūgh* is the kind known as *sanjān*.[42]

Another recipe for the method for *dūgh*: mix together *dūgh*, salt, sour-orange juice and fresh ginger juice. Fry asafoetida in vegetable oil, grind it and put into the *dūgh*. Another recipe for salt *dūgh*: bake cumin (*biryān*) and flavour it with asafoetida. Another recipe: put sour *dūgh* into fresh *dūgh*. Another recipe for *dūgh*: (*f.39b*) put radishes, salt, mustard seed and lime juice into *dūgh* and flavour it with asafoetida.

Another recipe for the method for curds: put potherbs, camphor, musk and rosewater into *māst* (coagulated milk) and flavour it with the perfume of roses. Another recipe for the method for *kaṛanba*:[43] fry *māst*, salt and asafoetida in vegetable oil and [*add*] *bhāt*. Another recipe for curds: beat it with half-*māst*, add rosewater, camphor, cardamoms, cloves and sour-orange leaves and put in *mūtha* beans[44] and white beans[45] or else have it plain. Another method for *dhīr dū'ī*:[46] having put a spoonful of *māst* into salt, strain

41 Catchword on f.37b is *va ān* but f.38a begins *bemānad*. The Farsi foliation indicates two missing folios.

42 'Double-boiled'.

43 A vegetarian dish.

44 *Phaseolus aconitifolus*.

45 *Vālā-yi safīd*.

46 Lit. '*quantity by spoon*'.

it through a cloth and, having grated a lot of garlic, (*f.40a*) add it. Bake coriander seeds, add them and put a quantity of chopped green onion leaves on top of it.

Another recipe is for the method for Ghiyath Shahi's congee: wash tamarinds well and put them into pure water. When they have become soft, knead them by hand and, having rinsed them, take their sour juice and put salt into it. Flavour it with aloes and perfume it with every kind of flowers. Add rosewater, camphor and musk. Another recipe for the method for double cooked congee: prepare very sour pure congee and add salt to it. Grind mustard seeds coarsely and throw away the husks. Mix fenugreek and sweet sesame seeds (*f.40b, with a miniature*) together and make the congee. Heat two earthenware pots. Put potherbs in one and, having placed the second one on top of it, scent the cooking pot four or five times and put the congee into the cooking pot. Another recipe, for the method for sherbet: mix lime juice, potherbs and pepper together and rinse them. Flavour them with aloes and scent them with the perfume of roses and add rosewater, (*f.41a*) camphor and musk.

Another recipe, for the method for Ghiyath Shahi's *baghrā*:[47] cut a quantity of pieces of gold leaf larger than the pieces of *baghrā*. Boil it[48] in water and in this way the gilding becomes sprinkled (*over the baghrā*). Remove it and then, using the *baghrā* water, grind together pine kernels, almonds, pistachios and raisins and put them into that *baghrā* so that it becomes delicious. Add vinegar that has been strained and flavour with garlic. If another variety is required, put it into *māst* curds or tamarind juice or lime juice or sour-orange juice or any acid fruit juice that is required, or else dissolve saffron, musk and camphor (*f.41b*) in water and put it into that *baghrā*. Cook stew well from pieces of meat and put it into the *baghrā* or, in place of that, if it is so wished, put in the brains of crows or small pieces of thin bread or put in *mūng* that has been cooked in ghee or, having boiled whey that has been strained from *dūgh* of the sour variety, put that in. Put in any of these that are required, one by one. There are a hundred versions of this recipe.

Another recipe for the method for *yakhnī* (broth): for the amount there may be of *yakhnī*, take half of that amount of onion. Mince half the onion with fresh ginger and also mince mint leaves of the quantity of two *dirams*. (*f.42a*) Mix them all together and sprinkle saffron, rosewater and lime juice on it and add some sweet-smelling ghee. That is one variety, and if it is flavoured with asafoetida that is another kind and if it is flavoured with vegetable oil, that is also a variety. Or else use the flavour of aloes essence or camphor or white

47 Triangular sections of paste or dough to be decorated. In this recipe the *baghrā* has clearly already been made.

48 Presumably 'them', the gold leaf and the *baghrā* are boiled together.

ambergris or the smoke of burnt betel leaves or the flavour of sour-orange leaves or the scent or the perfume of jasmine or of wheat.

Another recipe, for the method for *pūrī* bread: put sacred basil leaves into ghee and, having added camphor, heat it. (*f.42b*) Crumble the *pūrī* bread, put it in the ghee and fry it. Then add rosewater and honey (*shahd*). If tamarind juice is put in, then that is a variety and if lime juice is put in that becomes a version, as it does if syrup is put in. If mixed with different fruit juices, these are also varieties.

Another recipe, for the method for *bhāt*: cook the *bhāt* with the washed rice in congee or *dūgh* or syrup or sweet-scented water or in pumpkin juice and then cool it. Also having baked sesame seed (*f.43a*) and roasted or fried chickpea pulse, rice and cumin, mix them with fenugreek, cardamoms, cloves, lime juice, salt and ghee and add in asafoetida that has been fried in ghee. If another kind is required then each becomes a distinct variety. If *dūgh* and garlic are put in the rice, this is another kind. If fried aubergine soaked in sour milk is put in that is a variety and if wafers of *pāpaṛ* and ghee and lime relish are put in that is another kind. Put all these into rice *bhāt*, put in fresh ginger and mix into this same *bhāt, mūng* and ghee and this becomes another kind. If *mūng* (*f.43b*) and ghee and *bhāt* and *baṛa* are put together, it is a variety, as it is if soup and *baṛī* and meat and lime are mixed with *bhāt*. Also if *yakhnī*, ghee and *bhāt* are put together and also if honey (*shahd*) and ghee and *bhāt* are mixed, those are other kinds. If sour-orange juice, pumpkin juice, lime juice, sweet-orange juice and *sadāphal*[49] juice and *kamrak*[50] juice is taken, each one that is put into *bhāt* makes a different kind. If potherbs, ghee, *bhāt* and camphor are mixed together that becomes a variety, and if *bhāt* and *dūgh* and fresh ginger and onions and lime juice and salt are put together, that is another kind. If *bhāt*, potherbs, (*f.44a*) musk, rosewater and camphor are used that is another. If one *sīr* of *bhāt* and six *tūlchas* of honey (*shahd*) and four *tūlchas* of ghee are mixed together, then that is a different kind. If *bhāt* is fried in ghee to which rosewater and camphor are then added, serve it and that is another sort. If *bhāt, mūtha* beans, white beans, cardamoms and cloves are put together, it becomes a variety. If *bhāt, mūng baṛa* and *kaṛhī* and ghee are put together that is one sort. If *bhāt* and two *bakravī*[51] are mixed together that is a variety. If sugar-cane syrup and perfume are added, that is a variety as is date sugar and perfume. (*f.44b, with a miniature*) If ground almonds and ground pine kernels or ground pistachios or ground walnuts or ground *kaṛharī*[52] or ground water lily seeds mixed with perfume are put into *bhāt*, they become varieties.

49 Pampelmousse or shaddock.

50 *Averrhoa carambola*, starfruit, *kamarānga* in Sanskrit, *kamrakh* in Hindi.

51 A similar kind of citron to sour-orange, *taranj*.

52 The black kernels of a nut.

Another recipe for the method for *bhāt*: put in cumin *biryān* that has been cooked and ground and add soup and ghee.

(*f.45a*) Another recipe, for sherbet: flavour water and potherbs with asafoetida and vegetable oil and add saffron and a few potherbs.

Another recipe, for *zarat bhāt*: pound the *zarat* well so that it is not too fine nor yet too coarse. Put it in water and *dūgh*, stir it and when it is thoroughly soaked, cook it. Strain it and keep the liquid. Take the separated *zarat bhāt*, cool it and mix in lime juice or sour-orange juice, salt and finely cut fresh ginger equal in amount to the *bhāt*. Another recipe for *bhāt*: cook the *bhāt*, using either *zarat* or rice and cool it. Then take (*f.45b*) lime juice or tamarind juice or boiled corinda or boiled unripe mangoes, put salt into whichever is being used, and burn it in oil of sweet asafoetida and knead it by hand with that oil and mix rice with it. Another recipe for the method for *bhāt*: take mango syrup, camphor, musk and rosewater and, having flavoured sweet-smelling ghee with camphor, put them into that *bhāt*, cook it and serve it (*f.46a*). If cooked *jāman* fruit[53] is put into it, this becomes another variety, and by the same recipe as that use corinda and similarly use jackfruit. Another recipe for the method for *bhāt*: having boiled five small mangoes in milk, boil them again. Add *māst*, honey (*shahd*), sweet-smelling ghee, potherbs and camphor, and eat it.

Another recipe, for pasta (*tatmāj*):[54] prepare thin strands of pasta from the finest flour and boil it. Put together camphor, musk, rosewater, potherbs, cardamoms, three or four cloves, *bābrang*,[55] mace, spikenard and wild spikenard, grind them finely and add them [*as well as the pasta?*] to the sweetest *māst*.

Another recipe, for the method for pottage or gruel (*pūlānī*): (*f.46b*) put in tamarind, cardamoms, cloves, mace, potherbs, musk, camphor and a little rosewater and add sweet-smelling ghee.

Another recipe, for the method for *baghrā*: cut[56] the *baghrā* from the flour of plain boiled rice (*khashka*) and boil it in water. Remove the *baghrā* and keep the water. Put vinegar into the water and add ground almonds, garlic and salt so that it becomes delicious. Having cooked mince in sweet-smelling ghee, put that into it and add a few potherbs. Make sherbet and put all these into it. Another recipe for sherbet: take the juice of all kinds of fruit, put in a few herbs. In some . . . (*missing folio(s)*)[57] (*f.47a*) put them in some of it, and

53 The Java plum, fruit of the tree *Eugenia jambolana*.

54 *Tatmāj*, thin strands of pasta, vermicelli.

55 *Bābrang*, *Embelia ribes*, used medicinally for flatulence.

56 A strange choice of word here.

57 Catchword on f.46b is *kāfūr* but f.47a begins *bīyandāzad*. The Farsi foliation indicates one missing folio.

in some, put fresh ginger, onions and pepper. That amount is one variety. Flavour it with every kind of perfume. By the same method prepare it with *dūgh* or with mustard seeds or with juice. Prepare whichever is required by the same method.

Another recipe, for the method for bread (*nān*): according to the amount of grain available make that bread. Put potherbs in some and in some put sour fruit. Put fruit in some and then these are a quantity of varieties of bread. Put sour grapes (*ghūra*) in some flour and cook the bread. Put the juice of sour fruits in some.

Another recipe for *bhāt*: (*f.47b*) take cooked *bhāt*, and having dissolved four *rattīs* of white ambergris and one *rattī* of camphor in rosewater, knead it. Put some ghee which has been used to fry meat into the *bhāt*, also kedgeree, crushed parched grain, sugar, sherbet, melon and *dūgh*, whatever is required. Prepare perfume by the same recipe and use it as flavouring.

Another recipe, for the method for making flavoured foods. Grind four *rattīs* of rosewater, ten *rattīs* of white China rose, twenty *rattīs* of cardamoms, one *rattī* of cloves, four *rattīs* of mace and put them into whichever food is required. (*f.48a*) Another recipe for the flavouring of foods: grind a quarter of a *sīr* of mango syrup, two *māsas* of camphor and three *dirams* of saffron and use them in all kinds of food, it is wonderful. Another recipe for flavouring food: take nine leaves of the betel that is called *dīnat*, camphor, cardamoms and ground cloves. Add them to food, it is wonderful. Another recipe for flavouring foods: use sacred basil leaves and ground camphor because whatever food they are put into, it becomes good. Another recipe: chop mint and vinegar, add it to food and it becomes good. Another recipe (*f.48b*): *chavā*[58] should be used in all foods and with betel leaf (*tanbūl*) and, particularly, use it in perfume, it becomes good. Another recipe for flavouring: fry plenty of asafoetida in vegetable oil, then grind it and use it in food. That vegetable oil gives relish to food or greens or *kaṛhī* or *dūgh* or curds, it makes them tasty and it is good. Another recipe for flavouring: mix apples and rosewater together, flavour them and also put in white ambergris and scatter some musk on it. Also put sugarcane peel on food where required, flavour it and it becomes good. Another recipe for flavours of all kinds as follows: flavour of palm sugar, potherbs, (*f.49a*) sugar, gum lac (*lakha*), mastic (*masṭakī*), civet (*ghālihā*), chanpa oil, oil of jasmine (*mūgara*) and of white jasmine and of sandal, *rāl* (Saul tree resin), camphor juice, ambergris gum, amber, saffron, sesame seed, fenugreek, chickpeas, cumin, *sūnf*, coriander, essence of sour-orange leaves, essence of lime leaves, and the flavour of turmeric leaves. All these are separate flavours. Each food that is

58 The herb *Amaranthus oleraceus* or *A. gangeticus*, also known as *lālsag*.

required or each sherbet or each *dūgh* or juice or each meat or each vegetable, (*f.49b*) flavour it and make it tasty.

Another recipe for *rābaṛī: dūgh, jāman*, roast green potherbs, *zarat*, chick-peas, *'adas* lentils, *tūr* lentils, wheat, barley and *mūng* pulse separately and then grind them and put them singly into the *dūgh* and flavour it well. Put salt into some of it and use some without salt. Another recipe for *dūgh:* bake the kernels of *jāman* fruit, mangoes and jackfruit, and then grind them and put them in *dūgh* and flavour it with the same kernels.

Another recipe for the method for meat: boil the meat well, take it off, (*f.50a*) dry it and fasten it to a wooden skewer. Mix saffron, white ambergris and rosewater together and rub it on the meat. Put it in a cooking pot and add rice. Put in fresh ginger, onions and salt and cook it. Serve it with good gravy. Another recipe for meat: cut up the meat and cook it with turmeric, salt, fresh ginger, onions and *dūgh*. Flavour it with asafoetida fried in ghee. Add cardamoms, cloves, lime and pepper and serve it. Another recipe for meat: put the flanks of a sheep, bones of the breastbone, fat and the shoulder blade with all kinds of potherbs and mix them together. Add turmeric and (*f.50b*) rice flour. Make a broth, coloured yellow with sweet saffron and mango, and put in all the potherbs.

Another recipe for a delicacy: prepare balls made of *mūng* pulse stuck together, boil them and put them into minced meat. Prepare very small minced meat balls (*kūfta*) and cook them. Add raisins, almonds, pine kernels, pistachios, peeled kernels of the chironji nut,[59] peeled coconut, camphor, musk, rosewater and white ambergris and cook it. Fry it in ghee and add cardamoms and cloves.

Another recipe is for the method for the seeds of large watermelons: put together melon seeds and cucumber seeds and, having peeled them, grind them. (*f.51a, with a miniature*) Add some flour and, having made *baṛī* fried in ghee, bake it and put potherbs, camphor and rosewater on it.

Another recipe, for the method for *kaṛhī*: having put together mangoes, *dūgh*, salt, pepper, cumin, fenugreek, asafoetida, cardamoms and cloves, cook them and flavour with asafoetida. By the same method, make it from *kītha* (woodapple) and prepare (*f.51b*) by the same method any kind of *kaṛhī* that is required. Another recipe for *kaṛhī:* put in palm sugar and cook the *kaṛhī* and flavour it with asafoetida.

Another recipe for the method for *phāṭ* (split pulse): fry *mūng* pulse in ghee and add salt, water, asafoetida, fresh ginger juice, lime juice and onion juice.

59 From the tree *Chironjia sapida* or *Buchanania latifolia: chīrūnji* appears to be the word used for the nut, and *chārūlī* for the kernel. Babur calls them 'a thing between the walnut and the almond', much used in sweets and puddings.

Take it off when it is cooked and flavour it well. Another recipe, for kedgeree: fry the kedgeree[60] in ghee or bake it in almond oil or fry it in fresh butter and then, having added water and salt, cook it and put plenty of baked asafoetida in it (*f.52a*). Put in all kinds of relishes and put *pāpaṛ* layer upon layer on a dish and put sliced fresh ginger and onion on it. Another recipe for kedgeree: soak the kedgeree either in *dūgh* or congee or lime juice or tamarind juice or sour-orange juice or in perfumed water or in mint juice or in myrobalan juice or in pumpkin juice or in jackfruit juice or in *badhal* (monkey jackfruit) juice or in camphor juice or in musk juice. Select whichever is required from these and soak the *mūng* pulse and rice in it, then fry it in ghee. Cook the kedgeree and put relish and *pāpaṛ* in layers on a dish.

Another recipe for parched grain: (*f.52b*) put the parched grain into *dūgh*, add salt and pieces of onion and, having put in cumin, cook it. Also put parched grain into *kaṛhī* and cook it and, similarly, put parched grain into soup and cook it. Also having put cumin into congee, add parched grain and cook it.

Another recipe, for the method for *pīchha*: put rice water into a cooking pot, add some sacred basil and sweet basil and a handful of fresh leaves of sour-orange and lime and serve it.

Another recipe, for the method for *harsīya*:[61] cook the *harsīya* by the method used for *pīchha* until it is soft enough to eat with a spoon, or else cook it with partridge or quail or kid meat.

Another recipe (*f.53a*) is for the method for *rūda*: wash the entrails of a sheep until they are clean. Put potherbs of every kind into minced meat, stuff the entrails, boil them in a cooking pot and then bake them in ghee.

Another recipe, for the method for skewered meat (*sīkh*): mix meat with salt, onions and turmeric and boil it with whole potherbs. Cut it into very small pieces and strain it. Then fasten one segment of meat and one piece of onion on the skewer and rub ghee, caraway, lime juice, white ambergris, rosewater and salt on it. Bake it well and when it is tender, wrap it in thin bread and serve it.

Another recipe, for *zarat* bread: cook *zarat* bread (*f.53b*) and, having cooked it, turn it over and sprinkle rosewater on it. Then put either honey (*shahd*) and aromatic ghee on it or else ghee in which meat has been cooked.

Another recipe, for parched *zarat* (*thūmra*): cook parched *zarat* and fry it in ghee, then, having put honey (*shahd*), cardamoms and camphor on it, serve it.

60 Presumably meaning 'fry the mixture of rice and *dāl*' as indicated below.

61 Steingass (1957) defines *harsīya* as: 'a thick pottage of bruised wheat, boiled to a consistency, to which meat, butter, cinnamon and aromatic herbs are added'.

Another recipe: cook wheat *khīchra*[62] by the same method and also cook rice *bhāt* by the same method. Another recipe for *khīr* made of *zarat*: cook the *zarat khīr* and put plenty of poppy seeds on it and scatter honey (*shahd*) and aromatic ghee on it (*f.54a, with a miniature*), using plenty of honey (*shahd*) but only a small quantity of ghee.

Another recipe, for the method for buttermilk (*mhīrī*): cook the buttermilk in *dūgh* and bake it in ghee. Either make it sharp, sour or sweet, whichever recipe is appropriate, make that one.

Another recipe is for the method for *suhālī*:[63] (*f.54b*) mix cinnamon, cassia, cardamoms, camphor, white ambergris and onions with the dough of fermented dry bread and fry the *suhālī*.

Another recipe is for a vegetarian dish:[64] put together a quantity of those vegetables that are to hand, with aubergine, gourd (*kandūrī*), melon (*majaba*), gourd (*chachīnda*), grain, dill, zerumbet,[65] pumpkin and lentils. Cook them and flavour them with ghee. Fry asafoetida in vegetable oil, grind it and put it in and add salt.

Another recipe, for the method for sherbet: put together one cup of water with two *dirams* of sugar and add it to any fruit juice. This becomes a quantity of sherbet.

Another (*f.55a*) recipe, for the method for *kaṛhī*: put a quantity of screw pine (*kīyūra*) leaves into *kaṛhī*. When it has become well-flavoured, mix oil of aloes, *tagrī* (fragrant powder), sandal and rosewater and flavour it. Flavour it with aloes and throw away the debris of the screw pine. Another recipe for *kaṛhī*: put flowers of every kind into the *kaṛhī*, boil it and add some camphor, cardamoms, musk and cloves.

Another recipe, for thin soft *zarat* bread: rub flour on top and underneath the dough and cook it in a way that prevents it from becoming hard or broken. Then eat it with honey (*shahd*) and ghee.

Another recipe (*f.55b*) is for the method for split pulse (*phāṭ*): put *mūng* and chickpeas together and cook them. Make the pulse soft with potherbs and flavours, then sandwich this filling between two sections of bread made from double wheat flour. Add *sūnf*, cook it and put the filling into that bread and either fry it in ghee or cook it over a thorn fire or eat the bread with the ghee which has been used to cook the pulse.

62 Another kind of kedgeree, of rice, barley and pulse boiled together, according to Platts (1965).

63 Platts: 'wheat flour kneaded with water and made into very thin bread cakes and fried in ghee; a thin greasy cake'.

64 *dīg-i bāghi*, lit. 'cooking pot of a garden'.

65 A plant or its aromatic roots, *Curcuma zerumbet*, a variant form of zedoary, *Curcuma zedoaria*, related to turmeric, but used instead of ginger.

Another recipe, for white grain bread: cook it and scatter portions of musk on it. Another recipe, for *nān-i tang* (thin bread): make it wide and scatter sesame seeds on it or poppy seeds or coriander seeds or raisins or walnuts or almonds. Rub these ingredients into it in place of grain flour (*f.56a*) or else rub on *chārūlī* flour[66] or roasted chickpea flour and cook the bread.

Another recipe, for *kaṛhī*: put essence of *gāl*[67] into *dūgh*, boil it and add *māst*, honey (*shahd*) and ghee. It is good. Another recipe, for sherbet: mix onion juice and fresh ginger juice and flavour it with baked asafoetida. Another recipe for sherbet: grind pine kernels or walnuts, add syrup and have it with plain parched grain or with *bhāt*. Another recipe, for soup: fry a cup of turmeric in ghee. Prepare flour from roasted rice and mix it in water and turmeric. Grind saffron and pepper and mix it in. If it is wished, (*f.56b*) sweeten it or else make it sour and eat it with *bhāt*.

Another recipe, for the method of stuffing: soak chickpea pulse and boil it. Grind together dried pine kernels, walnuts and pepper and then mix them with onions and lime juice. This is called Ghiyath Shahi's stuffing.

Another recipe, for sherbet: mix vinegar and honey (*ʿasl*) and when it appears to be well-blended, add dried bread to it. Another recipe, for a dried relish (*āvāta*): mix mango chutney with mustard seeds and salt and put it on iron plates. Leave it in the sun for eleven days, then put rape seed oil on it. It is good. Put (*missing folio(s)*) . . .[68]

(*f.57a*) . . . Chop the meat with salt, coriander and fenugreek and also chop betel leaf. Grind cloves and cardamoms and mix them into it. Another recipe, for *kaṛhī* with *bhāt* and rice: if it is desired to cook this, then cook this recipe and put into it some *māst* and the cream of *māst*, namely clotted cream, and parched *zarat* and *bhāt* of barley meal, put all these in it.

Another recipe, for sherbet involves mixing together mango syrup, mango juice, palm sugar, ground cardamoms, cloves and musk. Another recipe, for *dūgh*: put chopped mango into *dūgh* (*f.57b*) and add palm sugar or salt. Another recipe, for sherbet: having mixed mangoes with sugar, chop them and take the juice and put cardamoms, camphor and cloves into it. Another recipe, for sherbet: chop fresh ginger with sugar and strain off the juice. Add cardamoms and cloves to the juice. Strain off radish and fresh ginger juice and add it to those cardamoms and cloves with a little salt.

Another recipe, for the method for bread: mix together fresh butter, ghee, salt, flour and *sūnf* and cook it. Another recipe, (*f.58a*) for *dūgh*: put salted lime

66 Ground chironji kernels, i.e. *Buchania latifolia*.

67 A kind of rose.

68 Catchwords on f.56b are *nuʿī dīgar* but f.57a begins *bīyandāzad*. The Farsi foliation indicates one missing folio.

into *dūgh* and chop it. Strain it and eat it or else put in salt and flavour it with asafoetida and cumin.

Another recipe, for kedgeree (*khichrī*): put *khichrī* in ghee, add salt, flavour it with asafoetida and cumin and then fry it. Cook the *khichrī* and add salted lime juice, also the juice of preserved fresh ginger and preserved *basnuta*.[69] Put all these onto the kedgeree and add *dūgh*, a portion of onion and salt to the *bhāt*.

Another recipe, for meat: cook the meat well and separate the broth, separate the meat and separate the ghee and cook the meat. Add aubergines and pumpkin (*f.58b*) and cook it. Another recipe, for the method for stuffing (*bhrat*): flavour a lot of onion well and soak dry bread or thin dried meat in ghee. Another recipe, for broken pulse (*phāṭ*): put a quantity of *mūng* pulse with meat and chickpea pulse. Add onion and cook it.

Another recipe, for the method for bread: make bread greasy with sweet-smelling ghee or with ghee in which meat has been fried. Another recipe is the method for (*cooking a*) head (*kalla*): cook a sheep's head by the Khurasani method, then cook *mūng* pulse by the rustic method and cook the sheep's foot, having added rice. It is very good.

Another recipe: flavour unleavened dough . . . (*missing folio(s)*) (*f.59a*) having cooked it over thorns. Another recipe for bread: (*take*) white grains, rosewater, salt and a little camphor relish and cook the bread. This camphor bread is a delicacy of Ghiyath Shahi. Another recipe, for *kaṛhī*: mix *kaṛhī*, rice flour, *dūgh*, salt, turmeric and saffron together. Cook the *kaṛhī* and add camphor. This is Ghiyath Shahi's golden *kaṛhī*. Another recipe for *khichrī*: put musk and rosewater in *khichrī*. Another recipe for *kaṛhī*: put white ambergris and rosewater in *kaṛhī* and cook it. This is known as ambergris *kaṛhī*.

Another recipe, for the method for skewered meat (*sīkh*): cook the skewered meat well, then fry it in ghee. Add salt and lovage (*f.59b*) and cook it. Then put vinegar, palm sugar and broth on it and put meaty broth (*lās*) over it. Grind a quarter of a *sīr* of almonds, walnuts, pine kernels, pistachios and raisins and make a stuffing, adding a little palm sugar. Cook bread with a double filling over thorns and sprinkle it with rosewater.[70]

Another recipe is the method for water: make pieces of new earthenware very hot on a fire and put them in water. When the water becomes sweet-smelling, add rosewater and palm sugar. If another variety is required, then put in asafoetida and salt and this becomes another kind.

69 The plant *Linum strictum*, which has yellow flowers.

70 i.e. first make *sīkh kabābs*, put them in a gravy, and eat them with stuffed bread.

(*f.60a*) Put parched grain or *bhāt* with *dāl* or *zarat* with plenty of onion. Fry it in ghee, add water and salt and cook it and flavour it with vegetable oil. Knead the meat with seven betel leaves, six *dirams* of cardamoms, one *diram* of cloves, asafoetida and saffron and add onion. Flavour it, put in water, rice, ghee and chickpea pulse and serve it with soup. Another recipe for meat: use three *dirams* of garlic, half a *sīr* of onion, one cooking pot of meat, the equivalent of one *diram* of asafoetida, a quarter of a *sīr* of fresh ginger and half a *sīr* of chickpea pulse. Flavour it with ghee, add water and cook it. Another recipe for meat: rub the meat with asafoetida and *dūgh* and, having added onion and fresh ginger, flavour it with vegetable oil. (*f.60b*) Put water in and make soup or else stew (*lās*) and add salt, lime juice and pepper. Another recipe for meat: mix the meat with fresh ginger, onions, garlic, ambergris, aubergines, rice flour, fenugreek and salt, and cook it in rape seed oil. Either make soup or have it as a stew (*lās*).

Another recipe, for rice: mix almonds and saffron in ghee and bake the rice. Add water and cook the rice, adding salt, pepper and cloves. Another recipe for rice: a quarter of a *sīr* of almonds, a quarter of a *sīr* of raisins, a quarter of a *sīr* each of walnuts and pine kernels, five *sīrs* of rice, a quarter of a *sīr* of asafoetida, a quarter of a *sīr* of salt, two *dirams* of cloves, two *dirams* of pepper, two *dirams* of date sugar . . . (*missing folio(s)*)[71] (*f.61a*) . . . mix it with soup and put plenty of cassia and ghee into it.

Another recipe, for sherbet: five *dirams* of lime juice, seven *dirams* of pot-herbs and two *sīrs* of water. Sprinkle rosewater on it. Another recipe for sherbet: one *diram* of cardamoms, one *diram* of cloves, five *dirams* of pot-herbs, two *sīrs* of water. Another recipe, for *dūgh*: take the whey of sour *dūgh* and add salt and asafoetida. Flavour it with vegetable oil or asafoetida.

Another recipe, for *bhāt*: soak the *bhāt* in rose and sugar water (*gulshakar*), and put rosewater on it. Another recipe for *bhāt:* chop wild figs (*anjīr jangalī*), namely *gūlar*, make sherbet, add two *dirams* of palm sugar and mix the *bhāt* with it. (*f.61b*) Another recipe, for meat: chop sweet-orange peel and betel leaves and rub them into the meat. Another recipe for meat: chop *ajvā'īn* (lovage) and rub it into all kinds of meat. Another recipe for *bhāt*: cook pieces of banana and cut it into slices similar to two gold coins. Chop ten pieces of banana and two *sīrs* of raisins in water and then mix this sherbet with the *bhāt*. Another recipe, for *kaṛhī*: grind rice flour, poppy seeds, almonds and raisins and boil them in water. Add some ghee, cardamoms and cloves and serve it. Another recipe for *bhāt* (*f.62a*): put jujube (*bīrchūn*), namely dried love fruit (*kunār*)[72] in water, mix it with *bhāt* and add rosewater. Another

71 Catchword on f.60b is *shakartarī* but f.61a begins *bā shūrbā*. The Farsi foliation indicates one missing folio.

72 *Zizyphus jujuba*.

recipe for *bhāt*: grind roast chickpeas and roast sesame seeds and mix them with *bhāt*. Another recipe: put boiled wheat, namely wheat in the husk, with one *sīr* of *chārūlī*, one *sīr* of wheat, one *sīr* of rice, a quarter of a *sīr* of cloves, a quarter of a *sīr* of cardamoms, two *dirams* of date sugar and a quarter of a *sīr* of raisins, in water and cook them. Add three *dirams* of potherbs, cook the wheat grains in the husk and add a small amount of ghee.

Another recipe for bread: take bread kneaded in rose and sugar water, and ghee. Put in plenty of ghee. Cook the bread. Cook a *gūjhā* stuffing[73] (*f.62b*) and cook *suhālī* in mustard seed oil. Another recipe for *suhālī*: fry the *suhālī* in rape seed oil. Chop onions and garlic, take the juice and put it on the *suhālī*. Another recipe for *suhālī*: fry them in ghee and sprinkle rosewater on them. Prepare sherbet from wild figs (*gūlar*) and honey (*shahd*) and drink it with the *suhālī*. Another recipe for sherbet: make sherbet from pumpkin juice and mango syrup and put in camphor and rosewater. Another recipe for sherbet is from pumpkin juice and honey (*shahd*), add camphor and rosewater. Another recipe for *kaṛhī*: take the juice of a white China rose and mix it with rice flour, and put it in. (*f.63a*) That is an excellent variety, and, if salt and pepper are put in, that is another kind and if relish is put in that becomes another variety. If mace, cardamoms and cloves are put in, then that becomes another kind. Another recipe, for the method for *chaklī* (a round flat cake), cook it from *zarat* or from rice. If a sweetener is put in, it becomes a variety, and if a relish is put in and it is cooked, that becomes another sort, and if salt and pepper are put in that is a variety, and if perfume is put in and it is cooked that is another kind.

Another recipe, for *darr ra* (a kind of milk pudding): mix milk, rice flour and palm sugar. Cook some with camphor (*f.63b*) and put a little palm sugar into it. Another recipe, for the method for parched grain: make the parched grain into *chakra* (i.e. *chaklī*) with milk, put in cloves and make it slightly sweet. Another recipe for baked *dabra*:[74] grind *bhāt* with clotted cream (*malāyī*) and boil it in milk. Add a little palm sugar. If desired the *dabra* can be made from flour or roast chickpea flour or from water chestnut flour or from almond flour, cook it by the same method. Another recipe for *darr ra*: grind pine kernels in water and cook *bhāt* in the same water. Cook chironji kernels, walnuts, almonds, coconut, water chestnuts and make *kaṛhī* by whichever recipe is required. It becomes several kinds. (*f.64a*) Another recipe for *darr ra*: cook the *darr ra* and cook every kind of sour fruit that is required. These make varieties. Another recipe for sherbet: mix fruit juices and *jāman* juice and flavour it with camphor. Then make the sherbet in a Chinese porcelain cup and, by the same recipe, if it is so desired,

73 i.e. of ground almonds and other nuts.

74 *Dabra* is unripe corn, but here meaning a kind of sweetmeat.

make mango sherbet or corinda or *fālsa*[75] or pumpkin or from pampelmousse or jackfruit or from monkey jackfruit – make the sherbet from whichever is required. Add palm sugar, camphor, cinnamon, cassia and cardamoms.[76]

Another recipe for *navāla* (snacks):[77] (*f.64b*) put a quantity of flour with the white of a hen's egg, knead it together and then knead it into the separated yolk and then cook it in a damp cloth over hot sticks. Use it as a stuffing for *pūrī* bread. Cook the *pūrī* bread well. Make a filling of almonds, cardamoms, potherbs, cloves and rosewater. Use this as stuffing as well as the hen's egg. Fry it in ghee and sprinkle rosewater on it. Also, by the same method, prepare *navāla* with walnuts and with pine kernels and with pistachio nuts. Ghiyath Shahi's *navāla* is made by the same methods, every kind of them. Subsequently from this *navāla*, we call (*the following*) to mind: having made *pūrī* bread, make the *navāla* and add a little palm sugar, and a portion of pumpkin as well as potherbs, rosewater, cardamoms (*f.65a*) and cloves and stuff the *pūrī*. Moisten camphor and fry it in oil and put syrup and date sugar on it. There are several varieties (*of navāla*). Also use water lily flowers, white China rose flowers, the leaves of *pū'ī*,[78] yam (*panḍālū*) leaves, garlic leaves, lentil leaves, *chīnach* (a herb) leaves, melon leaves, fresh shoots of the sour-orange bush, fresh young shoots of lime and tamarind and fig (*pīpal*) and mango and *jāman*. Rub them with chickpea flour and rice flour, fry them in ghee, rub in potherbs and sprinkle them with rosewater, camphor and cardamoms. If syrup is put in, (*f.65b*) then it is another variety and if salt, relish and pepper are added, this is another sort. Also if dry bread is cooked in perfumed ghee and vegetable oil or if *pūrī* is cooked in essence of turmeric and fenugreek or if *qarṣak* (a small sweet cake) is cooked, flavour it.

Another recipe, for rice: make rice water from rice and eat it with *dūgh* and turmeric. Another recipe for cold food (*sardāna*): boil milk, allow it to cool then add mango syrup and flavours. Another recipe for ghee: put bananas and dates into ghee. Boil the ghee, strain it and add date sugar (*f.66a, with a miniature*) and eat this ghee with food. Remove the bananas and dates from the ghee, put palm sugar on them and make sherbet. Another recipe for sherbet: mince coconut and leave it (*to soak*) in sweetened water. Strain off the coconut milk and, if desired, put syrup in it and also mangoes if so wished. (*f.66b*) Then drink it with *bhāt*.

Another recipe is for a method for ghee: put date sugar and jackfruit into ghee, boil it and eat it with food. Another recipe for soup: prepare minced meat, put chickpea *dāl* into it and cook the soup. Toss plenty of garlic into it

75 The sour purplish berry of *Grewia asiatica*, long known in India under the name *phālsa* as yielding a refreshing drink.

76 Note in margin below: '*navāla*'.

77 Platts (1965): 'a morsel or a dish of meat or a dish set before an unexpected guest'.

78 Indian spinach, or the potherb *Basella lucida*, white basil – probably the latter here.

and add fresh ginger, onions, lime juice, cardamoms, cloves, pepper, turmeric and fenugreek and flavour it with asafoetida.

Another recipe for skewered meat (*sīkh*): fry the *sīkh* well and chop some radishes and onions finely. Put together lime juice, fresh ginger juice, salt, asafoetida, turmeric, fenugreek, *āzmūda* and ghee. Rub them on the *sīkh* and revolve them over a fire. (*f.67a*) When they are roasted, stuff them into hot thin bread and serve them. Another recipe is for *yakhnī*: boil the fruit of bananas, cut them finely and flavour them well, with fresh ginger, onions, lime juice, salt, turmeric, fenugreek and asafoetida and make the *yakhnī*.

Another recipe, for relish: put mint and salt into lime syrup. Another recipe for sherbet: put lime juice into palm sugar syrup and sharpen (*the flavour*) with camphor. Another recipe for sherbet: chop vinegar, onions and mint together and add cardamoms and camphor. Another recipe for the same (*i.e. sherbet*): mix *dūgh* with rice flour, boil it and add pepper and salt. Put it in an earthenware dish (*f.67b*) and flavour it with asafoetida and vegetable oil.

Another recipe, for *palīv* (soup or broth): chop up partridge meat, cook it in *dūgh* and put it in asafoetida and vegetable oil in an earthenware pot, flavour it and it becomes partridge *palīv*. Another recipe for *palīv*: boil *zarat*, throw away the husks, wash it well and chop it up with *dūgh*. Having drained off the *dūgh*, take it and make the *palīv*. Flavour it with asafoetida and vegetable oil in an earthenware pot.

Another recipe for pickle (*āchār*): take figs (*pīpal*), wild figs (*gūlar*), *phīphar, jāman* fruit, sour corinda, *āmla* seeds, bananas, green chickpeas, roasted chickpeas and small cucumbers. Put in sourness (*tarshī*), sharpness (*tīz*) and salt and make the pickle. All these . . . (*missing folio*).[79]

(*f.68a*) . . . a quarter of a *sīr* of almonds and a quarter of a *sīr* of coconut into it. Another recipe for rice: cook the rice well. Put sour-orange leaves, lime leaves, *karna* (citron) leaves,[80] sacred basil and sweet basil into the rice and cook it or else, having put it into *khichrī*, cook it. After cooking take out the leaves and put in cardamoms and cloves. Another recipe, for *maṭṭhā* (curds): put palm sugar, vinegar, cloves, cardamoms, camphor and musk into the curds and add thin bread and broken *pūrī* bread and meat. This is Indian *baghrā*.[81] Another recipe for stuffing: mix water lily seed flour, cloves, (*f.68b*) camphor and palm sugar and fry it in ghee. Another recipe for *pālūda kūkū*:[82] prepare the *pālūda* from water lily seed flour. Make sherbet from cardamoms

79 Catchword on f.67b is *nū'* but f.68a begins *bādām*. The Farsi foliation indicates one missing folio.

80 A citron, with aromatic flowers.

81 'Sections of dough' normally.

82 *Pālūda* is a rich drink usually of water thickened with a certain type of flour or (latterly) sago, with added cream and fruit juices. *Kūkū* is a kind of fritter.

and palm sugar and put this sherbet into the *pālūda*. Another recipe, for meat *kūkū*: squeeze the seeds out of jackfruit, put them in the meat, add a relish and put in cardamoms and cloves.

Another recipe, for rice: stick cloves in a sour-orange and having removed the pulp, stuff the orange with cloves, cardamoms, musk, camphor, saffron and rosewater. Put this orange into rice and cook it.

Another recipe (*f.69a*) is for the method for *baṛa* (fried pulse balls): make *baṛa* from unripe wheat (*gūdī*) or make it from *mūtha* (mothi) beans or from parched grain or from *māsh* pulse or from *mūng dal* or from *zarat* or from any grains that are to hand. Make *baṛa* of every kind. Make it from small chick-peas (*batūṛī*) and from chickpeas (*nakhūd*) and from *zarat*. Prepare *baṛa* from each of these. Put fresh butter into flour, cook the *baṛa* and put relish into some and put perfume into some or put syrup into some and put potherbs of all kinds into some. Have some of the *baṛa* plain, some dry and make some of it moist.

Another recipe, for wheat *khichrī*: pound wheat *khichrī* well and having blanched it, (*f.69b*) take it and cook it in distilled water. When it is well-cooked, remove it and make it thoroughly cold. Strain *māst* (coagulated milk) through a cloth and put the thick part into the *khichrī*. Add salt and mustard seeds so that it can be used in *rā'īta* and eat it on the second day when it has become stale.

Another recipe, for sherbet: put six *dirams* of cardamoms and three *dirams* of cloves into water with enough potherbs to make it tasty and make the sherbet. Another recipe, for *dūgh*: put limes and cloves into *dūgh* and also put salt and asafoetida into *dūgh* and also put chopped betel leaves, cardamoms, cloves and camphor into *dūgh*. Another recipe, (*f.70a*) for sherbet: chop up two Sulayman (*white*) dates fried in ghee, dissolve them in water and make the sherbet.

Another recipe, for *baṛa*: put *mūng baṛa* into flummery (*anbalvānī*). Another recipe, for sherbet: chop up monkey jackfruit, mix it with water and add palm sugar or salt and mustard seed. Then make carrot *biryān*, chop the carrots up in water and add palm sugar and flavouring. Make the sherbet. Another recipe, for meat: put sorrel (*anbūta*) or orris root (*chūka*) with the meat and put greens with the meat. Another recipe, for sherbet: make the sherbet from vinegar, honey (*shahd*) and water, also serve it with duck and make *baṛī māst biryān*[83] (*f.70b*) and then make broth or stew from the meat and, having put the above-mentioned *baṛī* into it, cook it.

Another recipe for meat: when the meat is cooked, take it off and put in dried ground fenugreek. Another recipe, for the method for supper stew (*āsh shām*):

83 *Baṛī māst* is the modern *dāhi vadā*, i.e. wadas in yoghurt – perhaps these were then baked?

put together two half *sīrs* of *khichrī*, two half (*du nīm*) *sīrs* of meat and cook them. Put in plenty of ghee so that when it is cooked, the wheat and ghee are fused together (*congealed*), and flavour it with orris root or dill (*sūva*) and cook it. Another recipe, for chickpeas: flavour meat with asafoetida (*f.71a*) and cook it. Add chickpea pulse. Add cumin, fenugreek, asafoetida, salt, turmeric, pepper, lime juice and garlic, cook it until it is very tender.

Another recipe, for potherbs (*sāk*): flavour basil green (*pū'ī*) with asafoetida, cook it and add rice and salt. When it is cooked, take it off and serve it. Another recipe, for partridge: cook the partridge well, flavour it with asafoetida and put in chickpea pulse and add salt, cumin, fenugreek and turmeric. Another recipe, for chicken: cook the chicken using the same recipe explained for partridge and cook it well. Another recipe, for the method for pressed meat (*chachpīrak*): chop the minced meat finely (*f.71b, with a miniature*) and prepare a small loaf from fine white flour. Take two loaves, one below and one above, and stuff the mince between them. Make the sides firm and cook them with other meat. Add chopped cumin, fenugreek, asafoetida, salt, turmeric, pepper, lime juice, fresh ginger and onion, also put in *sūnf*. With the same kind of mince, make a gourd dish or a water chestnut dish and, having put in good potherbs, serve it.

(*f.72a*) Another recipe, for the method for *baṛī*: wash *māsh* pulse and grind it. Keep it overnight and put one portion of asafoetida in it. The next day put in an equal amount of asafoetida, and having baked cumin, pepper, onions, fresh ginger and fenugreek, mix them with crushed salt and beat the *baṛī*. By the same method prepare *baṛī* from *mūng*. Another recipe, for mango (*āmla*) *baṛī*: grind *āmla* in *pīṭhī māsh*,[84] add potherbs and beat the *baṛī* a great deal. Another recipe, for melon (*majad*): split the melon and remove the inside pulp. Add *māsh* pulse to it and put in baked asafoetida (*f.72b*), cumin and fenugreek. Mix it with poppy seeds and fresh ginger. Keep the ground *pīṭhī* for one day and beat the *baṛī* on the second day.

Another recipe, for *sakbā*:[85] put vinegar into meat broth, add cinnamon, cassia, cardamoms, flavouring and whole potherbs. Another recipe, for *tarīd*:[86] put ghee and different kinds of dried bread into broth. Sherbet: put pieces of dried bread in sherbet. Another recipe: put pieces of dried bread into *dūgh* and add onions, garlic and salt. Flavour it with asafoetida. Another recipe, for *dūgh*: flavour the *dūgh* well and put in salt, (*f.73a*) cumin and fenugreek. Another recipe, for meat: put cumin, pomegranate seeds and whole potherbs into meat broth. Another recipe, for *dūgh*: put palm sugar,

84 Pulse soaked in water, then crushed or ground.

85 Steingass (1957): a dish made with wheat, vinegar and wheat flour.

86 Steingass (1957): bread crumbled in milk; sop.

lime and asafoetida into *dūgh*. Another recipe, for *dūghbā* (dried buttermilk): put meat into *dūgh* and cook it.

Another recipe, for mince: for the amount of minced meat available, prepare an equivalent amount of minced onion and also prepare minced onion leaves and a quantity of half that amount of radish (*tarab*) leaves and a third of that amount of minced fresh ginger and two of garlic, lime juice and saffron. Having put in those amounts, cook the *yakhnī* and eat it with hot thin bread. (*f.73b*) Another recipe for mince: mix together chickpea pulse, garlic and mince, cook it and add lime juice and pepper. Chop radishes (*tarab*), fresh ginger and onions and put them in. Another recipe for mince: put *dūgh*, garlic, grape syrup and vinegar in mince and cook it. Another recipe for mince: put chickpea pulse, *sūnf* syrup and radishes in mince and make broth (*lās*) from it. Add fresh ginger, onions and lime juice, flavour it with vegetable oil and add asafoetida. Eat it with hot bread. Another recipe for mince: put pumpkin with mince and cook it. Then add mace, cassia and cardamoms and cook it well.

Another recipe, for *kūfta*: put together morsels of dried ginger (*zanjabīl*), morsels of radishes, (*f.74a*) morsels of asafoetida, morsels of onion and morsels of garlic. Prepare one meat ball (*kūfta*) and cook it with broth. Add lime juice, pepper and potherbs and serve it. Another recipe for *kūfta*: (*take*) seven cumin seeds, saffron, some mustard, musk, some mustard seeds and camphor and the same quantity of white ambergris. Mix them all together, make the *kūfta*, and make soup broth and cook it. Add pepper, lime juice and potherbs and cook it and then add the leaves of *kasūndī*,[87] mint, sacred basil and all potherbs. Another recipe, for the greens of orris root: having boiled orris root greens, mix them with mince. Form balls (*kūfta*), (*f.74b*) cook them and add pepper and relish. Another recipe for *kūfta*: put jackfruit into mince and prepare meatballs or else put in pumpkin or monkey jackfruit or mango syrup or unripe mango (*gīrī*) or fresh shoots of mango or sour-orange or fresh shoots of sour-orange. Use all the aforementioned varieties with mince and prepare meat balls.

Another recipe, for sherbet: chop together figs, *fālsa*, and dried dates with water. Make sherbet, flavour it and put in an equal amount of syrup. Another recipe for *kūfta:* steam orris, mint, dill and sorrel and make the *kūfta* with sumach juice (*āb-i samagh*). (*f.75a*) Fry it in ghee, put syrup, rosewater and camphor on it and serve it. Another recipe for *kūfta*: chop water lily flowers and put them with mince. Prepare the *kūfta* and fry it in ghee and flavour it with rosewater and camphor. Another recipe for *kūfta*: pound the meat and mix it with a scattering of poppy seeds, salt, *sūnf*, saffron, camphor and musk. Form it into balls and wrap the balls in lime leaves and put them into

87 Kasaundi, a green leafy member of the cassia family, *Cassia sophera*.

soup and broth. If the balls are wrapped in sour-orange leaves or in betel leaves these are other varieties.

Another recipe, for swollen parched grain (*khandvī*): put in *mūng* and whole potherbs (*f.75b*) and prepare the *khandvī*. Mix rice flour and *dūgh* and make *kaṛhī* and add it to the swollen grain (*khandvī*). If the *khandvī* is put into congee, it makes another kind as it does if put into soup or sour fruit juice or *kaṛhī*, or if asafoetida is put on to sour milk (*ḍaḍa*) this is another kind, and if it is fried in ghee and syrup, and flavouring is put on it, then that is a variety. If it is put into mustard juice or into sweet sherbet or into flummery (*anbalvānī*), (*f.76a, with a miniature*) these are other kinds.

Another recipe, for the method for sherbet: five *dirams* of sugar, two *dirams* of fresh ginger, two *dirams* of cloves, two *dirams* of cardamoms. Grind all these together, sift them and make the sherbet and put camphor on it. Another recipe, for *ḥarīra*:[88] grind poppy seed flour, coriander and cumin seeds and put them with *sūnf*, clove essence and cardamoms (*f.76b*) in water and boil them and add a little palm sugar and ghee. Another recipe, for sour-orange *ḥarīra*: prepare the *ḥarīra* from sour-oranges. Chop up all the fruit and put it in and add date sugar and syrup. This becomes orange *ḥarīra*. Another recipe for *ḥarīra*: put marsh melon (*kharbaza*) seeds with palm sugar and date sugar, make the *ḥarīra* and put cardamoms and cloves on it.

Another recipe, for supper food (*āshshām*) *khichrī*: cook wheat and meat together so that they amalgamate, add soft fresh butter, cloves and mace. If *mūng āshshām* is made, this is another kind and, if it is made from *zarat* or rice, (*f.77a*) then these are different varieties. Another recipe for the method for *zarat āshshām:* make *zarat āshshām* and add *āzmūda*.[89] Use the amount of grain that is available. If *āshshām* is made from different kinds of grain, then each grain makes a different variety of *āshshām*.

Another recipe, for sherbet: grind palm sugar, cardamoms and cloves, make sherbet and, if *bhāt* is added to it, it becomes *pānbhāt*. Another recipe, for the method for mango *khandvī*: put palm sugar, cardamoms, flour and cloves together and boil them. Make *rābaṛī*,[90] then prepare the *khandvī* and add ten *dirams* of honey (*ʿasl*), twenty *dirams* of ghee, dry bread crumbs and fresh ginger syrup (*f.77b*). This is one variety, and if sour-orange is put into some, that is another kind, and if greens water, chickpeas, fresh ginger juice, pepper and salt are put in, this is another sort.

Another recipe, for meat: cut *kabābs* of thin veal, add rounds of onion, fresh ginger, cardamoms, cloves and rice flour and flavour it with ghee. Add whole potherbs and, having roasted *āzmūda* seed, put that in. Another recipe, for

88 Platts (1965): 'a kind of pap made of sugar, milk, water, aniseed and cardamoms'.

89 *Ajmūd*, parsley; *āzmūda*, variously defined as parsley, celery seeds or caraway.

90 Platts (1965): 'a kind of food like pap; meal mixed with buttermilk; thickened milk'.

tied meat: take one portion of meat and one portion of onion. Put a portion of cardamoms, cloves and saffron on it and, on top of that, put a portion of onion (*f.78a*) and tie it with thread. Then add whole potherbs, fry it in ghee and put in lime juice and fresh ginger juice. When it is cooked, take it off and throw away the thread.

Another recipe, for soup (*shūrbā*): give a little flavour of garlic to fresh ginger juice and onion juice and then cook the meat soup. Add coriander, cumin, fenugreek, lime juice and asafoetida. It makes very good soup. Another recipe for soup: put a portion of meat into pure water with fresh ginger juice, lime, cumin, fenugreek, coriander and *sūnf* and then boil the meat. Take the strained liquid from it and, having tied whole potherbs in muslin, put them into it. Add relish (*f.78b*) and pepper and serve it. Put all the following in water and boil them: spikenard essence, wild spikenard, *mūtha* beans, small melon, wheat, cinnamon, cassia, cardamoms and cloves. Strain off the water, keep it and put in camphor and musk. Cook *bhāt* in that water or whatsoever is desired. Another recipe for meat: boil the meat well, add vinegar and mint and serve it.

Another recipe, for the method of flavouring food or *pān* or water: two *dirams* of sandal, one *diram* of musk, half a *diram* of white ambergris, rosewater, whatever is required use that flavouring. Another recipe for perfume or flavouring (*taʿṭīr*): put oil of aloes on potherbs, then distil *chūva* in (*f.79a*) a glass and put camphor, musk and rosewater into the aloes essence. Use it with whatever is required to be flavoured or perfumed. Another recipe for *taʿṭīr*: take saffron, rosewater, musk, camphor – whatever is desired, use this perfume or flavouring.

Another recipe, for meat: flavour meat and four aubergines and make them quite soft by cooking them. Put in sour and sharp flavouring and whole potherbs and cook them. Fry asafoetida in vegetable oil or in ghee and chop it and put it into the cooking pot. Another recipe, for 'foreign' (*gharīb*) food: boil green vegetables in water or boil them in lentil water. Cook *zarat* bread and flavour it. Whichever green vegetables are used in this food, flavour them with vegetable oil (*f.79b, with a miniature*) and asafoetida. Put fresh ginger, onions and pepper on them and, having put them all together, cook them and add asafoetida oil. Another recipe for green vegetables: boil vine greens in *dūgh* and water. Then take them off, squeeze them well and open them out and fan them. Then having roasted and ground cumin, salt and sesame seeds, add them . . . (*missing folio(s)*)[91]

(*f.80a*) . . . lime juice, roast lovage, fresh ginger, vegetable broth, cloves, cooked ghee, sweet sesame seeds, fresh cow's butter, coriander seed, white

91 Catchword on f.79b is *bīyandāzad* but f.80a begins with the word *āb-i līmū*. The Farsi foliation sequence is unbroken.

ambergris and tamarind. Also make *rā'ītā* of all kinds, sour or sweet or sharp, from leaves or shoots or roots. Prepare it from whatever is desired, put in *māst* and mustard seeds and this becomes *rā'ītā*. If it is made from good quality perfumes, these form other varieties as follows: flowers of *sapastān*,[92] or flowers of tamarind (*tamarhindī*) or of the horse radish tree (*sanhajna*) and rape seed, tamarind (*tantaṛīkha*), date sugar, ghee, cloves, asafoetida, young shoots of fig tree (*pīpal*), gherkins, cucumbers, flavoured vegetable oil, large gherkins, fresh ginger, Chinese cubebs,[93] orris root greens, loaf sugar, (*f.80b*) lime juice, aubergines, galingale,[94] turmeric, mustard, cassia, long pepper, *dūgh*, small gherkins, lentils, apples, green chickpeas, grain, pumpkin, *māst*, cardamoms, mace, lovage, pepper and white ambergris.

Again, use the method for cooking fish and, if there is no fish, then cook meat by the fish cooking method with rice flour. Should there be a long fish that resembles a snake, do not eat it after it has been cooked but eat the rest of every kind of fish. Again, do not eat milk and fish together nor aubergines and fish nor *māst* and fish. (*There now follows a list of foods that are, presumably, permissible to eat with fish, namely*): salt, sour-orange, rice flour, *tantaṛīkha*, roast lentils, dried ginger, roast sesame seeds, cloves, cumin essence, poppy seeds, garlic, roast *mūng* flour, (*f.81a*) cumin, tamarind (*tamarhindī*), fenugreek, chickpea flour, green coriander, congee, *karna*, almond oil, ghee, dried fresh ginger, vegetable oil, long pepper, rape seed oil, onions, mustard seed oil, *sūnf* essence, roast water chestnuts, jujube (*bīrchūn*). Also a recipe for the fish that is called *trikanṭak* ('three-spiked') in Hindi. This fish has three spikes and these spikes are poisonous so throw them away. The flesh is good, cook it and eat it. Also another fish, called the gall-fish. There is poison in the gall of this fish and in its fat. If a man eats it, he will die.

Again, recipes for the cooking of *pūrī* bread and dry bread (*kāk*) and *chapātī* and baked bread (*tanūrī*). (*f.81b*) Having rubbed on the seasonings suitable for that bread and (*also*) roast chickpea flour and sesame seed flour, cook the *pūrī* and then grease it with ghee and put it in a damp cloth. With other breads, cooked from different grains,[95] it is necessary that the flour for rubbing on the sides[96] should consist of flour of other grains.[97] Having rubbed the flour on it, cook the bread. (*Follows a list of suitable ingredients*): chickpea (*batla*), *zarat* (*rāla*), green chickpeas, *zarat* (*kanganīz*), parched wheat grains,

92 Sebestan plum, *Cordia myxa*.

93 Cubeb: the berry of the climbing shrub *Piper cubeba*, which resembles a grain of pepper and has a pungent spicy flavour.

94 Galingale (*khūlanjān*): aromatic roots of the *genera Alpinia* and *Kaempferia*.

95 Note between lines 4 and 5: 'namely *palīthan*', the dry flour put under or over dough (synonym *khashkī*).

96 *Balavan* (*sic*) = *palīthan*.

97 i.e. not the same as that used to make the dough.

salt, parched *chārūlī* kernels, almond flour, sesame seeds, *sūnf*, walnut flour, asafoetida, *tīvra*,[98] flavourings of all kinds, barley, lovage, *zarat*, lentils, coriander, *mūng* pulse, fine white flour, *gūdī*,[99] grain kernels (*bran*), nigella (*kalūnjī*) seed, chickpeas, wheat, plain boiled rice, also (*f.82a*) the potherb *kasūndī* (*smelling of*) camphor (*kapūr kasūndī*),[100] dry bread, rosewater, salt, chickpea pulse, musk, myrobalan, *karna*, beetroot (*chaghandar*), dill greens, fresh ginger, sweet basil, sorrel, fenugreek greens, pumpkin, gourd (*kankarū*), pomegranate seeds, cloves, lime leaves, cardamoms, boiled water, cinnamon, lime juice, cassia, onions, *dūgh*, turmeric, lovage, radishes, white ambergris, mustard seeds, ghee, vegetable oil flavour, *sūnf*, coriander, sour-orange leaves, rice, round peppers. Also, to boil milk: having strained the milk and taken the water that remains, do not drink the water of that milk with fish and do not drink milk with fish. Do not eat the following with milk: fish, radishes (*tarab*), *mūng*, flour, *mūtha* beans, lentils (*ʿadas*), *kaltha* (a pulse) and *zarat* greens (*f.82b*) nor with any green stuffs nor with sour fruit, do not drink milk with any of the preceding collection of foods. Also do not drink milk with salt. Milk that has gone bad should not be drunk nor should meat and milk be eaten together. Drink milk with the following: honey (*shahd*), almonds, raisins, coconut, wheatgrain, whey, wild dates (*khajūr*), dates (*khurmā*), myrobalan, honey (*shahd again*), melon seeds, thin bread, dried myrobalan, black bananas, *pūhīya* rice, walnuts, *chārūlī* kernels, pistachios, pine kernels, water chestnuts, *kasīrū* tubers, *kaṛhī*, water lilies, camphor, musk, cardamoms, cinnamon, cassia, date sugar, round peppers, long peppers, pepper roots, ghee, palm sugar, *laḍḍū, suhālī* bread, potherbs, *tal saklī* (sweetmeat), *khāja, phīnī*, (*f.83a*) all kinds of *bhāt*, milk, rice in the husk (*dhūnḍhan*), parched grain, *kītkī* and *zarat* – drink milk with all the aforementioned.

Also for the cooking of *baṛa* of all kinds: prepare the *baṛa* and fry it either in ghee or sweet sesame oil or in almond oil or rape seed oil or in ghee flavoured with burnt asafoetida. Add fenugreek, cumin and *sūnf*. Fry the *baṛa* in these things and also prepare *khandvī* having thoroughly roasted it. Use round pepper, bean pulse, onions, fresh ginger, honey (*shahd*), palm sugar, molasses, cane sugar syrup, flavouring; *chūlāā'ī*[101] and rice flour; vine leaves and rice flour; clove of garlic and rice flour; (*f.83b, with a miniature*) *chīnach* (a herb) and rice flour; mustard seed oil and *chārūlī* kernel flour, chickpea flour and *chārūlī* kernels; *mūng dāl* and almond flour; dates and rice flour; tamarinds and palm sugar and rice; white basil and rice flour; *sūnf* and rice flour; coriander, cloves, musk, cassia, cinnamon, burnt *sūnf* in vegetable oil;

98 Pungent strong hot relishes or spices.

99 Unripe wheat or barley parched in the ear.

100 *Kasūndī* is a green potherb, *Cassia sophera*, here apparently smelling of camphor.

101 The potherb *Amaranthus polygymus*.

vegetable oil in burnt fenugreek; cumin oil, oil in burnt asafoetida, ghee, walnuts and rice; (*f.84a*) parched grain and water chestnuts; bread and *māst*; camphor, plenty of *sūnf; zarat* and pine kernels; water lily seed flour, long pepper, *baṭlūn* (myrobalan and salt) and rice flour; oil of betel leaves (*tanbūl*); lentils, rice, *kaltha* pulse, *mūtha* beans, coriander seed, asafoetida, date sugar, *āzmūda, sūnf*, salt, rosewater, fenugreek, *baṛa* made from melons, tamarinds, *gūdī*,[102] *baṭlūn*, cumin, chickpea *dāl*, rape seed oil. Add honey (*shahd*), palm sugar, molasses, cane sugar syrup, camphor, musk and rosewater. Add flavouring to whole potherbs and also add flavouring to water or *dūgh* or buttermilk or *kaṛhī* or sherbet or congee or lime juice or sour-orange juice or unripe grape (*ghūra*) juice or barberry (*zarashk*) juice or mango syrup or myrobalan syrup (*f.84b*) and potherbs. Put the fried *baṛa* into these ingredients. It is also a remedy for pain caused by food indigestion, it brings relief.

This remedy was used by Sultan Firuz:[103] five *dirams* of *ajmūd*, five *dirams* of *jāpatrī* (mace), five *dirams* of cloves, five *dirams* of poppy seeds, five *dirams* of jasmine (*maghāra*) seeds and five *dirams* of saffron. Grind and sift this collection of ingredients for the remedy and then mix it in honey (*'asl*) and make it into balls (*pellets*) equal in size to prepared betel chews. Eat one pellet daily, the semen flows. (*Other ingredients are*) mustard seed, *zarat* grain, cardamoms, sugar, camphor, jujube, jackfruit, musk, mimusops, water lilies, sandal, corinda, *kankīrū*, bamboo shoots (*dhāman*), water chestnuts, *bhāt*, potherbs, (*f.85a*) starfruit (*kamrak*), salt, rosewater, monkey jackfruit, myrobalan, *kasīrū* root, *kītha* (woodapple), pungent bastard-saffron seed (*kazar-i tīvra*), oil of aloes, hog plum (*anbāṛa*), wild dates, cloves, *tīndū*,[104] honey (*shahd*), *fālsā*.

Also for pain, the (*following*) remedies produce lustful feelings and increase the flow of semen: long pepper, cardamoms, chironji kernels (*chārūlī*), fresh cow's butter, cow's ghee, sheep's milk, poppy seeds, cloves, date sugar, pine kernels, dried ginger, milk, dates, sugar, roasted chickpeas, *chārūlī*, almonds, figs, myrobalan, cow's milk, *'āqarqarhā*,[105] raisins and honey (*shahd*). Mix them, little by little, together and rub them on the penis. It makes sexual intercourse very pleasurable and comfortable. Also for good sexual intercourse and improved flow of semen, fry the following in ghee and eat them: flesh of a calf, flesh of sheep, (*f.85b*) brains of the domestic sparrow, pigeon, ghee, cow's milk, cardamoms, *'āqarqarhā, basbāsa* (mace), cinnamon and ten

102 Unripe barley or wheat parched in the ear.

103 Firuz Shah Tughluq of Delhi, 1351–88, from whom Dilawar Khan Ghori, the ancestor of the Sultans, received Malwa as a fief.

104 Fruit of *Diaspyros melanoxylon*, the Coromandel ebony, with an astringent fruit used in medicine and also for eating when quite ripe.

105 *Dranunculus anthemis pyrethrum*, used to treat headaches, toothache, paralysis of the tongue; it increases saliva.

domestic sparrows, they produce strong lust. (*Again*) palm sugar, roasted chickpeas, raisins, white *mūṣlī*,[106] *kankīrū* roots, honey (*shahd*), *ajmūd*, cloves, *kūchhā* seeds,[107] fine white flour, ground *zarat*, milk, haggis (*kīpā*), *gūkhrū*, white rock salt, chironji kernels, flesh of domestic sparrows, poppy seeds, dates, jasmine seeds, pine kernels, yolks of hens' eggs and wheat bread.

Again to prepare fresh pickle from ingredients: when the roots, leaves, flowers and blossoms have been broken up together, mix them with potherbs of every kind . . . (*possible missing folio(s)*)[108] . . . lovage, (*f.86a*) cinnamon, sour-oranges, melons, barberries, mace, asafoetida, fenugreek and the flowers of tamarind. Again the special quality of the following medicine is that it wards off bile and phlegm, purifies the blood and stops copious sweating. It is a purge and an aperient and also if it is rubbed on the skin, it purifies the pigment and the outer skin. This is the medicine: yellow myrobalan (*halīla*), balleric myrobalan (*balīla*), white China rose, fresh myrobalan (*āmla*), skin of *pterocarpus* (*bīya*), wild figs, catechu essence, *gulanbar* (mango?), figs, *phīphār*,[109] *jāman* kernels, *gulanbar* peel, *tīndū* peel, honey (*shahd*), *kānṭā sīlīyā*,[110] *kanval* (lotus) tubers, fresh pepper, cassia leaf, Coral tree (*marjān*) seeds, *mūtha* beans, mango (*anba*) tree bark, (*f.86b*) *barma*,[111] unripe wood-apple, unripe dates, skins of swollen parched grain, sesame oil, *ajmūd, kāyaphal* bark,[112] *lūd* bark,[113] bark of *mahva*,[114] *parīnag* or *phālī*,[115] ghee (*hūs*), *mūchras*,[116] sesame meal, pomegranate seeds, pomegranate skin, *dhāva* flowers,[117] *bandhāra*,[118] white water lily (*kīrav*) seeds.

Another aphrodisiac: the properties of this medicine are that it increases semen and strengthens desire. It is beneficial to the elderly and to youth and to children. It sharpens the intellect, makes the eyes shine, purifies the skin, enhances the hearing and the acuteness of the ear and it purifies the teeth and the tongue: *had ṣāgar*,[119] dried ginger (*zanjabīl*), round peppers, honey

106 White or black *mūṣlī* = a medicinal tuber, *Curculigo orchioides*, which is an aphrodisiac and a tonic.

107 A kind of tamarind.

108 Suspect catchwords on f.85b are *ajvā'īn dar ān* but f.86a begins with the words *ajvā'īn, taj, taranj*. The Farsi foliation sequence is unbroken.

109 *Gardenia latifolia*?

110 i.e. *kanta shelio* (frankincense).

111 *Tricosanthes incisa*, from the *Tricosanthes* species of gourds.

112 Wild nutmeg bark, *Myrica sapida*.

113 i.e. *ludhra*, medicinal bark of the tree *Symplocos racemosu*.

114 Tree with aromatic flowers, *Bassia latifolia*, or *Madhuca indica*, which when fermented were used for making spirits.

115 A medicinal and aromatic plant.

116 Gum of the Silk tree.

117 A red flower used in dyeing.

118 A drug.

119 Obscure, seems to mean 'dried deer bones'.

(*shahd*), (*f.87a*) jackfruit, almonds, *muhāmīd,*[120] grapes, mimusops and its fruit, *gūkhrū,*[121] white China rose, red rose, dates, *khārk,*[122] *kasīrū* root, fine white flour, *chūlā'ī* potherbs,[123] melon, piony (*khīyātūrī*), gourd, *ḍūḍī* (bottle gourd), *mahva* flowers, water lily seeds, milk, *rada barda,*[124] pomegranate seeds, cassia, date juice, *āmla*, garlic, cane sugar syrup, *jītī madd,*[125] *balbīj* seeds,[126] seeds of the rose (*kūza*), *mūṣlī* (medicinal tuber), chamomile, *āsanda* (Dragon's Blood),[127] figs, *khīr* made using *zarat*, sesame seeds, chironji kernels, pine kernels, pistachio nuts, walnuts, coconut, ghee, potherbs, bananas, *zarat*, gold leaf. The above-mentioned items make people fat and benefit those who are thin and those who are weak. Broken bones mend, wind and bile are cured and poison (*f.87b*) is warded off. They make for longevity and increasing comfort.

Also these (*following*) ingredients are effective in repelling fever. Cook the food and eat it. The fever of phlegm, biliousness, blood and wind is repelled. The ingredients are as follows: *pīpal* flowers, gourd, potherbs, *kalavī,*[128] yellow betel leaf, frankincense, roots of the caster-oil tree, cucumber, myrobalan, gentian (*charāyata*),[129] *mūng* pulse, peel of unripe mangoes, *andarjū* seeds,[130] the roots of *bal,*[131] black cumin, round pepper, Coral tree, *pīpal* root, *nasūt,*[132] *gūkhrū*, honey (*madhūrī*), small cardamoms, *raddha,*[133] stick liquorice (*jīthī*), *mākha vanā,*[134] *sadha* (nectar), Persian lilac (*bakā'īn*), salt (*sālūnī*), the milky fluid (*dūdhī*) found within wheat, cooked or boiled lentils,[135] a rose (*varda*), verbena (*sīvan*),[136] small lentils (*rinūka*), wild nutmeg bark, large lentils (*rīnkanīn*), (*f.88a*) sweet-orange, bamboo, roots of areca, round turmeric, mimosa (*rāsnī*),[137] *jīvak,*[138] hard dry bread, turmeric, rice in the husk, sesame

120 The Coral tree *Erythina indica.*
121 The plant *Ruellia longifolia* or *Tribulus lanciginosus.*
122 Swallow wort, *Calatropis gigantea.*
123 *Amaranthus polygamus.*
124 Obscure, a variety of *zarat*?
125 *Jītī* is a variety of euphorbia that yields oil.
126 *Balbīj*, seeds especially of the *Abutilon indicum*, used medicinally throughout western India.
127 *Dalbergia ougeinensis*. It has red gum and the bark extract is used medicinally.
128 *Gloriosa superba*, the Superb Lily, of which the tubers are used medicinally.
129 *Gentiana cherayta.*
130 Seed of the medicinal plant *Nerium antidysentericum.*
131 Medicinal plant, probably *Sida carpinifolia.*
132 Species of a purgative root, Indian jalap, *Ipomea turpe-tham.*
133 A medicinal plant.
134 Seed of the water lily *Anneslea spinosa*, taken for strengthening purposes.
135 This seems to be *masūr*, the pink lentil, *Lens culinaris.*
136 *Gmelina arborea*. Both root and fruit are used in medicine.
137 *Mimosa octandra* or *Ophioxylon sexpentaria.*
138 Name of a medicinal plant, one of the eight principal drugs classed together under the name *ashta varg.*

meal, deodar, *javāsa*,[139] *patpapra*,[140] figs (*baṛ*), *mūthi* beans, *pādal*,[141] screw pine (*kītkī*), dried acidulated milk (*patās*), preserved fruit or jam, *majītha*,[142] *tīntū* (*sic*) (i.e. *tīndū*) fruit, *zarat*, *khīr*, cardamoms, invalid food (*patha yanī*), date sugar, lovage, *ratānjan* (eye medicine), sandal, grain in the ear, cardamoms, *padmak*,[143] water or juice.

Also a method for warding off eye disease (cataract?): these medicines are effectual in repelling eye disease (*mantar gīrī*). Cook them in food or put prepared *phakī*[144] in food. The ingredients are as follows: root of the caster-oil tree, *nāg-i kīsar*,[145] *bhīyan guhla*,[146] cassia, *burnā*,[147] stick liquorice, *chūka*, sorrel, horse radish roots, *balbīj* roots,[148] green coconut, potherbs, cucumber, myrobalan, (*f.88b, with a miniature*) edible(?) mustard (*rā'ībhūg*), cucumbers, *tīndū* fruit, horse gram (*kalatt*),[149] *pāshan bīd*,[150] sugar, ghee, *zarat*, oleander, black cardamoms, betel leaf, *pīpal*, *kachlūn* (black salt),[151] root of the *kānis* grass,[152] *dhamāha* rice, cucumber, bamboo, sugarcane syrup, myrobalan, sugarcane roots, *dūb* grass, roots of *shāli* rice,[153] musk, *garmāla*,[154] cardamoms, grapes, large cardamoms, fruit from the *bahuphalī* fig, fragrant grass (*asīr*).[155]

Another medicine for making eyes bright: (*f.89a*) this medicine makes eyes very bright if it is put into food or meat or green stuff and vegetables and cooked and eaten. If it is boiled with herbs, strain the liquid and use it to wash the eyes. If the (*following*) ingredients are mixed together and put on the eyes, the eyes become very bright and diseases of the eyes are completely prevented. The medicine is as follows: *panj mūl*,[156] *māk vanī*,[157] leaves of

139 The prickly plant *Hedysarum alhagi*.
140 The medicinal plant *Oldenlandia biflora*.
141 Tree-trumpet flower, *Bignonia Sauveolens*.
142 A drug, manjith; the root of the plant yields red dye madder.
143 *Costus speciosus* or *C. arabicus*.
144 *Phankā*, the plant *Pistia stratioites*.
145 *Mesua ferrea*, the dried flowers are used in perfume and medicine.
146 A potion made with opium or bhang.
147 The tree *Cratoeva Roxburghii*.
148 *Abutilon indicum*.
149 *Dolichos uniflorus*.
150 *Plectantrus scutellarioides*.
151 A medicinal salt made by calcining fossil salt and the fruit of emblic myrobalan to promote digestion.
152 The tall grass *Emperata spontanea*.
153 *Shāli* is the generic name of all fine winter rices.
154 Steingass (1957): a certain kind of medicine.
155 *Andropogon muricatum*.
156 A collection of five roots or tubers. See Platts (1965), p. 272, for lists of these. He cites two collections.
157 Obscure. *Māk* is the medicinal plant *Eclipta alba*. *Mak* is of course *makka* or *Indian zarat*, but this was introduced from the Americas presumably somewhat later than this text.

lemon grass (*akhtia*), quince flowers, lemon grass flowers, *majītha,*[158] date sugar, horse radish tree, golden *kashta,*[159] stick liquorice, grapes, *ḍūḍī,*[160] cumin seed, *shapat* grass,[161] *ajmūd, halīla* (myrobalan), *lūd,*[162] camphor, round turmeric, honey (*shahd*), burnt cultivated potherbs,[163] *āmla*, fresh shoots of *sattavar,*[164] *bhiṛā,*[165] *sanbhālī,*[166] cloves, musk, blue water lily, (*f.89b*) sesame meal, sandal, red sandal, musk seeds, seeds of the *nīm* tree, leaves of the *nīm* tree, lentil pulse, *sapārī*, fruit of the monkey jackfruit tree.

Another medicine for curing itchiness of the body is as follows: *marva,*[167] pure sulphur, *ʿadas, tūr, mūng*, date juice, saffron, date sugar, pepper, lime juice, greens of the *panvār* (cassiatora) tree, *barmhī,*[168] *āsanda* bark,[169] frankincense, cardamoms, *sanbhālī* (chaste tree)[170] leaves, deodar, rice in the husk, round turmeric, turmeric, *sāngar,*[171] cucumber, *nāgbīl* betel, large cardamoms, cardamoms, liquidambar, round peppers, sesame meal, limes, *rīnūk,*[172] *khīr*, catechu, *karta,*[173] screw pine (*kītkī*), cinnamon.

Again, the method for making potherbs into pellets or for using eggs with potherbs or making many-coloured pumpkin with potherbs. (*f.90a*) Blow the fire and cook plump minced chicken, add onion, fresh ginger and whole potherbs and use it as a stuffing for the eggs of hens or of pigeons or of the eggs of any other bird that is required. Put together cardamoms, cloves, white ambergris, rosewater, camphor, musk, saffron and salt, rub it on the carcass and flavour it with ghee and cook it. Slightly cook some fresh onions, add lime juice and flavouring and put it in the mince. Flavour it with ghee and add whole potherbs.

Again, to stuff lime rind, throw away the pulp leaving the skin whole (*f.90b*) after the sourness and acidity have been removed. Then stuff it with flavoured

158 The drug from madder, *Rubia manjith*.
159 The medicinal plant *Costus speciosus* or *Costus arabicus*.
160 The milky fluid found in unripe wheat grains, also spelled *dūdhī*.
161 *Saccharum cylindricum*.
162 i.e. *lūdrā*, derived from the bark of the tree *Symplocos racemosa*.
163 *Hingsta repens*.
164 The vegetable *Asparagus racemosus*, of medicinal value.
165 Perhaps the belleric myrobalan, *Terminalia berica*, one of three myrobalans used in the medicine *triphala*, to combat debility.
166 The medicinal leaves of the Chaste tree.
167 *Ocimum pilosum*.
168 i.e. *barma*, the plant *Tricosantheses incisa*, used medicinally.
169 Dragon's Blood: the bark extract is used in medicine.
170 *Vitex trifolia*.
171 Uncertain: in Platts (1965) it is (1) the pod of the Shami tree or (2) a kind of bean or (3) the fruit of the Jant tree.
172 Small lentil.
173 Obscure.

mince and cover the top of it. Flavour it, cook it well and serve it. By the same method prepare citron fruit (*karna*) or sweet-orange or sour-orange and cook it. Also take flowers of the blue water lily and stuff them with *bhāt*, tie them up with thread, place them in a cooking pot and when cooked, serve them. Again make a cup from sour-orange leaves, put *bhāt* into it, tie it up with thread and cook it. When the stuffing is well-cooked, take it off and serve it in the leaf cup. Cook many varieties.

In the same way, there are also many kinds of *kaṛhī*. Make *pāpaṛ* and (*f.91a*) also make sherbet. Make some with *dūgh* and *māst* and put in the following ingredients: crushed *mūng* beans, date sugar, *lūh* broth,[174] sour-orange, *pāpaṛ*, shoots of citron, citron (*karna*), partridge broth, kedgeree, coconut milk, skewered lamb or kid, rose and sugar water, figs, honey (*shahd*), salt, vinegar, *kaṛhī*, white ambergris, yellow wheat, rice, fruit of the jujube tree, cardamoms, chickpea pulse, *nāg-i kīsar*, ground pepper, *zarat*, potherbs, *kīyalī* (medlar), palm sugar, ground cloves, *dūgh*, rosewater, *barmī*,[175] camphor, lime and ghee. Other foods (*are listed below*) that should be eaten after sexual intercourse and to increase the flow of semen. All these things should be eaten regularly (*f.91b, with a miniature*) to create well-being and to repel phlegm from the body. Impotence is cured, desire returns, joy is bestowed on the heart, there are erections and semen flows. It is good to sleep out of doors and to be fanned by cool breezes. Wash the body, rub in perfumes, smell sweet-scented flowers, tell stories with pleasant words and play *sarūds*; drink palm-wine (*sīndhī*) that does (*f.92a*) not cause drunkenness, eat bananas, almonds, walnuts, pistachios, pine kernels, chironji kernels, wheat, barley, *lassi, laḍḍū, sūr* fish, rice, sesame seeds, honey (*shahd*), potherbs, sugarcane, good food, *ghīvar* sweetmeats,[176] pulse *baṛa*, milk, water, broth, flavoured curds, *khīr*, and also cook *khīs* and *rābaṛī*.

If the following are mixed with a cup of *dūgh*, then they become sherbet. The sherbet is as follows: water chestnut flour, almond flour, *zarat* flour, sugar, honey (*shahd*), walnut flour, water lily flour, parched grain flour, flour of unripe wheat or barley, *dūgh*, rice flour, potherbs, sweet vegetable oil, fresh ginger, onions, coriander seed, flour made from pine kernels, *mūng* flour, whey, asafoetida burnt in ghee, (*f.92b*) lime, perfume, *zarat* flour, rose and sugar water, burnt asafoetida oil, fenugreek, lovage, tamarind, asafoetida, roasted wild rice, roasted chickpeas, salt. Again, another lot [*of ingredients*] to use with *māst* which is called *guṭhla*.[177] It is as follows: fresh shoots of sour-orange, fresh shoots of lime, asafoetida, roast cumin seed, musk, vinegar, *dūgh*, congee, hogplum, vine shoots, purslane (*lūnīyā*), onion leaves, fresh

174 *Lūh*, a bird similar to a partridge or quail.

175 Medicinal plant, *Trichosanthes incisa*.

176 Of flour, milk, ghee, coconut and sugar.

177 Platts (1965): a lump or mass as of curd in milk or of flour in broth.

shoots of ginger, camomile (*babūna*), garlic clove (*phārnak*), roast fenugreek, whey of *dūgh*, *bathala*,[178] whey of *māst*, white basil, lime juice, roast lovage, roast mustard seed, *chūlā'ī*, red cabbage, baked rice, roast sesame seeds, salt, garlic, chickpea greens. Also put pipless sweet lime into potherbs. Also (*f.93a*) all these (*the following*) leaves have been written down: scatter *tanbūl* leaves with them, perfume them and (*then*) fold the *tanbūl*. The leaves are as follows: fresh shoots of the mango tree with small leaves, sour-orange leaves, *karna* leaves, lime leaves, sweet-orange leaves, *jāman* leaves, sacred basil leaves, screw pine (*kīyūra*) leaves, and whole flowers and perfume of every kind. Having collected all these leaves, perfume the leaves of betel (*tanbūl*) and betel nut (*fūfal*), use the perfume of every kind of scented flower. The scent is immediately absorbed by all the other leaves. Rub the scent of these flowers into betel leaf. Also use oil of aloes, sandal, frankincense, *salā khal* (?oilcake essence), *salā ras* and white sandal wood. (*f.93b*) Use *marhaṭṭī* aloes and the other perfumes with *pān*, *fūfal*, *kāt* and *chūna*,[179] and also use the perfume of the peel of sour-orange and *karna* and lime and sweet-orange.

Again, with Ghiyath Shahi's *bīra*, the betel leaves are rubbed with camphor and rosewater. Eleven leaves are used to make one *bīra*. Make the lime yellow and boil the betel nut in extract of aloes oil, then rub it with musk scent and white ambergris and rosewater and make pungent perfume from flowers of the red rose. Another recipe for betel (*sapārī*): boil the betel nut in sandal juice, rub it with camphor and also with sandal (*f.94a, with a miniature*) and scatter rosewater on it. Make the *bīra* (chew) with twenty-five leaves and make a pungent extract of sandal. Mix the lime with saffron and rosewater. Make both these kinds of betel (*tanbūl*). In another *tanbūl* of Ghiyath Shahi, the *bīra* is made from fifty leaves and a little *chīkanī* betel and also from a little *sapārī*.[180] Prepare (*f.94b*) pungent essence from a lot of musk and having put it in the *tanbūl* which should not be too thin nor, alternatively, too thick, beat it.

Put in pounded ingredients as follows: one *tūlcha* of cardamom, half a *tūlcha* of musk, two *tūlchas* of camphor and half a *tūlcha* of sandal. Sprinkle rose-water on them and add one *māsa* of white ambergris, then fan it vigorously with a damp straw fan to cool it and then chew it. The property of this *tanbūl* is that it shrinks the anus, prevents vomiting, repels the harmfulness of hot

178 *Launaea nudicaulis*, 'used in sherbet'.

179 *Pān*, the betel chew or quid, also here called *bīra*, *sapārī* and *tanbūl*, consists of the leaf (*tambūla*) of the climbing vine (*Piper betle*), the nut of the *Areca catechu* (here called *fūfal*, and sometimes *sapārī*), a smearing of *kattha* or *kāt*, the astringent thick liquid from the heartwood of the *Areca catechu*, and *chūna*, a dab of slaked lime from crushed shells. Perfumes and flavourings of many kinds can be added.

180 G. Watt's *Dictionary* (1889–93), vol. 1, p. 300, describes the different methods of preparing the betel nut, all of which have different names. *Chikanī* is a way of treating the unripe nut which toughens it up.

wind and feverishness, the excess of blood that comes from over-heating, (*f.95a*) and also heartburn. Another *tanbūl* of Ghiyath Shahi: varieties of betel nut (*fūfal*) are ground coarsely with rosewater. The method for sandal and its leaves is to grind it finely on a stone and, having also ground pungent musk, add them together and mix them with cooked camphor and chew the *tanbūl*. The benefit derived from this is that it relieves toothache, makes the tongue soft and the mouth sweet-smelling. Another *tanbūl* of Ghiyath Shahi: having roasted the betel nut (*fūfal*), grind it finely on a grinding stone. Mix *pān*, lime and perfume with it and wrap it up in soft leaves, folding it into a triangle, and perfume it.

(*f.95b*) Again, finely pound together *tanbūl, pān*, perfume, catechu essence and *sapārī* and add the sap of cardamoms and the sap of cloves and pound it all into a paste.[181] Another *tanbūl*: moisten *sapārī* in the juice of jackfruit or of wild fig or of pumpkin. Then put a quantity of this *sapārī* with *pān*, catechu essence, lime, date sugar and galingale so that it is not too sour. Put all these into leaves and pound the *tanbūl*. Another *tanbūl*: having roasted oily *chīval*[182] and betel nut (*fūfal*), put together *pān*, catechu essence, musk and lime and pound them. Add essence of chanpa flowers, camphor, sesame oil, (*f.96a*) musk and saffron and pound them. Then sprinkle enough spirit (*ʿaraq*) of sweet-orange blossom on it to moisten it. Add a few wheat grains to the *tanbūl* and chew it, or add the quantity of one *diram* of coconut pieces and chew it. Also use cubebs, date kernels, tamarind kernels, *tīndū* kernels, Silk Cotton tree (*sīnbal*) kernels, *sapārī*, Butter tree, *marva* leaves,[183] *padmak* leaves,[184] flowers of the red rose and white China rose, myrrh flowers – all of these are fragrant and, if it is so wished, can be eaten in *tanbūl*. No harm comes from eating them but if, on the other hand, they become bitter, it is best not to eat them. Eat bamboo manna and eat a few potherbs. Also slightly flavour the *sapārī* with potherbs. Use *nāg-i kīsar* and cinnamon. Add all these things (*f.96b*) that have been written, one by one, to the *tanbūl*. Also put all the following, one by one, into the *tanbūl*: water chestnuts, almonds, water lilies, *karhaṛī*, dried sweet mango and a portion of the fruit of the palmyra palm (*tāṛ*) and chew it.

Another five examples of *pān:* having ground roast *fūfal*, pound together grain essence (*kāt-i bhakūra*), camphor, almonds, musk, *sapārī, pān, nāg-i kīsar* and saffron. Fan it with a fan, add rosewater and eat it. Another *pān*: put in *sapārī*, chickpea flour, sesame oil flavouring, musk and rosewater and fan it. Grind sandal flour, musk, rosewater, aloes extract, *pān*, (*f.97a*) *sapārī*,

181 Here the normal words for the chews also seem to mean specific types of areca nuts, as in the next recipe.

182 Fruit of the Indian Butter tree, *Bassia butyracea.*

183 *Ocimum pilosum*, a strongly scented plant.

184 The tree *Costus speciosus.*

lime, cardamom essence, oil of aloes, saffron, rosewater and camphor. Another *sapārī*: catechu essence, lime, *pān*, cooked camphor, rosewater and saffron. Another *pān*: catechu essence, *sapārī*, lime, camphor. The properties of catechu essence and lac are bitterness and astringency which wards off and alleviates fatty blood bile, hot phlegm and the kind of fever involving heavy sweating. It brings strength, increases good looks and repels white leprosy (*baraṣ*), leprosy (*jaẓām*) and leprous (*pīstī*) conditions, in addition to snakebite, coughs and poisons. Broken bones are mended. Lac may be used in illness as it is full of good qualities.

Another *tanbūl*: put catechu, *pān, sapārī*, lime, half a *tūlcha* (*f.97b*) of cardamoms, one *māsa* of camphor and rosewater on to a newly made flat clay dish so that it cools and then eat it. Or else use a clay cup or earthenware shards (*khazaf*) and put the ingredients into it. Another hot *tanbūl* of Ghiyath Shahi: mince the *tanbūl* and pound the *fūfal* nut finely so that its grains become soft. Grind five cloves and put them in or else put in ten whole cloves. Also put in four portions of long peppers or two portions of round peppers. One pepper equals date sugar or two peppers are equal to a galingale. Put a pellet of jasmine and its leaves or pieces of yellow myrobalan on the place where a tooth aches. (*f.98a, with a miniature*) Whenever a tooth aches and it is wished to alleviate the pain, take two *sarūla* (almond sweetmeats) and warm them, put *tanbūl* into them. Cover the *sarūla* and eat it when it becomes hot or else take a cup or a small goblet and put it into one or other of those or, having warmed some pieces of earthenware (*khazaf*), put them into the *tanbūl*. When the *tanbūl* turns black, add musk (*f.98b*) and cloves.

Another pleasant *tanbūl* of Ghiyath Shahi: put all the following into minced *tanbūl*, i.e. sandal, sesame oil, camphor, musk, potherbs and date sugar. Another soft *tanbūl* of Ghiyath Shahi may consist of *sapārī*, fat, catechu, camphor, *nūti pān*, or it may be *adākar*, or else, having put *kapūr-i bīl* into it, pound it.[185] Another dry *tanbūl*: put in *sapārī*, Butter tree fruit, mimusops leaves, date kernels, *tīndū* kernels, *jāman* fruit kernels, mango kernels, musk, rosewater and camphor. Another dry *tanbūl* [*is*] as follows: pure and sweet smelling *sapārī*, Butter tree fruit, leaves of the Sisoo tree,[186] *kahrvalī* (a pungent essence), musk, wild myrobalan, bamboo manna, camphor, (*f.99a*) musk, water lily, scents and perfumes of Ghiyath Shahi. If it is wished to chew this *tanbūl* immediately, then having put together musk, white ambergris and rosewater, make pellets. Another recipe for Ghiyath Shahi's perfumed pellets: mix together cooked camphor, bamboo manna, sandal, jasmine, cardamoms and saffron and take this mixture and make pellets. Eat the pellets with one *fūfal* made from four leaves with a little lime (*chūna*) and

185 These last three seem to be different kinds of betel leaves.

186 *Pān-i tahlī* (the Sisu tree *Dalbergia Sisoo*).

an equal amount of catechu essence. If the lime is of an equal amount, the colour will be good. Similarly, if the *fūfal* is of an equal amount, then the colour becomes good but if there is too much (*f.99b*) the colour does not become good. If there is plenty of *pān*, the colour becomes good. Bitter *tanbūl* prevents diseases of the throat and gullet as well as [*preventing*] leprosy, indigestion and dryness of the mouth. Eating sharp *tanbūl* relieves recent indigestion and phlegm. Feverish thirst, fever, gripes and heartburn, all these are prevented. The *tanbūl* can be minced if that is more palatable, but it is not a good thing to mix them for then there is no pleasure in eating them. Eating hot *tanbūl* is known to be advantageous; thirst and weariness are alleviated and fevers are prevented. Food can be digested, wind and phlegm[187] dispersed, the throat is cleansed, life is (*f.100a*) prolonged, the heart is strengthened and bile, wind and poisons are repelled.

When preparing *tanbūl*, put the ingredients in little by little. Either two or one, in the same manner that catechu essence is put in, add the same quantity. The qualities of that *tanbūl* are that the teeth are strengthened, diseases of the tongue, lips, gullet, throat and windpipe are prevented, as is inflammation of the chest. All the foregoing diseases are prevented and the intellect is strengthened, the eyes made bright, the quality of hearing is improved, the nose is purified, halitosis is banished and all illnesses (*f.100b, with a miniature*) are repelled. Hair becomes longer and shinier and is strengthened, broken bones mend and food that is bound up in the stomach is dissolved and digestion of food is assisted. Phlegm is prevented, the stomach is soft and an appetite for food is enhanced and it makes for a life of beauty and chastity. Coarse wind (*f.101a*) that may be in the stomach is relieved. It is astringent so bile and excess blood are decreased and phlegm is prevented. Blood is purified, ejaculation is delayed, gripes are cured and the stomach is tightened. If it is rubbed on the skin of the body, leprosy is driven away and the colour of the skin is made white and bad odours are prevented. It is the jewel of the mouth, the mouth is purified and the ardour of passion is increased. The ingredients are as follows: flowers of the white China rose, catechu peel, catechu wood, tamarind flesh, jasmine flowers, sesame seeds, thorns of the silk cotton tree, saffron flowers, tree-trumpet flowers, spikenard, large cardamoms, *padmak*, (*f.101b*) *marva*, ghee (*rūghan*), water lily seeds, ghee (*hūs*), sacred basil, acid *tanbūl*, date kernels, mace, *tīndū* kernels, walnuts, *pān-i kapūrī*,[188] *nāg-i kīsar*, *patkala* betel, *dasāvarī*,[189] *zarat*, camphor, date juice, pepper root, the membrane of a betel leaf (*pān-i kahlra*), *mūtha* beans, flowers of gum-myrrh, sesame meal, red roses, mace, round pepper, pepper, lac, wheat, coconut, almonds, bamboo manna, seeds of yellow myrobalan,

187 Note in right margin: '*balgham*', phlegm.
188 A yellowish betel leaf.
189 A kind of imported betel leaf.

date sugar, cubebs, sesame oil, cardamoms, camphor, cassia, *sapārī, pān*, catechu essence, lime, musk, white ambergris and cloves.

In the following few instances *tanbūl* must not be chewed, one of these is when blood comes from the chest by the way of the mouth (*i.e. tuberculosis*) and also when there is a bleeding vein, namely anyone who has a bleeding artery (*f.102a*). Also eat food that does not include ghee. Do not chew *tanbūl* in the case of eye-pain or in over-eating and, again, do not chew it after drinking wine. Do not chew it if there should be tuberculosis or a cough or in the case of a fluctuating disease. Do not allow *tanbūl* to be eaten in any of the above-mentioned diseases. Now, those illnesses in which chewing *tanbūl* is beneficial are as follows: put it on the food of anyone who suffers from insomnia and also chew *tanbūl* after headaches and after vomiting. In all these cases, chew *tanbūl*.

Another *tanbūl*: *pān* (*i.e. leaf*) of the betel vine, essence of catechu, *sapārī* (*f.102b*) and a shoot of fresh mango. Another *tanbūl* with water is an excellent perfumed one of Ghiyath Shahi. Use the water to wash the leaves and put a handful of them in *bakkha* (distillery dregs) and put them into perfume. Do not put them into drinking water. Put them into head lotion, moisten *kāt* (catechu essence) with it and also moisten *sapārī* in it. It consists of the following: two *mān* of water, sour-orange leaves, *karna* leaves, woodapple leaves, black cardamoms, white cardamoms, *mūtha* beans, spikenard, wild spikenard, cinnamon, *pannāg* (grain), *nāg-i kīsar*, wheat, cloves, cardamoms, sesame oil, sandal and zedoary. Put all these into water and boil them. When they have become well-flavoured, strain the water off. (*f.103a*) Then take the leaves and crumble them and put them into the perfume and into sandal and, having ground four *tūlchas* of fresh saffron, boil it and put it in. Grind up two *tūlchas* of musk, one *tūlcha* of camphor and two *māsas* of white ambergris and mix them with the water. Fill a glass, and use the perfume wherever it is required.

Put rosewater in a jug and if it is desired that rosewater should be distilled from that, then distil the rosewater and make *bakkha*[190] from the weight of that and put it into sandal and prepare the essence (*ghūl*).[191] Also equal amounts of chickpea flour, sandal and jasmine mixed with hand-pressed sesame oil becomes a wonderful perfume (*f.103b, with a miniature*). Heat it and put the following into it after they have been ground: mix one *tūlcha* of musk, half a *tūlcha* of camphor, half a *tūlcha* of saffron, one *māsa* of white ambergris and keep it in a glass. When the need arises, sprinkle it on clothes or put it into *ghūl*.

190 Aromatic black powder or debris left after distilling.
191 *Ghūl* or *ghūla*, essence or solution.

Another scent to use in *pān:* to one hundred betel leaves, use one *diram* of saffron, two *dirams* of musk, one *diram* of camphor, three *dirams* of cardamoms, half a *diram* of black ambergris, (*f.104a*) three *dirams* of bruised sandal and two *dirams* of cubebs. Grind all these with sandal and put in rosewater. Mix with water, knead it and rub both sides of the betel leaves with this liquid. Then place the betel leaves on a dish and scent them with aloes oil. Place the betel leaves, leaf by leaf, on the dish and place it on the embers turned on its side so that the scent does not run out. If it appears that the rosewater is running too freely, then put scented water on it. By this method put chanpa flowers, white jasmine flowers, screw pine (*kītkī*) flowers, white China roses, jasmine and red roses into water and leave them for an hour. Then take them out (*f.104b*) and throw them away, the water will have absorbed the scent. Add sandal and sweet-smelling flowers to this water and rub the betel-leaves (*pān*) with it.

Another perfume for scenting water: having tied camphor and one *tūlcha* of jackfruit (*panhas*) in a butter cloth with a cord, put it in the water. Do not touch the water with the hand, but take hold of the cord to put the fresh butter (*kara*) in the cloth and, similarly, use the cord to remove it from the water. Again a recipe for making water very cold: for five jars of water use half a *diram* of camphor, one *diram* of cardamoms, half a *diram* of *mūtha*, a quarter of a *diram* of *kapūr kachrī*, half a *diram* of *asīr*,[192] three *dirams* of tree-trumpet flowers (*pādal*), two *dirams* of white China rose flowers, a quarter of a *diram* of *barmī*,[193] a quarter of a *diram* of crushed sandal. (*f.105a*) Having ground all these ingredients together, tie them in a butter cloth and put them in the water.

Another recipe for scented water: as mentioned above, take four jars of water to half a *tūlcha* of musk, two *dirams* of sour-orange leaves, one *diram* of sweet-orange peel, one *diram* of wormwood (*dūna*),[194] three *dirams* of Bengal quince leaves (*bīl*), one *diram* of large *sūnf* seeds. Grind them all up and put them into the four jars of water. It makes a good perfume. Again, to mix the ingredients for *marhaṭṭī* aloes: [*take*] nine *dirams* of ambergris resin (*lādan*), nine *dirams* of frankincense, a quarter of a *sīr* of sandal, nine *dirams* of gum lac, nine *dirams* of small white cardamoms, nine *dirams* of *tagrī* powder,[195] nine *dirams* of spikenard, three *dirams* of ground sesame seed essence, six *dirams* of wheat, nine *dirams* of *gūṭṭha*,[196] nine *dirams* of *barmī*, (*f.105b*) thirty-two *dirams* of sesame oil, half a *tūlcha* of camphor, six *dirams* of saffron, eighteen *dirams* of liquidambar (*salāras*), thirty-six *dirams* of honey

192 Roots of two fragrant grasses, respectively *Hedychium spicatum* and *Andropogon muricatum*.

193 A medicinal plant, *Tricosanthese incisa*.

194 *Artemisia indica*, the Indian wormwood or fleabane.

195 The shrub *Tabernae montana coronaria*, of which fragrant powder is made.

196 A preparation of coriander seeds, coconut and cardamoms.

(*shahd*), nine *dirams* of roasted sweet-scented mollusc shell (*nākhan būyā*), nine *dirams* of wild spikenard – mix all these together to combine them. Collect together half a *sīr* of the first pressing of aloes oil, one and a half *tūlchas* of musk, a quarter of a *diram* of camphor, three *māsa* of black ambergris and moisten them in a little rosewater and make the mixture thick.

Another recipe for a principal perfume: sour-orange, sweet-orange, pampelmousse, Bengal quince, citron (*karna*), pumpkin peel, jackfruit, of which take the pulp and throw the rest away, screw pine (*kīyūra*), *sūn* (flowers?), screw pine (*kītkī*). Moisten all these and put them into a perfumed cloth bag, cover it with flour dough and cook it (*f.106a*). Take the flowers of jasmine, *pāch*,[197] yellow *sūn*, and the Poon tree. Also the flowers of gum myrrh, jasmine *grandiflorum*, wild Poon Tree, *chanbīlī* (jasmine) and flowers of the water lily – take such sweet-smelling flowers as these, tie them together and put them into a pan. Take that pan holding the above-mentioned flowers in a bag, cover it with flour dough and put a lid on it and cook the perfume.

Another method for producing pure essence and another method for manufacturing perfume is also prepared as mentioned above. Take two or three of those ingredients and cook the perfume and, if it is wished that they should all be cooked together (*f.106b*) then, having collected them all, cook the perfume. From this, if required, make a solution and, if so wished, use it to perfume water and flavour food and flavour fruit and to prepare scent. This is as follows: black cardamoms, small cardamoms, sesame meal, betel nut (*sapārī*), zedoary, cinnamon, cubebs, white ambergris, white cardamoms, figs, *mūtha* beans, acid gourd, wheat, cucumber, *nāg-i kīsar*, saffron, chickpea flour, cassia, rosewater, red roses, white China roses, wild spikenard, spikenard, sesame seed oil, cardamoms, camphor and musk. Another recipe for preparing perfume: take two or three from the collection of ingredients listed above and, having mixed them together, cook them. Then give this perfume the scent (*f.107a*) of every kind of flower. The ingredients are as follows: water, extract (*gulāb*) of every flower, mace, white cardamoms, black cardamoms, *sūnf*, spikenard, cloves, *nāg-i kīsar*, rosewater, camphor, Chinese zedoary, cucumber, musk seed, chickpea flour, cassia, wild spikenard, *mūtha* beans, date sugar, acid gourd, betel nut (*fūfal*), *bābrang*,[198] aloes, cinnamon, liquidambar, musk, *kalat*[199] and sandal.

Another recipe for making that cold perfume which is manufactured everywhere, is as follows: red rose flowers, wheat, spikenard, *parīnag, pāch*(*ak*), white cardamoms, betel nut (*sapārī*), tamarind seeds, *marva*, artemisia, nutmeg, *nāg-i kīsar*, catechu essence, bamboo manna, white China rose,

197 i.e. *pāchak*, the costus (*Saussurea lappa*), of which the roots have valuable perfume.
198 Medicinal seed of *Embelia ribes*.
199 *Dolichos uniflorus*.

padmak, (*f.107b*) fresh sandal, sandal (*malākara*), aloes, white ambergris, camphor, cardamoms, *kapūr īlīya*,[200] *asīr* grass, and saffron (*kīs*) flowers. Another recipe for perfume and for scenting clothes and for flavouring food and water and for scenting betel (*pān*) and betel (*sapārī*) and for scenting head lotion and for scenting the hair of the head is as follows: liquidambar, musk, chickpea flour, camphor, sweet-orange peel, camphor, rosewater, white ambergris, *tagrī* powder, red rose flowers, white cardamoms, zedoary, cinnamon, *barma*, chanpa flowers, finely ground cinnamon, *muthha, bhadr*,[201] saffron, hand-pressed sesame oil, sandal, cardamoms, cloves, cooked camphor. Another recipe for making and distilling aromatic paste (*chūva*): add perfume and rosewater to water and soak the following: *sala-i khāl* (essence of oil cake?), liquidambar, (*f.108a*) frankincense (*labān*), white sandal, sesame seeds, rosewater, spikenard, wild spikenard, the perfume of flowers washed in rosewater, lac, resin of Saul tree (*rāl*), ghee, *dhanāsrī* (cream?), sandal (*malākara*), *zarat*, beeswax, musk, camphor, okra, sandal, *mūtha* beans, small cardamoms, cinnamon, *barmā*, essence of Saul tree, saffron, sesame oil, potherbs, sugar, mountain camphor, rice (*dhan*), white ambergris, black ambergris, red rose flowers, cooked camphor, civet (*ghālīya*), sweet oil.

Another recipe for preparing a solution from the scent of complete flowers, the ingredients are as follows: green pumpkin, cardamoms, flowers of gum myrrh, flowers of screw pine (*kīyūra*), chanpa grass, date sugar, white China rose, spikenard, scent of jasmine flowers, wild spikenard, grain, *tagrī* powder, vinegar, deodar, banana, (*f.108b*) flowers of the blue water lily, mango (*naghzak*), jackfruit, *kapūr kachrī*,[202] white sandal, camomile, cooked sandal, musk, saffron, hand-pressed sesame oil, *zarat*, wild fig roots, wild fig peel, *barmī*, chickpeas, sweet-orange peel, rosewater, black ambergris, limes, star-fruit, lime juice, catechu extract, turmeric, cinnamon, sandal (*malākara*), liquidambar, sandal (*chānd*), civet, wheat, *mūtha* beans, camphor, small cardamoms, *asīr* roots, zedoary, white ambergris, blue lotus, sandal.

Another method, for mango fool (*gaṛanba*): *māst* strained through a cloth, camphor, salt, sweet *māst*, minced onion leaves, cream or crust from sweet *māst*. Another recipe: grape juice, pure water, cloves, palm sugar, cardamoms, crust of *māst*, camphor. Another recipe, for nourishing *bhāt*: (*f.109a*) whey, buttermilk from the crust or cream of *māst*, wheat kedgeree, *zarat bhāt, gūdi bhāt*,[203] *zarat bhāt*, buttermilk taken from coagulated milk that has been strained through a cloth, camphor, musk and cloves. Roast some cumin and put in sufficient to make it black. Date sugar, honey (*shahd*),

200 Another variety of camphor.

201 Fragrant grass, *Cyperus rotundus*.

202 Fragrant grass, *Hedychium spicatum*.

203 *Gūdi*, unripe wheat or *zarat* parched in the ear.

palm sugar, rose and sugar water, sugar, potherbs, raisins, mustard seeds, salt, cubebs, *mūtha* beans, cinnamon, cassia, fresh ginger, grape syrup, pure water. Also use seasoning flavours: ghee, asafoetida flavour, garlic, *dūgh*, sour-orange, roasted coriander seed, limes, minced onion leaves and also coriander, water, salt, cumin, *sūnf*, camphor, cloves, cardamoms, buttermilk, also sugar potherbs, palm sugar, tamarind, *māst*, jujube, (*f.109b*) ghee and *bhāt*.

Another recipe for preparing *paṭū* (a leaf recipe) is as follows: rice flour, chopped aubergine leaves, leaves of the snake gourd (*chachīṇda*),[204] leaves of lentils (*tūrī*), garlic leaves, yam (*panḍālū*) leaves, pulse flour, minced *kandūrī* gourd, melon leaves, vine (*raz*) leaves, betel leaves, chopped leaves of *kandūrī* gourd, chopped cucumber leaves, black gourd leaves, tamarind, white basil leaves, date sugar, pulse flour, *nīm* tree leaves, cloves, *pīpal* tree leaves, cumin, water lily flowers, asafoetida, *sūnf*, salt, fenugreek, fresh ginger, vegetable oil, ghee, cassia, cardamoms, pepper.

Another recipe, for preparing aubergine *būrānī*:[205] tamarind, citron (*karna*), *tantaṛīkha* (tamarind), pomegranate seeds, barberries (*zarashk*), flavour of oil, scented foods of all kinds, perfumes of all kinds, vinegar, (*f.110a*) lime juice, cumin, fenugreek, cardamoms, cooked beans, flavoured oil, *kandūrī* gourd, snake gourd (*chachīnda*), cloves, date sugar, salt, fresh ginger, figs (*pīpal*), yellow lentils, *mūng* pulse, melon, *dūgh*, mustard seeds, garlic, buttermilk, congee, peppers, gourd (*kadū*). Another recipe for preparing *pān bhāt*: make essence (*or juice*) of potherbs and essence (*or juice*) of camphor, add cardamoms to it and make sherbet. [*Use*] white rock salt (*sīndhā*), cumin and date sugar for special date sherbet. [*Make*] starfruit sherbet, raisin sherbet, sweet pomegranate sherbet, potherb sherbet, honey (*shahd*) sherbet, palm sugar sherbet, Khurasani fruit sherbet, sherbet made from the syrup or jelly of acid fruit, *bhāt* made from grains of every kind, sugar sherbet, (*f.110b*) sugarcane sherbet, watermelon sherbet, raisin sherbet (*faqāʿ*), *tīndū* sherbet, wild date sherbet, roses and sugar water sherbet, *kasīrū* root sherbet, wild fig sherbet, coriander, *sūnf*, Indian fig sherbet, corinda sherbet, fig (*pīpal*) sherbet, plum (*ālū*) sherbet, *jāman* fruit sherbet, camphor, saffron, scum of vegetable oil (*ḍaḍa*), scum of ghee, monkey jackfruit sherbet, tamarind sherbet, jackfruit sherbet, *mūtha* beans, asafoetida, onions. For making other scented or flavoured liquids soak fruits in pure water so that their flavours are absorbed by the water, then add a small amount of a sweetener. Drink that water or put it into the beverage *pān bhāt*.

[*Prepare*] the flavour of jackfruit, perfumed water, cold water, pure water, camphor, musk, saffron, (*f.111a*) the flavour of white ambergris, flavour of

204 The snake gourd, *chachīnda* in Sanskrit, *Tricosanthes anguina*.
205 *Būrānī* is a dish made from aubergines.

black cardamoms, the seven-sided flower, the flavour of wheat, the flavour of sugar, of honey (*shahd*), potherbs, flowers of the Poon (*pūn*) tree, the flavour of sweet basil, perfume of *nāg-i kisar*, flavour of sour-orange, flavour of banana, flavour of limes, flavour of screw pine (*kītkī*), flavour of unripe mango (*kīrī*), flavour of corinda, flavour of hogplum, flavour of *jāman* buds, flavour of mango buds, flavour of sacred basil, flavour of water lily flowers, flavour of *jāman*, lime flowers, flavour of pampelmousse, flavour of *mūtha* beans, leaves of citron (*karna*), of screw pine (*kīyūra*) flowers, scent or flavour of mango leaves, cucumber juice, cardamoms, jasmine flowers, scent of citron (*karna*), cardamoms, flavour of fenugreek and of roasted asafoetida, jasmine flowers, tree-trumpet flowers, flavour of sesame meal, white China rose, gum myrrh flowers, citron (*karna*) flowers, flavour of myrobalan, (*f.111b, with a miniature*) scent or flavour of camphor, scent or flavour of zerumbet, flowers of jasmine (*chanbīlī*), scent or flavour of sour-orange leaves, flavour of sesame oil, white ambergris, chanpa flowers, scent of jasmine (*jā'ī jū'ī*) flowers, scent of lime leaves, scent or flavour of monkey jackfruit, scent of citron (*karna*) rind, liquidambar, scent of *bālā*,[206] cloves, scent or flavour of banana, sour-orange flowers, scent of sandal. Other recipes for scents or flavours: sesame meal, *asīr* grass roots, *bālā*, sacred basil, sweet basil leaves, and make it from sour-orange leaves (*f.112a*) and from lime leaves and mango leaves and citron leaves and pampelmousse leaves and chanpa leaves, cardamom essence, cloves, saffron. Squeeze a quantity of juice from these and flavour or scent it with water lily flowers, from *kīyūra* (screw pine) flowers and from *kītkī* (screw pine) and from red rose flowers and from mint leaves. Cook meat or bread or pulse or grain in the husk or whatever is required using these flavours or scents. The food becomes well-flavoured and well-scented.

Boil vine shoots and hogplum shoots, orris root, tamarind shoots, corinda and sorrel (*asbūtī*). Season with ghee and put in plenty of onion. Add roasted asafoetida, salt and fresh ginger. Flavour it with asafoetida essence and add lime juice and pepper. (*f.112b*) Also if it is so wished, the herbs can be cooked separately in it. Another recipe, for stuffing (*bhrat*): roast the *bhrat* in hot ashes and make the stuffing: roasted cumin, roasted fenugreek, lovage, pot-herb stalks or sprigs, pomegranate seeds, roasted nigella seeds, tamarind, *khīyātūrī*, grain, roasted sesame seeds, *tīndū* fruits, wild myrobalan, gourd, aubergine, *khalī*, tamarind, cloves, cardamoms, salt, woodapple, jackfruit, monkey jackfruit, catechu, lentils, *kakūṛā* gourd, *sūran* (yam),[207] hogplum, fat corinda, *zarat*, carrots, onions, lime, asafoetida, red yam, mint, cassia, garlic (*lahsan*).

Again, to prepare recipes (*f.113a*) for fresh pickles (*āchār*): having put the *sūran* (yam) into a new earthenware cooking pot, remove the pulp and throw

206 *Hibiscus tortuosus*.
207 The 'elephant foot yam', *Amorphophallus campanulatus*.

away the peel and add relish as follows: pickled yellow myrobalan, partridge, Saul tree flowers, *kangar*,[208] cooked *jāman* fruit, salt roasted in earthenware, oil of burnt asafoetida, wild tamarind pulp, cultivated mango, fresh water chestnuts, aloe flowers, rind of *bhānvar* fruit,[209] cloves, hot water, rape seed oil, mustard seed oil, saffron, fresh water lily seeds, *sūran* yam, quail, fish, gourd, turmeric, roasted cumin, roast fenugreek, limes (*līmū*), cardamoms, *fālsa* fruit, bamboo shoots, hogplum, cooked mango, mustard, mulberries, fish, *dūgh*, jasmine, lime (*nībū*), *khalī* bark (*or rind*).[210]

Another recipe for medicinal plants that repel illnesses of the chest (*f.113b*) and enhance the appetite and make for great strength: make pickle, put it in food and eat it. It is made as follows: fresh grapes, hogplum seeds, sweet-orange, hard grains, tamarind leaves, sorrel, lime, sherbet, banana, orris root, wild vine shoots, *bīdhamī* bread[211], *kaṛhī*, swollen grain, citron (*karna*), congee, cooked *jāman* fruit, *āmal-i bīdas* orange, wild sour-oranges, wood-apple, buttermilk, sour-orange, fatless *māst*, mango, myrobalan, tamarind, chironji fruit, *tantaṛīkha* tamarind, corinda, starfruit, pomegranate, hog-plums, *janbhīra* lemon, vinegar, *dūgh*, yellow myrobalan, Indian jackfruit. The properties of the above-mentioned ingredients are those that sharpen the appetite and hunger and ward off illnesses of the chest (*f.114a*). They enable food to be digested and when they are taken, they warm the body, undigested food is softened and is digested and no longer feels heavy.

Another recipe, giving particulars of some remedies that relieve phlegm, is as follows: red *bathala*,[212] cloves, betel leaves, tree-trumpet flower, turmeric, sesame oil, sandal, cucumber, *phālī kara*,[213] fresh vine, sesame flour, *kamvī* medicine,[214] catechu essence, horse radish leaves, rape (*sarsūn*), *bathala*, dill, elephant's foot yam, honey (*shahd*), dates, sour gourd, *mūthi* beans, mango, long peppers, lime, aubergines, asafoetida, garlic, radish, *pīpal* figs, date sugar, pepper, *chāb* figs,[215] *bahuphalī* figs, *chatrak*,[216] mustard, (*f.114b*) poppy seeds. The above-mentioned items are those that keep diseases of the throat at bay and get rid of phlegm. Pustules, leprosy, bad digestion, tumours, abscesses and sweating are repelled, hunger comes, food is digested and the stomach and intestines are purified.

208 A tuber.
209 *Ipomoea eriocarpa*.
210 Obscure.
211 Obscure.
212 *Launaea nudicaulis*, renamed *Chondrilla nudicaulis* – Watt (1889–93): *batthal*, common weed throughout north India; sand-binding plant – used medicinally in sherbet in the southern Punjab.
213 Possibly *Cyamopsis psoralioides*, guar gum.
214 This includes cumin.
215 From the Gujarati *pipal* tree.
216 *Plumbago zeylanica*.

Another recipe, for making *malīda* as follows:[217] roses and sugar water, sugar, roasted sesame seeds, cloves, palm sugar, honey (*shahd*), rape seed oil, sweet sesame oil, almond oil, molasses, parched grain bread, camphor, musk, date sugar, bread cooked on ashes, bread with two fillings, oil from the kernel of the chironji fruit, coconut oil, fresh butter, raisins, wholemeal bread, whole grain bread, *garṣak* cake, dried bread, onions, *gūkhrū* (*f.115a*), baked thin bread, *angākṛī* cakes, *pūrī* bread made with lightly leavened white flour, cardamoms, ghee, honey (*ʿasl*), almonds, chironji kernels, pulp of the marsh melon, date sugar, galingale, garlic, *sūnf*, poppy seeds.

Another recipe, for the method for making halva: it is necessary that equal amounts of pomegranate to sugar are used or else use less pomegranate. The recipe is as follows: parched grain fried in ghee, plain boiled rice fried in ghee, *mūng* flour fried in ghee, flour of washed rice fried in ghee, wheat flour fried in ghee, bean flour fried in ghee, roasted chickpea flour fried in ghee, roasted rice flour fried in ghee, almond flour, (*f.115b, with a miniature*) pine kernels flour, flour of chironji kernels, essence of all kinds of aloes, scent of all kinds of flowers, pepper, cloves, dates, raisins, palm sugar, potherbs, camphor, rosewater, honey (*shahd*), *sūnf*, musk, saffron, galingale, cassia, cardamoms, date sugar.

Another recipe, for making *pālūda*. The method is as follows: take chironji kernels and almonds, and add them to cardamoms, (*f.116a*) almond paste, parched grain paste, water chestnut paste, rice paste, *kalatt* paste,[218] blue water lily seed paste, zedoary paste, sesame meal paste, grape sherbet, parched *zarat, zarat* paste, lentil flour paste, musk, sugar, cloves, tamarind, plum (*ālū*) sherbet, date sherbet, potherbs, camphor, pomegranate seeds, rosewater, cassia and cinnamon, and cook the *pālūda*.

Another recipe for *bhūjī* (fried vegetables): use pumpkin or grains or melon, whatever is required, prepare it, cut it finely and rub crushed salt into it by hand. Squeeze the juice out, throw the rest away and flavour the liquid. The flavouring is as follows: *tīndū* kernels, flowerets of bamboo, zerumbet, tamarind sap, horse radish, (*f.116b*) mango, date stone kernels, onions, beans,[219] *jāman* fruit kernels, *mūng* beans, mango kernels, *asīr* grass, figs (*pīpal*), aubergines, gourd, grains, *khattākar* paste[220] *nabakī* (myrobalan),[221] bamboo shoots, roast cumin, jackfruit, gourd, pepper, tamarind, buds or flowers of tamarind, cumin seeds, oil of burnt asafoetida, rape seed oil, vinegar, lime juice, radishes, oil of burnt fenugreek, asafoetida, *dūgh*, lentils,

217 Broken bread with sugar and ghee.

218 *Zarat* or horse gram, *Dolichos uniflorus*.

219 *Sīm*, broad beans (*Delichos lablab*) here referred to as *takhm-i sīm*, i.e. bean seeds.

220 According to Platts (1965), it is a preparation of opium, alum, turmeric, lemon juice, all heated in a copper vessel and applied to the eyes for headaches or on sprains.

221 *Terminelia chebula*.

water chestnuts, roast sesame seeds, rice water, gourd, salt, mustard, congee, buttermilk.

Another recipe for the making of butter ghee: when the ghee has become hot, add camphor and small cardamoms, also betel leaves, potherb juice, camphor, (*f.117a*) small cardamoms, ghee, sandal, sesame oil, white China rose, red rose, the scent of appropriate flowers, saffron, musk, holy basil, rosewater and ghee beaten together, white ambergris, sweet-orange peel, sour-orange peel, sweet-scented flowers – having heated them, add them. Make sections of earthenware hot and put them into the ghee. Also use cumin, coriander, wheat, garlic, onions, mint, fenugreek, fresh sprigs of citron (*karna*), flowers of *mūtha* beans, flowers of the white water lily, cardamoms, cinnamon, roasted chickpeas, *sūnf*, date sugar and asafoetida.

The Betel (*Tanbūl*) Book and the Perfume (*ʿAttār*) Book of Ghiyath Shahi: leaves of the Sissoo tree (*pān-i tahlī*)[222] of Shadiyabad (*i.e. Mandu*), *kapurkānti*,[223] pungent essence (*kahṛvalī*), kernels of mango stones, *ghāghra*,[224] fresh *kapūr bīlī* (yellow betel leaves) picked at the time of (*i.e. when the moon is in*) Chitra (*the 14th Lunar Mansion*), leaves of (*or juice of*) *katra*,[225] *lānjī pān* (betel), *adākar* (fresh ginger), hogplums, *patkūla pān* (betel). (*f.117b*) Wash all these (*aforementioned*) leaves and clean them and likewise also wash the shoots of this *pān* and also the seeds of the *pān*, and clean them.

(*There follows a list of betel chews*): betel nut boiled in milk and cut up (*sapārī chīval-i chikanī*), betel nut of superior betel (*sapārī pānḍvā nādra*), *sapārī* of catechu essence, *sapārī* of *kapūr kānti, sapārī atsār* (fresh betel nut), lime for the centre of the *sapārī*, betel nut boiled in milk with pieces of lime, catechu essence, essence of grains, very pure betel (*chīkanī*), essence of screw pine (*kītkī*), essence of rosewater, chanpa essence, white China rose essence, essence of citron (*karna*), sandal paste on *pān*, camphor paste, musk paste. Having filled the betel basket (*chūlī*), take the *pān* (betel leaves) and then, having put camphor in water, sprinkle it on the *pān* (*f.118a*) so that it hardens and then chew the *pān* with plain *sapārī* (betel nut). Make a paste of camphor, cardamoms and cloves, make paste of *barmhī*, wheat paste, camphor paste, cassia leaf paste, cinnamon buds paste, *bahuphalī* (fig) paste, woodapple paste, small cardamoms paste, zedoary paste, sesame oil paste, potherbs and oil, and also make paste of the following: white ambergris, white ambergris juice, frankincense, frankincense juice, saul tree juice, sesame oil, *marhaṭṭī* aloes, camphor juice. Scatter some of these kinds of juice on to the betel leaves (*pān*) and fold them into bundles. Also make paste and also scent and

222 The Sissoo tree, *Dalbergia sissu*. Oil from the wood is used internally and externally.
223 Betel leaf which is yellowish-green, pungent like pepper and smells like camphor.
224 The wetland plant *Xanthiumi indicum*.
225 Obscure.

perfume these juices and also perfume (*f.118b, with a miniature*)[226] the *pān* and the *sapārī*. Also perfume the catechu essence and the . . . (*damaged*) and also perfume the lime and the *tanbūl*.

Another pleasing benefit recounted in the Book of Enjoyment (*Kitāb-i Hārat*) is the most pleasant that refers to the benefits derived from *tanbūl* and its qualities: camphor, cinnamon, wheat, cloves, cubebs, cardamoms, catechu essence, lime, *sapārī* (betel nut), *pān* (betel leaf), all these ingredients make for a good *tanbūl*. (*f.119a*) The properties of *pān* are that it purifies the mouth, when it is foul and bitter and it wards off flatulence. The qualities of *sapārī* are that it is a laxative, it takes hold of the throat, it produces much bile and it induces an appetite for food. The properties of lime are that it gets rid of bitter and sweet phlegm. The properties of *tanbūl* are that it gets rid of wind, bile and phlegm, produces well-being and desire, gets rid of halitosis, purifies the mouth, brings serenity, induces intelligent talk and produces an appetite for food. It softens the tongue, purifies the teeth and throat, changes the disposition, restricts saliva, repels diseases of the chest and cures the throat. (*f.119b*) Fever, thirst, phlegm and wind are got rid of, libido is strengthened, desire is awakened and erections are induced. The heart is invigorated and the intellect strengthened and it is a purification. The *sapārī* (*consists of*) one *pān* (*and*) two *chūna*. The catechu essence and the water lily thoroughly perfume the lime. If the lime of the *sapārī* is thoroughly perfumed and likewise the *pān* of the *sapārī* is thoroughly perfumed then the *pān* of the *tanbūl* becomes pleasantly tasty. If the *pān* (leaves), *sapārī* (nut), *chūna* (lime) and the *kāt* (catechu essence) are compatible and of the correct proportions, the colour will be good and it will be sweet, pleasantly perfumed and tender. If there is too much *sapārī* the colour will come out and it will not be sweet. If there is too much *chūna*, the mouth will become blistered and sore and the breath will be bad. If there is too much *pān*, (*f.120a*) it will become excessively coloured and too highly scented.

Some say that *sapārī* can be eaten at any time but that *chūna* is best eaten in the morning in preference to other times. Diseases of the mouth are collectively prevented, appetite is created and the trickling of urine is prevented. Every day upon waking from sleep, chew *tanbūl* and also eat it on food, after washing the face and after vomiting. Chew it when indisposed as it helps indisposition, gets rid of sexual diseases, rheumatism and tonsillitis and prevents all illnesses and flatulence. However some people have been forbidden to chew *tanbūl*, (*f.120b*) for example someone who has excess of bile or shortness of breath or weakness (*impotence*) or who has fasted or who has painful eyes or someone who has taken poison or suffered from giddiness or blindness (*migraine?*) or who has galloping consumption – do not give these people

226 Note in the margin near the miniature 'leaf-eating'.

tanbūl. Do not swallow the saliva that is first formed because it reveals many kinds of illnesses and do not swallow the second lot that collects as it will cause diarrhoea and fever but do swallow the third lot of saliva that has collected as this is very beneficial.

(*f.121a*) Equally, to achieve immortality, it is necessary to chew *pān* in this way. By chewing wild *pān* which is called *dīnat*, success is driven away, poverty and ill-health are induced and troubles occur. The veins in the *pān* (betel leaves) should not be eaten as they damage the constitution. Do not eat the head of the *pān* because it will shorten life. The veins of the *pān* destroy the intellect and if a *pān* is eaten with that *chūna* it takes away quality of life. If a quantity of *pān* is continually chewed, some of the following troubles and defects are caused: it brings ill-health, the colour of the face becomes yellow and blindness and illnesses of the mouth are caused. However, if the *pān* is perfumed and if flowers and scent are rubbed into it, the benefits are as follows: (*f.121b, with a miniature*)[227] seminal fluid increases, well-being is established, the body becomes comfortable, bad sight is prevented and feverishness, restlessness and stiffness are reduced.

Another recipe, for making parched grain: having put parched grain into all kinds of vegetable oil, cook it and grind it. Fry it and mix it with grain flour of every kind and it becomes good body paste (*abtāna*). The ingredients for the most part are as follows: civet, chickpea flour, apple peel, sweet-orange peel, rosewater, (*f.122a*) frankincense, liquidambar, lac, ground seeds of small cardamoms of both kinds, black and white, ghee (*hūs*), cinnamon, spikenard, wild spikenard, deodar, *barmā, chapāvati* (*chironji*), Chinese cubebs, flowers of every kind, beeswax, bananas, screw pine (*kīyūra*), *mūtha* beans, large and small cardamoms, camphor, cardamoms, large cloves, cloves twigs, cloves, Chinese cassia, cassia bark, *kapūr kachrī*, cooked camphor, both kinds of camphor, hand-pressed sesame oil, saffron, sugar, oil of every kind, sandal of every kind, red roses, musk, camphor, white ambergris. Another recipe for preparing *abtāna* (paste): turmeric, saffron, gold leaf, pollen of the red rose, spikenard, baked perfumed mollusc shells (*nākhan būyā*), deodar, leaves of the Indian fig after they have turned yellow, (*f.122b*) wild fig, mango, sugar-cane syrup, turmeric leaves, lime juice, starfruit, catechu essence, barley, wheat bran, long turmeric, rice, lentils, *panvār* seeds,[228] camphor, almonds, vinegar, *mūtha* beans, pollen of water lily flowers, white China rose pollen.

Another recipe for an unusual perfume: collect together the following ingredients, sprinkle warm water on them, then, having dried them, grind them finely and perfume them with many flowers. Eat this or rub it on the body, put it in food, flavour *pān* with it, scent head lotion with it, put it in

227 Note in the margin 'to chew leaves'.

228 Seeds of *Cassia tora*, a traditional tranquilliser.

sherbet, scent clothes with it and scent anything that is required with it. (*f.123a*) The method is as follows: musk, white ambergris, artemisia, beans, *ghālīya* (civet), chickpea flour, rosewater, sweet-orange peel, *parīnag*,[229] bamboo manna, catechu essence, citron (*karna*) flowers, *malākara* sandal, sesame oil, camphor, *nāg-i kīsar* blossoms, chironji (*chapāvati*), white sandal, red rose flowers, saffron, cloves, *mūtha* beans, wheat, cinnamon, cardamoms, cucumber, liquidambar, *barmā*, zedoary, spikenard, wild spikenard, aromatic powder (*tagrī*), small black cardamoms, small white cardamoms.

Another recipe, for making flavourings for vegetable oils from the following ingredients. Press them (*the ingredients*) together with sesame seeds or put them into vegetable oil and boil and flavour them. The ingredients are as follows: mangoes, spikenard, mango gum, mango buds, (*f.123b*) screw pine (*kītkī*) flowers, jujube flowers, chanpa flowers, jasmine, lime, vinegar, starfruit, turmeric, red sandal, madder, Toon tree flowers, beans, sweet-orange peel, sour-orange peel, camphor, saffron, *marva* fruit,[230] Indian myrtle (*ḥanā*), artemisia, small cardamoms, wheat, *chūva sūla* (aromatic paste), ambergris, pumpkin, banana, musk, quince flowers, cooked quince, lime peel, *chūva* (paste), jackfruit tree flowers, jackfruit, jujube. Another recipe for making pungent essence, the ingredients are as follows: sandal, sesame oil, zedoary, cubebs, sacred basil, *mūtha* beans, fresh mango shoots, sour-orange peel, chickpea flour, flavoured sugar, white China roses, saffron, chanpa essence, freshly picked lime shoots, cardamoms, cloves, (*f.124a*) freshly picked citron (*karna*) shoots, liquidambar, *barmā*, red rose flowers, camphor, civet, citron (*karna*) flowers, rosewater, mango syrup, white ambergris, catechu essence.

Another recipe for an aloes mixture and its ingredients: it is for perfuming clothes, hair of the head, water or whatever is required, and for making perfume. The ingredients are as follows: honey (*shahd*), potherbs, gum lac, Saul tree resin, jasmine, small cardamoms, molasses, rind of sugarcane, catechu essence, wild spikenard, spikenard, aromatic paste (*chūva*), white sandal, oil seed, ambergris, white China rose, wax, sandal, gum resin, scented mollusc, musk, sugar, cardamom oil, saffron, camphor, rosewater. Another recipe for perfume to be used in the banqueting hall and the house if it is required to be perfumed. (*f.124b, with a miniature*) If it is so desired, rub the walls with perfume or, having put perfume in water, sprinkle it on the walls. The ingredients are as follows: put in *ʿabīr* (scented paste or powder), *basant* seeds,[231] bruised or coarsely ground grain, *chūva* paste, Chinese camphor perfume,[232] leaves of trees. Make the perfume, put it in and sprinkle it. Use

229 Medicinal plant sometimes called *phālī*.

230 *Ocimum pilosum, Artemisia vulgaris* or *Origanum majorana*, all strongly scented plants.

231 *Linum strictum*, ridged yellow flax, seeds used as an emollient.

232 *Kafūr-i chīnī*.

mango, ambergris, beans, *marhaṭṭī* aloes, perfumed fat, bruised grain, *chūva*, essence of mouse-ear plant (*marzangūsh*), Chinese camphor, boiled juice of spikenard, (*f.125a*) and put in flowers scented with aloes, white sandal essence, scent from shoots, sesame oil scent, sweet basil essence, chanpa essence, artemisia essence, turmeric leaves essence, sacred basil essence, cardamom juice, sandal juice.

Another recipe for *ʿabīr* of Mahmud Shahi: four *dirams* of spikenard, four *dirams* of wild spikenard, four *dirams* of *mūtha* beans, two *dirams* of zedoary, four *dirams* of catechu essence (*kattha*), four *dirams* of cloves, four *dirams* of sandal, four *dirams* of *barmā*, four *dirams* of *malākara* sandal, four *dirams* of small cardamoms, four *dirams* of cinnamon, four *dirams* of turmeric leaves, four *dirams* of *tagrī*, two *dirams* of *marva* fruit, four *dirams* of cassia, one *diram* of *bahuphalī* figs, four *dirams* of ghee (*hūs*), four *dirams* of *chapāvatī* (*chīrūnjī*). (*f.125b*) Chop up all these ingredients and mix them with hot water and dry them in the sun. Then, when grinding a quantity of them, add them to other ingredients as follows: four *dirams* of wheat, three *dirams* of zerumbet, three *dirams* of chickpea flour, four *dirams* of roasted cassia, nine *dirams* of sweet sesame. Put them into vegetable oil and grind the above-mentioned ingredients, then add scented mollusc shells and grind them again and then sift them through a cloth. Then take six *dirams* of musk and one *māsa* of camphor and put in three times the amount of flower perfumes.

Another favourite of Mahmud Shahi: nine *dirams* of ground sandal, one *diram* of zerumbet, one *diram* of wheat, one *diram* of sweet-orange peel, three *dirams* of ground sandal (*malākara*), (*f.126a*) two *dirams* of bamboo manna. Grind and sift all these, mix them together and add four times the amount (*karrat*) of jasmine flower perfume. Mince and sift half a *tūlcha* of musk, two *rattī* of camphor and one *māsa* of white ambergris and mix them together. Another recipe of Mahmud Shahi: take nine *dirams* of ground sandal, six *dirams* of sandal (*malākara*), three *dirams* of saffron, two *dirams* of wheat, two *dirams* of *kapūr kachrī*. Grind all these in three *dirams* of sesame oil, and put them into an earthenware cooking pot scented with fresh red roses and put in two *dirams* of sesame oil and boil it. Strain it into a glass, dry the sandal, add one *tūlcha* of musk, one *māsa* of white ambergris, (*f.126b*) four *rattīs* of camphor, and pound it all together. Another *ʿabīr* paste of Ghiyath Shahi: four *dirams* of bruised sandal wood (*malākara*), four *sīrs* of ground sandal, nine *dirams* of *tagrī* powder, . . . (*damaged*) three *dirams* of *kapūr kachrī*, two *dirams* of wheat, six *dirams* of catechu essence, six *dirams* of spikenard, six *dirams* of wild spikenard, six *dirams* of cinnamon, two *dirams* of small cardamoms, six *dirams* of cloves, three *dirams* of dregs from the perfume distillery (*nakh*). Mince and sift all these. Roast the *nakh* in a hot pan and when it has turned red, take it out of the pan and put it with the above-mentioned ingredients. Add three *tūlchas* of ground musk and one *māsa* of ground camphor and perfume it with three times this amount of flower scent.

Another recipe . . . (*missing folio(s)*) . . . (*f.127a*)[233] . . . a quarter of a *sīr* of . . . two *dirams* of *kapūr kachrī*, two *dirams* of wheat, nine *dirams* of pounded sesame, six *dirams* of ground sandal (*malākara*). Put all these together, grind them and, having mixed them with rosewater, boil the mixture in a cooking pot. Distil it in a glass and add three *dirams* of sesame oil, one *diram* of sandal, one *diram* of small cardamoms, one *diram* of liquidambar, and one *diram* of jasmine oil, and distil it. Add six *dirams* of saffron and dry it. Then having ground together one *tūlcha* of musk, one *māsa* of white ambergris and half a *māsa* of camphor, mix them together.

Another of the principal perfumes of Ghiyath Shahi: half a *diram* of *bahu-phalī* figs, one *diram* of sour-orange peel, half a *diram* of white ambergris, (*f.127b*) three *māsa* of camphor. Grind them all together and mix them with rosewater. Form the mixture into quarter-*diram* pellets. Another of the principal perfumes of Ghiyath Shahi: two *dirams* of sour-orange peel, two *dirams* of mango peel, one *diram* of camphor, one and a half *dirams* of musk, a quarter *diram* of ambergris and one *diram* of white sandal. Form into pellets with rosewater. Another recipe for Ghiyath Shahi's essences: grind together four *dirams* of hand-pressed sesame oil and the equivalent amount of rosewater, put in three *māsa* of musk, four *rattī* of camphor, and one *māsa* of white ambergris. Another (*recipe for*) an essence of Ghiyath Shahi: pound nine *dirams* of sandal with rosewater (*f.128a*) and add three *māsa* of musk, one *māsa* of camphor, four *rattīs* of wheat and one *diram* of zerumbet, put it in the essence and perfume it with three times the amount (*karrat*) of *marhaṭṭī* aloes. Another (*recipe for*) essence of Ghiyath Shahi: pound four *dirams* of hand-pressed sesame oil with three *māsa* of musk, four *rattīs* of camphor and white ambergris and then prepare the essence.

Other recipes for the perfumes of the *House of Pleasures* are for the method of distilling for *chūva* (aromatic paste). Mix the ingredients and use scented water or essence and, if it is required, prepare *bakkhā*. The ingredients are: musk, camphor, white sandal, *chūva*, sandal, essence of sandal shoots, rosewater (*f.128b*), essence of *jāman* seed, civet scent, grain seed oil, liquidambar, fragrant grass roots, *nāg-i kīsar*, wheat, *chūva*, frankincense, sesame seed oil, roasted rice, musk plant, musk (*from the musk deer*), minced civet, broken scented mollusc shell, fat, civet, all kinds of oils, shoots of oleander, minced musk-bag (*and*) minced musk (*from the musk deer*), saffron.

Another recipe for scented ointments for women. Rub perfume separately into each joint. (*Use*) pellets of perfumed paste. Wash the hands in rosewater.

233 Again a suspect catchword (f.126b), for although it appears (*sāvīda*) at the top of f.127a, the preceding word or words related to it are missing according to the punctuation. The Farsi foliation sequence is unbroken.

Take the sap from the bark of the mango tree and from the bark of the wild fig tree and from the *pīpal* tree and wash the body (*with it*). Rub aromatic paste, perfume and musk into the armpits. (*f.129a*) Rub *chūva*, rosewater and musk onto the private parts and rub sandal on the throat. Essence of musk is good for the mouth, (*also*) put aloes perfume into the mouth. Rub ointment made from bodily oils on the face, rub rosewater on the forehead, sniff flowers, scatter spikenard on the head, rub saffron on the face, use scented flower oils of every kind, make *'abīr* (*scented powder*) with the sweet scent of jasmine flowers, polish the two front teeth, rub perfume into the handkerchief, wash the whole body with rosewater. Put on a white *chādor* and apply scent to it. Rub the body with twigs and wash in cold water.

Another recipe for making drinking water cold: place waterpots, one on top of another, and make a (*f.129b, with a miniature*) small hole in the bottom of one so the water runs down. Fill an earthenware pot with water and use that water during a drought. And, because of drought, it is necessary to prepare it during that season in winter that is called *māh mās* (*waxing of the moon*). Water skins, also, should be prepared during *māh mās*. Put perfumes (*flavourings*) of all kinds into the water and fasten the necks of the water jars with fresh clay. (*f.130a*) Drink the water. Rub water pots with sandal juice and put camphor into them. Drink water from a gold vessel. Also, having filled water pots with water, put them down and fan them. Place a water pot in a string net, suspend it and shake it. Take water pots into a cave and fan them. Soak a clean cloth in water, fan it and then squeeze it out and drink the water. Put monkey jackfruit (*katakphal*)[234] in the water and add a handful of small cardamoms and cassia. Put pearls and a small nugget of gold into the water.

Also (*follows*) a reminder of things that are useful in the summer weather. If the heat is overwhelming and too much bile is produced (*damaged*) and thirst is produced and (*f.130b*) pain becomes chronic and if, from riding out hunting and galloping a horse in the hot sun, sunstroke is caused, then turn to the following remedies. Give flowers of every kind and fruit of every kind on a cushion. Bring witty men who are his boon companions before him. Give cucumbers, gherkins, wild figs and perfume. Turn a water wheel before him and throw water in the air. Burn camphor and rosewater and put cucumber leaves on the body. Moisten clothes with water and put them on the body. Fill water pots with water and make holes in the pots and put them on a high place. Make bedclothes from skins . . . (*damaged*) a garment of fine linen (*kattān*); (*f.131a*) (*Take*) rosewater, sandal and camphor; soak a *chādor* in the rain; moisten a cloth with rosewater, sandal and camphor, place it over the eyes; moisten a *chādor* with camphor, sandal and rosewater, put it on and

234 *Lakūch, Artocarpus lacucha.*

shake it. Place a net of pearls on the head, fan with a metal tray, place a net of pearls over the eyes and chest. Moisten a muslin *chādor* in water and hang it in the breeze. Take cold drinks and food. Rub perfumes of every kind into a cloth and use it as a fan. Make jasmine flowers and pieces of crystal cold and place them on the eyes. Place flowers on the eyes (*damaged*) . . .

(*f.131b*) Dress her in white clothes and a string of pearls, sprinkle water on her. If a woman is comatose, wash her body in cold water and put pearls on her. Put quince (*bīl*) leaves on her, also water lily leaves, grass (*dūb*) and *pīpal* leaves. Make a lotion of cold water and rosewater and wash her face with it. Put a pellet made from cardamoms, camphor and rosewater in the mouth.

Another recipe, for inducing sleep: take every kind of fruit. Bring before him a woman of sweet words, play the *sarūd*, place flowers and fruit of every kind before him. Kiss the lips (*lit. strike the lips together?*). Play musical instruments that are played by movement of the fingers, they are called *sarūds*.[235] (*missing folio(s)*)[236]

(*f.132a*) . . . cardamoms, rosewater, red roses, white China roses, *marva* (*fruit*), *padmak*,[237] rice in the husk, fruit of mimusops, box myrtle (*kayaphal*),[238] sesame meal, camphor, *sūnf* roots, catechu extract, bark of musk willow, wild fig roots, Persian lilac, *līnab* (palm juice?), Coral tree, *kasīs* (date wine?), *phatkarī*, roots of sorrel. Another recipe for substances that induce the penis to increase the flow of semen is as follows: wheat bread, meat, chickpea, beans (*faba baklāris*), pigeon, cow's ghee, walnuts, potherbs, pine kernels, baked sparrow, date sugar, yellow sandal, raisins, round peppers, honey (*shahd*), pistachio nuts, almonds, cooked dates, white sesame seeds, saffron, milk boiled with dates, white ambergris, white chickpeas, wild carrots, mint, . . . (*damaged*), coconut, cooked grapes, dry bread, (*f.132b*) musk, red and white beans, duck eggs, cooked meat, sheep meat, leeks, onions, hens' eggs, palm sugar, duck, chicken, fresh baked fish, olives.

Another recipe for ingredients that increase the flow of semen and strengthen sexual desire is as follows: ten *sīrs* of white Khurasani onions cut into rings and fried either in cow's ghee or sesame seed oil. Fry a young pigeon and mix it with the ghee. Then pound red beans and white chickpeas and mix them together, add some water so they become well-cooked. Seal the lid of the cooking pot and cook until the pulse becomes soft. (*f.133a*) Mix with it one

235 The sarud is a plucked instrument related to the sitar.
236 The catchword on f.131b is *sarūdhā*, but f.132a begins with *alā'īchī, gulāb*. The Farsi foliation sequence is unbroken.
237 *Costus speciosa* or crepe ginger.
238 *Myrica esculenta* or box myrtle.

diram of cassia, half a *diram* of galingale (*khūlanjān*) and dried bread. Cut chapatti finely, mix it in and boil it by the *baghrā* method,[239] put the chapatti in or else, having cooked the chapatti on embers, put it in the broth and eat it. Another recipe for food: cook meat of every kind and hens' eggs and pigeons and birds of every kind and onions and fat young pigeons. Cut them into tiny pieces and fry them in duck fat, add salt and roughly minced white chickpeas. Make it produce enough liquid to cook it thoroughly, then seal the lid of the cooking pot and cook for long enough to cook the pigeon and chickpeas. Then add one *diram* (*f.133b, with a miniature*) of cassia and half a *diram* of galingale (*khūlanjān*) and add the acid juice of citron (*karna*). Eating this food makes the semen flow, increases strength and increases sexual desire making it much stronger. Another recipe: fry fat lamb (*or kid, halvān*) in walnut oil and two portions of white onions. When it is well-fried, add salt, cloves, cardamoms and cinnamon. (*f.134a*) Then perfume a fresh clay cooking pot with the flavour of asafoetida. Add three or four times this amount of vegetable oil, put in potherbs, then shake the cooking pot and put the lid on it. When it has become savoury and well-baked, add lime juice, vegetable oil and asafoetida.

Another recipe for *bhrat* (mash or stuffing): fry aubergine on hot embers, add onions, fresh ginger, salt, pepper and much relish. Flavour it well. Add aniseed, then cook chapatti and eat the *bhrat* with it. Another recipe for food: extract juice from every kind of fruit and boil it. Fry flour in ghee, put it into the juice and add a little palm sugar, (*f.134b*) cardamoms and camphor and serve it. Another recipe for bread made from all kinds of grains: cook the bread, hollow it out and put in ghee. Another recipe for potherbs: chop sweet-smelling potherbs finely, add salt and asafoetida and boil them. When they are boiled, take them off and flavour them with asafoetida or fenugreek in ghee, put the potherbs into them and add either roasted sesame seeds or coarsely ground cumin seeds. Add three parts of potherbs and one part of fresh ginger, finely cut.

Another recipe, for the method for *bhāt*: add one portion (*f.135a*) of *bhāt* to *baghrā* and barley gruel (*yavūk*) and three portions of *jāman bhāt*. Mix them together, add salt and put in camphor, musk and some rosewater. Another recipe: if it is a fact that digestion has become difficult, eat light food at that time. The method for *bhāt*: add *mūng* pulse and broken pulse to *bhāt*. Put asafoetida, salt, fresh ginger, cardamoms and cloves with the broken pulse and cook it. Make a stew from neck of lamb and add rice, fresh ginger, turmeric, pepper, asafoetida, *sūnf* and coriander.

Another recipe, for broth with pulao (*pilav*): take well-flavoured pieces of meat and add finely cut fresh ginger, dried ginger juice and lime juice

239 See f.41 etc. above.

and cook it. Eat finely cut dried ginger with it. Another recipe, (*f.135b*) for partridge *yakhnī* (broth) and plain rural *kabābs* and plain rural *sīkh* (skewered meat). Put fresh ginger, onions, caraway, salt and asafoetida with all kinds of potherbs and prepare it. Another recipe, for *kaṛhī*: take sour cow's *dūgh* and cook skewered lamb taken from the five places[240] with whole potherbs and put it into the *dūgh*. Also flavour it with buttermilk and also cook parched grain and onion and also kedgeree from parched grain and also *bhāt* made from wheat. Flavour these foods with buttermilk or else eat it with *dūgh*. Also, having put date sugar into ghee, boil it, also use liquidambar, also gourd and *bathala* (*f.136a*) and *bhrat-gandūrī* (meat and vegetable stuffing),[241] also melon *bhrāt* and meat and aubergine and meat and pumpkin. Cook all these foods. Another recipe: take a melon and cut a little out of the top of it with a knife. Remove the inside of the melon and place an ember (*charcoal*) in it. Put asafoetida on it, wrap potherbs in flour, fasten up the mouth and roast it on embers. Add salt, asafoetida, pepper and lime juice, make *bhrat* (stuffing) and flavour it. By the same method make aubergine *bhrat* and by the same method make . . . (*damaged*) *bhrat* and by the same method make gourd *bhrat*. (*f.136b, with a miniature*) Also lentil juice and split lentils are good for cooking. When soft foods are required then cook the following: soup made from plain *dūgh*, soup of the flesh of myrobalan, *mūng* and sweet-smelling (*sūvās*) rice.

Fry some rice, namely parched rice (*khīl*) and cook all the following with rice water and with relish of every kind and vinegar of all kinds: (*f.137a*) thin cake cooked on charcoal (*angār manda*), dry bread (*kāk*), thin bread of unleavened flour, thin baked bread, parched grain bread, parched barley grain and barley bread, barley meal, starch (*āhaṛī*), *būranī*,[242] kedgeree, *chaklī, khīs, rābaṛī* (pottage) of parched grain, *ghāṭā* (pounded) barley, barley buttermilk, parched grain, *lūh* (partridge) broth, *kabābs* of *lūh, lūh* soup, dishes flavoured with *lūh, sīkh* of the kite or similar bird, split peas, split *mūng*, split lentils, sweet-smelling ghee or ghee that has been used to cook meat, *pāpaṛ*. Add lime relish and pieces of cut-up fresh ginger . . . (*damaged*) and also cut-up pieces of liquorice root and cumin with lime . . . (*damaged*). Also add cumin, (*f.137b*) mint, *dāl*, coriander and salt to meat soup, cook it and sprinkle rosewater on it. Put salt and potherbs on skewers and cook it until it is thoroughly soft. Another recipe, for mixed meats that is called *sūndna*: pound the meat until it is very thin, cut it finely, add turmeric, asafoetida, coriander and salt to it. Mix it up and put it into a cooking pot and flavour it. When the meat's own juices have been brought out, put hot water on it and cook it. When it is half-cooked, add ghee. Sprinkle lime juice on it before serving.

240 i.e. five succulent cuts of lamb.

241 A mash of boiled or fried vegetables or a mash of melon or of meat with aubergine or meat with pumpkin.

242 Aubergines stewed in sour milk.

Another (*f.138a*) recipe for aubergine *bhrat*: mix minced meat, minced onion and portions of aubergine, that have been cooked with meat, with aubergine *bhrat*. Mix them all together, add ground asafoetida and the flavour of asafoetida and put cooked ghee on it. When the aubergine is cooked, mix together mustard seed, lentil seed, gourd, butter beans, pumpkin, white basil and potherbs. Put them in water, cook them and add ghee. At the time of serving, sprinkle fresh ginger juice or lime juice on it. Another recipe, for cooked mince: grind cardamoms, cloves and turmeric, add them to the mince and then, (*f.138b*) having put ghee into a cooking pot and flavoured it with turmeric, fry the above-mentioned mince. When it has become soupy, add water and stir with a spoon so that the mince becomes mixed with the water and thickens. When the soup is mixed and cooked, and is ready to serve, add fresh ginger. Put in onions and lime juice, take it off, and having put parched grain into that soup, either eat it as it is or add it to *bhāt*.

Another method, for buttermilk (*mhīrī*): cook the buttermilk in *dūgh* and add roasted caraway, roasted fenugreek and roasted asafoetida. Cook the buttermilk with roasted rice, add salt and flavour it with ghee . . . (*missing folio(s)*)[243]

(*f.139a*) . . . fasten the lid of the cooking pot with a clean cloth and place the above-mentioned filling (*pūran*) on the cloth and steam it. Add onions and then, having fried asafoetida in vegetable oil or in ghee, grind it and add it to that filling. Prepare two loaves from flour dough. Put the filling on one of the loaves and place the second one on top of it (*i.e. to make a sandwich*) and strengthen the sides of the sandwich and fry it in ghee. Another recipe for *lāpasī* (pottage) . . . (*damaged*), fry it in ghee and then grind it, add palm sugar, lime juice and (*f.139b*) fresh ginger juice and cook the *lāpasī* for a short time. Put cardamoms and cloves on it. If fruit is added that is another version. Another recipe for *lāpasī* of fried wild rice (*shāl*): mash the wild rice roughly on a stone, fry it in ghee, add water and put in syrup and pomegranate. Add cardamoms, cloves, rosewater, camphor and musk and serve it.

Another recipe, for the method for *mūṛṛkī*: boil *mūng* in water, grind it into pieces, add pepper, fresh ginger, coriander, asafoetida and salt and beat them all together and fry them in ghee . . . (*damaged*) and either eat it like this (*f.140a*) or, having put it in sherbet, drink it. Another recipe, for the method for *mūng* bread: put in asafoetida and salt, then first of all soak the *mūng* in water, then wash the *dāl*, fan it a little and crush it coarsely and put ground salt, pepper, asafoetida, lime juice and fresh ginger into it. Then coarsely

243 Another highly suspect example of skulduggery. The catchword on f.138b (no doubt correctly) is *nū'ī dīgar*, indicating a new recipe, but f.139a does *not* begin with a new recipe, although the words *nū'ī dīgar* have been squeezed in above *sar-i dīg*.

grind cardamoms and cloves and mix them all together. Wrap them up in a fig leaf or a banana leaf and enclose it all in flour dough. Place it in hot ashes and when it is time to eat the food, take it out of the dough and throw the dough away. Take it out and eat it and, by the same method prepare . . . (*damaged*) and by the same method (*f.140b*) prepare it from finger *zarat* (*mand vā*).[244] By the same method, prepare it from beans, having first salted and boiled them. Take them out, knead them by hand and mix them with cardamoms, cloves, pepper and ghee. Wrap them in a leaf and enfold it in dough. Place it on hot ashes and at meal time throw away the dough and eat the contents. This is called 'foreign food'. Prepare lentils in the same way and, by the same method, prepare beans (*sīm*).

Another recipe, for preparing 'foreign' bread: having baked plain boiled rice in plenty of ghee . . . (*damaged*) bake it hard . . . (*damaged*) roast some *sūnf* seeds . . . (*damaged*) add . . . (*damaged*) and put a little (*f.141a*) water into it, enough to moisten it and make thick coarse bread. Place a piece of bread on it and under it, these pieces also made from dough. Make the edges of these breads strong, then bake it on hot embers so that it will become baked and cooked. When it is well-cooked, take it off and throw away the bread above and below it and eat the bread between.

Another recipe for 'foreign' food: cook soft *bhāt* from yellow chickpeas (*yavūk*).[245] Cook broken yellow chickpea pulse, put it into the dish of *bhāt* and add . . . (*damaged*) sugar to the *bhāt* and minced fresh ginger and sweet-smelling ghee. Cook strips of dough (*pāpaṛ*) (*f.141b*) on hot embers, cut the *pāpaṛ* finely and put it, piece by piece, into the *bhāt*. Another recipe for 'foreign' food: marinate portions of meat in ghee and cook it well. When it is cooked, add pieces of dried bread to it. Then place the meat on a leaf, wrap it up and enfold it in layers of dough and bake it in hot embers. Take it off at meal time and throw away the dough and eat the meat. Another recipe for 'foreign' food: put whole potherbs into minced meat and cook it. Put the broth (*yakhnī*) into earthenware cooking pots, bake it and eat it. Another recipe . . . (*damaged*) for mince: likewise (*f.142a*) make *kabābs* fried in ghee, and also make mince well-fried in ghee.

Another recipe: the advantages of *bhāt* are that it repels thirst, cools fevers, gives strength to the body and makes semen flow. Add one or two raisins or dates, or put in four or five. Boil bananas or jackfruit or monkey jackfruit or coconuts or almonds or sour pomegranate or potherbs or honey (*shahd*) or ghee or *maṭṭhā* or *sūndhī* or pepper or cardamoms or cassia or cinnamon or *nāg-i kīsar*, as well as saffron, camphor and musk, in water and beat it with

244 Known as *rāgi* or *manduā*, the grain of *Eleusine coracana*.
245 Bengal gram, *chanaka, Cicer arietnum*.

a churning stick and drain off the liquid and cook varieties of *bhāt* in the liquid.

Some . . . (*damaged*) and also other medicines (*f.142b*) that make the following troubles go away such as abundant phlegm, excess wind, excess bile, excessive thirst and lack of appetite – these are some of the afflictions that are warded off by them and they make for great strength and for increase of semen and are as follows: congee or warm water or sour pomegranate juice, mustard seed, salt and sweet pomegranate juice. Mix them all together and then, having also mixed together pepper, round pepper, dried ginger, cardamoms, cassia, cinnamon, cumin, coriander, saffron, musk, camphor and ambergris, prepare it and take the pure liquid from it. There are all kinds of . . . (*damaged*) water chestnuts, fried rice, chickpeas, various kinds of *kaṛhī*, (*f.143a*) almonds and pine kernels. Put one or two items from the above-mentioned into it, having ground them, and prepare them small enough to enable him (*i.e. an invalid*) to take it with his fingers. This is called *līhīya* (*i.e. food that can be licked*). If it is made thinner, this is called *pīhīya* and can be eaten with a spoon. The healing properties are twofold as follows: the *līhīya* is thick and the *pīhīya* is light. Make whichever kind and to what quantity is required.

Pickle (*āchāl*) makes food digestible and induces hunger. Make pickle from sour fruit, corinda, mango, hogplum, . . . (*damaged*). After seven days . . . (*damaged*) the pickle becomes good. Remove it (*f.143b*) and slice it and add mustard seed, cardamoms and cloves to it and put in some cumin, pepper, fresh ginger, some garlic and, having cut them, put in segments of onion. Add it to all foods or to vegetables or to meat when required. It is beneficial in that it produces hunger, weight is gained and feelings of pleasure and well-being are induced. Another recipe: bake fried new shoots of mature vine in ghee. When put into potherbs, they become well-flavoured. Another: take new shoots of mature orange and from lime and from . . . (*damaged*) and fresh coriander and onion leaves. Fry them all in ghee and put them with potherbs and then put these potherbs (*f.144a*) into food and into meat and into green vegetables. Another recipe for chutney for the digestion of food: myrobalan, raisins, white water lily, pulp of *tīndū* fruit, figs, apples, *kūndī* fruit,[246] *kākṛā* stones,[247] *mīnha* (plum) stones, mustard seeds, myrobalan, lentil sprouts, fresh ginger, lime, pepper, fresh betel nuts (*sapārī*), mangoes and also fruits that are tender and all leaves that are tender and all roots that are tender. Take all these and make pickle for, eaten with food, it helps digestion.

246 *Gūndī* in Hindi, *Cordia Rothii* or *C. angustifolia*, yielding a sour fruit used in pickles.

247 *Pistachio* (or *Rhus*) *integerrima*, of which the gall-like growths (*kākṛā sangī*) on the leaves are used medicinally.

Another recipe for pottage (*lāpasī*): lightly fry dry flour in ghee . . . (*damaged*) put it in water and boil it well. When it has become well-cooked put in . . . (*damaged*) and serve it with *meze* (titbits). Put in (*f.144b, with a miniature*) pomegranate and palm sugar, then put in a small amount of ghee. By the same method prepare it from rice or make it by the same method from chickpeas and cook it from every kind (*of grain or dāl*) that is required. It can become several varieties. Mix in vinegar and honey (*shahd*), this is a sweet version and put . . . (*damaged*) on it. Also soak rice in water and bake it. Fry (*f.145a*) it, then pound it and mix in sourness and sharpness or make it sweet. Also roast potherbs and one *diram* of sesame seeds and roast half of a *diram* of fenugreek, two *dirams* of rice, two *dirams* of parched chickpeas, half a *diram* of oilcake (*khal*), one *diram* of asafoetida, four *dirams* of vinegar (*sarka*), the juice of one lime, four *rattīs* of musk, four *rattīs* of camphor. Flavour with vegetable oil and put potherbs into meat or food or sherbet or *dūgh* or put them into anything so desired.

Also give flavours of every kind to foods as follows: the flavour of sugar, of sugarcane juice, of camphor, of musk, rosewater, (*f.145b*) sandal, aloes oil, cassia, cinnamon, cardamoms, white ambergris, liquidambar, white sandal, essence of oilcake (*khal*), civet, small cardamoms, cloves, spikenard, wild spikenard, liquorice roots, *tagrī* powder, saffron, chanpa flowers, jasmine flowers, turmeric leaves, jasmine (*mūgarā*) flowers, red roses, beans, screw pine (*kīyūra*), jujube flowers, banana leaves, sandal leaves, sour-orange leaves, apples, artemisia flowers, *marva* flowers, white China roses, sacred basil (*tulsī*), sweet basil (*raiḥān*), all these when thoroughly cooked and burned give out flavours, use whichever are required.

Another recipe: put myrobalan and fried rice into it, boil it and add . . . (*damaged*). Put in salt (*f.146a*) and pepper and take it off. Flavour it with asafoetida and add cassia, cinnamon, mint and lime juice. Put plenty of asafoetida flavouring into it and also fresh ginger juice. Another recipe, for rice water (*pīchha*): put in *mūng* pulse, water, cassia, cinnamon, cardamoms and cloves and flavour it. If fried rice has been put into it, cook it. This makes another version. And if rice (*presumably plain rice*) is put in and cooked, this is another version.

A method for making bread: put *sūnf*, onions, ghee and salt into wheat flour and cook it. Make chapatti bread from fermented dough and cook thin chapattis. The method for pine kernel relish: grind the pine kernels . . . (*damaged*) then put honey (*shahd*) or sugar . . . (*damaged*) in it. Other relishes are made (*f.146b*) from pumpkin seeds, there is also almond relish, parched rice relish, roasted chickpea relish and walnut relish, *chārūlī* relish, poppy seed relish, roasted sesame seed relish and pistachio relish. Prepare all these varieties of relish (*chashnī*). Just as the method for pine kernel relish has been explained, so prepare the rest of the relishes in the same way. These are called Ghiyath Shahi's relishes.

Another recipe, for meat soup, put a tamarind into meat soup and cook the soup. Another recipe for soup: put . . . (*damaged*) into meat soup. Another recipe for meat soup: put myrobalan into meat soup and cook it. (*f.147a, with a miniature*) The following is a method for cooking *kaṛhī* with two kinds or with three kinds of potherbs. Mix the ingredients together and it becomes a variety of well-cooked *kaṛhī*, the ingredients are as follows: *dūgh*, salt, rice flour, unripe grain parched in the ear, barley, chickpea flour, cloves, cardamoms, . . . (*damaged*), hogplums, tamarind, congee, lime juice, . . . (*damaged*) juice, corinda, citron (*karna*) juice, musk, (*f.147b*) cinnamon, camphor, *mūng*, whole chickpeas, rice, ground *mūng baṛī*, mixed with spice and made into dough, swollen grain, dried ginger, large pieces of *baṛī*, pepper, vegetable oil burnt with asafoetida, asafoetida fried in vegetable oil, palm sugar, pumpkin, woodapple, four portions of Bengal quince relish, salted lime, thin slices of pasta (*tatmāj*), sliced *baghrā*, *pūrī* bread, dry bread, yellow *zarat* bread, *zarat* bread, potherbs, *gulshakar*, whey, cardamoms, *dūgh*, cumin, fenugreek, black nigella seeds, *āzmūda*. Other potherbs are used in conjunction with ingredients for meat soup: palm sugar, cardamoms, musk, asafoetida essence, walnuts, coconut, water lilies, *karhaṛī* nut, . . . (*damaged*), fried sesame seed, fried chickpeas (*f.148a*), salt, mint, red roses, pepper, fenugreek flavouring, *marvā* flowers, potherbs, myrobalan, honey (*shahd*), dates, raisins, sacred basil, onions, walnuts, cumin flavouring, jujube, dried ginger, sour-orange juice, small unripe mangoes, saffron, aloes oil flavouring, tamarinds, coriander, citron acidity, pistachios, cinnamon, tamarind (*tantaṛīkha*), lime juice, cumin, barberries (*zarashk*).

Other seasonings and flavourings for recipes are as follows: potherbs, tubers, honey (*shahd*), date sugar, starfruit, saffron, figs (*gūlar*), *tīndū* fruit, tamarind, wild figs (*anjīr*), jackfruit, raisins, white China rose, red roses, pumpkin, corinda, palm sugar, garlic, . . . (*damaged*), roasted new shoots of corinda, roasted new shoots of . . . (*damaged*), myrobalan, camphor, peaches,[248] Indian fig, (*f.148b*) figs (*pīpal*), monkey jackfruit, sorrel, *bīr* fruit,[249] hogplums, limes, fresh ginger, sour-orange.

Another method for the preparation of varieties of pickle: if the ingredients are all mixed together, the pickle is delicious. They are as follows: cardamoms, green chickpeas, seed of bastard saffron (*gazar*), linum, garlic, rape (*sarsūn*) shoots, radish shoots, onions, mango flowers, horse radish flowers, fresh lime shoots, fresh sour-orange shoots, *jāman* fruit, green fennel, fruit of the jackfruit tree, fresh shoots of *pīpal*, mango kernels, fresh ginger, potherbs, sour-oranges, sweet vegetable oil, roast sesame seeds, vinegar, mustard seed oil, coriander seed, cloves, tender pods of the Agati tree,[250] fresh shoots

248 *Shaftālū*.
249 Indian jujube, or Chinese date, *Zizyphus jujuba*.
250 *Agathīya*.

of . . . (*damaged*), mustard seeds, coriander, asafoetida, cooked mangoes, asafoetida milk, . . . (*damaged*) of roast lovage, (*f.149a*) roast coriander, rape seed oil, cumin, salt, roasted *sūnf*, limes, whey, baked rape seeds, baked fenugreek, shoots of Bengal quince, cucumber, fenugreek, gourd (*kandūrī*), horse radish roots, tender pods of the *kachnār* tree,[251] tender pods of the *āsītrā* tree.[252]

Also the mixing of cold foods, the cold ingredients are as follows: figs, raisins, *jāman* fruit, *tīndū* fruit, monkey jackfruit, mimusops, jackfruit, wild fig, cardamoms, palm sugar, saffron, rosewater, camphor, figs (*pīpal*), potherbs, fresh ginger root juice, garlic, pomegranate seeds, whey, tamarind (*tantaṛīkha*), congee, betel leaves, lime juice, *fālsa* berries, . . . (*damaged*) juice, pumpkin, large peas, pomegranate, peaches, . . . (*damaged*), cinnamon, sweet-oranges, cassia, jujube, musk, (*f.149b*) *bhāt*, white ambergris, barberries.

The following should also be used when cooking *khīr*: walnut flour, coconut flour, pulse flour, well-flavoured ghee, mango syrup, long peppers, grain flours, chopped raisins, ground almonds, ground pistachio nuts, ground pine kernels, crumbs of thin bread, thin white bread, thin baked bread, rosewater, Sulayman dates,[253] fresh ginger, poppy seeds, parched grain, dried bread, *zarat*, roasted *shāl* (wild rice), *pūrī* bread, dried ginger, pepper, cardamoms, water, single dates, palm sugar, cloves, milk. (*f.150a*) Serve it and eat it. It greatly strengthens libido.

Another recipe: cut pieces of meat very small and rub the meat with potherbs of all kinds. Make stones very hot and put the above-mentioned meat on them so it becomes well-roasted and then eat it. Another recipe for aphrodisiac food: fry green chickpeas in cow's ghee and mix two equal parts of pine kernels and two equal parts of walnuts in palm sugar and cook them. Put them into a bowl immediately and eat them before food and also at evening prayers. Another recipe: get a young pigeon or a chicken or a sparrow and having cleaned it well, (*f.150b*) rub it with potherbs, skewer it on a stick and rub it with galingale, cassia, salt and flour and either bake it or else cook it in soup. Another recipe: rub all kinds of potherbs into fish roe, fry it in ghee or walnut oil and add five hens' eggs to it. Another recipe: bake fresh fish and white onions in walnut oil, add salt and then eat it with chapatti bread. The advantages of it are that it has a powerful sharpness and causes erections and, at the time of intercourse, semen is emitted. This is not brought about by medicine . . .[254]

251 *Bauhinia variegata*, or mountain ebony. Watt (1889–93): 'the buds are eaten as vegetables when prepared with animal food'.

252 *Bauhinia racemosa*?

253 Special white date.

254 Damaged and smudged, but the gist seems to be that the above food is more effective than any medicine.

(*f.151a*) *Ṭālīsfar*[255] is of great benefit. Put the required amount of *ṭālīsfar* bark in water overnight, then throw away the rind and mix the water with pure honey (*ʿasl*). Keep it for twenty days and when thirsty drink ten *dirams* of it. That amount helps copulation, prevents impotence and strengthens intercourse. For anyone whose ejaculation causes discomfort, by taking this preparation at the time of seminal effusion, he will find that ejaculation will give pure delight.

Because of the increase of semen, this medicine is a sovereign remedy and the cause of wonder. It is made up as follows: kernels of cotton seeds, . . . (*damaged*), half a *diram* of boiled rice mixed with ghee, . . . (*damaged*) and rub it on the penis. (*f.151b*) The patient sees improvement in himself no one else would notice. Also smear the penis with balsam oil, olive (*zīt*) oil and one *diram* of pure Tibetan musk.[256] Grind it, mix it with the above-mentioned oils and rub however much is required on to the head of the penis. Copulation is then possible and does not get sated. Another recipe to combat obstruction of seminal flow: a saffron yellow silk ring is beneficial, warms the penis and thus, by degrees, warms the semen. Also prepare a ring from a band of wool. It is very good and these methods are very effective and . . . (*damaged*) prepare the fur to the width of four fingers . . . (*damaged*). In winter weather (*catchword*) . . . (*missing folio(s)*)[257]

(*f.152a*) . . . also rub it in the ashes of sweet-smelling wood burned on the ground, shake the earth off the wood and clean it. Moisten the earth with rosewater, put it on a clean cloth and place it on the female private parts. The moisture that comes from her womb is dried up and becomes fragrant. Also the smell of those from the country of Abyssinia goes away and pain in the loins caused by copulation with Abyssinians and Negroes goes away. Also, in winter and in summer, do not allow her to lie down on her breasts. Give the bride . . . (*damaged*) burnt aloes, honey (*shahd*), frankincense roots . . . (*damaged*) skin of burnt myrobalan. (*f.152b*) Having ground them, mix together the following: burnt coconut skin, burnt almond skins, lime, white rock salt, burnt coconut, saffron, burnt aloes, burnt barley, burnt betel (*fūfal*), the white pieces to be found in mimusops stones, ground brick (*khasht, for an abrasive?*), burnt sandal, catechu extract, ground *aqīq* (cornelian or agate). Mix them all together, and put them in perfumed water of every available kind, and rub it (*the mixture*) on the teeth. Another recipe for colouring the teeth: pomegranate skin dye, flowers or fruit of *majītha*,

255 According to Steingass (1957), it is the bark of an Indian olive tree which when applied to the mouth, is a cure for certain diseases. *Ṭālīsfar* is the *Rhododendron anthropogon* or *lepidotum* according to Watt 1889–93, with strongly aromatic leaves of medicinal benefit.

256 *Musk-i tabatī*.

257 The catchword on f.151b is *zamastān*, but f.152a begins with *dīgar dar mīyān*. The Farsi foliation indicates two folios missing.

the juice of the skin of coconut which runs out when the skin is burnt, Abyssinian *al-ḥadīd*,[258] namely . . . (*damaged*), yellow myrobalan, myrobalan, lime cooked with sulphate of iron (*kasis*),[259] . . . (*damaged*) the teeth. Place it on the teeth, (*f.153a*)[260] rub good lac (*mahāvar*) on an iron board and stand it upright in congee water for hours. Gargle with alum (*phatkaṛī*) and lime juice, smear the teeth with *sapārī* betel and *pīṇḍ* (ball of meal). The teeth turn red and also turn black.

Again, to doubly perfume clothes, put musk into smelly armpits. Fill pockets with musk and sew them up. Rub *chūva* (scented paste) into every belt and into the armpits. Sew a bag of green silk and fill it with musk. Again, to make the breath fragrant hold a white China rose in one side of the mouth and turmeric leaves in the other side. Take Saul tree resin,[261] saffron, red roses, (*f.153b, with a miniature*) jasmine flowers, *marhaṭṭī* aloes, sandal, gum resin, sugarcane peel, sesame seed oil, potherbs, aloes, camphor. Use them for scenting the nostrils.

Another recipe (*or list*) of necessities (*associated with*) the monsoon season and for the weather of that season: stuffing (*bhrat*), skewered meat (*sīkh*). Add dried meat, fresh butter, *sūnf* bread, *biryān, talā dabī*,[262] fried cake of pulse meal, samosas, *para*,[263] *galgalla*,[264] having rubbed . . . (*damaged*) (*f.154a*) coarsely ground pulse, *pūrī* bread, wheat flour cakes, bread fried in butter, almond *yakhnī* (soup), vinegar, chickpeas, onion juice, bean *yakhnī, lās*, fenugreek, lovage, fresh ginger, lime, radishes, Mongol *yakhnī*, Yazd *yakhnī* (meat hash). Another list of foods suitable for winter: kedgeree, fenugreek, nourishing *lās*, fresh ginger, sugar, fresh breadcrumbs, thin bread cooked on a skillet, thin baked bread, *zarat* bread and ghee and honey (*shahd*), relish (*kasūndī*), hot dried bread, hot dates, kedgeree of bean pulse (*māsh*), meat and aubergines, meat and fenugreek leaves, ghee, . . . (*damaged*) pickle *yakhnī*, sorrel, *kashk* (thick pottage), *bhāt* and sheep's trotters (*pācha*).

Everything cool, is suitable for summer: flummery (*khīs*) . . . (*damaged*) (*f.154b*) having made it full of flower perfume, cold milk solids, cold milk pudding, . . . (*damaged*) camphor, buffalo milk, betel, essence of crushed *pān, bhāt*, flavoured curds (*sakhrān*), flummery (*ambalvānī*), milk *dūgh, dūgh*, palm sugar, syrup, pap (*rābaṛī*), mango fool with fresh *māst*, date sugar, sherbet, *pālūda*, flavoured curds (*rasāla*), mango fool. Other recipes for food for

258 Obscure.

259 Used as an astringent according to Watt (1889–93).

260 Lacks a Farsi foliation number.

261 The *sāl* tree, *Shorea robusta*, yields an aromatic resin, i.e. *rāl*.

262 Obscure.

263 Damaged in text, obscure.

264 Balls of swollen rice mixed with molasses.

banquets: . . . (*damaged*) of *laḍḍū*, one hundred *mān* of *phīnī* and two or three times of *gaz* (*all three sweetmeats*).

The hospitality of Ghiyath Shahi: a roast whole cow with radishes and onions placed in its mouth, *rīvaṛī* cakes, five *sīrs* of peppers, large loaves, . . . (*damaged*) of all kinds of chopped potherbs, roast whole camel, . . . (*damaged*) of whole . . . (*damaged*) (*f.155a*), serve cups of palm sugar, large vessels of palm sugar, Ghiyath Shahi's samosas, potherb shoots, a pinch (*qaraṣ*) of potherbs, a large pure loaf cooked on a palm-leaf mat (*būrīyā*), green shoots covered in gold and silver or dyed with saffron or coloured, cakes of halva and of *malīda* cake, serve green radishes, fill a watermelon with thin pieces of gold and whoever eats the melon keeps the gold leaf. Put gold leaf on flowers, use the stems of tubers and cooked greens and the green leaves of the shoots of jasmine. Bring food to the Moon of the World on a tray of seven colours and (*bring*) a tray laden with gold and every kind of . . . (*damaged*).

Another list of items that give pleasure: (*f.155b*) Ghiyath Shahi delights in perfume during battle; cold camphor; *mūtī*[265] is a source of comfort to Ghiyath Shahi; pomegranate syrup, intensely cold tamarind syrup, fresh ginger halva, *bhāsak*,[266] red sandal wood, salves of every kind, syrup (*ras*), *mūtī* sweetmeat, white sugar candy and rosewater, melon halva, nourishing *laḍḍū*, kedgeree made of Khurasani fruits of every kind, perfumed sandal wood, saffron. Give them at the time of fierce fighting when the sword strikes the enemy on the head, reward the military commander with gold and silver rings. (*Take*) mead, fresh cumin, *laḍḍu*, gold and silver vessels full of Himalayan (*himachal*) sherbet, a jug of rosewater, *gulshakar*, vessels full of *chūva*, . . . (*damaged*) of sweet-smelling twigs, and betel (*tanbūl*) and distribute it that evening . . . (*damaged*). Moisten camphor . . . (*damaged*). (*f.156a*) (*Take*) myrobalan, honey (*ʿasl*), corinda syrup, myrobalan halva, oils for wounds, medicines for wounds, medicines of every kind for healing wounds, for preventing fatigue and for staunching bleeding. Rub ground sesame seed and myrobalan into the body.

Again (*follow*) details relating to items suitable to take for the sport of hunting: take plenty of water, provisions, rosewater and camphor, sparrow-hawks and cheetahs and Khurasani dogs and spotted lynxes. Take falcons for scattering partridges and also female champions clad in armour and girt with swords. Take medicine (*mūmyāʾī*) along, also *pāzhar*[267] . . . (*damaged*) and take all kinds of medicines for staunching blood and medicines . . . (*damaged*) and take remedies of all kinds. Take round upon round (*f.156b*) of gold and silver

265 Sweetmeat of flour, curds and sugar.
266 Obscure, possibly *Calatropis gigantea*.
267 A treacle antidote for snakebite.

necklaces for the owners of the castles who own the houses of the lowest caste people (*halālvar*). Also take along elephants that should not be in must. Pay for the hunting and game. Ride a horse of proven temperament and when mounted on the horse, recite a prayer. Have the fangs and the skin of the head of a snake, with the snake's head, on the quiver. Take humble villagers and people of the lowest caste. Whichever direction the wind is blowing from, go in that direction. In order to ascertain the direction of the wind take along a fine handkerchief. Take flowers (*phūl*) and palanquins, with slave girls as palanquin bearers. Take provisions and food for cooking carried on a horse. . . . (*damaged*) rub the face with saffron and almonds. If . . . (*damaged*) also take along *sarūds* (*musical instruments*) and singers of songs. (*f.157a, with a miniature*) Put camphor in shoes and fasten them up. Take along the likeness (*shakl*) of the beautiful beloved. Drink from hunting cups. Agreeable women should come, also take along a conversationalist and a boon companion. Rub the feet with sandal and camphor, change into stockings. At the hunting place, take up a position at the back and take aim. Take along a goatskin . . . (*damaged*) to put under the feet. (*f.157b*) In order to be able to tell the time, take along the wheel of an astrolabe. Take eminently brave men.

Another piece of advice for using a hunting circle,[268] fill the bottoms of quivers with gold and silver coins, both small and large (*i.e. for rattling*). Take along one war-horse and entrust it to the hand of an intelligent man. It is sensible to take tiger (*shīr*) and male buffalo skins and it is wise to be in the vicinity of plantain plants. Be alert in places where snakes may be hiding. Take a small curtain, take a sickle for use wherever it might be required, take a parasol to provide shade, take a rug, a chair pillow, take a pusteen.[269] Snares and traps must also be taken along. Take forceps, tweezers, pincers; take sharpeners (*i.e. for arrows, spears etc.*) and . . . (*damaged*).[270] There must be a travelling bath and readily available hot water . . . (*damaged*) and take along stones (*f.158a*) and flints to light fires.[271] Take beds and bedding and oil. Take a white cockerel. Take one hunting horse. Take thumb rings (*shast*), weighing scales, fish hooks and tackle, provisions, snares, travellers' shoes, blowpipes of hollow bamboo, take ground traps for birds and resinous fruit[272] and quail traps.

When it is intended to hunt deer, take along two men of the lowest caste (*halālvar*) for skinning.[273] Take along arrows, crossbows, swords, daggers, wax

268 i.e. driving game up in a circle by use of beaters.
269 Fur or sheepskin jacket.
270 Note in the lower margin: 'it all becomes moist, damp'.
271 Note in the margin: 'so that a tiger does not approach'.
272 Used with lime to entangle birds.
273 Who can handle carrion.

cloth, protection for light rain, *tufak*,[274] some rebecks, axes, double bows, wax for fastening blades to handles, lamps, small daggers (*kitārī*), daggers, fur bedclothes, knives, *bāna*,[275] a weighing balance, maces and clubs, . . . (*damaged*) large shields that men hold behind themselves for protection when standing up.

(*f. 158b*) If, when out hunting, you are galloping a horse, carry a long spear in the hand and remember the places where snakes and wolves are. Avoid the area where there are narrow lanes and small scorpions that is known as 'the desert of the scorpion'. Do not go where there are many spiders. Take women's head-ornaments. Take female hawks (*bahrī*), falcons (*dhūtī*), falcons (*jarra*),[276] female falcon (*bāz*), falconer's drums, earmuffs, outer garments, bamboo bows, slings, skin drums, arm coverings. Do not gallop a horse over ground that is full of holes, gallop a horse in water, (*take*) a cat, do not urge the leading horse forward on a mountain, take along chairs and juice and water and wine and potherbs and myrobalan, take civet and musk and rub them on the body. . . . (*damaged*).

(*f.159a*) Take rosewater, medicines and some *pān*. Do not go near a village that might have small chieftains as it will be fortified. Take Mahmud Shahi's travelling throne (*takht-i ravān*) and Ghiyath Shahi's throne. Take a dog carrier and a palanquin, a basket of silver, hollow bamboos or needles, armlets and beds. Fold the bedding and make it into a bundle to be carried on a horse. Another advice for hunting: put shops in the hunting jungle and organise goods and the manufacture of everything. Also organise the *khāns* of the *māst* sellers and their districts and the purchasing of milk from their houses. Also organise the buying of food and the throwing of sand on marshy places. Fill empty skins with *zarat* straw, (*f.159b, with a miniature*) use them as floating mattresses. Take mattresses. Fill a gourd with water in order to make the water cold and fasten the gourd to a bedstead with tapes. Take wax candles. Have sacks filled with *zarat* straw for the purpose of floating them on holes and ditches, emitting smoke (*to drive out game*). Do not urinate near them. Do not urinate near the place where wounded wolves (*gurg-i mār*) may have fallen. Do not go out in wind and lightning.

(*f.160a*) Take oboes (*shahnā'ī*), food for the royal court, galingale (*k͟hūlanjān*), cubebs, date sugar, cassia, round pepper, pepper, water skins, large baskets, fine linen cloth, large kettledrums, straight trumpets and round trumpets, potherbs of all kinds, vessels of ghee and vegetable oil, rice, *mūng*. Put skewers everywhere so that they are readily available when required and can be brought out and food can be cooked. Put goatskins of water before him

274 Tubes for shooting clay balls by blowing.
275 A kind of *patta* (sword) with a thick-edged blade and a wooden hilt.
276 The male of the *bāz*.

and provide him with shade. Another tip for hunting: take camels along, pusteens, sewing thread, thread for clothes, sticks for striking rabbits, . . . (*damaged*) a net for catching fish (*when*) seated under an umbrella, . . . (*damaged*) for catching deer, sticks for catching quails, sticks for making quails (*f.160b*) and partridges fly up.

For the purpose of capturing animals alive, take living animals (*i.e. as decoys*) of every kind, thumb rings (*zhakīr*) and finger/thumb rings (*angashtāna*), tree nets, rings on ropes to use on trapping nets, circular nets, belts, milk-giving animals, suitable clothes, take traps for catching deer (*chītal*), have it fried in oil, catch a mountain goat in a trap and hold it by its beard. When hunting mountain goats, beware of snakebite. Do not go near the mountains, stay far away from them.

Another recipe for perfuming clothes, sesame oil, flowers of every kind, frankincense, sugar, yellow myrobalan, . . . (*damaged*), sesame, camphor, musk, sandal, saffron, cinnamon, . . . (*damaged*) (*f.161a*), *barmhī* medicine, spikenard, cloves, *tagrī*, garlic, . . . (*damaged*), a quantity of two mustards. Another recipe for making preserves from Khurasani fruits: soak them in sweetened water and when they have become well-soaked, throw the water away. Put in camphor, musk and rosewater, *gulshakar*, white sugar candy, wild figs, *tīndū* fruit, *tagrī*, apples, quinces, jujube fruit, love fruit, potherbs, raisins, rosewater, almonds. Perfume it with flowers of all kinds and boil it in fruit juice. Add saffron, musk, camphor, . . . (*damaged*), water chestnuts, Sulayman dates, sugar, almonds, . . . (*damaged*), blue water lilies, raisins, *kaṛhī*, peaches, (*f.161b*) dried cooked meat.

Another recipe, for baking fruit: put the following on hot roasting embers: yellow wheat, sesame seeds, small chickpeas, lentils, *zarat*, mango kernels, wheat parched in the ear, *zarat*, *mūng*, bruised *zarat*, *mūtha* beans, green chickpeas, barley, pistachios, pungent potherbs, sugarcane, unripe chickpeas, tamarind kernels, date sugar, almonds, kernels of *jāman* fruit, jackfruit kernels. Fry *baṛa* in oil. Fry *pūrī* bread in ghee and then roast it in hot embers. (*Use*) blue water lily seeds, dried coconut, pine kernels. Allah the All-wise and the Just.[277]

(*f.162b*) 'The Book of the *Niʿmatnāma* of Nasir Shah'[278] and the *ʿAṭṭārnāma* ('Book of Perfume') and the methods for perfumes and for *chūva* (paste) and the methods for sweet-smelling oils and the method for cooking camphor and the methods for extracting flower essences and the methods for obtaining

277 This section ends on f.161b. Folio 162a has been foliated in Farsi numerals and words but only has 'God the Merciful', etc. written in a large hand, almost as a writing exercise, on it.

278 Folio 162b has a very fine but damaged *ʿunvān*, the illuminated border enclosing the title as given, and the text follows straight on.

essences of every kind and the methods for aloes and for sour-oranges and for the chief perfumes and the methods for mixing perfumes and the methods for sherbets. These are explained in this book and, if God the Exalted wills it, we will explain the methods for cooking food and [*also*] (*f.163a*) the methods (*or recipes*) for meat and for pasta (*baghrā*) and for skewered food and for samosas and for cooking fish and for stew (*yakhnī*) and for cold foods and for flummeries and for rice and for royal (*or court*) meat and for cooking *baṛa* and for flavoured curds and sweetmeats (*pakvān*) may be written, as also the method for sweetmeats (*māshī phindhā*) and *laḍḍū* and (*also*) sweetmeats of every kind, as well as *tal-i sakhlī* (sesame sweetmeats) and *pūrī* bread and *kapūr-i nalīhā* (?camphor stems).[279]

Also methods for *bakkhā* (*perfume distillation*) and for *pān* and *sapārī* and the method for . . . (*damaged*) and the methods for chutneys and for rustic *kabābs* and the methods for . . . (*damaged*) and the methods for perfumes of every kind. (*f.163b*) The method for essences (*ghūl*) has been written and is as follows: one *tūlcha* of sandal, half a *tūlcha* of zerumbet, a quarter of a *tūlcha* of wheat, one *tūlcha* of the leaves (*barg*) of red roses, half a *tūlcha* of saffron, half a *tūlcha* of camphor, half a *tūlcha* of musk. Mix all the above together, grind them and rub them on the body. Another recipe for essences: one *tūlcha* of sandal, one *tūlcha* of camphor, one *tūlcha* of musk, a quarter of a *tūlcha* of civet. Grind them with rosewater and rub them on the head and on the body. Another recipe for essences: grind one *tūlcha* of sandal, one *tūlcha* of camphor, one *tūlcha* of musk and a quarter of a *tūlcha* of civet with rosewater, and rub it on the head and the body. Another recipe for essences: (*f.164a*) one *tūlcha* of chickpea flour, half a *tūlcha* of camphor, half a *tūlcha* of musk, a quarter of a *tūlcha* of saffron. Mix all these together with rosewater and rub it on the body. Another recipe for *chūva* or *ghūl*: put two *tūlchas* of sesame oil in a cup and perfume the sesame oil. Add four *tūlchas* of musk, one *māsa* of camphor, grind it with rosewater and rub it on the body. Another recipe for essences: mix two *tūlchas* of sandal in a cup and perfume it with *marhaṭṭī* aloes and with the scent of flowers of every kind. Grind a quarter of a *tūlcha* of musk and two *māsa* of camphor . . . (*damaged*) and rub it on the body. Another recipe for essences: having ground one *tūlcha* of chickpea flour with one *tūlcha* of sesame oil (*f.164b*), put it into a cup and scent it with aloes and rub it into the body.

Another recipe for essences: roast perfumed mollusc shells on pieces of new earthenware and then grind one *diram* of musk and half a *tūlcha* of camphor with rosewater and rub it on the head and body. Another recipe for essences: grind one *tūlcha* of sandal, a quarter of a *tūlcha* of ambergris, one *tūlcha* of zerumbet, one *tūlcha* of wheat and a quarter of a *tūlcha* of saffron. Put them

279 Smudged and obscure.

together in a cup with half a *tūlcha* of camphor and half a *tūlcha* of musk and grind them all together and rub them on the body. Another recipe for essences: leaves of the red rose, . . . (*damaged*) one *tūlcha* of sandal (*f.165a*) that has been scented with jasmine flowers, one *tūlcha* of musk, one *tūlcha* of white ambergris, one *diram* of cooked camphor. Bind these with rosewater and rub it on the head and the body. Having perfumed two *tūlchas* of sandal with jasmine scent, perfume one *tūlcha* of unadulterated musk, four *tūlchas* of ambergris and one *māsa* of camphor and rub it into the head and body.

Another recipe for essences: one *tūlcha* of sandal perfumed with flowers, one *tūlcha* of musk, one *diram* of white ambergris and one *māsa* of cooked camphor. Grind these with rosewater and rub on the head and on the body. Another method for *chūva* paste has been written: three *tūlchas* of choice sesame oil, coarsely ground barley. Add one *diram* of potherbs and knead it with rosewater and add one *tūlcha* of finely ground white flour to it, to thicken the *chūva*. Another recipe for *chūva*: one *tūlcha* . . . (*damaged*), knead it in a cup and turn that cup upside down. (*f.165b, with a miniature*) Put some water into a cooking pot and distil the *chūva* on it. Mix three *tūlchas* of sesame oil, one *tūlcha* of fine white flour and one *diram* of potherbs and moisten them with rosewater. Fill a glass and the cup in which the *chūva* has been kneaded and place it below the *chūva* and make the *chūva* on top of it. Add one *diram* of musk and one *māsa* of camphor and rub it on . . . (*damaged*) and the body.

(*f.166a*) Another recipe for *chūva*: three *tūlchas* of sesame oil, one *diram* of potherbs, one *māsa* of musk, half a *māsa* of camphor, half a *māsa* of saffron and two *tūlchas* of fine white flour. Put them together, grind them, mix them and fill a glass and then distil the *chūva*. Add half a *māsa* of camphor to half a *māsa* of musk, grind them with rosewater and rub the *chūva* on the body. Another recipe for *chūva*: two *tūlchas* of sesame oil, spikenard, wild spikenard, *tagrī*, *mūtha* beans, deodar, take a number of *māsa* of each of the above. [*Take*] three *māsas* of frankincense, one *māsa* of *salā rās*, and two *tūlchas* of fine white flour. Grind all these together and fill a glass and distil the *chūva*. Add one *māsa* of camphor and one *māsa* of musk . . . (*damaged*) grind it and rub it on the body.

(*f.166b*) Another recipe for pure *chūva*: moisten three *tūlchas* of sesame oil, one *diram* of potherbs and one *tūlcha* of civet with rosewater and put them into a glass and distil them. Having taken one *māsa* of camphor and one *māsa* of musk, grind them in the *chūva* and rub it on the body. Another recipe for *chūva*: one *tūlcha* of sesame oil, one and a half *dirams* of potherbs, cassia, cinnamon, *tagrī*, *mūtha* beans, turmeric leaves, yellow myrobalan, Saul tree resin (*rāl*), *nāg-i kīsar*, spikenard, wild spikenard, perfumed mollusc shell on pure liquidambar, frankincense, sandal, zedoary: of each of the above take one *māsa*. Collect them all together, add one and a half *tūlchas* of sweet sesame and one *tūlcha* of white flour, fill a glass and distil the *chūva*. Mix . . .

(*damaged*) and one *diram* of musk (*f.167a*) with it, grind it and rub it on the body. Another recipe for *chūva:* put one *tūlcha* of fine white flour into a container over hot embers, add *marhaṭṭī* aloes and perfume it. When it has become well-scented, take it and put into it one *diram* of civet, one *diram* of camphor and one *diram* of musk. Sprinkle some rosewater on it and grind it finely, then scent it with jasmine flowers. It becomes wonderful and good. Rub it on the head and the body.

Now for the methods for every kind of aloes (*ʿūd*)[280] that have been written down and are as follows: take half a *sīr* of finely pounded sesame seed, add one *sīr* of ground . . . (*damaged*) to it and put it into a silver bowl or a copper bowl. (*f.167b*) Take it out and pour rosewater on it. The amount of sesame seed oil that is in it becomes absorbed and the rosewater rises to the top. Put it on hot embers in a pot and boil it until the rosewater becomes completely dried up. Then take it off and add four *tūlchas* of musk, one and a half *tūlchas* of white ambergris and a quarter of a *tūlcha* of finely ground camphor and put it into sesame seed oil and mix it well. Make it into balls and dry it in the shade. Whenever it is required take a ball, place it on hot embers and use it for scent.

Another recipe . . . (*damaged*): a quarter of a *sīr* of sesame pounded small, . . . (*damaged*), potherbs, half a *tūlcha* of civet, (*f.168a*) one *tūlcha* of musk, one *diram* of camphor. Mix all these together, dry them in the shade and when it is required for rubbing on the body or for perfuming clothes, then use it. Another recipe, for the manufacture of *marhaṭṭī* aloes: spikenard, wild spikenard, *tagrī, mūtha* beans, cassia, small white cardamoms, ghee, *barmā*, perfumed mollusc shell, Saul tree resin, deodar, yellow myrobalan, red dye *kattha* which colours cloth, sandal – use one *sīr* of all the foregoing. Take two *sīrs* of sesame oil, one *sīr* of frankincense, one *sīr* of *salā rās* and put them all together. Then add a quarter of a *sīr* of honey (*shahd*) to them and dry them in the sun. . . . (*damaged*) put it on clothes so that they absorb the scent, then put . . . (*damaged*) into the clothes. They become very good and absorb (*f.168b, with a damaged miniature*) the scent very well.

Another recipe for aloes: mix together three *sīrs* of sesame oil, a quarter of a *sīr* of frankincense, one *tūlcha* of saffron, one *tūlcha* of camphor, one *tūlcha* of musk and one *sīr* of potherbs, it becomes good aloes. Now the perfumed oils have been written down: mix together one *tūlcha* of oil of jasmine, one *māsa* of camphor, two *māsa* of musk, one *māsa* of civet and rub it into the body and head. Another recipe: (*f.169a*) finely grind one *tūlcha* of jasmine oil, four *tūlchas* of sweet-orange peel and one *māsa* of camphor and rub it on the

280 *ʿūd*, the highly perfumed resin from aloe wood (*Aquillaria agalloca*), an eastern Indian tree with a fragrant wood. In these recipes, the presence of *ʿūd* seems taken for granted, and the other ingredients are added to it.

body. Another recipe, for oil: finely grind one *diram* each of jasmine oil, chanpa oil, *chanbīlī* jasmine oil, citron (*karna*) oil, two *dirams* of musk, two *māsas* of camphor and rub it into the body. Another recipe for oil: put together one *tūlcha* of the scented flowers of citron (*karna*), one *tūlcha* of pure musk, half a *māsa* of camphor, one *māsa* of white ambergris, grind them and rub them on the body. Another recipe for oil . . . (*damaged*): put together two *tūlchas* of jasmine oil, half a *tūlcha* of red rose flowers, one *diram* of . . . (*damaged*), half a *māsa* of cooked camphor, rub them on the head and the body. (*f.169b*) Another recipe for oil: take four *tūlchas* of oil scented with jasmine. Put very finely cut peel of sour-oranges into oil and when the oil has thoroughly absorbed the flavour of orange, then remove the peel from it. Add one *tūlcha* of musk and half a *māsa* of camphor, grind it finely and rub it on the head and the body. Another recipe for oil: grind one *māsa* of each of the following: spikenard, *tagrī*, cinnamon, *mūthi* beans, zerumbet, *barma*, cloves, dried sweet-orange peel, dried sour-orange peel, *salā rās*, kedgeree, wheat, cardamoms, . . . (*damaged*), one *diram* of musk and one *māsa* of camphor, (*f.170a*) rub it on the body.

Another recipe for oil . . . (*missing words*)[281] scent it with sesame oil and when the scent is well-absorbed . . . one *tūlcha* of musk, a quarter of a *tūlcha* of camphor, one *māsa* of civet . . . grind them finely and perfume them with the scent of flowers . . . rub it into . . . Now the method for cooking camphor . . . finely grind twelve *tūlchas* of camphor . . . put in one *tūlcha* of finely ground musk . . . grind it and squeeze it, half a *tūlcha* of saffron . . . *salā rās* . . . mix it together with the camphor . . . *tagrī*, cumin, sandal, . . . (*f.170b*) put it in and put on it half a *tūlcha* of sesame oil . . . put it in and mix it and put in it the above-mentioned camphor . . . mix it together evenly and on . . . place, then a white rose and gum together . . . and having ground it finely, moisten it with that white rose and gum . . . seal it and put another cloth on it . . . seal it with gum on it. When one day has elapsed . . .[282]

(*f.171a*) . . . place the camphor on it and when the distillery becomes very hot, moisten the cloth in water, and hour by hour, rub the distillery with it. Cook twelve *tūlchas* of camphor in twelve perfumes. Do not make the fire from more than two pieces of wood, catechu wood must be used and must be the thickness of the thumb. Then take off the distillery and unseal it and take a small pot. Then put water into a tight-lidded cooking pot, wrap its lid in a cloth and place it on hot embers. When the water is hot, put the small pot in it . . . (*damaged*). When it has become hot, take it off and take wood of thick bamboo and thin . . . (*damaged*) and use the wood to remove the pot of camphor (*f.171b, with a miniature*) out of the china pot.

281 In folios 170a and 170b one-third of each line is missing.
282 Missing words, also the last two lines of 170b are too smudged to make sense of.

Another recipe for the method of cooking camphor: put broken pieces of sandal into a distillery of rosewater, add water and put in the number of *tūlchas* of camphor that are required. Having ground that amount, put it in *yakhnī*, seal the distillery with dough . . . (*damaged*) distil rosewater, take a glass . . . (*damaged*) (*f.172a*) when it is hot, throw away the water and again put in cold water so that the camphor becomes cooked. Then take it off and stir it with a bamboo stick. This camphor will be very cold.

Now the methods for distilling flower and rosewater (*gulāb*) perfumes have been written down: finely pound one *sīr* of sesame, sift it through a cloth and soak it in two *sīrs* of water overnight. The next day put the *gulāb* into a distillery and distil it. Put the thoroughly distilled *gulāb* into a glass and when it is all distilled seal the top of the glass well so that . . . (*damaged*). When the time comes for it to be used rub it on the body . . . (*damaged*) and perfume *pān* and *sapārī* with it until they become well-scented. (*f.172b*) Remove the sesame oil that has remained in the distillery and dry it and then use it to prepare whatever is required with it and prepare perfumes.

Another spirit (*ʿaraq*) of saffron: a quarter of a *sīr* of fresh saffron, three *sīrs* of water. Soak the saffron in the water and leave it for one night. The next day put it into the distillery of *gulāb*, distil it and rub it on to the head and the body and put it into food and water and scent *pān* and *sapārī* with it and put it into whatever is required. Take the saffron that has remained in the distillery and dry it and put it wherever it is required. Another (*f.173a*) recipe for spirit of sandal: take one *sīr* of the sweetest-smelling sandal, grind it finely and sift it through a cloth. Put three *sīrs* of water on it and leave it for a whole night and the next day put it into the distillery and distil it. It becomes sandal spirit (*ʿaraq*). Perfume it and rub it on the body and sprinkle it on clothes and put it in food and in water and put it wherever it is required. Another spirit is of citron (*karna*) flowers: dry the citron flowers thoroughly, take one *sīr* of them and pound them gently. Put them into three *sīrs* of water and leave them overnight. The next day put them into the *gulāb* distillery and distil them. This is called *ʿaraq* of . . . (*damaged*) and, of the *ʿaraqs*, this is the best. (*f.173b*) Put it wherever it is required and rub it in whenever it is required.

Another flower essence is made from jasmine (*mūgara*) flowers: pluck the cut flowers of the jasmine from the twigs, remove the moisture from the immature flowers and dry them. Then take one *sīr* of those flowers and add two *sīrs* of water. Cover them overnight and fix them so the perfume does not run out. Cover them thus and, on the second day, put them into a *gulāb* distillery and distil them. The result is a good flower essence and whatever is dried in a cloth (*i.e. the residue*), the stronger the perfume becomes, and by the same method distil flower essence from whatever flower is required. Another method for making cardamom *ʿaraq*: pound a quarter of a *sīr* of cardamoms hard and add . . . (*damaged*) of water (*f.174a*) and leave it overnight. Put it into the *gulāb* distillery the next day and distil it. Rub it wherever it is required and put it wherever it is required. By the same method make *ʿaraq* of cloves and *ʿaraq* of cassia and *ʿaraq* of *marva* flowers and *ʿaraq* of artemisia (*dūna*) and distil every kind that is required by the same method. If a method has been spoken of then it has been written down.

Dry *chanpa* flowers in the sun. Take ten *sīrs* of those dried flowers, add ten *mān* of water. Boil them until they are cooked and only five *sīrs* of water remains. Take it off, strain off and keep the water and throw the flowers away. Put the water into a glass vessel and boil it so that it thickens, (*f.174b, with a miniature*) then take it off and put it into any perfume that is required. Another is of frankincense. Put a clay pot on to embers and heat it thoroughly. Remove it with tongs and put broken frankincense into it and put a silver bowl full of water on it. When it is known that the essence has been distilled, then take the bowl and remove . . . (*damaged*) take it (*f.175a*) and put it in a cup and, by the same method, make whatever quantity is required and distil it.

Another method for cooking sour-oranges: take a really fresh orange and remove the top of the skin that is nearest the stalk. Cut a small ring from it, make a hole in that side of the orange and remove the pips, pith and flesh. Stuff it with the following ingredients: take two *tūlchas* of well-pounded cardamoms, then grind half a *māsa* each of spikenard, wild spikenard, *tagrī*, *barmā*, dried peel of sweet-orange, zerumbet, cloves and *mūtha* beans and one *māsa* of saffron. Sift them in a sifting cloth and add one *tūlcha* of ground musk, one *diram* of white ambergris, and two *tūlchas* of camphor. (*f.175b*) Grind them all thoroughly with one *tūlcha* of finely ground sesame seed. Collect all these ingredients in the sifting cloth and moisten it with rosewater. Perfume sandal with jasmine and put one *māsa* into the above ingredients. Stuff the orange with all of it, place the ring of orange, that had been cut off, on top and seal the top of the orange with dough. Rub the top of the dough with flowers. Then put the orange on a charcoal or cow dung fire and cook it: do not overcook the orange but cook it equally all over. Remove it from the fire and throw away the flowers and the dough. Wrap it in a clean cloth and eat it when required. If it is desired (*f.176a*) to keep it for many days, then remove the stuffing from the orange and dry it. Whenever it is required for eating, moisten it with rosewater and eat it. If an orange is not available, sew orange leaves together to form a basket, put the above-mentioned stuffing into it and cook it. A little is very good.

Another recipe, for strong perfume: one *tūlcha* of musk, one *tūlcha* of camphor and one *tūlcha* of sesame seeds. Pound the musk and camphor and grind the sesame seeds finely and sift them in a cloth. Add a quarter of a *tūlcha* of ground white ambergris . . . (*damaged*). Put together half a *tūlcha* of jasmine and put it with rosewater (*f.176b*) in dough and eat it. Another strong perfume: break one *tūlcha* of cardamoms into small pieces. Take a quarter of a *tūlcha* of camphor and a quarter of a *tūlcha* of musk and also grind these coarsely. Mix them with rosewater and eat them. Another strong perfume: grind two *tūlchas* of dried red roses, one *tūlcha* of musk and half a *tūlcha* of camphor. Mix them with rosewater and eat them. Another strong perfume: half a *māsa* of *chanpa* essence, one *diram* of saffron, one *tūlcha* of finely ground cardamoms, half a *tūlcha* of musk, one *tūlcha* of finely ground camphor. Mix them together and eat them with rosewater. Another strong perfume: half a *tūlcha* of sandal perfumed with jasmine, one *māsa* of cooked camphor, one *māsa* of white ambergris. (*f.177a*) Grind them, make the perfume and, having mixed them with rosewater, eat them.[283] That section has been completed.

Now the methods for sherbets have been written down. Sherbet: grind one *tūlcha* of saffron with water, then take five *sīrs* of the juice of potherbs and put the saffron in that juice. Slowly make it soft over the fire, stir it with a spoon and boil it. When it has thickened, add rosewater. Also grind one *māsa* of white ambergris, two *rattīs* of camphor and two *rattīs* of musk. Put it into a receptacle and drink it when it is required. Another sherbet of lime: take four *sīrs* of potherb juice and put it into . . . (*damaged*) then take one *sīr* of lime juice (*f.177b, with a damaged miniature*) and put it into the potherb juice and cook it slowly over the fire until soft. When it has thickened add the following ingredients: half a *tūlcha* of saffron, quarter of a *māsa* each of nutmeg, cinnamon, spikenard, cloves and *tagrī*. Pound them and sift them and put them into the juice. Finely grind two *rattīs* each of musk and camphor and one *māsa* of white ambergris, add them to the above. Keep the sherbet in a stone (*f.178a*) receptacle and drink it whenever it is required. Another method for sandal sherbet: grind four *sīrs* of good potherbs, two *sīrs* of strongly scented sandal juice with water. Put it into a clean sifting cloth, squeeze out the liquid and put this liquid into the above-mentioned juice and cook it slowly over the fire. When it has thickened, take it off and keep it in a receptacle and when the need arises, drink it. Also, by the same recipe, make sesame sherbet.

Other recipes for sherbets have been written down. Sherbet: take five *sīrs* of pure clean potherbs, grind them finely and sift them in a cloth. Put in the same amount of well-sweetened juice as of lime juice (*f.178b*) so that it becomes well-flavoured and add pepper that is well-flavoured. Mix them all together and strain them through a straining cloth. Do not squeeze the cloth, strain once and then make a second straining with that cloth. It should be well-strained. Perfume the receptacles with *marhaṭṭī* aloes and when the containers have absorbed the perfume well, then put the sherbet into them. Seal the mouths of the containers carefully and when the sherbet has absorbed the

283 Literally, *bekh̲ūrand*.

flavour of the aloes, throw away the husks of the jasmine flowers and put them into the sherbet. Also put in fresh buds of jasmine if available and when the sherbet is well-flavoured and cool (*f.179a*) add camphor, musk and rose-water and drink it. Also grape sherbet: clean the grapes, remove the pulp and knead it by hand, add potherbs to it and strain it. Put the sherbet into ewers having first perfumed them with the scent of *marhaṭṭī* aloes. When the sherbet has absorbed the perfume of the aloes, then add jasmine buds and also put in some rosewater, camphor and musk. Make tamarind sherbet by the same method and make whatever sherbet is required by the same method.

Now the methods for cooking meat have been written down: (*f.179b*) take meat from a fat mountain sheep and cook *kabābs* from it. Add turmeric, asafoetida, green coriander, onions and salt and boil it. When the meat has become thoroughly cooked, flavour some ghee with asafoetida and put that meat into it. When it has become well-stewed, add roasted ground cardamoms, cloves, cumin and fenugreek and put in coriander and cook it for an hour. Take it off after adding one *rattī* of camphor and two *rattīs* of musk. Put extracted lime juice in one china pot and make vinegar in another pot. Offer whichever is preferred, put it on to the dressed meat and eat it.

Another recipe (*f.180a*) for meat: put a game bird (*ṭaghrān*) into a cooking pot and pour water on it. Add salt, asafoetida, turmeric, green coriander and onions. Cook it until it is tender so that it becomes thoroughly cooked, then add cardamoms, cloves, fenugreek, cumin, pepper and lime juice. Then put the *ṭaghrān* on a large dish, put sweet-smelling ghee on it and add one *rattī* of camphor and one *rattī* of musk. Then put lime juice and vinegar, to taste, on it and eat it. Another recipe for meat: take the tender flesh of mountain sheep, cut off the tender roasting flesh and fat, and boil it well and take it off. Then thoroughly flavour ghee with asafoetida and put it on the meat (*f.180b, with a damaged miniature*) and add cumin, cardamoms, cloves, fenugreek, lime juice and some lovage. Add onions and eat it.

Another recipe called 'pungent' for meat: take mountain sheep meat that is plump and fat, cut it into very small pieces, cutting a little of it into tiny crumbs. Mix it together, wash it well and put it into a cooking pot. Add salt, green coriander, (*f.181a*) onions, fresh ginger and asafoetida and boil it well and put greens into the middle of it. When it has become thoroughly cooked, put in lime juice and pepper and take it off. It is not necessary to add asafoetida. Heat two earthenware cooking pots, the kind that become red hot over charcoal. Put one new earthenware pot cold into a cooking pot and put a hot earthenware pot on to it. Put a mixture of cumin, fenugreek, cardamoms, cloves, asafoetida and sesame oil into the hot cooking pot and put the second hot earthenware pot on top of it. Seal the lid, flavour it and eat the meat.

Another recipe for meat: (*f.181b*) take good meat and mince it after washing it. Add turmeric, cumin, fenugreek, coriander, cardamoms, onions and cloves and mix them all together. Flavour ghee with asafoetida, put the mince into it and add water. When it is thoroughly cooked, put in lime juice and pepper, take it off and add one *rattī* each of camphor and musk and serve it. Another recipe for tender meat: cut the meat finely with a knife and boil it. Flavour ghee with asafoetida and when ghee is well-flavoured, put the meat into it without turmeric. Add *māst*, (*f.182a*) cardamoms and cloves, also one *rattī* each of camphor and musk. Add salt, take it off and eat it.

Another recipe for partridges and quails: prepare tender partridges and quails. Rub in turmeric, asafoetida and salt. Put a cooking vessel (*dathāra*) into a cooking pot, add water and put it on the fire. When the water is hot, put the quails and partridges in the *dathāra*. Seal the lid of the cooking pot well and cook thoroughly. Then put the partridges and quails on skewers and rub them with potherbs of all kinds. Roast the skewered meat and put some camphor and musk into ghee. Rub the ghee onto the skewered meat and roast it. When the meat is required for eating (*f.182b*) add lime juice or vinegar and eat it. Also put some boiled meat into a *dathāra* and add potherbs of all kinds. Put some sweet-smelling ghee into a skillet and when it is hot, put the meat in, gently stir the ghee with a spoon and baste the meat with it. Cook it well, put it on a dish and add some camphor, musk and rosewater. When it is required for eating, roll it in vinegar or lime juice.

Now the methods have been written for cooking partridges, quails or *ṭaghrān* or the flesh of fowls or the flesh of deer or of hares or of the preparation of the flesh of any of these meats (*f.183a*) or for hares' tongues or heifers' tongues or mountain sheep tongues. Put them into a *dathāra* and boil them. When they are well-boiled, take them off. Add turmeric, salt, asafoetida and coriander and boil them. When thoroughly cooked take them off. Mix together lime juice, turmeric, cumin, asafoetida . . . (*damaged*) and rub potherbs into the meat. If it has become overcooked, then tie it up with cotton and roast it over embers. Then put one *rattī* of camphor in sweet-smelling ghee and rub it on the skewered meat. When it has become well-grilled, take it off. When it is time (*f.183b, with a miniature*) to eat, dip it in lime juice or vinegar and eat it.

The method for *pūrī* bread has been written down: mince the flesh of mountain sheep finely, or the flesh of deer, and rub in turmeric and salt. Flavour ghee with asafoetida essence and put the mince into it. Add enough hot water to it to cook it until no water remains and only ghee is left. Then mix together one *rattī* of each of the following: cumin, fenugreek, cardamoms, cloves, camphor and musk. (*f.184a*) Put pepper and lime juice into the cooking pot and take it off. Then arrange petals of the red rose or the white China rose or the leaves of mint on *pūrī* bread and put the mince on top. Secure the stuffing, tie it with cotton and wrap it in a clean, thin, small cloth. When it is required for eating, dip the meat, wrapped in the bread, in vinegar or in lime juice and eat it. Take mince from the same meats, stuff screw pine (*kīyūra*) leaves and tie them with cotton. Also take some of the same mince, sew a basket of sour-orange leaves and stuff it with mince and wrap it in cotton. Put it in a cooking pot and when it is required for eating, (*f.184b*) eat it with vinegar or with lime juice.

Again, the methods for *baghrā* (pasta): take one *sīr* of vinegar, a quarter of a *sīr* of lime juice, one *tūlcha* of salt, one *sīr* of potherbs, a quarter of a *sīr* of peeled and ground almonds. Cook the cut *baghrā*. Take one *sīr* of water and two *tūlchas* of garlic and mix them together. Put them into the cooked *baghrā* and put well-stewed fat meat onto them. The *baghrā* becomes very good. Another recipe for rice *baghrā*: cook pure rice and also well-cook the mince separately in another cooking pot, also cook the cut *baghrā* separately. Then mix them all together and add one *tūlcha* of ground garlic and put in half a *sīr* of vinegar, (*f.185a*) it makes good *baghrā*. Another recipe for *baghrā*: cut it and cook it and add one *sīr* of water, half a *sīr* of vinegar, a quarter of a *sīr* of lime juice and one *tūlcha* of salt to it. Put in the amount of flavouring that flavours it pleasantly and put the cooked *baghrā* into it. Add one *tūlcha* of garlic and mix it well in and put well-cooked *lās* or broth on it. The *baghrā* becomes good.

A method for samosas: mince tender mountain sheep meat or deer meat finely. Mix together turmeric, cumin, fenugreek, coriander, cardamoms and cloves and flavour them with ghee that has been given the flavour of asafoetida. When it has become well-flavoured put the minced meat into it and simmer it so that it becomes well-cooked. (*f.185b*) Put in lime juice and pepper and then add a quarter of a *sīr* of fresh ginger or one *sir* of chopped onion. Take it off and put in one *rattī* of camphor and one *rattī* of musk. Prepare a few very large samosas and prepare a small number of tiny one-portion samosas. Stuff them, fry them in sweet-smelling ghee and before serving them dip them in vinegar or in lime juice and eat them.

Another method of preparing lamb's meat: chop well some fat meat and make finely ground mince and, again, put it on the grinding stone and grind it finely. Add turmeric, cumin, fenugreek, cardamoms, cloves, salt and pepper to it and mix it together. Put in one *rattī* each of camphor and musk (*f.186a*) and also some finely cut onions. Add some fresh ginger, onions, garlic, salt and lime juice, mix them and put in a quantity of cardamoms and cloves and whole *sūnf* seeds. Then make two portions of small amounts like small loaves from that mince. Make it wide and use it as stuffing for the hollow bread of *pūrī*. Similarly put fresh ginger and the cut-up onion into portions of meat and strengthen the sides of the two portions. Put the above-mentioned portions in a cooking pot, and boil it. Take the equivalent of two *sīrs* of ghee and flavour it with asafoetida. When it has become well-flavoured put the lamb meat into it. Then (*f.186b, with a damaged miniature*) add cardamoms, cloves, pepper, lime juice and onions. Take it off and at the time of serving put vinegar and lime juice on it and then eat it.

Another recipe: cut the mince finely, then grind it on a grinding stone. Add turmeric, a quantity of asafoetida, cumin, fenugreek, cardamoms, cloves, whole *sūnf* seeds, also add finely cut fresh ginger and onion, as well as lime juice and salt. (*f.187a*) Then using lime juice, make small balls. Put the amount of water needed to cook it well into a cooking pot and place the first cooking pot onto a pot holder and heat the water. When it has become hot, that is the time to put the balls into it. Cook them well, add pepper, lime juice and salt and take them off. Put in some sweet-smelling ghee and very large pieces of cut-up onion and take it off.

Another method for Mongol *yakhnī*: take mountain sheep and *ṭaghrān* and grind the flesh twice or grind the flesh of deer. Boil it well and add asafoetida, cardamoms, cloves, cumin, fenugreek, pepper, onions, fresh ginger and salt. Put sweet-smelling ghee on it, then take it off (*f.187b*) and, at the time of eating it, cut it thin, dip it in lime juice and eat it. Another recipe for *baṛa* (pulse dough) *yakhnī*: put in partridge, asafoetida and salt, cook it and take it out. Make the *yakhnī* using *baṛa*. Cut some onions finely and a quantity of fresh ginger and put them into it and flavour it with asafoetida. Place a quarter of the leaves under it and a quarter on top of it and put the *yakhnī* on to the leaves. Put the leaves on to fine wooden skewers, put flour dough on it and bury it in hot ashes. When the *yakhnī* is required, remove it from the leaves, put vinegar and lime juice on it and eat it.

Another method, for cold food. (*f.188a*) Cold rice (*bhāt*): mix water, lime juice and salt to obtain a good flavour. Scent the receptacle (*sabū*) ten or twelve times with *marhaṭṭī* aloes perfume. Take the lid of the *sabū* in a cloth and put the lime juice mixture into the *sabū* and put in the amount of *bhāt* that has been made. It will be absorbed by the lime juice. Take it out and rinse it seven times. Put it into the juice, add flowers of all kinds and when the perfume of the flowers has been well-absorbed, remove the flowers, add rosewater and serve it. Another recipe for cold food . . . (*damaged*) take good tamarinds and soak them in water. When they have become well-soaked, throw away the (*f.188b*) tamarinds and strain the liquid through a silk cloth, and add salt. Perfume the *sabū* with *marhaṭṭī* aloes. When the perfume has been thoroughly absorbed, put a cloth round the lid of the *sabū*. Put the tamarind juice into the *sabū* and put jasmine flowers in. When it has become well-scented, throw the flowers away. Add a small quantity of rosewater and drink it. Another recipe for cold food: wash rice well and cook *bhāt* thoroughly and knead it by hand. Sift it through a muslin cloth and rinse it. Chop finely some potherbs of the highest quality and make sherbet. Put the above-mentioned *bhāt* into the sherbet after the *bhāt* has been sifted. Mix them together, (*f.189a*) pour in some water to thin it down and leave it thus for two days. Then put jasmine flower buds into it and when the scent of the flowers has been absorbed, throw away the flowers, add a quantity of rosewater and drink it.

The method for cooking *khīs* (flummery): take fresh whey of the amount needed to cook the flummery, add a small quantity of lime juice to it and put it on the potholder (*dīgdān*). When it comes to the boil, namely when . . . (*damaged*) comes, then put in rice flour mixed with *dūgh* and stir it well with a spoon so that it does not curdle. Wash the rice well, soak it in water and then grind it on a grinding board and take its residue in a sifting cloth. Mix the residue with whey (*f.189b, with a damaged miniature*) and put it into a cooking pot and add one *tūlcha* of finely cut fresh ginger. Add one *diram* of lovage and some salt. When it has become well-cooked, take it off and flavour it with vegetable oil and asafoetida and then drink it. Another recipe for flummery: wash rice thoroughly and when it is well-soaked, grind it. Make thin gruel from tamarinds (*f.190a*) and boil it. When it has become well-boiled, mix the rice flour that has been ground, with water, and put it into a cooking pot. Stir it with a spoon so that it does not stick and it becomes cooked. Then when it is cold, throw away the scum that has risen to the top and scent it with jasmine flowers. Then drink it with sherbet and those cold liquids that have been mentioned.

Now the methods for rice have been written: wash rice well and put in enough saffron to make it a good yellow colour. Put two *sīrs* of ghee into a cooking pot and flavour it with saffron, then add the above-mentioned rice to it and fry it well. Pour water on it, enough to cook the rice well, add salt (*f.190b*) and rosewater and eat it. Another rice: wash the rice well and put in enough water so that it comes to the boil. Put three *tūlchas* of ground saffron into the boiling rice and also, when it has become well-boiled, put in enough salt to make it flavoursome. When the *bhāt* is cooked, pour off the surplus water. Put in two *sīrs* of sweet-smelling ghee and the equivalent of one *sīr* of lime juice and steam it. Take it off and beat in rosewater and eat it. Another recipe for pure rice: put it in boiling water and add (*f.191a*) tiny morsels of mountain sheep meat and also put small pieces of fat into it and add salt and asafoetida. When the meat and fat are thoroughly cooked, then add the rice. When the rice is cooked, remove the surplus water and add two *sīrs* of sweet-smelling ghee. Put in one *sīr* of lime juice and some salt, and steam it. Then take it off and eat it.

The method for roasting in the earth: make a ditch or hole in the ground. Take whatever amount of meat is available for cooking and light a fire in the ditch so that it becomes very hot. Place very small stones all round the ditch, ring upon ring, make a fire on the stones so that they become hot. Wash the carcass of a cow well. (*f.191b*) Put together turmeric, salt, cumin, fenugreek, cardamoms, cloves, coriander and a little asafoetida, pour lime juice on to them and add onions and fresh ginger. Mix potherbs with ghee and rub them on to the flesh. Then spread plantain in the above-mentioned ditch, place the meat on top of the leaves and, again, put plantain leaves on the meat to cover it. Then place hot stones on top of the plantain leaves and, again, spread plantain leaves on top of the stones and on top of them put meat and, once more, spread plantain leaves on top of that meat and put tiny stones on top of the leaves. Arrange as much as is required by this method, put plantain leaves on top of it and put a layer of heated stones (*f.192a*) and again put more plantain leaves on it. Then fasten the mouth of the ditch (*oven*) with a mixture of clay and water to a quarter of a thickness so that steam does not escape. Set fire to two or three wooden props on top of it. When it is time to eat, dispose of the fire on top of the ditch and turn the oven (*kūdāl*) upside-down. Take the meat out and eat it either with vinegar or lime juice.

A method for cooking *baṛa*: boil the pulse (*dāl māsh*), then rinse it and grind it finely. If there are five *sīrs* of pulse, then mix ten finely ground *kasīrū* tubers with it and add half a *sīr* of fresh butter and beat it so that it becomes as one (*blended*). Add some asafoetida and put in salt. Then prepare the *baṛa* and cook it in sweet-smelling ghee. (*f.192b, with a damaged miniature*) Take it out of the ghee and scatter some chopped potherbs on it, also camphor and musk, and eat it. Another recipe for *baṛa*: wash pulse (*dāl māsh*) well, grind it finely, pound it and knead it by hand. Put in asafoetida, coriander and whole peppers and mix them all together. Prepare the *baṛa* and fry it in ghee or vegetable oil. (*f.193a*) Then make flummery (*ambalvānī*) from tamarinds, put potherbs into it, sweeten it and add some camphor, musk, rosewater, cardamoms and cloves. Mix it well and put the *baṛa* into it.

Another recipe, for *baṛa* of *dāl māsh*: prepare good *baṛa* and then take some fresh *dūgh* and boil rice in it. Then put salt, asafoetida and green coriander into that which has become broken (*i.e. the soaked rice*) and boil it. When it is well-cooked, add cumin, fenugreek, cardamoms, cloves and pepper, and, having made some water very hot, put the *baṛa* into it. Flavour this *kaṛhī* with asafoetida, put the *baṛa* into it and eat it.

Now the method for making *sakhran* has been written: (*f.193b*) take good *māst*, put ground potherbs into it and strain it through a cloth. Add camphor, musk, cardamoms, cloves and rosewater and prepare it with the perfume of flowers. When the flower perfume has been absorbed, throw away the flowers. Then cut up sections of the fruit of bananas very small and put them into it. Put the pulp of a bunch of twelve bananas into the *māst*. Another recipe for watermelon *sakhran*: take a sweet watermelon and cut up its flesh very small, throw away the seeds and knead it by hand. Add potherbs and strain it through a thin cloth and flavour it with flower essence. When it has absorbed the scent of the flowers, throw them away. Then add some camphor and musk and sprinkle rosewater on it (*f.194a*) and eat it.

A method for bruised rice: take a quantity of kedgeree, wheat, saffron, sandal, bruised sesame and the same amount of finely ground chickpea flour. Strain it through a thin cloth and sprinkle some rosewater on it and flavour it with *marhaṭṭī* aloes. A method for an aromatic rice dish (*shūla*): moisten sesame, camphor, musk and saffron in oil of jasmine. Put water into a dish and stand a trivet on it. Heat the rice and pulse (*shūla*) on embers, then remove it and put it on the trivet. Mix the above ingredients and put them on the *shūla*. Anoint a china bowl with jasmine oil (*f.194b*) so the *shūla* becomes perfumed. Moisten a cloth, rub it on the receptacle, dye it red and perfume it with *marhaṭṭī* aloes. Crush some saffron, put it in jasmine oil and grind it finely. Add camphor, musk, liquidambar, civet and some rosewater and knead it. A method for *pāpaṛ*: if using one *mān* of pulse flour, then take eight *tūlchas* of asafoetida, four *sīrs* of salt, three *sīrs* of water, six *sīrs* of sesame meal, one and a half *sīrs* of grape juice . . .[284]

(*f.195b*) The method for the rice of Nasir Shahi, Eternal Ruler and Sultan: put plenty of ghee into a cooking pot and strained greens water. Flavour it with Khurasani cumin or celebrated (*mashhūr*) cumin. Put garlic juice into the cooking pot, then when it comes to the boil, add three *sīrs* of rice, almonds, walnuts, garlic, cardamoms and pepper. Also a recipe for Nasir Shah's *labūb*:[285] thoroughly wash two handfuls of long rice and grind it finely. Strain it through a thin cloth and put ghee into a skillet. Fry flour in the ghee and mix it with fresh ginger juice, lime juice and garlic juice. Mix the three juices together and make dough. Take the cooking pot off and, having cut up portions of meat and washed it clean (*f.196a*), put it into the cooking pot. Bring the pot to the boil and take it off. Strain off the liquid and then mix together fresh ginger, onions and lime juice and put them into the cooking pot. They call this *safīd* (pure or white) meat.[286]

284 The remainder of f.194b is missing and there is nothing at all on f.195a.

285 Kernels, essences.

286 Folio 196 ends here, as does the text, except for a *mīm* (letter 'm') at the bottom which probably stands for *tamām*, i.e. completed, indicating the end of the MS. Underneath is written 'The assembled *Ni'matnāma* 207 pages'.

Glossary

Note on units of weight

There were no universally accepted standard measurements in India before the nineteenth century, despite the attempts of the Mughals to impose such a scheme. The precise measurements of weight indicated in the *Niʿmatnāma* are therefore not fully recoverable. However, the general sequence between the smallest and the largest weights is clear enough, and here is given such a sequence (taken from *Hobson-Jobson* (Yule and Burnell 1985)) as standardised in 1833:

8 *rattīs* = 1 *māsa* = 15 troy grains
12 *māsas* = 1 *tola* = 180 troy grains (the weight of a one rupee coin)
80 *tolas* = 1 *sīr* (seer) = 2½ lbs troy
40 *sīrs* = 1 *mān* (maund) = 100 lbs troy

It can be readily seen that the *rattī*, in which measurement quantities of the otherwise worrying camphor are added to recipes, is in fact a minute amount, so small that its presence is simply a token symbol of the cost and wonder of the dish, rather like the presence of ambergris and musk (ingredients which also went into seventeenth-century Stuart cookery in England). The author of the *Niʿmatnāma* does not use the *tola*, preferring instead what appears to be the similar *tūlcha*, or else the Persian *diram* (direm), which is the equivalent of a drachma, i.e. the weight of a coin, as was the *tola*, standardised as the weight of one rupee.

ʿabīr	aromatic powder, *see also tagrī*
ʿadas	lentils, pulse
ʿanbar	ambergris
ʿanbar ashhab	white ambergris
ʿāqarqarhā	medicinal plant, pellitory (*Anthemis pyrethrum*)
ʿaqīq	agate or cornelian
ʿaraq	spirit
ʿasl	thin honey, *see also madhūrī, shahd*
āb	water, juice
abhal	juniper

ablūch	white sugar, candy
abtāna	aromatic paste, *see also chūva*
āchāl or *āchār*	pickle, relish, *see also āvāta, chashnī*
adākar	ginger, *see also adrak, sūnth, zanjabīl*
adrak	fresh ginger
āhaṛī	gluten, starch
ajmūd	parsley, caraway, celery seed, *see also āzmūda*
ajvā'īn	lovage
akhrūt	walnut, *see also gardagān*
akhtīya	aromatic grass
alā'īchī	cardamom
ālū	Bukhara plum (*Prunus communis*), *see also mīnha*
āmal-bīdas	variety of orange
ambadī	okra, *see also bhinḍī*
ambal	flummery, *see also anbalvānī, khīs*
amchūr	dried mangoes
āmla	myrobalan, *see also balīla, halīla*
āmlī	dried tamarind
amrūd	guava or pear
anār	pomegranate
anbalvānī	flummery, *see also ambāl, khīs*
anbāṛa	hog-plum
ānbūta	sorrel, *see also asbūta*
andarjū	seed of medicinal plant (*Nerium antidysentericum*)
ānḍī	musk of the musk deer
angākṛī	small cakes baked on live coals or cinders
angār manda	thin cake
angashtāna	thumb rings, *see also shast*
anjīr	wild figs (*Ficus carica*)
ārad	flour
āsanda	Dragon's Blood (*Dalbergia ougeinsis*)
asbūta	sorrel, *see also ānbūta*
āshshām	supper food
ashṭa varg	the eight principal drugs
asīr	fragrant grass (*Andropogon muricatum*)
āvāta	dried relish
āzmūda	parsley, caraway, celery seed, *see also ajmūd*
bābrang	medicinal seed of *Embelia ribes*
bābūna	camomile
bādām	almond
badhal	monkey jackfruit, *see also katakphal*
baghār	spices fried in hot fat
baghrā	sections of dough
bāgla	beans (*Faba sativa*)
bahrī	female hawk

bahuphalī	figs (from the opposite-leaved fig tree)
bakā'īn	Persian lilac
bakhūr	perfume
bakkhā	aromatic distillery dregs, *see also nakh*
bakla	bean (*Vicia faba*)
bakravī	a sour citron
bal	*Sida carpinifolia*, with medicinal roots
bālā	small cardomoms
balbīj	*Abutilon indicum*, seeds especially used in medicine, also roots and leaves
balīla	myrobalan, *see also āmla, halīla*
bandhāra	a drug
bānsa	bamboo manna
baṛ	fig
bara	lamb or kid
baṛā	dried pulse cake, *see also baṛī*
barāhī	stuffing, *see also bhrat*
baranj	rice
barg	leaf
baṛī	dried pulse cake, *see also baṛā*
barma, barmī, barmhī	medicinal plant (*Trichosanthes incisa*)
barnī	millet
basbāsa	mace
basnuta, basant	the plant *Linum strictum*
bathala	sherbet ingredient, *Launaea* or *Chondrilla nudicaulis*
batla	chickpea
batlūb, batkūb	food made with walnuts
baṭlūn	medicine of black salt and myrobalan
batūṛī	small chickpeas
bāz	female hawk
bhadr	fragrant grass (*Cyperus rotundus*)
bhānvar	the plant *Ipomaea ericarpa*
bhāsak	the plant *Calotropis gigantea*
bhāt	cooked rice or maize
bhinḍī	okra
bhiṛā	belleric myrobalan
bhoj	birch
bhrat	stuffing, *see also barāhī*
bhūjī	fried potherbs or vegetables
bhūlsārī	gum myrtle
bīdas	musk willow
bīl	quince
bīr, bīrchūn	jujube, *see also kunār*
bīrā	betel nut
biryān	baked food

bīsan	chickpea flour
bīsara	female hawk
būrānī	aubergine stew
būrīya	plaited palm-leaf mat
carom	ajowan (*Carum copticum*)
chāb	fruit of the Gujarati *pīpal*
chachīṇḍa	snake gourd, *Tricosanthes anguina*
chachpīrak	meat loaf (pressed meat)
chādor	female gown
chaghandar	beetroot
chaklī, chakrā	round, flat cake of maize, rice or pulse
champa	aromatic flowers of *Michaela champaka*
chanbīlī	jasmine (*J. grandiflorum*)
chānd, chāndan	white sandal
chanpa	aromatic flowers of *Michaela champaka*
chapātī	flat bread
chapāvatī	the tree *Chironjia sapida* or *Buchanania latifolia*
chāptarī	bran
charāyata	gentian
chārūlī	kernel of the chironji nut from the tree *Chironjia sapida* or *Buchanania latifolia*
chashnī	relish, flavouring
chatrak	medicinal plant
chavā	amaranthus
chhaṛ	spikenard
chhaṛīla	wild spikenard
chikanī, chīkanī	treated betel nut
chīla	ball of fried pulse
chīnach	a herb
chīrūnjī	nut of the tree *Chironjia sapida* or *Buchanania latifolia*
chītal	spotted deer
chīval	fruit of the Butter tree (*Bassia butyracea*)
chūk, chūka	orris root
chūlā'ī	potherbs, amaranthus
chūlī	betel basket
chūnā	lime or crushed shells (for betel)
chūva	aromatic paste
dabra	unripe corn? a kind of sweetmeat
ḍaḍa	sour thick milk
dākha	grapes
dāl	pulse
dālchīnī	cinnamon
dampukht	cooking in a sealed pot, steaming
dangrī, dangra	green pumpkin
darkā	clay oven

darr ra	milk pudding
dathāra	cooking pot
dhamāha	a variety of rice
dhāman	bamboo shoots
dhān	rice in the husk
dhanīyā	coriander
dhatūra	thorn apple
dhāva	red dye
dhūdhī	milky fluid found in wheat (*gandum*) grains
dhūnḍan	rice in the husk
dhūtī	male falcon
dīg	cooking pot
dīnat	betel leaves
diram	drachma, unit of weight
dūb	grass (*Panicum dactylon*)
dūdh	milk
ḍūḍī, dūdhī	milky fluid in wheat (*gandum*) grains
dūg͟h	churned sour milk, used to make drinks such as *lassī*
dūg͟hba	dried buttermilk
dūna	leaf cup, the plant *Artemisa indica*
fālsa	*phālsa*, the sour berry of *Grewia asiatica*, yielding a refreshing drink
faqāʿ	barley or raisin beverage
fīlfīl	pepper
fūfal	areca nut used in betel chews
gāgā	food given at entertainments
gāgra, gāgrī	water pot
gāl	a rose
galgalla	balls of rice and molasses
ganā	sugarcane, *see also nīshakar*
gandum	wheat
ganvārī	'rustic food', *see also rūstā*
gaṛamba	a vegetarian dish, also *kaṛamba*
gardagān	walnut, *see also ākhrūt*
garmāla	medicine
garṣak	cake
gaz	(1) sweetmeat (2) measurement, just less than a yard (33 inches)
gazar	carrot, *see also shaqāqal*
ghāghra	medicinal plant (*Xanthium indicum*)
g͟hālīya	civet, *see also shāk͟h*
g͟halūla	ball, pellet
g͟harīb	foreign
ghāṭā	pounded barley
ghī	ghee, clarified butter, oil, *see also rūg͟han, hūs*

ghīvar	sweetmeat of flour, ghee, milk, coconut and sugar
ghīvrā	cucumber
ghūl	buttermilk, *see also mhīrī*
ghūl, ghūla	essence, solution
ghūra	unripe grapes
gīhūnlī	wheat, grain
gīrī, kīrī	unripe mangoes
gūdī	unripe grain parched in the ear
guhla	medicine made with opium
gūjhā	nut pastry or stuffing
gūkhrū	*Ruella longifolia*, or *Tribulus lanciginosus*
gulāb	rosewater
gulanbar	mango
gūlar	fig (*Ficus glomerata*)
gul-i surkh	Damask rose
gulshakar	roses and sugar, honey
guṭhlā	lumps of curd in milk, or dumplings in broth
guṭṭha	preparation of coriander or cardamoms
ḥab	grain
halālvar	meat-handling caste
haldī	turmeric
halīla	yellow myrobalan, *see also āmla, balīla*
ḥalva	sweetmeat
halvān	lamb or kid
ḥanā	Indian myrtle
harīra	pap, pottage
harsīya	pottage
hāshamī	breadcrumbs
hing	asafoetida
hūbīr	green lac
hūs	ghee, *see also ghī, rūghan*
jā'ī jū'ī	jasmine (*J. auriculatam*)
jā'ī patrī	cinnamon
jā'ī phal	nutmeg
jāhī	jasmine (*J. grandiflorum*)
jalgūza	pine kernels
jāman	the java plum, *Eugenia* or *Syzygium jambolana*
jambū	rose-apple
janbhīra	citron
jāpatrī	cinnamon, mace, *see also patraj*
javārī	sorghum, millet
javāsa	the plant *Hedyscrum alhagi*
jāvatrī	mace
jazām	leprosy
jīra	cumin, *see also zīra*

jīṭhī, jīthī madd	liquorice
jītī	euphorbia
jīvak	medicinal plant, one of the eight *ashṭa varg*, q.v.
ju	barley
kabāb	skewered meat, *see also sīkh*
kabāba	cubeb (*Piper cubeber*)
kabīkaj	cockroach
kachār	cucumber, *see also kachrā*
kachlūn	white rock salt, *see also sīndhā*
kachrā	cucumber, *see also kachār*
kachrī	kedgeree, *see also khichrī*
kachūr	aromatic root of zedoary, *Curcuma zedoaria*, related to turmeric
kadū	pumpkin, gourd
kāfūr	camphor, *see also kapūr*
kahṛvalī	pungent essence
kā'īphal	wild nutmeg
kāk	dry bread
kakṛā sangī	*Pistachio* or *Rhus integerrima*
kakṛī	cucumber
kakūṛā	a vegetable
kalandā	watermelon
kalanjāra	vine greens
kalanjī	nigella seed
kalatt, kalthī	millet, horse gram
kalavī	lily tubers used medicinally
kalt	*see kalatt*
kamrak	starfruit
kamvī	medicine
kanār	banana, *see also mūz*
kandūrī	gourd (*Bryonie grandis*)
kāngar, kanganīz	millet
kānis	grass (*Emperator spontanea*)
kānji	congee, sour rice gruel
kankarū	gourd
kankīlī	the Asotra tree (*Bauhinia racemosa*)
kānṭā sīlīya	frankincense
kāntha	extract, essence
kanval	lotus
kanvār	aloes plant (*Aloe perfoliata*), *see also 'ūd*
kapūr	camphor, *see also kāfūr*
kapūr bīlī	yellow betel leaf variety
kapūr kachrī	the roots of the fragrant grass *Hedychium spicatum*
kapūr kantī	betel leaf
kapūr-i nalīhā	?camphor stems

kara	fresh butter, *see also maska*
kaṛāhī	cooking pan
kaṛanba	see *gaṛamba*
kaṛharī	medicinal nut
kaṛhī	chickpea pulse dressed with spices and sour milk
karīla	bitter gourd
karna	citron with aromatic flowers
karrat	(*so many*) times
karūnda	corinda fruit, *Carissa carandas*
kās	cup, bowl
kāsa	a royal meal
kashk	thick pottage, made of wheat flour and cream
kasīrū	tubers of *Cyperus tuberosa*
kasīs	sulphate of iron
kasīs	date wine
kasūndī	green potherb, *Cassia sophera*
kāt	catechu essence used in betel chews
katakphal	monkey jackfruit tree
kaṭhal	jackfruit tree, *see also phanas*
kaṭkī	medicinal plant
kattān	fine linen
kattha	catechu essence
kāyaphal	wild nutmeg (*Myrica sapida*)
kāzar	bastard saffron
khājā	sweetmeat
khajūr	wild dates
khal	oilcake
k͟hamar-i ʿasl	mead
k͟hamīr	dough
khand	sugar
khandvī	swollen parched grain
k͟harbaza, k͟harbūza	marsh melon, *Curcunus melo*
k͟harīza	mimusops
khārk	swallow wort
khārq	broken shells
k͟hashka	plain boiled rice
k͟hashkī	dry flour to put on dough, *see also palīthan*
khattākar	medicine for easing eye pain
k͟hāzaf	earthenware shards
khīchra	rice, barley and pulse boiled together
khichrī	kedgeree, normally of both rice and pulse, *see also kachrī*
khīl	parched rice
khīlvar	parched grain
khīr	pudding of rice or maize with milk

khīs	flummery
khīyār	cucumber, gherkin
khīyātūrī	piony
khūlanjān	galingale
khurmā	date
khurma'i sulaymānī	white dates
kīpā	haggis, *see also rūda*
kīrī, gīrī	unripe mangoes
kīs	saffron, *see also za'faron*
kīsar	saffron
kishmish	raisins, *see also mū'īz*
kītkī	screw pine, a smaller version of *kīyūra*, q.v.
kīthā	woodapple
kīyālī	medlar
kīyūra	screw pine (*Pandamus odaratissimus*), *see also kītkī*
kūchhā	tamarind
kūdāl	clay/stone oven
kūfta	meat balls
kūkrū	cucumber
kūkū	fritter
kunār	jujube
kūndī	medicinal plant
kunjud	sesame
kūrtha	grain in the ear
kūsāla	a calf
kūza	a rose
labūb	kernel, essence
lādan	ambergris resin
laḍḍū	sweetmeat
lahsan	garlic, *see also phānak, sīr*
lāk	lac
lākha	gum lac
lakūch	monkey jackfruit tree (*Artocarpus lakoocha*)
lānjī pān	betel
lanvās	stew, meaty broth, *see also lās*
lāpasī	pottage, pap, *see also rābaṛī*
lās	stew, meaty broth
lassī	milk or yoghurt drink
līhīya	thin pottage, pap
līmū	lime (*Citrus acida* or *C. medica*)
lūbān	frankincense, *see also kānṭā sīlīya*
lūbīyā	beans, *Dolichos sinensis*
lūd, lūdhrā	bark of *Symplocos racemosa*
lūh	bird similar to a partridge
lūnīyā	purslane

madār	medicinal plant
madhūrī	honey, *see also ʿasl, shahd*
maghāra	jasmine (*Jasminum zambac*)
mahāvar	lac, *see also lāk*
māhīcha	slices of paste, dough (from pulse)
māhīcha āradī	slices of flour paste?
māh mās	waxing of the moon
mahva, mahū'à	tree with aromatic flowers, *Bassia latifolia*, distilled into spirits
majdaba	white gourd melon
majītha	madder
makhā vanā	water lily seed
makka	?millet
malākara	sandal, *see also chānd, sandal*
malāyī	clotted cream
malīda	cake made of breadcrumbs, butter and sugar
mān	maund, weight approx. 38 kg
mandvā	finger millet, *Eleusinia coracana*
manqāsh	tweezers
marchūnī	peppers
marhaṭṭī	from Maharashtra, see *ʿūd*
marjān	potherb
marva or *marvā*	strongly scented plants *Ocimum pilosum, Artemisia vulgaris* or *Origanum majorana*
māsa	a small weight, 17 grains troy weight approx.
maʿṣafra	dyed with saffron
māsh	pulse (*Phaseolus radiatus*)
māshī phind	sweetmeat of pulse
maska	butter, *see also kara*
māst	sour coagulated milk, thick and creamy yogurt
maṣṭakī	gum mastic
masūr	lentils, *see also tūr*
māt	large cooking pan
maṭṭhā	curds
meze	titbits, hors d'œuvres
mhīrī	buttermilk, *see also ghūl*
mīda	fine flour
mīd-ikham	yam flour
mīnha	plum, *see also ālū*
miṭhā nīm	curry leaf
mīṭhī	fenugreek
mūchras	gum of the Silk tree
mūgarā	double jasmine (*Jasminum zambac*)
mūhamīd	Coral tree
mū'īz	raisins, *see also kishmish*

mūm	wax
mūmyā'ī	medicine
mūng	bean pulse (*Phaseolus mungo*)
mūng vānī	lentil pulse
muṛṛkī	*mūng* dish or drink
mūṣlī	a medicinal tuber, *Curculigo orchioides*, either in white or black form, used as an aphrodisiac and a tonic
mūtha, mūthi	kidney bean pulse (*Phaseolus aconitifolus*)
muthha	fragrant grass (*Cyperus rotundas*)
mūtī	sweetmeat of flour, curd and sugar
mūz	banana, plantain, *see also kanār*
mūz kūla	banana, plantain
nabakī	myrobalan
nabāt	potherbs
nāfa	musk bag (of the musk deer)
nagbīl	*Piper betel*
naghzak	mango
nāg-i kīsar	the *nāgakeśara* tree, *Mesua ferrea*, with beautiful white flowers, which when dried are used in medicinal salves; the fruit yields a resinous oil
nakh	aromatic distillery dregs, *see also bakkhā*
nākhan būyā	perfumed shell of freshwater mollusc
nakhūd	chickpea
nal	bamboo, *see also bānsa*
namak	salt, *see also kachlūn*
nān	bread
nān-i tang	thin bread
narangī	sweet-orange
narhaṛ	shin bone, shank
narjīl	coconut palm
nashank	potherb, *Marsilia dentata*
nasūt	purgative root (*Ipomeaturpe-tham*)
navāla	food for a guest, a snack
nībū	lime, *Citrus medica*
nīlūfar	blue water lily
nīshakar	sugarcane, *see also ganā*
nūtī pān	betel leaf
pāch, pāchak	costus, roots used in perfume
pācha	sheep's trotters
pādal	tree-trumpet flower (*Bignonia sauveolens*)
padmak	tree (*Costus speciosus*)
pakvān	sweetmeat, cake
palag	spinach
palīthan	dry flour to put on dough, *see also khashkī*
palīv	broth, soup

pālūda	a rich drink usually of water thickened with flour and honey
pān	betel leaves
panḍālū	yam
panhas	jackfruit
pān-i kapūrī	yellow betel leaf
pān-i tahlī	leaves of the Sisoo tree (*Dalbergia sisoo*)
panj mūl	five roots for medicinal use
pannāg	nutmeg
panvār	cassia
pāpaṛ	wafers of *dāl* dough, fried
para	*obscure*
parbatī	mountain sheep
parīnag	medicinal plant
pasta	pistachio
patās	dried acidulated milk
patkala	betel
patraj	cinnamon, mace, *see also jāpatrī*
pātravalī	leaf plate
paṭṭal	leaf plate
paṭū	a leaf recipe
pāzhar	snakebite antidote
phakī	medicinal plant
phālī	see *parīnag*
phānak	garlic clove, *see also pharnak*
phanas	jackfruit tree, *see also kaṭhal*
pharnak	garlic clove, *see also phānak*
phāṭ	split or broken pulse
phaṭkarī	alum
phīnī	sweetmeat, bundles of wheat dough strands, served with milk and sugar
phīphar	gardenia
pīchha	rice or pulse water
pīhīya	meat gruel
pinḍ	ball of meal
pīpal	sacred fig tree (*Ficus religiosa*)
pīstī	leprosy
pīṭhī	ground and soaked pulse
pīyāz	onion
pūdīna	mint
pū'ī	white basil, *Basella alba*
pūlānī	gruel, pottage
pūṛan	filling
pūrī	balloon bread
pūstīn	fur or sheepskin jacket

qalīya fricassee
qaṛamba mango fool
qaranfīl cloves
qarṣak small sweet cake
qatagh soured milk or buttermilk
rābaṛī pottage, pap, of meal cooked in buttermilk or curds
rada barda millet
raddh medicinal plant
rā'ī mustard
raiḥān sweet basil
rā'īta yogurt based vegetable or fruit dish
rāk molasses, syrup
rāl resin of the Saul tree (*Shorea robusta*)
rāla millet
ramphal custard apple (*Annona reticulata*)
ras syrup, sap, juice
rasāla flavoured curds
rāsnī mimosa
ratānjān eye medicine
rattī seed of *Abrusprecatorius*, used as a very small weight approx. 1.75 grains
raz grape, vine
rīnūka small lentil
rīvaṛī small cake of sugar topped with sesame seeds
rūda haggis or sausage, *see also kīpā*
rūghan oil, ghee
rūḥ grains, essence
rūstā 'rustic food', *see also ganvārī*
sabū jar, water pot
sadāphal pampelmousse
sadha nectar
safīd white, pure
ṣafrā bile
sāg, sāk vegetables, potherbs
sakbā a meat and wheat recipe
sakhran flavoured curds
sāk-i chūka greens of the orris root plant
salā ras liquidambar, storax
sālī, shālī rice
samagh sumach
sambūsa samosa, stuffed pastry fried in ghee
samūr fur
sanbhālī the Chaste tree (*Vitex trifolia*)
sandal sandal, *see also chānd, malākara*
sang tāra citron

sanghāṛa water chestnuts
sanjān method of double boiling food
sapārī areca nut or betel chew
sapastān Sebestan plum (*Cordia myxa*)
sardāna cold food
sarka vinegar
sarpan the Poon tree (*Calophyllum inophyllum*)
sarsūn rape seed
sarūd musical instrument, lute
sarūlā sweetmeat, paste (flour, sugar, ghee, poppy seeds and almonds made into a paste and boiled in small portions of solidified milk)
sarva Indian dill
sattāvar medicinal plant
shabat aniseed
shaftālū peach
shahd thick honey
shahnā'ī oboes
shakartarī palm sugar
shākh civet, *see also ghālīya*
shāl, shālī rice
shapat grass (*Saceharum cylindricum*)
shaqāqal wild carrot, *see also gazar*
sharīfa custard apple
shast thumb rings
shūla pulse, aromatic rice dish
shūrbā soup, *see also yakhnī*
sīb apple
sīkh skewered meat or fish
silāras liquidambar or storax
sinbāl Silk Cotton tree
sīndhā white rock salt, *see also kachlūn*
sīndhī toddy, palm wine
sīndhū wild date juice
singhāra water chestnut
sīngrī radish pod, siliqua
sīr weight, approx. 1 kg
sīr garlic, *see also lahsan, phānak*
sīsūn the Sisoo tree (*Dalbergia sisoo*)
sitāphal custard apple (*Annona squamosa*)
sīvan verbena
sīvatī highly scented white China rose
sīyāhdāna coriander seed
suhajnā horse radish tree, *Moringa pterygosperma*
suhālī thin fried bread, *paratha*.

sūn	red sugarcane, *Bignonia indica*
sundhī	date sugar
sūndna	mixed meats
sūnf	aniseed or fennel seed
sūnth	dried ginger, *see also zanjabīl*
sūr	a fish
sūran	a yam, *Arum campanulatum* or *Amorphophallus campanulatus*
sūs	liquorice
sūva	dill
sūvās	'sweet-smelling' rice
ṭabaqzar	gold leaf, *see also varq*
tabāshīr	bamboo manna
tag͟hār	provision bag, earthenware dish
ṭag͟hrān	small game birds
tagrī	fragrant powder
taj chīnī	nutmeg
tajpat, taj	cassia
takht-i ravān	travelling throne
tal-i sakhlī	sweetmeat (sesame)
ṭālīsfar	medicinal bark of Indian olive tree
tamarhindī	tamarind
tanbūl	betel chew
tantaṛīkhā	tamarind
tanūrī	baked bread
taṛ	palmyra palm
tarab	radish
taranj	sour-orange
tarbūz	watermelon
tārī	palm wine
tarīd	pap, bread and milk
tatmāj	thin pasta
taʿṭīr	flavouring
thālī	tray or plate
thāliya	spiced pulse lumps
thūlī	cooking pan, plate
thūlī	dish of wheat with spices
thūmra	parched millet
thūrī	parched grain
tīl	sesame
tīlīya	sesame oil
tīndū	resinous fruit of the Coromandel ebony (*Diospyros melanoxylon*), also used as a medicine
tītar	partridge
tīvra	pungent strong hot relishes or spices

trikanṭak	a fish with three spikes, also called *siluras*
tufak	blow pipe
tūlcha	a weight, apparently equal to a *tola*
tulsī	sacred basil
tūn	Toon tree (*Cedrela toona*), a red cedar
tūr	lentils, pulse
tūt	mulberry
‘ūd, ʿūd-i marhaṭṭī	aloes, Marhatti aloes
vālā-yi safīd	white beans
varda	a rose
varq	gold or silver leaf for decorating food
yak͟hnī	soup, broth, *see also shūrbā*
yavūk	yellow chickpea pulse, pulse gruel
yazdā'ī yak͟hnī	meat soup or hash
zaʿfarān	saffron, *see also kīs*
zanjabīl	dry ginger
zarashk	barberries *(Berberis aristata)* dried in the sun
zarat or *ẓarat*	a kind of millet
zard chūba	turmeric, *see also haldī*
zīra	cumin
zītūn	olive

Bibliography

Abu'l-Faẓl: *The Ain-i Akbari*, pts 1–3 trans. H. Blochman, pts 2–3 trans. H. S. Jarrett, *Bibliotheca Indica*, vol. 61, Calcutta, 1873–1894.

Achaya, K. T.: *Indian Food, a Historical Companion*, Delhi, 1994.

—— *A Historical Dictionary of Indian Food*, Delhi, 1998.

Aziz, Khalid: *The Encyclopaedia of Indian Cooking*, London, 1991.

Beveridge, A. S.: *The Baburnama in English*, Calcutta, 1922 (repr. London, 1969).

Briggs, John: *History of the Rise of the Mohamedan Power in India till the Year* AD *1612*. Trans. from the original Persian of Mahomed Kasim Ferishta, 4 vols, Calcutta, 1910.

Budhwar, Meera (ed.): *The Complete Indian Cookbook*, 1992.

Chaghatai, M. A.: *Painting during the Sultanate Period*, Lahore, 1963.

Day, Upendra Nath: *Medieval Malwa: A Political and Cultural History, 1401–1562*, Delhi, 1965.

Dey, K. L.: *The Indigenous Drugs of India*, Calcutta, 1867, 1896.

Dutt, Uday Chand: *Materia Medica of the Hindus*, Varanasi, 1980.

Dymock, William: *The Vegetable Materia Medica of India*, London, 1885.

—— and N. K. Gadgil: *A Glossary of the Vernacular Names of the Principal Plants and Drugs found in Bombay and on the Western Coast of India*, Bombay, 1883.

Ettinghausen, R.: 'The *Bustan* manuscript of Sultan Nasir Shah Khalji.' In: *Marg*, vol. 12(3), pp. 39–43, Bombay, 1959.

Heal, Carolyn and Michael Allsop: *Cooking with Spices*, Newton Abbot, 1983.

Losty, J. P.: *The Art of the Book in India*, London, 1982.

Mahindra, S. N.: *Spices in Indian Life (f. 6500* BC*–1950* AD*)*, Delhi, 1982.

Morarjee, Sumati: *Tambula: Tradition and Art*, Bombay, 1974.

Norman, Jill: *The Complete Book of Spices*, London, 1991.

Penzer, N. M.: 'The romance of betel-chewing.' In: *Poison-Damsels and Other Essays in Folklore and Anthropology*, London, 1952. Privately printed.

Platts, John T.: *A Dictionary of Urdu, Classical Hindi and English*, Oxford, 1965 (from the 5th impression of 1930).

Playfair, George: *The Taleef Shereef or Indian Materia Medica*. Trans. from the original, Calcutta, 1833.

Prashad, Baini (ed.): *A History of India to the 38th year of the Reign of Akbar*, vol. III, pt II, *Bibliotheca Indica*, vol. 225, Calcutta, 1939.

Roxburgh, William, *Flora Indica*, ed. William Carey, Serampore, 1820–4.

Shaida, Margaret: *The Legendary Cuisine of Persia*, Henley-on-Thames, 1992.

Shurreef, Jaffur: *Qanoon-e- Islam or the Customs of the Moosulmans of India*, trans. G. A. Herklots, London, 1832.

Skelton, R.: 'The Niʿmatnāma: a landmark in Malwa Painting.' In: *Marg*, vol. 12(3), pp. 44–50, Bombay, 1959.

Steingass, F.: *A Comprehensive Persian–English Dictionary*, 4th impression, London, 1957.

Stewart, J. L.: *Punjab Plants Comprising Botanical and Vernacular Names and Uses*, Lahore, 1869.

Titley, N. M.: 'An illustrated Persian glossary of the 16th century.' In: *British Museum Quarterly*, vol. XXIX, 1964–5, pp. 15–19.

—— *Miniatures from Persian MSS: Catalogue and Subject Index*, London, 1977.

Watt, George: *A Dictionary of the Economic Products of India*, 10 vols, Calcutta, 1889–93.

Yazdani, G.: *Mandu: The City of Joy*, reprinted edn, New Delhi, 2000.

Yule, Henry and A. C. Burnell: *Hobson-Jobson: A Glossary of Colloquial Anglo-Indian Words and Phrases, etc*, 2nd edn, ed. William Crooke, reprinted, London, 1985.

Index

ʿ*ajā'ib aṣ-ṣanā'i* xi
agate 75, 109
almonds 9, 13, 15, 21–3, 25, 28–30, 32–3, 41, 43, 46, 48, 50, 58 61, 66, 70–2, 74–6 78, 80, 90, 94, 96; *see also* flour, oil
aloes 6, 14, 19, 21 27, 38, 47–9, 52–4, 57–9 62–5, 75–6, 81, 83, 87, 88, 91, 93–4, 101, 110, *nn. 27, 280*
alum 76, 106
amaranthus 24, 40, 98, *nn. 58, 101, 123*
ambergris 5, 13, 19, 22, 24–7, 29, 30, 36, 38–40, 45–7, 49, 51–6, 59, 61–4, 66, 71–2, 74, 81–4, 86–7, 95, 103
animals *see* birds, camels, cats, cheetah, civet, cows, deer, dogs, elephants, goats, horses, kids, lambs, lynx, meat, rabbit, sheep, skins, wolves
antidote *see* snakebite
aphrodisiacs xix, 41–3, 60, 66–7, 74–5, *Pl. 36*
apples 24, 39, 61, 71–2, 80, 108
areca 43, 45, 99, 108, *n. 181*
artemisia 53, 62–3, 72, 86, 99, *nn. 194, 230*
asafoetida 12, 13, 15–19, 22–30, 33, 35–42, 46, 55–9, 67–9, 72–4, 88–94, 100
ashes, hot 56, 58, 70, 91
Asotra tree 101
astrolabe 78
aubergines 1, 2, 22, 27, 29, 30, 38–9, 55–8, 67–9, 76, 98, *nn. 205, 242*

bamboo 41, 43–4, 57–8, 78, 85, 99, 105; manna 48–50, 53, 62–3, 97, 109
bananas 30, 32–3, 40, 43, 46, 54, 56–71, 61–2, 70, 93, 101, 105; leaves 11, 12, 70, 72, 78, 92–3
banquets, food for 76
barberries 41–2, 55, 73–4, 110
bark used in: cooking 57, 61, 103; medicines 42, 43, 45, 65, 75, 109, *nn. 113, 162, 169, 255*; *see also* peel
barley 8, 25, 28, 40, 46, 61, 67–8, 73, 75, 80, 82, 99, 101; parched 68; pounded 68, 99
basil: sacred 15, 18, 22, 24, 26, 33, 36, 47, 50, 56, 62–3, 72–3, 110; sweet 15, 18, 26, 33, 40, 56, 59, 63, 72, 107; white 32, 40, 47, 55, 69, 106, *n. 78*
baskets 78, 79, 86, 90, 97–8
battles, preparation for 77
beeswax 54, 61
beetroot 40, 98
berries *see* falsa, barberries, mulberries
betel xvii, 22, 24, 25, 45, 47–52, 59–60, 71, 74–7, 79, 81, 97–9, 103, *nn. 179–80, 185, 188–9, 223*; advantages of 47–51, 60, 61; basket 59, 88; dangers of 51, 60, 61; perfumed 38, 47, 49, 51–4, 59–60, 85; preparation of xvii, xviii 47–52, 59–61, *Pls 26–9, 32*; *see also* areca, catechu, leaves, lime
bile 42–3, 49–50, 60, 65, 71, 107
birds: used in recipes 11, 34, 42, 67–8, 74, 88–9, 91; traps for 78, 80; *see also* chickens, crows, hawks, partridges, pigeons, sparrows, *ṭaghrān*
blowpipes 78, 79, 109, *n. 274*
bones 11, 16, 42–3, 49, 105, *n. 119*
bouquet garni 38
brains, cooked 21
bran 40, 61, 98
bread xv, 24, 42, 58, 66, 68, 74, 76–7, 98, 105, 109, *Pl. 71*; balloon 8, 22, 32–3, 39, 73, 76, 80–1, 89–90, 106; camphor 29; crumbs 37, 76, 100; dry 8, 29, 32–3, 39, 40, 43, 58, 66–8, 73, 76, 101; recipes

for 7, 26–9, 31–2, 39, 67, 69, 70, 72, 89, *nn. 95, 97*; stuffed xx, 3–4, 19, 26, 29, 32–3, 35, 58, 69, 70, 89, 90, *Pl. 49*; thin 7, 26, 28, 40, 58, 68, 76, 105, 108; used in food 8, 21, 27–9, 32–3, 35, 37, 58, 67, 70, 73–4, *n. 217*; *see also* dough, flour
Būstān of Sa'dī xi
butter 5–7, 15, 18, 26, 34, 37–8, 41, 52, 58–9, 76, 93, 102, 104
Butter tree 48–9, 98, *n. 182*
buttermilk xvii, 15, 27, 41, 54–5, 57, 59, 68–9, 100, 104, 107, *Pl. 18*; dried 36, 99

cakes 27, 31–2, 58, 77, 96, 98–9, 104, 107, *n. 63*
calf xvi, 103, *Pl. 1*
camel 80; roast 77
camomile 43, 47, 54, 96
camphor 3–15, 18–27, 29, 31–4, 36–8, 41, 45–56, 58–66, 70–2, 74, 76–8, 80–9, 93–4, 101; recipe for cooking 80, 84, 85, *nn. 200, 232*
candles 79
cane, sugar *see* sugar cane
caraway 26, 33, 37–8, 41–2, 68–9, 73, 96, *n. 89*
cardamom 3–10, 12–19, 22, 24–8, 30–41, 43–5, 47–67, 69–74, 83–94, 96–7, 100
carrots 34, 56, 66, 99, 108
cassia 7, 13, 16, 18, 27, 30, 32, 35–6, 38–40, 42–4, 51, 53, 55–6, 58–9, 61, 63, 65, 67, 70–2, 74, 79, 82–3, 86, 106, 109, *nn. 87, 100, 228*
caster-oil tree 43–4
cat 79
catechu 45, 48–50, 56–7 59–60, 84
catechu essence 42, 50–1 53–4, 59–63, 66, 75, 102
chador 65–6, 98
chanpa 18, 24, 48, 52, 54, 56, 59, 62–3, 72, 84, 86–7, 98
charcoal 68, 86, 88
Chaste tree 45, 107, *n. 166*
cheetah, hunting 77
chicken 11, 13, 19, 34, 45, 66, 74, 78, 89
chickpeas 8, 17, 24–5, 31–5, 37, 39–42, 46–7, 54, 59, 66–8, 70–4, 76, 80, 97, 105; *see also* flour, pulse
chironji 25, 28, 31, 40–3, 46, 57–8, 61–3, 72, 98, *nn. 59, 66*
chutney *see* relish
cinnamon 4, 7, 13, 17–18, 27, 32, 35, 38, 40, 42, 45, 48, 51, 53–5, 58–63, 67, 70–2, 74, 80, 82, 84, 87, 98, 100, 106
citron *see karna*, lime, orange
civet *see* musk
clay ovens 11; *see also* pot shards, pots
clothes 64–7, 78–80; perfume for 51, 54, 76, 80, 83; *see also* chador, linen, muslin, pusteen, shoes
cloth: bag 53; in cooking 89, 94; distilling 84–5; sealing 84, 91; sifting 85, 87, 91–4; *see also* fans, linen, muslin
cloves 3–10, 12–19, 22, 24–5, 27–8, 31–4, 37–42, 45–6, 48–9, 51, 54–8, 60–3, 69–70, 72–4, 84, 86–93, 107
cockroach (*inscription*) xii, 101, *n. 5*
coconut 4, 9, 15, 25, 31–3, 40, 43–4, 48, 50, 58, 66, 70, 73–6, 80, 105
coins 30, 78, *n. 268*
congee xvi, 6, 14, 20–2, 26, 37, 39, 41, 46 55, 57, 59, 71, 73–4, 76, 101, *Pl. 15*; double-cooked 21; tamarind 21; *see also* pap, pottage, rice
cooking: by boiling 2, 8, 20, *n. 22*; by frying 3, 4, 9, 12, 19–20, 68–9; by roasting 8, 11, 77, 92; by steaming 8, 69; *see also* pots
Coral tree 42–3, 66, 104, *n. 120*
coriander 3, 6, 8, 9, 11–14, 16, 24, 28, 38–40, 55, 59, 67–8, 71, 74, 88–90, 92–3, 99, 100; seed 21, 28, 37–8, 41, 46, 73, 108, *n. 106*
corinda 16, 23, 31, 33, 41, 55–7, 71, 73, 77 102, *nn. 31, 32*
costus 45, 48, 50, 53, 66, 105, *nn. 143, 159, 184, 197, 237*
cotton seeds 4, 75
cows: food for xv, 4; roasted 11, 77, 92; *see also* calf, milk, veal
cream 4, 28, 31, 54, 104
crows' brains 21
cubebs 39, 48, 50, 52–3, 55, 60–1, 79, 101, *n. 93*
cucumber 13, 33, 39, 43–4, 53, 55–6, 65, 74, 100, 101–3; seed 25
cumin 3, 6–9, 11, 13–16, 19, 22–4, 26, 28, 35, 37–9, 41, 45–6, 54, 57–9, 67–8, 71, 73–4, 77, 88–92, 94, 100, 110, *n. 214*
cups 31, 49, 82, 86, 88, 94; gold 65, 77; leaf 46, 99
curds 18, 20, 33, 70, 76, 81, 93, 104, 107
curry leaf 104
custard apple 107, 108

date: kernels 45, 48, 50, 58; sugar 4, 18, 22, 30–2, 37–8, 40–1, 44–6, 48–9, 51, 53–5, 58–9, 66, 68, 70, 76, 79, 80, 108
dates 32, 36, 40, 42–3, 45, 57–8, 66, 70, 73–4, 76, 102–3; sulayman 34, 74, 80, *n. 253*
decoys 79, 80
deer 78, 80, 98, *n. 119*; spotted 78, 98; *see also* musk, venison
deodar 44–5, 54, 61, 82
dill 27, 35–6, 40, 57, 108–9
diram (*weight*) 95, *passim*
dogs, hunting 77, 79
dough 9, 21, 23, 27, 29, 53, 69, 70, 90–1, 94, 96, 102, 104, 109, *nn. 47–54*; for sealing pots 19, 85–6; *see also* bread, flour, pulse
Dragon's Blood 43, 45, 96, *n. 169*
drinks *see* bread, mead, milk, sherbet, water
dye *see* madder

ebony fruit 12, 41–2, 44, 55–6, 71, 73–4, 80, 109, *nn. 104, 251*
eggs: duck 66; fish roe 74; hen 32, 42, 45, 66–7, 74; stuffed 32, 45
elephant 78
embers, hot 67–8, 80, 83–4, 86, 93; *see also* ashes
entertainment xix, 46, 66, 77, *Pl. 39*; food for xv, 32, 46, 77, *Pl. 7*; *see also* banquet, hospitality
essences 24, 28, 32, 37–8, 47–9, 51, 53, 55–6, 58–9, 62–4, 80–2, 85, 94, 100–1, 103, *nn. 191, 285*; *see also* flavourings, paste, pellets, perfumes, powder, solution
euphorbia 43, 101, *n. 125*
eyes, care of 44–5, 65–6, *n. 220*

falcons *see* hawks
falsa berries 32, 36, 41, 57, 74, 99, *n. 75*
fans *xv*, *xix*, *xx*, 3, 46–8, 65–6, *Pls 8*, *42*, *52*
fennel 10, 12, 13, 18–19, 24, 27, 35–6, 40–2, 52–3, 55, 58–9, 66–7, 70, 72, 74, 90–1, 108–9
fenugreek 3, 4, 6, 8–11, 13, 15–16, 18–19, 21–2, 24–5, 30, 32, 35, 38, 40–1, 46–7, 56–9, 67, 69, 72–4, 76, 89–93, 104
fever, remedies for 43, 47–50, 60
fig peel 54
figs 30–3, 36, 41–2, 44–6, 48, 53–5, 57, 61, 63–6, 71, 73–4, 80, 96–8, 100, 106, *n. 215*
fires: charcoal 68; thorn 27, 29; *see also* ashes, embers, stoves
Firuz Shah Tughlugh of Delhi 41, *n. 103*
fish: food to eat with xx, 52, 57, 66, 80, 81, 109; food forbidden with 39, 40; hooks 78; poisonous 39; recipes 11, 12, 16, 39, 46, 74; roe 74; skewered 12; stuffed 12
fishing xx, *Pl. 52*; lines 78
flavourings 4, 5, 38, 40–1, 53, 55, 56, 59, 62, 65, 71–3, 109; *see also* betel, essences, perfume, relish, solution
flax 62, *n. 231*
flour 5, 8, 39, 43, 46, 58, 61, 67, 71, 74, 82–3, 96, 102, 104–5; almond 17, 31, 40, 46, 58; chickpea 8, 16–17, 31–2, 39–40, 48, 51, 53–4, 58, 61–3, 73, 81, 93, 98; dough 53, 70; millet 8, 46; pine kernel 46, 58; poppy seed 37; pulse 16, 39, 55, 58, 74, 94; rice 4, 8, 16, 29, 32–3, 37, 39–41, 46, 55, 58, 73, 92; sesame seed 17, 57; walnut 40, 74; water chestnut 31, 46; water lily 33, 41, 46
flowers: used in cooking 11, 18, 27, 42, 46, 56, 58–9, 61, 65, 80, 91, 93; used in perfume 39, 44, 47–8, 52–6, 59, 61–4, 76, 80, 184; *see also champa*, gentian, jasmine, roses, water lily
flummery 19, 20, 34, 37, 46, 76, 81, 91–3, 96, 102, *n. 40*
food: accompanying betel *see* betel; accompanying milk *see* milk; aphrodisiac xix, 41–3, 46, 66, *Pl. 36*; cold 32, 66, 74, 76, 81, 91, 108; flavoured 5, 24, 38, 45, 54–6, 58, 93; forbidden 39, 40, 51, with betel 51, with fish 39, 40, with milk 39, 40; foreign 38, 70, 99; for guests 32, 77, 104–5; invalid *see* pottage; medicinal xvii, 42–5, *Pl. 24*; preparation of *Pls 5–24*, *31*, *36–8*, *40*, *50–1*; rustic xvi, 12, 16, 68, 81, 99, 107, *n. 26*, *Pl. 12*; seasonal xix, 65, 66, 76, 77, *Pl. 40*; supper 34–5, 37, 96
frankincense 42–3, 45, 47, 52, 54, 59, 61, 64, 75, 80, 82–3, 86, 101, 103, *n. 110*
fricasee 15, 106, *n. 28*
fritter 33–4, 103, *n. 82*

fruit 24, 31, 55, 71, 77, 80; *see also* apples, banana, barberries, citron, ebony, falsa, figs, grapes, guava, jackfruit, *jāman*, lime, mangoes, monkey jackfruit, mulberries, myrobalan, oranges, pampelmousse, peach, pear, plums, preserves, quince, sherbet, starfruit, woodapple
fur 65, 107

galangale 39, 48–9, 58, 67, 74, 79, 103, *n. 94*
garden, Ghiyath Shahi in *see Plates*
gardenia 33, 42, 106, *n. 109*
garlic 3, 4, 8, 15, 16, 21–3, 30–2, 35–6, 38, 43, 47, 55, 57–9, 71, 73–4, 80, 90, 94, 103, 106, 108
gentian 43, 98, *n. 129*
ghee 3–9, 11–20, 23–33, 35, 37–9, 41–2, 44, 46, 50, 54–6, 58–9, 61, 63, 66–72, 74–6, 79, 80, 83, 88–94, 99, 100
gherkins 39, 65, 102
Ghiyath Shahi i, vii, ix, *Pls 4–29, 31–53*; Betel Book of 59; Book of Perfumes of 59, 80; favourite recipes of 28–9, 32, 47–9, 51, 59, 63, 72, 77; fishing *Pl. 52*; gold shoes of x, xi, *Pls 51, 53*; on hunting expedition xix, 77–9, *Pl. 41*; supervising his cooks *Pls passim*
ginger: dried 3, 4, 6–8, 10, 19, 36, 39, 41–2, 67, 71, 73–4, 96, 109, 110; fresh 9–13, 16–17, 19, 22–6, 28–30, 33, 35, 37–40, 45–6, 55–6, 59, 67–71, 73–4, 76–7, 88, 90–2; juice 7, 8, 17–18, 20, 25, 28, 33, 36–8, 67, 69, 72, 74, 94; syrup 37
goat: mountain 80; skin rug 78, 79; *see also* kid
gold 65; in recipes 14, 21, 77; *see also* coins, cups, necklaces, rings
gold leaf 21, 43, 61, 77, 109, 110
gourds 27, 35, 40, 42–3, 53, 55, 57–9, 68–9, 74, 79, 98, 101–2, *nn. 111, 204*
grain 27, 39, 44, 54–5, 57–8, 67, 100, 103, 107, 109; parched 8, 14–15, 24, 26, 28, 30–1, 34, 37, 39, 41–2, 58–9, 61, 68–9, 73–4, 100, 102, 109, *n. 17*; pounded 9; puffed 20; *see also* barley, millet, pulse, rice, wheat
grape sugar 17, 36, 41, 55
grapes 24, 43–5, 54, 57, 66, 88, 94, 98, 100, 107
grass, aromatic 44, 45, 54, 56, 58, 64–5, 96–7, 99, 101, 105, 108, *nn. 152, 155, 192, 201–2*
guava 96
gum 24, 42, 62, 76, 84, *n. 213*; *see also* resin
gum lac 24, 62, 103
gum mastic 24, 104

haggis 26, 103, 107
halva 58, 77
hawks 77, 79, 96–9, *n. 276*
health, advice on 41–4, 46–50, 57, 60, 64–7, 71, 74–7
heatstroke 65
hibiscus 56, *n. 206*
hog plum 41, 46, 56–7, 59, 71, 73, 96
honey: thick 22–3, 26–8, 31, 34, 40–3, 45–6, 52, 54, 56–8, 62, 66, 70, 72–3, 75–6, 83, 108; thin 28, 37, 41, 58, 75, 77, 103, 109; *see also* mead
horse radish: roots 44, 57, 58, 73–4; tree 39, 45, 108
horses xix, xx, 65, 78–9, *Pls 41, 47*; skewbald xix, *Pl. 42*
hospitality 76–7; food for 32, 77, 105, *n. 77*; *see also* banquets
house, perfume for 62
hunting xix, 77–8, *nn. 268–76, Pl. 41*; methods 78–9; preparation for 77–9; supplies 77–9; *see also* decoys, dogs, snares

illnesses 60; care of 44–5, 65–7; medicines for 41, 43–51, 57, 60, 71, 75; *see also* betel, bile, chest, eyes, heatstroke, impotence, indigestion, insomnia, itchiness, leprosy, phlegm, toothache
impotence, remedies for 41, 46, 50, 60, 67, 75
indigestion, remedies for 41, 50, 57, 60, 67, 71
inscriptions, seals xii, xiii, *n. 6*
insomnia, remedies for 66
instruments, musical xix, 78, 79, *Pl. 39*
invalid food *see* food, pottage
iron, sulphate of 76
itchiness, remedies for 45

jackfruit 6, 23, 26, 32, 36, 41, 43, 48, 52, 54–5, 57–8, 62, 70, 73–4, 80, 102, 106, *n. 13*; seeds 8, 25, 34, 80
jāman 8, 23, 25, 31–3, 42, 47, 49, 55–8, 64, 67, 73–4

jasmine 22, 24, 41–2, 49, 52–4, 56–7, 62–5, 72, 76–7, 82–5, 87–8, 91–4, 98, 100–1, 104
juice used in recipes 18, 26–7, 31, 41, 48, 59, 63, 67, 73, 80, 94; *see also* fruit, ginger, lime, onion, orange, pampelmousse, pumpkin, sumach, tamarind
jujube 30, 39, 41, 46, 55, 62, 72–4, 80, 97, 103, *nn. 72, 249*
juniper 95

karna (citron) 33, 39, 40, 46–7, 51, 55–7, 59, 62, 67, 73, 84–5, 102, *n. 80*
kebabs: fish 12; meat 12, 37, 68, 70, 88
kedgeree 15, 24, 26–8, 34, 46, 54, 68, 76–7, 84, 93, 101–2, *n. 62*
kernels used in cooking 5, 8, 13, 15, 48–50, 58, 80, 94, 103, *nn. 18, 52, 285*; ground 22, 31; *see also* chironji, dates, jackfruit, *jāman*, mangoes, pine kernels, tamarind, wheat
kid, recipes for 12, 26, 46, 67, 97, 100

lac 49, 50, 52, 54, 61, 76, 100, 103–4
laddu 9, 40, 46, 77, 81
lamb, recipes for 46, 67–8, 90, 97, 100, *n. 240*; *see also* sheep
lassi 46, 103
leaf baskets 86, 90; plates and cups 4, 11, 98, 106; recipes 11, 18, 32–3, 47, 49, 51, 55–6, 70, 72, 91–3, 106; rose- and sugar *see* roses; *see also* bamboo, bananas, basil, betel, curry, garlic, lentil, lime, mangoes, melon, mint, onion, oranges, quince, screw pine, turmeric, vegetarian, yam
lentil 8, 25, 27, 32, 38–41, 43, 45, 55, 58, 61, 68–71, 80, 95, 104–5, 107, 110, *nn. 135, 172*
leprosy 49, 50, 57, 100, 106
lilac, Persian 43, 66, 97
lime (*fruit*) 25, 34, 45–7, 54, 56–7, 62, 71–6, 87, 103, 105; juice 4, 7, 8, 10–17, 20–3, 25–6, 29, 30, 33, 35–6; 38–41, 45–7, 54–6, 58, 61, 67–9, 73–4, 76, 87–94; leaves 15–18, 24, 26, 32–3, 36, 40, 46–7, 73; peel 17, 47, 62; (*alkaline*) used in betel chews 47–51, 59, 60, 98
linen, fine 65, 79, 102
liquidambar 45, 52–4, 56, 61–2, 64, 68, 72, 81, 94, 107–8
liquorice 43–5, 68, 72, 109
lotus *see* water lily
lovage 10, 29, 30, 38–40, 42, 44, 46–7, 56, 74, 76, 88, 92, 96
lynx, spotted 77

mace 8, 23–4, 31, 36–7, 39, 41–2, 50, 53, 97, 100, 106
madder 44–5, 62, 75, 83, 94, 104, *nn. 142, 158*
Mahmud Shah x, xii, 63, 79
Mandu ix, x, xi, xiii, 59, *Pls 1, 2*
mango fool 54, 76, 106
mangoes 6, 13, 25, 28, 31, 35, 42–3, 45, 56–7, 61–4, 73–4, 96, 100, 105; dried 48; leaves 47, 51; syrup 23–4, 28, 31–2, 36, 41, 74; unripe 13, 23, 36, 56, 73, 100, 103
marinades 9, 11, 13, 14, 15, 16, 70
marva 48, 50, 53, 62–3, 66, 72–3, 86, 104
māsa (*weight*) 95, *passim*
maund (*weight*) 95, *passim*
mead 77, 102, *n. 31*; *see also* honey
meal: barley 28; *see* sesame
meat xv, 67, 76, 80, 109; balls xx, 25, 36, 91, 103, *Pl. 50*; loaf 10, 98; minced xvii, 3, 4, 9, 10, 18, 25–6, 35–6, 69, 70, 88–91, *Pl. 20*; recipes xx, 8–11, 13, 14, 18–19, 24–5, 28–30, 35–8, 67, 76, 81, 88–91, 94, *Pl. 48*; roast 8, 11, 74, 92; saffron 12; skewered xvi, 11, 25–6, 29, 33, 46, 68, 74, 76, 89, *Pl. 9*; soup xvi, 7–8, 10, *Pl. 10*; stews xv, 4, 10, 13, 30, 34, 67, 76, 103, *Pl. 4*; stuffed 10, 13; stuffing 3, 12, 26, 35, 89, 90; *see also* birds, cows, deer, haggis, kid, lamb, sheep, veal, venison
medicines 41–4, 47–50, 57–8, 60, 71, 74–5, 77, 79, 96–109, *nn. 43–5, 118, 122–57, 159–72, 175, 255*; *see* antidotes, food, illnesses, invalid, remedies
melon 24, 27, 32, 38, 41–3, 55, 58, 68, 93, 101–2, 104, 109; seeds 25, 37, 40; stuffed 35, 68, 77
Miftaḥ al-fuẓāla x, xi, *Pl. 53*
milk 2, 42, 43, 59, 66, 74, 76, 79; buffalo 4, 15, 76; churned 10; coagulated 8, 10, 11, 15–17, 20, 28, 34, 39, 41, 46–7, 54–5, 57, 76, 79, 89, 93, 104, *n. 177*; cow's 3, 4, 15–17, *Pl. 3*; curds 8, 18, 20, 21, 46, 93, *n. 177*; dried 44, 106; forbidden 39, 40; recipes 4, 5, 31, 40, 99; sheep's 4, 41; soured 5, 6, 8, 10–12, 15, 20, 22–30, 33–7, 39–41, 46–7, 55,

57–8, 68–9, 73, 76, 92–3, 98–9, *nn. 11, 42*; wheat grain 43, 99; *see also* buttermilk, food, *lassi*, rice, whey
millet 7, 8, 15, 17, 23, 25–8, 30–1, 33–4, 37, 39–44, 46, 50, 53–4, 58, 70, 73–4, 79–80, 97, 100–1, 104, 107, 109–110, *nn. 16, 199, 203, 218*; *see also* bread, flour, parched, soup
mimosa 43, 107, *n. 137*
mimusops 41, 43, 49, 66, 74–5, 102
mint 16–18, 21, 24, 26, 33, 36, 38, 56, 59, 68, 72–3, 89, 106
molasses 40–1, 58, 62, 76, 107, *n. 264*
mollusc, perfumed shell of 53, 61–3, 64, 81–3, 105
monkey jackfruit tree 26, 32, 34, 36, 41, 45, 55–6, 65, 70, 73–4, 96, 102–3
monsoon xix, 76, *Pl. 40*
moon: 14th lunar mansion 59; waxing 65, 104
mouse-ear 63
Muhammad ibn Da'ud ibn Muhammad ibn Mahmud Shadiyabadi x, xi
mulberries 57, 110
musicians xix, 78–9, *Pl. 39*
musk: civet 24, 54, 61–2, 64, 72, 79, 81–4, 94, 99, 108; deer 64, 96, 105; tibetan 75, *n. 256*; (*vegetable*) 3–7, 9–13, 18, 19, 21, 23, 25–8, 33–4, 36, 38, 40, 41, 44–9, 51–4, 58–9, 62–5, 67, 69–74, 76, 80–4, 86–90, 93–4
muslin 13, 38, 52, 66, 91, *n. 36*
mustard 16, 36–7, 39, 44, 57, 59, 80, 107; seed 10, 12, 20–1, 24, 28, 34, 36, 39–41, 47, 55, 69, 71, 74
myrobalan 16–18, 26, 33, 40–5, 49, 50, 56–8, 68, 71–3, 75–7, 79–80, 82–3, 97, 100, 105, *nn. 151, 165, 221*
myrtle 62, 66, 97, 100, *n. 238*

Nasir Shah i, ix, x, xii, 80, 94
necklaces 77
nectar 43, 107
nets, string 65
nigella seeds, 40, 56, 73, 101
Nim tree 45, 55
nut recipes 13, 15, 21–2, 25, 29, 31–2, 46, *nn. 30, 73*; stuffing 32, 100
nutmeg 4, 18, 42–3, 53, 87, 100–2, 106, 109, *n. 112*
nuts *see* almonds, areca, chironji, coconut, kernels, pistachios, walnuts

oil 11, 46–7, 58, 61–2, 64, 72–5, 77, 83–4, 102, 107; almond 26, 39, 40, 58; aloes 6, 27, 38, 41, 47, 52, 72–3, 83; perfumed xix, 24, 47, 64–5, 80–1, 83–5, *Pl. 44*; sesame 40, 42, 48–9, 51, 54, 56–66, 76, 80–5, 109; vegetable 12, 16, 20–1, 23–4, 27, 30, 32–3, 36, 39–41, 46, 55, 61–3, 67, 69, 72–3, 79, 92–3; walnut 67, 74; *see also* butter, ghee, olive, rape seed
okra 54, 96–7
oleander 44, 64
olive 66, 75, 110, *n. 255*
onion 3, 4, 6, 8–13, 15–16, 19, 24–7, 29, 30, 33, 35–8, 40, 45–6, 55–6, 58–9, 66–74, 77, 88, 90–2, 106; leaves 21, 36, 46, 54–5, 71
opium 100, *n. 146*
orange leaf plates 11, 12, 46, 86, 90
oranges 57, 96; leaves 2, 13, 18–20, 22, 24, 26, 32–3, 36–7, 40, 46–7, 51–2, 71–2, 89; peel 13, 17, 30, 47, 54, 59, 61–4, 83–4, 86; pulp 5, 34; sour 5, 12–15, 17–19, 23, 26, 37, 39, 41–2, 46, 53, 55–7, 73, 81, 86, 109, *n. 51*; stuffed 34, 86; sweet 13, 43, 46, 48, 53, 57, 74, 105
orris greens 36, 39, 107; root 34–5, 44, 56–7, 98
ovens 11, 92–3, 98, 103

palanquins 78, 79, 109
palm sugar 4, 8, 17, 18, 24, 25, 28–30, 32–5, 37, 40–2, 46, 54–5, 57–8, 66–7, 69, 72–4, 76–7, 108
palmyra tree fruit 48, 105, 109
pampelmousse 22, 32, 53, 56, 107, *n. 49*
pān see betel
partridge 57, 77, 80, 103, 109, *n. 174*; eggs 4; recipes for 12, 13, 16, 18–19, 26, 33–4, 46, 67–8, 89, 91
pasta *see* dough
paste: aromatic xviii, xix, 1, 5, 38, 54, 58–9, 61–5, 76–7, 80–3, 96, 98, *Pls 33, 43*; dough 73; fried 3, 6
pavilions, garden *Pls 6–10, 13, 15, 20*
peach 73–4, 80, 108, *n. 248*
pear 96
pearls 65–6
peel *see* figs, lime, orange, sugarcane
pellets, aromatic 49, 64–5, 83
pepper 4, 6–7, 10, 11, 13–19, 21, 24–5, 28, 30–46, 49–50, 55, 57–8, 66–8, 70–4, 77, 79, 88–94, 99, 104

perfume 56, 61–5, 76, 77, 82–8, 97; in betel recipes 38, 47–9, 51–2, 59, 60; for clothes 51, 54, 62, 65–6, 76, 80–3, 85; in cooking 5, 6, 17, 21–2, 28, 31, 34, 38–9, 46, 54–6, 58, 61–2, 87–8, 91–3; distilled xix, xx, 38, 51, 63, 64, 81–2, 84–6, 97, *n. 190*, *Pls 45–6*; domestic use of xviii, 62–3, *Pl. 34*; mollusc shell *see* mollusc; preparation of 38, 51–4, 61–4, 80–8, *Pl. 30*; *see also* essences, musk, oil, paste, pellets, powder, rosewater, solution, water
pestle and mortar 3, 9, 17
phlegm, remedies for 42–3, 49, 50, 57, 60, 71, *n. 187*
pickles *see* relish
pigeons 11, 13, 19, 45, 66–7, 74
pilao 67
pine kernels 13, 15, 22, 25, 28–32, 40–3, 46, 58, 66, 71–2, 74, 80, 100
piony 43, 103
plantain *see* banana
plates 16, 17, 28, 49, 88, 109; lapis lazuli 17; leaf 11, 12
plum *see* hogplums, myrobalan, sebestan
pomegranate 14, 35, 40–3, 55–8, 70–5, 77
Poon tree 53, 56, 108
poppy seeds 27, 28, 30, 35–6, 39, 41–2, 57–8, 72, 74
pot shards 29, 49, 59, 81, 91–2, 102
potherbs xvii, 3, 5–8, 10–16, 20–5, 30–8, 41–9, 54–9, 66–77, 79–80, 82, 87–93, 97–8, 102, 104–5, *Pl. 22*; *see also* bouquet garni
pots: clay 6, 12, 18, 20–1, 33, 56, 59; cooking 3, 10–15, 25, 38, 46, 56, 84, 88–94, 99, 102, 104, 109, *Pls passim*; metal 3, 9; scented 20, 63, 67, 87, 91, 94; sealed 19, 66–7, 69, 84, 87–9, 91, 98; steamed 69, 92, 98
pottage, pap recipes xv, xix, 4, 23, 25–6, 35, 37, 44, 46, 68–9, 71–2, 76, 100, 102–3, 106–7, 109, *nn. 3, 61, 83, 86, 88, 90*, *Pls 3, 37, 38*
powder, aromatic 27, 52, 54, 62–3, 65, 72, 80, 82–7, 95, 109, *n. 195*
preserves, fruit 44, 80
pulse 95–8, 102, 105–6, 108–110; bean 5–10, 15–18, 20, 25, 29–31, 34–40, 43–5, 50–7, 61–3, 66–73, 79, 80, 82–6, 96–7, 103–5, *nn. 6, 14, 44–5, 84, 219, 241*; chickpea xix, 6–7, 14, 16–17, 22, 25, 27, 29–32, 35–6, 40–1, 46, 70, 102, 110, *n. 10*; dough 5, 9, 22, 26, 46, 68, 73, 90–4, 104; recipes xvii, 5–7, 16, 25, 27, 29–30, 34–5, 40–1, 46, 67, 69, 73, 76, 93, *Pl. 17*; split 17, 18, 25, 27, 29, 68, 106; wafers 9, 22, 26, 68, 94, 106, *n. 20*
pumpkin 17, 22, 27, 29, 31–2, 36, 39, 40, 45, 48, 53–4, 58, 62, 68–9, 72–4, 98, 101
purslane 46, 103
pusteen 78, 80, 106, *n. 269*

quails 12, 13, 16, 18, 19, 26, 57, 78, 80, 89, *n. 174*
quince 62, 73–4, 80, 97
quivers 78, *n. 268*

rabbits 11, 12, 13, 18, 80
radish 13, 16, 20, 28, 33, 40, 45, 57–8, 73, 76–7, 108–9; leaves 36–7
raisins 13, 21, 25, 28–31, 40–2, 55, 58, 66, 70–4, 80, 99, 103–4
rape seed oil 12, 16, 28, 30–1, 39–41, 58, 74, 108
ratti (*weight*) 95, *passim*
relish, recipes for 22, 26, 28–9, 31–4, 36, 38, 40, 42, 56–7, 67–8, 71–4, 76, 81, 96, 98, 109, *n. 98*
remedies *see* aphrodisiacs, antidotes, betel, bile, chest, eyes, fever, illnesses, impotence, indigestion, insomnia, leprosy, medicines, phlegm, toothache
resin, Saul tree 24, 54, 62, 76, 82–4, 107, *n. 261*; *see also* gum
rice xvi, 13–16, 22–6, 30–4, 41–7, 54, 66–72, 74, 76, 79, 90–4, 97, 99, 102, 109, *nn. 29, 33, 153, 264*, *Pls 5, 11*; boiled xvi, 5, 6, 8, 14, 23, 40, 58, 61, 66–70, 75, 92, 94, 102, 108; with gold 14; plain 4, 14, 40, 58; saffron 14, 92; flour 4, 5, 16–17, 20, 23, 25, 28, 31, 37, 39, 92; water xvi, 7, 8, 17–18, 26, 32, 59, 68, 72, 106, *Pl. 13*; *see also* congee, fricasee, kedgeree, pilao
rings 75, 78, 80, 108; gold and silver 77; silk 75
roe *see* fish
rose apple 100
roses 43, 48, 53–4, 59, 61–2, 66, 72–3, 76, 84, 87, 89, 99, 100, 103, 110, *n. 67*; leaves of 4, 12, 81–2; perfume of 3, 7, 9, 14, 20, 47, 54; white China 14, 18, 24, 31–2, 42–3, 48, 50, 53–4, 56, 59, 66, 72–3, 76, 89, 108

rosewater 3–6, 11–41, 45–54, 58–74, 77–100
rustic food *see* food

saffron: in recipes 3, 4, 7, 12, 13, 15, 24–5, 28–30, 34, 36, 38, 41, 45, 47–62, 65–6, 70–87, 93–4, 102–4, 110; rice 14, 92; spirit of 85
samosas xii, xv, xvii, 3, 4, 19, 76–7, 90, 107, *Pl. 23*
sandal: in recipes 17, 24, 27, 41, 44–66, 72, 76–87, 93, 98, 104, 107; spirit of 85
sarūd 46, 66, 78, 108, *n. 235*
Saul tree flowers 56–9; *see also* resin
scorpions 79
screw pine 18, 40, 44–5, 59, 61, 72, 103, *n. 35*; leaves 11, 27, 47, 89, 90; used in perfume 52–4
sebestan plums 39, 108, *n. 92*
seeds *see* caraway, coriander, cotton, cucumber, jackfruit, melon, mustard, nigella, pomegranate, poppy, rape, sesame, water lily, woodapple
sesame 6, 8, 10, 80, 85, 93, 103, 109; meal 42–5, 50, 53, 56, 58, 66, 94; seeds 8, 11, 16, 17, 21–4, 28, 31, 38–40, 43, 46–7, 50, 54, 58–9, 63–4, 66–7, 72–3, 77, 80–3, 86–7, 107; *see also* oil
sheep 106; bones 12, 25, 29; head 29; intestines 26; meat 3, 11, 12, 13, 25, 66, 76, 89–92, 105; milk 4; shank 25; *see also* haggis, lamb
shells: broken 102; perfumed 53, 61–2, 64, 81–3, 105
sherbet, recipes for xvii, xx, 14, 21, 23–37, 41, 46, 55, 57–8, 62, 69, 76–7, 81, 87–8, 91–2, 97, *Pls 19, 21, 47*
shoes x, xi, 78, *Pls* 51, 53
Silk Cotton tree 48, 50, 104, 108
sīr (*weight*) 95, *passim*
Sisoo tree 49, 59, 106, 108, *nn. 186, 222*
Skelton, Robert vii, x, xi, 112
skewered: fish 12, 108; meat xvi, 11, 25–6, 29, 33, 46, 68, 74, 76, 79, 81, 89, 91, 101, 108, *Pl.* 9
skin, treatment of 45; *see also* fur, goat
slave girls x, 77, 78
snakebite, antidote for 49, 77, 80, 106, *n. 267*
snakes 78–9
snares, traps 78, 80, *n. 272*; *see also* birds, nets
soldiers, female x, 77
solution 53, 100, *n. 191*; *see also* essences, flavouring, perfume
sorrel 34, 36, 40, 44, 56–7, 66, 73, 76, 96
soup 7, 8, 10, 18, 19, 21–2, 28, 30, 33, 46, 67–9, 76, 91, 105, 108, 110, *n. 22*; fish 12; meat xvi, 7, 8, 10, 13, 32, 36, 38, 68–9, 73, 91, *Pls 9, 10, 14*; mongol 13, 76, 91; rabbit 11, 13, 18; *see also* food, invalid
spiders 79
spikenard 23, 38, 50–4, 61–3, 72, 80–7, 98
spinach 105, *n. 78*
spirit (*ʿaraq*) 48, 85–6, 95; *see also* saffron, sandal
starfruit 22, 41, 54–5, 57, 61–2, 73, 101, *n. 50*
stones, heated 11, 74, 92–3
stoves 11, 92–3, *Pls passim*
stuffing 28, 29, 31, 33, 45–6, 56, 68–9, 76, 97, 100, 106, *n. 81*; for aubergines 67, 69; for bread 3, 4, 19, 26–7, 29, 32–3, 35, 69, 89, 90; for eggs 32, 45; for fish 12; for haggis 2, 26; for meat 10, 13, 68; for melon 35, 77; for oranges 34, 46, 86; for samosas 3, 4, 19, 90; *see also* nuts
sugar 17, 18, 24, 27–8, 37, 39, 41, 44, 46, 54–8, 61; cane 4, 17, 22, 40, 46, 72, 80, 96, 108, *n. 34*; peel 24, 62, 70, 76; *see also* cane, date, grape, molasses, palm, syrup
sumach 36, 107
summer food *see* food, seasonal
swallow wort 43, 102, *n. 122*
sweetmeats 6–8, 31, 40, 46, 49, 77, 81, 99, 100–6, 108–9, *nn. 7, 74, 176, 265*; coloured 6; halva xviii, *Pl. 31*; *laḍḍū* 9, 40, 46, 77
syrup *see* ginger, mango, sugar, tamarind

ṭaghrān 11, 89, 91, 109
tamarind 39, 41, 42, 46, 50, 55, 58, 74, 80, 103, 109, *n. 107*; congee 21; dried 96; flummery 20, 92–3; juice 20–3, 26; in recipes 6, 13, 14, 32, 40, 48, 50, 53, 57–8, 73, 88, 91, 92; syrup 13, 77
teeth, care of 60, 65, 75–6; *see also* toothache
thumb rings 78, 80, 108
Tipu Sultan xiii
tongs, cooking 86
tonics *see* impotence, medicines, remedies

tools *see* tongs, tweezers
Toon tree 62, 110
toothache, remedies for 48–9
traps *see* snares
Tree-trumpet flowers 44, 50, 52, 56, 57, 105, *n. 141*
trees *see* Asotra, Butter, Caster Oil, Coral, Deodar, Horse Radish, Jackfruit, Monkey Jackfruit, Nim, Palmyra, Pipal, Poon, Saul, Silk Cotton, Sisoo, Soon, Toon, Tree-trumpet
tubers: edible 5, 40, 55, 57, 73, 77, 93, 102, *nn. 9, 208*; medicinal 41–3, 101, 105, *nn. 106, 128*; *see also* water lily
tulcha (*weight*) 95, *passim*
turmeric 3, 4, 7–11, 14–17, 19, 24–5, 28–9, 32–3, 35, 39–40, 43, 45, 54, 61–3, 68–9, 82, 89, 90–2, 100–1, 110; leaves 63, 72, 76
tweezers 7, 78, 104

umbrella 80
'*unvān* 80, *n. 278*

veal 37
vegetable recipes 16, 58–9, *n. 43*
vegetables 47, 107; green 12, 18, 34, 38, 71, 77, 88, 94; root 16, 34, 56, 66, 99, 108
vegetarian recipes 16, 27, 99, *nn. 43, 64*; *see also* leaf
venison 3, 12, 16, 89–91
verbena 43, 108
vine leaves 38, 40, 55, 101, 107; shoots 46, 56–7, 71
vinegar 13, 21, 23–4, 28–9, 33–8, 46, 54, 57, 61, 68, 72–3, 76, 88–93, 108

walnuts 22, 28–30, 41, 43, 46, 50, 66, 72–3, 94, 96–9
water 65, 79, 95; chestnuts 31, 35, 39–41, 48, 57–9, 71, 80, 108; cooling xviii, xix, xx, 52, 65, 79, *Pls* 35, 42, 52; flavouring 29, 38, 41, 53, 55, 65; perfumed 26, 51–5, 64–5, 75; pots 65, 99, 107; skins xviii, 65, 79, *Pl. 35*
water lily 40–1, 45, 48–9, 73, 80, 101, 105; flowers 32, 36, 46, 53–6, 59, 60; leaves 66; seeds 8, 22, 33, 42–3, 50, 57–8, 80, 104, *n. 134*; stuffed 46; tubers 42
wax 62, 78–9, 104; bee's 54, 61
weapons: battle 77; hunting 77–80, *n. 275*
wheat 8, 22, 25, 27, 30, 34–5, 46, 50–1, 56, 59–64, 68, 80–1, 84, 93, 100, *nn. 99, 102*; bread 27; flour 4, 8, 27, 46, 58; grains 3, 6, 7, 9, 39, 40, 58; kernels 5; milky fluid of 43, 45, 99; parched 8, 39, 40, 46, 80, *n. 203*
whey 18, 21, 30, 40, 46–7, 73–4, 91–2, *n. 39*
wine 79, 102; palm 46, 108–9
winter food *see* food, seasonal
wolves 79
women, advice on hygiene for 65, 66, 75, 78; *see also* chador, slave girls, soldiers
woodapple 16, 25, 41, 51, 56–9, 73, 103
wormwood 52, *n. 194*

yam 6, 57, 104, 106, 109, *nn. 12, 207*
yam leaves 32, 35
yogurt salad 34, 39, 107

zedoary 51, 53, 54, 58–9, 62–3, 82, 101, *n. 65*
zerumbet 27, 56, 58, 63–4, 81, 84, 86

نعمت نامه در علم طب بخط نسخ جلد
پسرخ بابت ملک الملک ... جمع کتابخانه
معمور شده بتاریخ ۵ ماه ربیع الاول
سنه ١٠٢٤

ا ب ت ث ج ح خ د ذ ر ز س ش ص ض
ط ظ ع غ ف ق ک ل م ن و ه لا ی
تمت ... والسلام

دوم

این کتاب نعمت نامه

ا ب ب ب

بکرا

کتاب در پختن سنبوسه غیاث شاهی

یا کیبلجی

کتاب نعمت نامه در طب بخط نسخ

جلد سرخ بابت ملک الماس جمع کتابخانه

عامره شده بتاریخ ۲۲ ماه ربیع الاول

١٥٤٤

نعمت نامه ناصر شاهی در ترکیب الوان طعام

و حلوا و ماهی و ساختن گلاب و عطریات وغیره

پاتیلی بیارند خواه از زر یا از نقره یا از برنج و در پاتیل دیگر

از مس یا از آهن باشد بنهند و آب بیندازند و علف بالای او

بنهند چنانچه آب بالای علف بیاید و بالای آن طبقی بنهند

و بارد مهر کنند و شیر گاو تازه دوشیده که آب با و نیامیخته

باشد بیارند و یك وصله جامهٔ پاك بر چوبی بطریق بادبیزن

بپیچند و بآن جامه شیر را بردارند و بر بالای طبق بمالند ساعت

بساعت تا شیر بالای طبق بطریق نان غلیظ شود فرو آرند و

به آلت آهنی شیر را بردارند و سنبوسه راست کنند و

در میان ان سنبوسها پر کنند بچیزی که گفته میشود

نوعی دیگر سنبوسهٔ غیاث شاهی بیارند روهٔ خوب از گندم

صاف پنج سیر و یك سیر روغن خوشبوی دران اندازند

و بدست بمالند و بدسته چوبی بکوبند چون خوب امیخته

شود ماهیچه راست کنند بسطبری انگشت و در میانهٔ

روغن برشته سازند و ان ماهیچهٔ برشته را در میان گل بنهند

تا کسب خوشبویی کند بعد ازان بدست بمالند و خورد

کنند تا باریك شود و در میان ان نبات و مشك و کافور و الاچی

و قرنفل بیندازند و یکجا امیخته کنند و در میان سنبوسه

بنهند و بسیار پر کنند و با همسنگی بردارند بسیار لذیذ و خوب

خوب باشد نوعی دیگر سنبوسهٔ غیاث شاهی قیمهٔ

خوب پخته با هم چندان پیاز قیمه کرده و زنجبیل خورد

کرده ربع ان و نیم توله سیر اش کرده همه یکجا

بیامیزد و زعفران سه توله در گلاب اش کرده

با قیمه بیامیزد و از میان شوربای بادنجان بیرون آرند

و با قیمه یکجا کرده در سنبوسه پر کنند و در میان

روغن برشته سازند خواه از نان تنک خشک باشد یا

از نان میده یا از خمیر خام هر سه جنس سنبوسه پزد

لذیذ و خوب باشد نوعی دیگر سنبوسه غیاث

شاهی از گوشت آهو قیمه باریک کرده بیارند و روغن را

بکهار میتهی بدهد و قیمه را بزعفران آمیخته در روغن
اندازد بعد نمك و زیره بریان کند و الاییحی و قرنفل و
کشنیز و پل رتی مشك در قیمه انداخته یك پزد و
مقدار نیمهٔ قیمه پیاز و ربع آن قیمه زنجبیل در گوشت
اندازد چون خوب پخته شود گلاب بزند و
فرو آرد و سنبوسه پر کنند و بچوب سنبوسه را
سوراخ کند و در روغن خوشبوی برشته کند
و نرم فرو آرد و بهمین نوع سنبوسهٔ هر گوشت
که خواهند میشود ترتیب سنبوسهٔ گوشت نرم
پرپتی یا گوشت آهو باریك قیمه کنند

ومیان آن زرد چوبه و زیره و میتهی و کشنیز

والایچی و قرنفل انداخته بیامیزد و در روغن

خوشبوی بگهار هنگ اصلی بدهد چون بگهار

خوب شود قیمه را درو اندازد و بگذارد تا خوب

پخته شود بعده آب لیمو و فلفل بیندازد

بعد از آن زنجبیل ربع سیر و پیاز یک سیر بریده

درو اندازد و فرو ارد بعده کافور یک رتی و مشک

یک رتی بیندازد و اندك سنبوسه را بزرك راست کنند و

اندکی کوچك بمقدار یك نواله راست کنند و قیمه درو پر کرده در

بریده بخورد

روغن خوشبو برشته سازند و وقت خوردن در سرکه یا آب لیمو فرو

نوعی دیگر ماده گاو زرد یا سیاه را نیشکر

وگیاه سبز و پنبه دانه و سوند و نارگیل و جوز بویا

وجاپتری و ماش و تخم کنج وبرگ تنبول بخورانند

یا گوسفند را یا گاو میش را و شیر ایشانرا بگیرند

وبجوشانند وچیزی آنرا که بالا آید جدا کنند

آن شیر را نیم گرم بیاشامند وچیزی آنرا جامه

بیز کنند و در میان آن آرد گندم انداخته

و کشک ساخته در میان روغن برشته

کنند و کافور و الایچی و قرنفل و سوندهی و فلفل

گرد مقداری بیندازند خوش مزه باشد

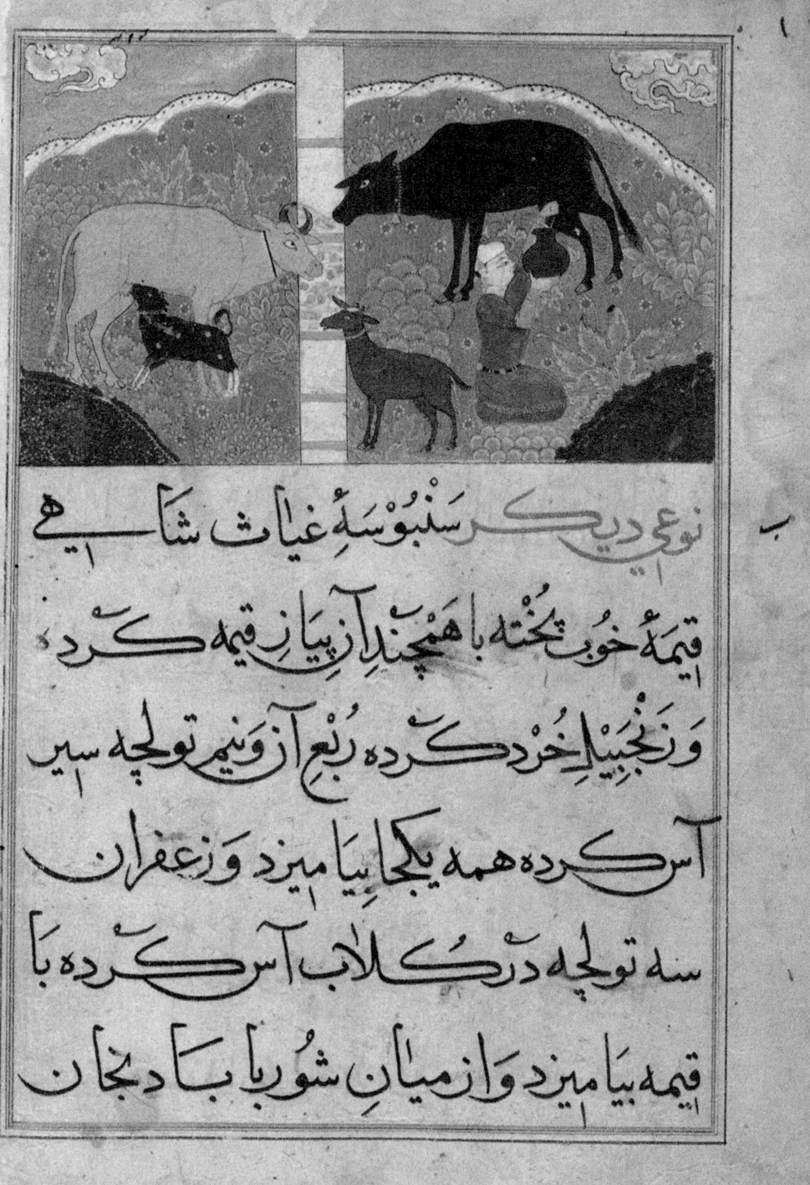
نوعی دیگر سنبوسهٔ غیاث شاهی

قیمهٔ خوب پخته با همچند آن پیاز قیمه کرده

و زنجبیل خرد کرده ربع آن و نیم تولچه سیر

آس کرده همه یکجا بیامیزد و زعفران

سه تولچه در گلاب آس کرده با

قیمه بیامیزد و از میان شوربا بادنجان

بدروا

بیرون آرند و با قیمه یکجا کرده در سنبوسه
پر کنند و در میان روغن برشته سازند خواه که
ازنان تنک
خشک
باشد یا ازنان
میده یا از
خمیر خام هر سه جنس سنبوسه بپزد لذیذ باشد
دیگر لنواس غیاثشاهی وصلهای تنک از گوشت
بگیرند و در روغن بگهار هنک و میتهی
بدهند و گوشت را با زردچوبه قدری پیا میزنند

وخوب نرم کرده بپزند وروغن خوشبوی بالای
آن بسیار بینداززند وبالای آن قدری الاچی وقرنفل
واندک کافور وآرد برنج انداخته بپزد چون
خوب پخته باشد وصلهای پیاز بزرگ بزرگ و
زنجبیل نیز وصلهای بزرگ بینداززد وبالای آن
فلفل خشک آس کرده بینداززند ولیمو بیفشارد
لذیذ بود دیگر برنج ساده غیاثشاهی از شربت
شکرتری دهن بدهد وچون بجوش آید برنج را در آن اندازد
وچون نیک پخته باشد فرو آرد ودر آن آب که
ازین برنج گرفته باشد الاچی وکافور وقرنفل

آن برگهای برهم دوخته شیر را سرد کنند

لذیذ باشد دیگر در ساختن بره از شیر

برنج را در آب خویسانیده باریک آس کنند چون در

دیگ شیر گرم شده باشد آرد برنج در آن بیندازد

اگر پنج سیر شیر باشد چهار سیر آرد بیندازد و

بگذارد تا خوب تخته شود فرو آرد و یک مشت

آرد میده میان آن بیندازد و بره راست کرده در میان

روغن بپزد و بالای بره نبات و کافور و مشک

و الاتچی و قرنفل بیندازد و سبوی گل معطر سازد

دیگر ترتیب شیر برنج شیر را خوب بجوشانند و در

میان آن برنج را خوب شسته بیندازد یا آنکه روغن

گندم که بسیار سفید باشد بیندازند یا سر و له آرد

بیندازند یا ماهیچهٔ باریک بیندازند و بالای آن کافور

و مشک و گلاب و اندکی عنبر اشهب بیندازند

و چون خوب پخته باشد فرو آرند نه بسیار غلیظ

باشد و نه تنک موازنه بپزند

نوعی دیگر شیربرنج پنج سیر شیر خوب بجوشانند
نیم سیر برنج شسته با شیر آش کنند و جامه بر کنند و
در آن شیر اندازند و نبات آن مقدار بیندازند که نه سخت
شیرین باشد و نه کم مزه چون خوب پخته باشد
مغز ترنج شیرین دانه کرده بیندازند و
اگر ترنج شیرین نباشد و ترش موجود باشد پس
مغز ترنج ترش را چند از در آب بشویند که ترشی
از و برود و آنرا در شیر بیندازند و گلاب و کافور
و مشک انداخته فرو آرند و سرد کنند لذیذ باشد
نوعی دیگر بوره ماست ماست را در جامه بسته بدارند

وخوب بیفشارد تا غلیظ شود ویک مشت آرد میده در و

اندازد و در روغن خوشبوی بره راست کرده تخته برشته

کنند و بالای بره الاچی و کافور و مشک و نبات

و قرنفل بیندازد و بخوشبویی کل معطر سازد دیگر

بره کسیر و پنج سیر دال ماش خوب بشوید و باریک

آس کنند و پنجاه عدد کسیر و آس کرده در آن

بیامیزد و پنج سیر مسکه تازه در آن اندازد و بدست

بمالد و هنگ و نمک قدری انداخته بکف دست بپزد

روغن خوشبوی و کافور و مشک و نبات و الاچی

و قرنفل بالای بره اندازد و بوی کل معطر سازد

وجند عدد

وچند عدد ازین بره بغیر شیرینی بدارد ودر میان همین
بره کرهی خوب راست کرده یا دوغ داغ داده باشد یا
کانجی بوی داده باشد وبره را آن زمان در کرهی یا دوغ
یا کانجی بیندازد وفی الحال بخورند تا درمیان آن حل نشود
مشت
دیگر بره پنداله را خوب آس کنند ویک
آرد میده در وی بیندازند ودر روغن خوشبوی بره کرده
برشته کنند وبالای بره نبات وکافور مشک کلاپچی
فلفل قرنفل آس کرده بیندازد دیگر بهمین نوع
بره رتالو کنند وبهمین نوع بره کتهل وبهمین نوع
بره انبه کنند دیگر بره ماش طریق بهتر راست

کنند و از تمر هندی قتغ کنند و در میان آن
نبات و گلاب و کافور و مشک و الاچی و قرنفل
بیندازند و بخور عود بتیلید بدهند و بره را در آب
سخت گرم اندازند
و بیرون آرند و در قتغ
بیندازند
و بهمین
نوع بره
نمک راست
کنند نوعی دیگر بره ماش را از شیر ماش را

خوب شسته با ریك آس کنند و در میان آن هنك

و پیاز و زنجبیل و زیره و منتهی بیامیزند و بره راست کنند و

بالای آن بره دیگر از مسکه بسازند و بر و نهند و دیگر

بره از ماش راست کنند و بالای بره مسکه نهند و

همچنین چند عدد بره طبقه طبقه یکی از مسکه و یکی

از ماش بالای یکدیگر نهند و در روغن برشته

کنند و شیر را گرم کنند نبات و کافور و مشك

و گلاب در شیر اندازند و قدری از این شیر بغیر

شیرینی نگاه دارند و در هر دو نوع شیر برهاء

گرم گرم بیندازند و بالاء شیر سایه دوغ بدهد یك طبقه

ازان ماست باشد ویك طبقه ازان بره باشد لذیذ باشد

نوعی دیگر بره گرهی بیارد دوغ ترش و برنج را خوب

شسته آس کرده در آن اندازد کشنیز تر و زیره و

میتهی بریان کرده بیندازد الاتچی و پیاز و قرنفل و ادرك

آس کرده بیندازد و گرهی را خوب بجوشاند فلفل

ونمك بیندازد چون جوشیده باشد فرو آرد و دو وصله خزف

گرم کند بالای یکی هنك و زیره و میتهی و الاتچی

و قرنفل و کنجد بیندازد و بالای وصله دوم نهد

و بالای آن هردو دیگی بپوشاند چون خوب بوی گرفته باشد

در آن دیك گرهی بیندازد و در آن گرهی بره بندازد

کرم کو

گرم گرم دیگر ترتیب پهینی روه صاف از گندم ب
پنج سیر روغن ربع سیر وقت کوفتن روه بیندازند تا بسیار
خوشبوی و صاف شود و در میان آن برنج شسته آس کرده
بیامیزد و طریق ماهیچه آردی بسازند و اورا بپیلند
و بالای آن مسکه بمالند و بکارد ببرند پهینی راست
کرده در روغن خوشبوی برشته سازند و اگر هر
ورقی نوعی دیگر خواهند پس یک ماهیچه سرخ و
یک ماهیچه سفید بالای هم بپیچند و ورقهای هر جنسی
شود و پهینی رنگین شود دیگر نسر کماجه پنج سیر ب
روه را یک سیر روغن بیندازند و بکف دست بمالند

وخوب بکوبند وروغن اندك اندك مي اندازند و

وبه بیلن ببیلند وطریق نان سازند وبالاي آن آرد برنج

مسکه بمالند وآن نان را ته کنند ویکیك کهاجه را

موازنه آرد بکارد ببرند وببیلند وکهاجه تنك راست کنند

وبه منقاش یا ناخن نقش کنند ودر روغن برشته کنند

وشیرهٔ صاف بقوام آورده بالاي آن بیندازند وبوي

گل معطر کنند دیگر پهیني از منك

دال منك شسته باریك آس کنند وباب گرم نخود سا ننند

[illegible] نان ببیلند وباکارد طریق پهیني ببرند و

[illegible] کنند طریق پهیني بهن

کرده

کرده در روغن برشته کند و بالای آن شیرهٔ صاف

بیندازد و بهمین ترتیب پهینی نخود بسازد و بهمین ترتیب

از عدس نیز راست کند که لذیذ باشد

دیگر ترتیب نان تنک

نبات را با روغن خوب

آس کند

کافور و

مشک

الائچی قرنفل

بیندازد چنانچه روهٔ سفید بجهة نان تنک خمیر میکنند

همان طریق خمیر کنند این روده را و آن مقدار
قطعه که برای نان تنك میگیرند آن مقدار
قطعه خمیر بگیرند نبات انداخته نان تنك
بپزند نوعی دیگر نان تنك دال منك یا دال نخود آب ب
و نبات انداخته خوب بپزند چنانچه بالای سنك بجهة پوولی
آرد خمیر میکنند همچنان خمیر کرده قطعه قطعه کنند در
میان انداخته بپزد نوعی دیگر نان تنك از روده پاك سفید ب
نان تنك بپزد و کافور و مشك و الاچی و نبات و
روغن بهم الدوده کنند و در روغن برشته کنند و بوی
گل معطر سازد این را تنك نان شکری خوانند

نوعی دیگر

نوعی دیگر ترتیب نان تنك از کلت دال کلت نورا
در میان آب نخود خیسانند و باریك آس کنند و با آب آمیخته از
جامهٔ تنك بیرون کنند و تاوهٔ کالی گرم کنند و بروغن
تاوه را چرب کنند و آرد را که پالوده داشته است بجامهٔ
پاك آلوده کنند و آن جامه را بالای تاوه بگسترانند
دیگر ترتیب شوربا آب که از برنج پخته بر میگیرند بستانند
و زردچوبه و زعفران و الاچی و قرنفل و فلفل و زیره و گوشت
پخته با هم آمیخته بار دیگر بپزند و هنگ و نمك
وقت فرو آوردن و روغن بیندازند و آب لیمو نیز بیندازند
دیگر ترتیب شوربا گندم کوفته و گوشت با تمام

حوائجات انداخته شوربا بپزند نوعی دیگر شوربا

گوشت تخته درمیان کرهی انداخته بجوشانند تخم

و پترج والاچی وکافور وآب زنجبیل وآب لیمو و نمک

انداخته در دیگ اندازد لذیذ باشد نوعی دیگر شوربا آرد زرت

دوغ و زیره و نمک و پیاز انداخته بپزد آب لیمو والاچی و

قرنفل انداخته فرو آرد سرد کرده بخورد هناک و کنجد بدهد

نوعی دیگر شوربا آرد برنج یا آرد زرت یا گندم درشت

آس کرده که آنرا تهولی خوانند یا کنکنی یا دال منگ

شسته درمیان شیر انداخته بجوشانند و شکر تری موا زنند

بیندازند بسباسه وکافور بالای آن ریزند نوعی

۱۳
سیزده

دیگر ترتیب آب درمیان آب برنج و زرت و گندم و
جو و تور و نخود برشته همه یکجا کرده بپزند نمك
بیندازد و دو درم روغن بیندازد و از بالا آب صاف
بردارد و آن آب را بخور روغن یا کنجد بدهد بعده یا شیرین
کند یا ترش کند یا خوشبو کند یا تیز کند یا
آب لیمو و سیر اندازد پس جنس دیگر شود و دانهایی
میان آب را شیرینی و خوشبویی انداخته یك جنس شود
نوعی دیگر ترتیب آب کاك کاك را درمیان آب
نخود بیاند و بدست کاك را مالیده آب صاف ازو بگیرد
و درمیان آن خوشبویی و شیرینی اندازد دیگر ترتیب باکره

برنج را نرم اندام بپزد طریق رابری و وقتِ فرو آوردن آرد
نخودِ برشته بیارند یا کرهی برشته یا بادامِ برشته
یا تخمِ نیلوفر برشته یا تخمِ کتهل برشته یا استهٔ انبهٔ برشته
یا استهٔ جامن برشته میانِ آن انداخته بپزد نوعی دیگر
جهکلی زرت را سفید کرده بکوبند و در میانِ دوغ
زیره انداخته بپزد و سرد کرده با ماست و زیره و نمک
انداخته که آنرا متهه کویند بخورند نوعی دیگر کوشت ساک
پله دار روغنِ خوشبوی در دیك اندازد و چون ک
شده باشد بکهارِ زیره و پیاز و میتهی بدهد و چون
بکهار خوب کرفته باشد زردچوبهٔ خشك آس کرده

بیندازد

۱۴
بچهارده

بینداٰزند و چون زرد چوبه سرخ شود گوشت را در دیگ کنند

و چون گوشت خوب برشته شود آب بینداٰزند و سونف

و کشنیز و زیره و میتهی و ساگ را جوشانیده آب او

بیفشارد و دور کند و ساگ را در گوشت کند و نمک بینداٰزد و چون

خوب پخته

شود و صلها ی

بزرگ بزرگ

و آب بیل و

لیمو با اندک

نمک انداخته فرو آرند نوعی دیگر ترتیب پوری پوری

ب

راست کنند و در میان آن کنجد دانهٔ مقشّر و برشته

نبات و کافور و مشک و الاچی و قرنفل یکجا آمیخته در و اندازد

و لبهای پوری را استوار کنند و در روغن برشته کنند

ب و بوی گل معطر سازد نوعی دیگر لدو روهٔ

سفید پنج سیر و ربع سیر روغن یک درم نمک انداخته خوب

خمیر کنند و بالای سنک بکوبد یکسیر روغن

وقت کوفتن اندک اندک بخوراند و مزوارها سازد

یا ماهیچه و در روغن برشته در شیرهٔ صاف قوام آورده

ب لدو بندد و بوی گل معطر سازد نوعی دیگر لدو آرد ماهیچه

روه یکسیر روغن یک تولچه نمک یکماسه انداخته خمیر کنند

وچون

و چون خوب تر شده باشد بالای سنگ بکوبد و چنانچه
بجهت پاپر لویی بدست پاره آرد را آنچنان بشکنند و ماهیچهٔ مهین
باریک چون موی راست کنند و درمیان جامهٔ باریک
انداخته در روغن برشته کنند و از آن نیم ماهیچه زیر
و نیمی بالا و میان آن از نبات و کافور و مشک بیندازد و بوی
گل معطر سازد نوعی دیگر لدو منگ دال منگ را خوب
بشوید و اندک بجوشاند و در نبات و کافور و مشک
بیندازد لدو بندد بالای آن آرد میده با آب حل کرده بیالایند
و در روغن برشته کنند و بوی گل معطر سازند
نوعی دیگر لدو که کرسنگی آرد روه سفید بنج سیر نیک بخوسانند

و با دسته چوبینه بالای سنگ بکوبد و یکسیر و نیم روغن را

بخوراند و مقدار سطبری انگشت ماهیچه راست کند و در

روغن برشته کند و معطر بگلاب سازد و ماهیچه را زیره

کند و در میان آن بادام کوفته مقشر دو سیر نارگیل

کوفته دو سیر نبات و کافور و مشک و الاچی و قرنفل یکجا آمیخته

لدو بندد نوعی دیگر ترتیب گوشتها پنج سیر گوشت و

ربع سیر هلد و نیم تولچه قرنفل الاچی یک تولچه زیره میتهی برشته

از هر یک ربع تولچه و ربع تولچه کشنیز هر همه یکجا کرده و

روغن خوشبوی در دیگ اندازد و در بر نهد چون ک شده

باشد سنگ و الاچی و قرنفل و کشنیز تازه در آب انداخته بگهار

۱۶ ۱۶
شانزده

چون بکهار خوب شده باشد کوشت بیندازد

چون لنواس شده باشد آب بیندازد و دو تولچه نمك بیندازد

چون خوب پخته باشد یك رتی کافور و یك رتی مشك

بیندازد فلفل ربع تولچه و آب دو عدد لیمو در آن اندازد یا ساك

چیزی در آن اندازد یا همچنان بدارد دیکر ترتیب قیمها

پنج سیر قیمه سه تولچه هلد یکتولچه الاچی نیم تولچه قرنفل

ربع تولچه کشنیز و میتهی یك تولچه زیرهٔ برشته ربع تولچه

کشنیز تر و ادرك و پیاز هر یك ربع تولچه آس کرده یکجا بیامیزد

و ما... دو سیر روغن در دیك انداخته در بر نهد چون کرم

شده باشد اول بکهار هنك بدهد و میتهی بیندازد چون

ب

میتهی سرخ شده باشد آنگاه گوشت قیمهٔ گوشت بیند د

و اندک هنک خام بیندازد و دو رتی کافور و یک رتی مشک

و آب دو لیمو همه یکجا کرده بپزند و نیم سیر پیاز قیمه کرده و

چهار تولچه قیمهٔ زنجبیل و ربع تولچه فلفل دراز انداخته فرو

آرد ترتیب لنواس گوشت چهار سیر گوشت و چهار تولچه ب

هلد و دیگر حوائجات که پیشتر ذکر کرده شد بیندازند

و بهمان نوع پخته فرو آرند وقت فرو آوردن یک تولچه

اجوان بدست بمالند و بیندازند و وصلهای پیاز بزرگ

بزرگ و ادرک نیز بیندازند نوعی دیگر گو

گوشت را باریک ببرند چنانچه بالا گفته شد بزنند

و دوغ

و بگهار هنك و میتهی بدهد و گوشت را با حوائجات
مذکور در دیك اندازد چون خوب پخته باشد شوربای
بگیرد گوشت را دور کند زیره میتهی هنك الاتچی قرنفل
را بگهار دهد نوعی دیگر شوربای بی روغن
گوشت را با حوائجات مذکور در آب اندازد و در بر نهد
چون پخته باشد فرو آرد و شوربا آنرا بگیرد صاف کند
و گوشت دور کند و بگهار میتهی هنك بدهد نوعی
دیگر قیمه را چنانچه پیش گفته شد بهمان بسلس بپزد
را به ماست و هلد و نمك و آب لیمو یکجا بیامیزد و کنجد
شیرین در دیك انداخته در بر نهد چون خوب گرم شده باشد

بکهار هنك بدهد و کوشت را بار ایی ماست آمیخته در دیك

انداز د چون نخته باشد فرو آرد نوعی دیکر ترتیب بره از

کوشت و ماش قیمه را باریك کند و در میان آن هلد و زیره

و میتهی الاتچی قرنفل کافور مشك کشنیز تر هنك نمك

فلفل آب لیمو ادرك پیاز آس کرده و اندکی روغن همه یکجا کرده

بیامیزد و قیمه پیاز ادرك جدا بکند و در میان آن

کشنیز خشك سونف الاتچی قرنفل کافور مشك آب لیمو

و نمك بیامیزد و از قیمه کوشت دو عدد نان بسازد و در میان

آن نانها این پور ز ببندد و کنارهاء نان [illegible]

بهمین نوع چند عدد نان بسازد و در تهاره بالا کنه

کیاه

طعام خوردن باشد از زیر خاکستر بیرون آرد و در صحن

کشیده پیش نهد و بهمین نوع تخنی خرگوش کند

و هر تخنی که

خواهد بهمین نوع کند

نوعی دیگر ترتیب سیخ هر جانور که باشد یا طغران

گوشت گوسپند اول بسیار کارد زنند و با هلد و آب

خوب بشویند و بجوشانند نمك و هنك حوتج که پیش
گفته شد انداخته بجوشانند و چون خوب تخته باشد
فرو آرند اگر بسیار مهرا شده باشد پس بر ریسمان بپیچد
و حوتج هر جنسی با آب لیمو بر گوشت بمالند یکجا کرده
ساعت بساعت و بریان کنند چون حوتج در گوشت
سرخ شد و در خورده باشد در روغن مشك کافور کلاب
انداز و بر گوشت بمالد و دیگر بریان کنند چون خوب
تخته باشد وقت خوردن ریسمان دور کنند نوعی دیگر
ترتیب گوشت درگاه کودالی دو گز عمق یك گز و نیم پهنا بکنند
و اندرون کودال را گل مالیده اندود کنند و در میان

آن

۱۹ ۱۹
۲۱
بیست یک

آن هیزم انداخته آتش بسوزاند و کودال را نیک گرم کند
و در کنارهای کودال سنگها گرم کند گوشت گاو
یا گوشت گوسپند یا طغراز گوسپند باشد بالای
آن برگ موز بپیچد و در میان کودال سنگها بیندازد و
بالای سنگها برگ موز بیندازد و بالای آن برگها گوشت
را که در برگ موز پیچیده است بنهد و باز بالای آن
گوشت بر برگهای موز بیندازد باز سنگ گرم
بیندازد و بالای آن سنگها برگ موز بیندازد گوشت را
بالای آن برگها بنهد و دیگر بالای گوشت برگ موز اندازد
همچنین هر چند که خواهد طبقه می نهد گوشت را یا

مرغ را و کبوتر را و بالاء کوداک بسیار برک مور اندازد

و بالاء آن بگل مهر کند آنچنانکه بخار از هیچ جای بیرون

نرود این نوع یک گاو یا دو گاو هر قدر که خواهند

بیندازند و تمام شب بگذارند تا بپزد و بالاء کوداک دو سه پشته

هیزم بسوزانند وقت طعام خوردن گوشت بیرون آرند

و بخورند نوعی دیگر ترتیب ماهی خارهای ماهی را

بیرون آرند و با دوغ هلد و هنگ بشوید و هنگ خالص را

در تیل بسوزانند و همان هنگ را آس کنند و زیره و میتهی

بریان کرده هلد فلفل کشنیز کنجد دانه برشته یکجا آمیخته

در ماهی بمالد بسیار ادرک آس کرده بیندازد و تیل که در آن

اول تختر ماهی در روغن کفنه همچنان این قیمه اندک
روغن داده بپزد و پاتل از برک ترنج بدوزد و در میان آن
قیمه بیندازد و بریسمان بپیچد و دتهاره بالاء سفید بدهد
آب بیندازد دتهاره خوب شده باشد و پاتلهاء پیچیده را
در دیک نهد چو زیک جوش آمده باشد فرو آرد بنهد بهمین
نوع قدری قیمه در میان برک کیوره نهاده بپزد و
و بهمین نوع بالاء برک موز برک کل سرخ و کل
سیوتی بکسترد و قیمه بالاء آن نهد و پوره ببندد
و همین نوع کوشت راست کند و تیتر و بتیر و
خرکوش و آهو هر کدام که خواهد راست کند

نوعی دیگر ترتیب سیخ ماهی چنانچه پیش قیمه در روغن
پختن گفته بودیم بهمان نوع ماهی را پخته فرو آرد و کشنیز
برشته و سونف برشته نیم کوفته با آن بیامیزد و قیمه را با حوائج
آمیخته طریق خوب کوفتها مقدار تیند و بندد و بریسمان بپچد
و در سیخ کشد کافور مشک گلاب در روغن بیامیزد هر ساعت روغن
را بر سیخ بمالد چون خوب سرخ شده باشد فرو آرد نوعی دیگر کباب
ماهی روسنا یعنی کنواری خزف خوشبوی آب نادیده بالای دیگدان
نهاده گرم کنند و پرکالهاء ماهی بی خار با دوغ هنک و آب بشوید
و نمک هنک فلفل الاچی قرنفل خشک آس کرده برو بمالد و آب لیمو
همه بر ماهی بمالد و بالاء خزف یعنی کراهی کالی بریان سازد چون

خوب برشته باشد نخورهنك اصلي بدهد و بهمين نوع كباب
تيهو و بتير و حلوان و مرغ و كبوتر بكند و بهمين
نوع كباب خرگوش نيز بكند نوعي ديگر تخني
ماهي شستن ماهي چنانچه پيش گفته بهمان نوع
دتهاره و بالا دهد يا از برك ترنج دتهاره دهد و بالاء آن
جامه بگسترد و بالاء آن ماهي را با آب ليمو و نمك
ماليده بنهند و ديك را سر بنهند چون تخته باشد فرو آرند
و آب و بيفشارند دور كنند و طريق تخني بوره كنند
الاچي قرنفل فلفل آب ليمو نمك ادرك پياز باريك بريده همه
يكجا بياميزد و بهنك اصلي نخورد دهد و برك ترنج را با تل

دو عدد بدوزد یکی را زیر و یکی را بالا نهد و در میان آن تخنی

نهد چو وقت طعام خوردن شود آن زمان بیرون کشد و

بهمین نوع تخنی هر گوشت که خواهد بکند نوعی دیگر

گوشت گوسفند پر بتی با استخوان بگیرد و نیک

بشوید و در میان آن آزهنک و پیاز ادرک نمک و ساق ساک

و کشنیز تر همه را یکجا کرده بپزد آب بسیار بیندازد

چون خوب پخته باشد قدری فلفل و آب لیمو انداخته فرو

آرد یا همچنان بدارد یا نخورهنک بدهد نوعی دیگر ترتیب

برشتن ماهی ماهی را چنانچه پیش گفته بشوید و چون تمام

که کفته بیامیزد و در تیل سرسوز یا تیل رایی برشته سازد و

چنانچه

۲۵

بعث پنج

چنانچه پیش گفته بپزد و در تیل رایی یا تیل سرسون
بگهار هنگ بدهد و بپزد نوعی دیگر ترتیب گوشته زعفران
گوشت را خوب بشوید و روغن خوشبوی در دیگ
انداخته در بر نهد چون گرم شده باشد زعفران گلاب کافور
بگهار بدهد و گوشت را با زعفران آمیخته بگهار بدهد چون
لنواس خوب شده باشد بمقدار آب بیندازد و الایچی قرنفل
گشنیز سونف تج پترج زیره میتهی آس کرده در کره
جامه بسته در گوشت اندازد و بادام چلغوزه پسته مویز
کشمش شیره تمر هندی خوب تخته باشد بیندازد گلاب
کافور مشک عنبر بیندازد فرو آرد و بهمین نوع بتیر و تیتر

و مرغ و کبوتر بپزد نوعی دیکر کوشت را خوب بشوید
و در روغن بکهار هنک داده کوشت را با زعفران آمیخته
بیندازد و چون لنواس شده باشد آب کرم بیندازد و نمک و
الایچی قرنفل سونف کشنیز زیره میتهی بیندازد چون خوب
پخته باشد آب لیمو فلفل انداخته فرو آرد و برک ترنج درست
بیندازد یا پوست نارنکی نوعی دیکر چنانچه پیش کفته
کوشت را بپزد و در بعضی دیکها برک بیندازد و در بعضی
انبه و در بعضی کیری بیندازد نوعی دیکر روغن
کرم کند عنبر کلاب مشک را بکهار بدهد چون بکهار خوب شده
باشد کوشت را با کلاب و زعفران آمیخته بیندازد چون

لنواس شده باشد آب گرم بیندازد و خوب بپزد چون

پخته باشد ادرك پیاز مغز ترش از ترنج بیندازد فرو آرد

و در بعضی پیاز

بیندازد و خیار

هم بیندازد

نوعی دیگر تخنی یزدایی بیارند گوشت گوسفند یا تیتر

یا گوشت گاو یا هر گوشت را که تخنی خواهد کند و گوشت را

درهم مالیده تخنی یزدایی بپزد و هلد نمك و هر جنسی حوائج

انداخته در روغن بکهار دهد و آب انداخته شوربا کند و پیاز

بسیار اندازد خوب شوربا شده باشد فلفل و آب لیمو بیندازد و

فرو آرد نوعی دیگر تخنی مغلی پر کالهاء گوشت بزرگ

بزرگ با پیاز و ادرك خوتج انداخته و نمك بجوشاند و گوشت

را تنك تنك ببرد و اگر خواهد درست بدارد و اگر در

شوربا خواهد در شوربا اندازد نوعی دیگر تخنی مغلی

وصلهای گوشت با استخوان بگیرد و در میان آن پیاز و

ادرك نمك هر جنسی خوتج انداخته بجوشاند چون خوب

پخته باشد آب لیمو یا روغن آمیخته بیندازد نوعی دیگر

گوشت گوشت را خوب شسته در سرکه اندازد و

نگاه دارد

۳۷

بیست هفت

نکاه دارد و در روغن بکهار هنك بدهد و کوشت را

با حوایجات هر جنسی آمیخته در دیك انداز د چون خوب تخته

باشد آب لیمو فلفل ادرك انداخته فرو آرد نوعی دیکر کوشت

وصلهای بزرك بزرك بجوشاند و بیرون آرد و باریك تخنی ببرد

و

همچون بوره و در میان آن پیاز و ادرك ترب بریده بیندازد

بخور هنك بسیار دهد نوعی دیکر تخنی ادرك پیاز ببرد

باریك و نمك بیامیزد و تخنی را باریك بریده با او بیامیزد آب لیمو

بدهد و بخور روغن نوعی دیکر کوشت کوشت را ببرد

یك وصله کوشت و یك وصله پیاز در ریسمان کشد بسیار بهمین

ترتیب و در روغن بکهار داده انداز د و لنواس کند و آب بیندازد

وخوب بپزد الاچی قرنفل نمک زیره هلد کشنیز بیندازد چون
خوب پخته باشد فلفل و آب لیمو انداخته فرو آرد و اگر خواهد
لنواس بدارد و اگر خواهد شوربا دار کند نوعی دیگر
ترتیب برنج نیمی روغن نیمی آب و نیمی کانجی باهم آمیخته
ادهون بدهد چون بجوش آید برنج را شسته و زعفران آس
کرده مالیده در دیگ اندازد چون خوب پخته باشد آب
زیادتی بپالاید و آنرا علی حده بدارد و در آن مقدار نیم سیر برنج
بیندازد و قدری روغن خوشبوی و بالا گلاب کافور نوعی
دیگر برنج ساده تمر هندی را در آب بخیسانند چون خوب پسیده
باشد بمالند و آب را بپالایند بگیرند و تمر هندی را دور

کنند

کنند و از آب را بعود مرهتی بخور دهند و بوی گل
معطر کنند و آب را ادهوز بدهند و برنج را خوب شسته
در آب بخوسانند و چون نزدیک بجوش آمده باشد برنج بیندازد
بپزد و آب زیادتی بالا آید دور کنند و برنج را گلاب
انداخته فرو آرد و از آب پالوده را کرهی بپزد یا
نبات انداخته شربت کند و بهمین نوع تهولی بپزد و بهمین
نوع ترشی ترنج یا آب انار ترش انداخته بپزد نوعی دیگر
برنج ساده ادهوز آب بدهد و برنج بیندازد چون پخته
باشد بالا آید و در آن برنج گلاب بیندازد و گل
سیوتی و کافور انداخته فرو آرند نوعی دیگر برنج

ساده بیارند دو حصه آب و یک حصه شیر در دیگ اندازد

ادهون بدهد چون بجوش آید برنج بیندازد چون پخته

باشد آب زیادتی بپالاید دور کنند و برنج با

بخار بردارد

نوعی دیگر برنج ساده زعفران در میان آب انداخته

ادهون بدهد چون بجوش آید برنج بیندازد چون پخته باشد

بپالاید و آب دور کند زعفران عنبر گلاب کافور مشک

بیکجا

یکجا آمیخته در برنج بیندازند و با روغن خوشبوی دست مالیده

برنج بیامیزد و بخار داده فرو آرد نوعی دیگر برنج ساده

زرنگ را ادهو ز آب بدهد چون بجوش آید برنج بیندازد

چون تخته باشد فرو آرد برنج را سرد کند و در صحن بکشد

و بگذارد تا دانه دار شود و ورقهای زر را بالای برنج زرنگ

کند نوعی دیگر برنج ساده نبات را در آب تمر هندی انداخته

ادهو ز بدهد چون بجوش آید برنج بیندازد چون تخته باشد

بپالاید و از آن آب شربت سرد راست کند و بالای برنج کافور

مشک گلاب بیندازد وقت روان کردن قدری فلفل

بیندازد نوعی دیگر برنج با روغن روغن خوب در دیگ

انداز چون گرم شده باشد کافور گلاب عنبر اشهب را
بگهار دهد بعده برنج را با زعفران و نمک آمیخته در
روغن اندازد و خوب بریان کند بعده آب بیندازد
و چلغوزه و پسته و بادام مقشر و الایچی و قرنفل و نارگیل
مقشر سپید ریزه گرده ناکوفته هر همه را یکجا کرده
در دیگ اندازد و خوب بپزد بعده برگ ریحان یا برگ
تلسی یا برگ ترنج انداخته فرو آرد نوعی دیگر
قلیه برنج روغن در دیگ اندازد چون گرم شود
بگهار هنگ و سیر بدهد بگهار خوب گرفته باشد
حوائجات که بالا گفته شد در گوشت آمیخته در روغن

اندازد

اندازند چون لنواس شده باشد آب بینداز دو موازنه یکسیر شیر

گاو بینداز چون بجوش آید برنج شسته بینداز چون خوب

پخته باشد فرو آرد و بهمین نوع دیگر برنج بپزد و لیکن

شیر گاو نکند بلکه مقدار ربع سیر یعنی لهسن بینداز د

و فلفل درست بینداز فرو آرد نوعی دیگر ترتیب

تهولی چون روغن خوشبوی در دیگ گرم شده باشد

بگهار زیره یا پستهی بدهد یا هنگ یا پیاز را بگهار بدهد

بعده تهولی دران اندازد و خوب بریان کند بعده آب

آن مقدار در و اندازد که بپزد فرو آرد نوعی دیگر

تهولی چون روغن خوشبوی گرم شده باشد بگهار

تلسی و کافور بدهد بعده تهولی را با زعفران آمیخته در دیگ
اندازد و خوب بریان کنند بعده آب و نمک بیندازند
چون تخته باشد قدری گلاب بالای آن اندازند و فرو آرند
نوعی دیگر بهات از زرت زرت را خوب سفید
کرده بکوبند بعده آنچه ریزه شده باشد دور کنند
و آنچه درست مانده باشد بستانند و در شیر گاو میش اندازند
و مایهٔ دوغ در آن اندازند روز دوم آن ماست را بر هم زنند
و آن زرت را که در زیر ماست باشد بیرون آرند
و دوغ جدا بستانند و مسکه جدا نگاه دارند و زرت
را نیک بشویند و آبی صاف که بالای دوغ مانده باشد

آهسته

۳۱ 28

بچ یار

آهسته بر گیرند بدارند و بعد از آن اد هوز آب در

بر نهند چون بجوش آید زرت را در آن بیندازند چون

خوب تخته باشد آب بپالایند دور کنند زرت تخته

بستانند و از آن میان اندکی سر کنند و در میان دوغ

از هنک بکهار داده بیندازند و در بالای آن

برکهاء تازهٔ لیمو بیندازند نوعی دیگر ترتیب

کهچری سه حصه دال منگ شسته و یک حصه

برنج در روغن خوشبوی که بکهار میتهی داده باشد

بیندازند و خوب بریان کنند بعده آب و نمک

انداخته نیک بپزد بعده فرو آرد نوعی دیگر کهچری

کرهی ادهو از آب بدهد چون بجوش آید دال کرهی زرد

بیندازد چون پخته شود برنج شسته بیندازد و نمک بیندازد

چون نیک پخته باشد روغن خوشبوی بیندازد فرو آرد

نوعی دیگر ترتیب ماهی گوشت ماهی را بستانند

و خار تمام دور کند بعده در تیل شیرین یا تیل سرسون

هنک بسوزاند و آنرا آس کند بعده برگهای لیمو تازه

و الایچی قرنفل زیره میتهی نمک آب لیمو هر همه را با گوشت

و تیل آمیخته یکجا کند و یکشب بدارد روز دیگر

ازان گوشت نانهاء کوچک راست کند در آفتاب

خشک کند و در مات نهد و هر وقتی که خواهد

قدری را

قدهی را در روغن برشته کند بخورد یا بالای آتش برشته

کند بخورد و بهمین نوع گوشت تیتر و گوشت آهو

و بتیر و کهل کنجد دانه هر کدام که خواهد راست

کند

نوعی دیگر ترتیب روستایی سبزی بیخها گرفته خوب

بجوشاند فرو آرد و در میان روغن کنجد هنگ برشته

کند و آنرا آب لیمو و نمك و تیل داغ داده مذکور بیامیزد

بعضی از آن بگیرد و بگهار داده بپزد و بهمین نوع

تخم ترب که آنرا سینکره خوانند بپزد و بهمین

نوع ساگهای خشك هر همه بپزد نوعی دیگر

ترتیب کروندہ در ماست رایی و نمك و آب لیمو انداخته

یکجا ... کرونده را اندك جوشانیده در همین ماست

بیندازد بعده کنجد شیرین در دیك انداخته در بر نهد

و قطعهٔ از هنك اصلی در آن اندازد چون خوب برشته باشد

پس ماست و کرونده را در آن اندازد و چون نیم جوش

خورده باشد فرو آرد نوعی دیگر ترتیب کهندوی

دال مُنگ

دال منك خوب در آب بخوسانند بعده باريك آس كنند
و در ميان آب نرم بپزد بعده بالاي طبق كه آنرا تهال كويند
تيل كه بكهار هنك داده باشند بمالد و آن دال نرم تخته
را در آن تهال بيندازد و پهن سازد چون غليظ شده باشد
پس فلفل و آب ليمو هنك داده تيل يكجا بياميزد و قدري بكف
دست برداشته بالاي آن بمالد و بكارد ببرد و از بالاي
تهال بردارد در ظرف ديكر بدارد نوعي ديكر
ترتيب كرهي دوغ ترش را بيارند و در ميان آن آرد برنج
يا آرد نخود بيندازند و در ميان آن هلد هنك نمك انداخته
بجوشانند چون تخته باشد فرو آرد هنك زيره ميتهي الايچي

تیل را نخور بدهد بعده از آرد نخود یا آرد مُنک بری راست

کند در میان روغن یا تیل برشته در کرهی بیندازد

نوعی دیگر ترتیب کرهی سفید دوغ ترش بیارد

و در میان آن ادرک و کشنیز تر یا خشک بیندازد

و نمک و بجوشاند چون نیم جوش خورده باشد الاچی

قرنفل ادرک پیاز فلفل انداخته فروآرد و چنانچه بالا نخود

کفته بودیم همان نوع نخود دهد و بهمین نوع کرهی

از کیتهه و آمله و منک و سنبهالی و سیر هر کدام که

خواهد راست کند نوعی دیگر ترتیب کرهی

دوغ ماده گاو و سوندهی ادرکی انداخته بپزد و هلد

و نمک

و نمک بیندازد و سوندهی آن قدر اندازد که دهن
نسوزد و قدری آرد برنج نیز داخل کند و بجوشاند
نوعی دیگر ترتیب کرهی دوغ ماده گاو
آمله منک برنج شال برشته تج پترج الاچی قرنفل نمک
بیندازد و بجوشاند فرو آرد نوعی دیگر ترتیب
کرهی آرد بادام دوغ قند الاچی قرنفل یکجا آمیخته
در بر نهد و بجوشاند چون پخته باشد فرو آرد نوعی
دیگر کرهی در میان دوغ برگ لیمو آس کرده
بیندازد و آب لیمو نیز بیفشارد و پوست لیمو نیز بینداzد
بعده نمک الاچی قرنفل انداخته بجوشاند چون پخته باشد

فرو آرد نوعی دیگر ترتیب کرهی از دنکره

دنکره را دست مالیده آب او صاف کرده بگیرند

و گوشت را جوشانیده آب او بگیرند بعده شکرتری

الاچی قرنفل انداخته بجوشاند چون پخته باشد فرو آرد

نوعی دیگر ترتیب پیچهه یعنی آب زیادتی که

از دیگ بر میدارند بعد پختن برنج و جزآن منک

برشته را در آب انداخته بجوشانند و بعده صندل

تازه آس کرده آب او بگیرد بعده آمله الاچی

در آن انداخته بپزد نمک بیندازد چون پخته باشد

چند برگ پودنه در آن اندازد و فرو آرد نوعی دیگر

پیچهه

پیچهٔ آب برنج پخته را بستانند و در میان آن شیرهٔ انگور

بسیار انداخته و الایچی و کافور قرنفل گلاب

بیندازد چون خوب پخته باشد فرو آرد نوعی دیگر

ترتیب پیچهٔ از نخود نخود را جوشانیده

آب آن بستانند بعده نمک زیره هنگ الایچی قرنفل

فلفل آب ترنج انداخته بجوشانند چون پخته باشد فرو آرد

نوعی دیگر پچهه منک در میان روغن برشته آب
زنجبیل نمک هنک را بکهار بدهد نوعی دیگر
پهت منک در روغن بکهار هنک بدهد و دال منک
را در آن اندازد برشته کند بعده آب بیندازد
و نمک بیندازد چون پخته باشد آرد کنجد دانه برشته
یا آرد نخود برشته در آن اندازد بیامیزد و قدری روغن
خوشبوی در آن اندازد فرو آرد نوعی دیگر
پهت دال نخود سوز دال غیاثشاهی دال نخود و مغز
زردچوبه خالص باریک آس کنند و در جامه
انداخته بپالایند و آب بستانند بعده زعفران خوب

تازه

تازه آش کرده دران اندازد یکجا کرده بپزند تا آنزمان
که دال و شوربا یکی شود و رنکها باهم آمیخته
شوند بعده نمك آب لیمو آب زنجبیل بیندازد بعده پوست
نارنکی و پوست ترنج انداخته فروآرند بعده
صحن لاجوردی باشد یا صحن فیروزی باشد دران
برنج بهات بکشند و در یك کنار از بهات این دال
بکشند و روغن خوشبوی در کاسه علاحده
کشیده پیش روان کنند و سوز دال غیاثشاهی
رابه این خوشبوییها معطر سازند خوشبوییها اینست
کل چنبه کل سون زرد معطر سازد و در سون کیتکی

دالِ نخود را که تخته داشته اند بنهند و بریسمان

بپیچند و اندک دتهاره بدهند و گل سرخ و گل سیوتی

و گلاب در آن اندازند یا گل ترنج یا گل نارنج

یا گل نارنگی بیندازند و اگر خواهند چندین جنسها

را علاحده علاحده بپزند نوعی دیگر پهت مُنك

مُنك درست را تخته در کره جامه ببندد و گلهای هر جنسی

در یك جامه بگسترند و بالاء آن کره پهت را

بنهند و جامه گل را بالای آن کره بندد و در دیگی

آب انداخته و کره نهاده سرپوش نهند و چون بوی گلها

پهت را در خورده باشد بعده آنرا برگیرند و بالای آن

گلاب

گلاب کافور انداخته بخورند نوعی دیگر ترتیب
ساگ ساگ سبز را در دیگ اندازند و در میان آن هینگ
نمک روغن انداخته بپزند چون پخته باشد برگ تلسی
برگ ریحان برگ تازهٔ درخت انبه برگ لیمو تازه برگ ترنج
تازه بوده هر یک را جدا جدا دسته ببندد و این
دستها را بالای ساگ نهد و این دستها ساگ را در صحن
کشد و پیش آرد بعده دستها را بیرون آورد
و ساگ بخورد نوعی دیگر ترتیب متهه ماست
نبات شکر تری شکر الاچی قرنفل تج
پترج جاپهل جاپتری سوندهی فلفل سونف کافور

مشك یکجا آمیخته صاف کرده بگیرند متهه

خوب شود نوعی دیگر ترتیب پیچهه منك

را در خزف بریان کنند بعده در دیك اندازند

آب بینداز ند و نمك و آب ادرك و آب ترنج بینداز

و چون خوب تخته باشد فرو آرند و بخور هنك بدهند

نوعی دیگر پیچهه برنج بریان کرده منك

بریان کرده در آب بسیار انداخته بجوشاند و

طبرزد بیندازد و سه چهار آمله نیز بیندازد چون خوب

تخته باشد بخور هنك و میتهی بدهد نوعی دیگر

پیچهه شالی بریان کرده باریك آس کنند و در آب

۳۸

دوغ ترش بیندازند و نمک طبرزد بیندازند چون خوب
پخته باشد زیره بریان کرده آس کرده بیندازد
یکنوع همین جنس بپزند و یک نوع در آب شیرین انداخته
بپزد نوعی دیگر ترتیب شوربا خواه گوشت باشد
یا تیتر یا بتیر در آب صاف اندازد و در میان آن هنگ
زیره کشنیز نمک انداخته بپزد چون پخته شود آب
ترنج بیندازد فرو آرد بخور هنگ دهد نوعی دیگر
شوربا گوشت هلد زیره میستهی الایچی قرنفل نمک هنگ
انداخته بجوشاند بپزد چون خوب پخته باشد شوربا
صاف کرده بگیرد بعده الایچی قرنفل هنگ زیره

میتهی نمک هر همه را یکجا آمیخته بخورد هد نوعی دیگر

شوربا گوشت را با زعفران آمیخته در روغن بگهار

داده بیندازد و الایچی و قرنفل کشنیز سونف نمک

در آب انداخته بپزد چون خوب پخته باشد قدری

فلفل و آب ترنج بیندازد و گلاب بزند فرو آرد

٣٩ 36

نوعی دیگر ترتیب گوشت جوشانیده

آب بسیار در دیگ انداز و برگ ترنج یا والا یا برگ انبه

راد تهاره بدهد و بالای آن پر کالهاء گوشت بنهد یا

مرغ یا کبوتر یا تیتر یا بتیر هر کدام که خواهد

آنرا بنهد و آنرا هینگ زیره میتهی قرنفل هلد الایچی نمک

یکجا آمیخته بمالد و بالا پیاز انداز و سر دیگ بپوشاند

و به آرد خمیر مهر کند چنانکه بخار بیرون

نیاید چون خوب پخته باشد فرو آرد و حوائجات که

مالیده است پاک کرده دور کند بعده زعفران

گلاب عنبر اشهب یک رتی کافور یک رتی

مشك هر همه را یکجا آمیخته بدان گوشت بمالند

و در همان دیگ تهاره نهاده بپوشانند نگاه دارد وقت

طعام پیش بردن قدری روغن خوشبوی بر آن

مالیده پیش برد و اندکی بغیر روغن پیش ببرد

نوعی دیگر ترتیب سنبوسه از گوشت آهو

قیمه باریک کرده بیارند و روغن را بگهار هنگ

و میتهی بدهد و قیمه را بزعفران آمیخته در روغن

اندازد بعده هنگ نمک زیره میتهی بریان کند

و الایچی قرنفل کشنیز و یک رتی کافور و یک

رتی مشک در قیمه انداخته نیک ببرد و مقدار نیمه

قیمه

۴۵ 37

بجهل

قیمه قیمهٔ پیاز و ربع آن قیمه زنجبیل در گوشت

اندازد چون خوب پخته باشد گلاب بزنند و

فروآرد و سنبوسه پر کند و بچوب سنبوسه را

سوراخ کند و در روغن خوشبوی برشته

کند و نرم فروآرد و بهمین نوع سنبوسهٔ هر

گوشت که خواهند میشود نوعی دیگر

ترتیب چونکه گوشت قیمه سخت باریک بیارد

و در میان آن زعفران یا هلد والایچی قرنفل کشنیز

فلفل نمک آب لیمو کافور مشک پیاز ادرک هر همه یکجا

بیامیزد چون روغن گرم شود بکهارهنک بدهد

بعده قیمه را در آن اندازد بعده عنبر اشهب و گلاب را

چاشنی داده فرو آرد بعده آرد را خمیر کرده دو عدد

نان بسازد و در میان آن این قیمه را انداخته نان بالای

کریله ببرد و بگدازد تا نیک پخته گردد

و چون پخته باشد فرو آرد و در میان روغن خوشبوی

کافور مشک گلاب بیندازد و نان مذکور را

چونکه کرده این روغن را بالای آن نان

بیندازد **نوعی دیگر ترتیب کهیس** برنج را خوب

بشورد و بالای سل آس کند و آرد را بجامه بیزد

بعده دوغ و نمک و زنجبیل باریک بریده و زیره بریان کرده

و آن

بماند این را آنبل گویند یا بدوغ بخورند یا با شیر
بخورند یا با آب بخورند نوعی دیگر کهیس بستانند
آرد برنج باریك و با آب و آب لیمو یا کانجی و نبات
مقداری که شیرین نشود بپزد چون پخته باشد
فرو آرد نوعی دیگر کهیس از تمر هندی آرد
انبل
برنج در آب تمر هندی بپزد فرو آرد نوعی دیگر
ترتیب آنبلوانی آرد برنج و نبات و آب تمر هندی یکجا
کرده بپزد چون پخته باشد فرو آرد کافور
گلاب بیندازد نوعی دیگر کهیس
کهیلور کند که میباشد کهیلور آن بیارند

وخوب بتراشند وتنك تنك ببرند ودر آفتاب خشك

كنند بعده باريك آس كنند در آسيا وآرد

آن بگيرند بعده دو حصه كاچي واگر كاچي

نباشد دوغ بيندازد واندك نبات بيندازد و آرد

كهلور انداخته كهيس ببرند چون پخته باشد

فرو آرد سرد كند وبا شير سرد يا دوغ سرد بخورند

وكهيلور خشك كرده در روغن برشته بخورند

نوعي ديگر تتيمه دوغ در دوغ ترش نمك

بيندازد وهنك لاچي قرنفل زيره ميتهي تيل بينداز

يكجا كند ودو وصله خزف گرم كند

بالاي

بالای یک تهیکری قدری از همین حوایج بنهد
و تهیکری دوم بالای آن بنهد و بالای هر دو دیک
را بنهد و بخور دهد پنج شش نوبت بخور بدهد بعده
دوغ را در آن دیک اندازد این دوغ دون سنجان را
جنس است نوعی دیکر ترتیب دوغ دوغ نمک
آب ترنج آب ادرک و هنک در تیل برشته آس کرده
بیندازد نوعی دیکر دوغ نمک زیره بریان کرده
بخور هنک بدهد نوعی دیکر دوغ ترش شده را
در دوغ تازه اندازد نوعی دیکر دوغ در دوغ
مولی الایچی قرنفل بیندازد و نمک بیندازد نوعی

دیگر دوغ در دوغ مولی نمک رایی آب لیمو بیندازد

و بخور هنک بدهد نوعی دیگر ترتیب متهه

در میان ماست نبات کافور مشک گلاب بیندازد

و بوی گل معطر سازد نوعی دیگر ترتیب

کرنبه ماست نمک هنک در تیل برشته و بهات

نوعی دیگر متهه در ماست نیم برهم زده

گلاب کافور الاچی قرنفل برگ ترنج بیندازد

و موتهه و والاء سفید بیندازد یا ساده بدارد نوعی

دیگر ترتیب دهیر دوی ماست را نمک

انداخته جامه بیز کند و بسیار سیر آس کرده

درو

درو اندازد و سیاه دانه بریان کرده نیز بیندازد و
بالای آن برگ پیاز سبز بریده بسیار بیندازد نوعی دیگر
ترتیب کانجی غیاثشاهی تمر هندی را خوب شسته
در آب صاف اندازد چون نرم شده باشد بدست بمالد
و صاف کرده آب ترش او بگیرد و در آن نمک
بیندازد و بخور عود بدهد و بگلهای هر جنسی
معطر سازد و گلاب و کافور و مشک بیندازد نوعی
دیگر ترتیب کانجی دو سنجان کانجی سخت
ترش صاف را نمک بیندازد و رایی نیم کوفته کند
و پوست آن دور کند بعده میتهی و کنجد شیرین

یکجا آمیخته کند و دو پر کاله خزف گرم کند

بالای یکی این حویج بنهد و دوم را بالای آن نهاده

دیک را چهار پنج کرت بخور دهد بعده کابچی را

در دیک انداز د نوعی

دیگر

ترتیب

شت

آب

لیمو نبات فلفل یکجا آمیخته صاف کرده بستاند

و بخور عود بدهد و بوی گل معطّر سازد و کلاب

وکافور

و کافور و مشك بینداز د نوعی دیگر

ترتیب بغراء غیاثشاهی ازتنکه زرد قدیمی

بزرگتر بغرا ببرد در آب بجوشاند و همچون

پالوده لرزنده شود بیرون آرد بعده چلغوزه بادام

پسته مویز یکجا آش کند با آب بغرا و در آن

بغرا انداز د چنانکه لذیذ شود بعده سرکه

صاف کرده بینداز د و چاشنی سیر بدهد

و اگر نوع دیگر خواهند در متهه ماشت

یا در آب تمر هندی یا آب لیمو یا آب ترنج یا ترشی

هر میوه که خواهند بیندازند یا زعفران مشك

کافور در آب حل کنند و در آن بغرا بیندازد

ببزند
بعده لنواسار از گوشت چکتله خوب

مغز
و در بغرا اندازد و در جای آن بغرا اگر خواهند

کاک بیندازند یا نارنک پاره کرده

بیندازد یا منك در روغن پخته بیندازد یا آب

زد
صاف ازان دوغ جغر چکر جوشانیده بیندا

آنرا کرنکت خوانند این نوع هزار جنس میشود

جدا جدا نوعی دیکر ترتیب تخی آن مقدار ب

که تخی باشد نیمه از پیاز و نیمه پیاز ادرك

قیمه کنند و از برك پودنه نیز مقدار دو درم

قیمه کنند بعده یکجا بیامیزد و بالای آن زعفران
با گلاب بپاشد و آب لیمو بیفشارد و قدری
روغن خوشبوی در او اندازد پس یکجنس شود
و اگر بخور هنک دهد پس یکجنس باشد و اگر
بخور تیل بدهد یک جنس شود یا بخور عود تیلیه یا
بخور کافور یا بخور عنبر اشهب یا برگ تنبول سوخته
دود دهد یا برگ ترنج را بوی دهد یا بخور غالیه دهد
یا از گل موگره بوی دهد یا بوی
کیهونله بدهد نوعی دیگر ترتیب
نان پولی برشتن در روغن برگ تلسی اندازد کافور

اندا خته کرم کند در میان آن نان پولی را
پاره پاره کرده بیندازد تا برشته شود بعده
گلاب بزند و عسل اندازد و اگر آب
تمر هندی اندازد پس جنسی شود و اگر آب
لیمو اندازد جنسی باشد و اگر باب شکری
اندازد جنسی شود و باب هر میوه که بیا میزند
یک جنسی باشد نوعی دیگر ترتیب بهات
در کانجی یا در دوغ یا در آب شکر یا در آب
خوشبویی یا در آب دنکره برنج را شسته
بهات بپزند و سرد کنند بعده کنجد دانه بریان

کرده

43

۴۷ چهل هفت

کرده و نخود برشته و برنج برشته زیره برشته
و میستهی الایچی قرنفل آب لیمو نمک روغن هنگ که
در روغن برشته باشند هر همه را یکجا بیامیزد
و اگر نوع دیگر خواهد که هر جنسی
علاحده شود پس اگر در برنج متهه باسین
بیندازد یکجنس شود و اگر بورانی بادنجان
بیندازند یکجنس شود و اگر پاپر و روغن و
آچار لیمو بیندازند پس جنسی شود اینها همه در برنج
بهات بیندازند و ادرک بیندازد و در همین بهات
نمک و روغن بیامیزند جنسی دیگر شود و اگر

منك و روغن و بهات و بره بيندازند جنسي شود و اكر

شوربا و بري و كوشت و ليمو در بهات بيا ميزند

يك جنس شود و اكر بوره يخني بهات و روغن يكجا

كنند پس جنسيي شود و اكر شهد و روغن و

بهات بيا ميزند يكجنسي شود و اكر آب ترنج و دنكره

و آب ليمو و نارنكي و آب سدا پهل و آب قمرك از ينها

هر كدام كه در بهات بيندازد هر يك يكجنس شود

و اكر نبات و بهات و روغن و كافور يكجا بيا ميزد

يكجنس شود و اكر بهات و دوغ و ادرك و پياز و آب

ليمو و نمك بيندازد يكجنس شود و اكر بهات نبات مشك

كلاب

۳۸۱
44
چهل و هشت

گلاب کافور بینداز ند جنسی شود و اگر بهات
یک سیر و شهد شش تولچه روغن چهار تولچه یکجا بیامیزد
پس یکجنس شود و اگر بهات را در روغن برشته کند
و گلاب بزند و کافور انداخته فرو آرد جنسی
شود و اگر بهات و موتهه و و الاء سفید الایچی
قرنفل یکجا کند یکجنسی شود و اگر بهات و
برهٔ منک و کرهی و روغن یکجا کند یکجنسی شود
و اگر بهات و دو بکوری بینداز د یکجنس شود و اگر
شیرهٔ نیشکر و خوشبویی بینداز ند یکجنسی شود
و اگر شیرهٔ خرما و خوشبویی بینداز ند جنسی شود

واکر بادام آش کرده و جلغوزه آش کرده یا

پسته آش کرده یا کردگان آش کرده یا

کرهری آش کرده و یا تخم نیلوفر آش کرده اینها

همه با خوشبویی

آمیخته

بیندازند

چنسها

شود

نوعی دیکر ترتیب بهات دربهات زیره بریان

کرده آش کرده بیندازند و شوربا و روغن بیندازند

نوعی دیکر

نوعی دیگر ترتیب شربت آب و نبات هنك و
تیل را بخورد دهد و زعفران بیندازد و نبات کمتر
اندازد نوعی دیگر بهات زرت زرت را
خوب بکوبند چنانکه نه بسیار خرد شود و نه
بسیار درشت باشد آنچنان بستانند و در آب و دوغ
انداخته بشورد و چون در اداهرن تخته باشد بپالایند
و آب او جدا کنند و بهات جدا بگیرند و سرد
کنند و آب لیمو یا آب ترنج و نمك و برابر بهات
ادرك باریك ببرد و یکجا بیامیزد نوعی دیگر
بهات از زرت یا از برنج بهات بپزد و سرد کند بعده

آب لیمو یا آب تمر هندی یا کروندە جوشانیده
یا کیری جوشانیده و نمک در میان هر کدام
که خواهد بیندازد و در تیل شیرین هنگ
بسوزاند و بآن تیل دست بیالاید و برنج را باهم
بیامیزد نوعی دیگر ترتیب بهات رایی
آب لیمو نمک هنگ در تیل برشته زیره برشته میتهی
برشته یکجا بیامیزد و در بهات اندازد نوعی دیگر
ترتیب بهات شیره انبه کافور مشک گلاب
در روغن خوشبو بگهار کافور بدهد و در میان
آن بهات بیندازد پخته باشد فرو آرد و در میان همین

اگر خواهی

اگر جامن پخته بیندازند جنسی دیگر شود
و بهمین نوع از ازگرونده میشود و بهمین نوع
از ازکتهل نیز میشود نوعی دیگر ترتیب
بهات پنج انبرت شیر جوشانیده را باز بجوشانند ماست
شهد روغن خوشبوی نبات کافور انداخته بخورد
نوعی دیگر تماج از آرد میده تماج ببرد و
بجوشانند بعده در ماست شیرین کافور مشک
گلاب نبات الایچی قرنفل سه چهار عدد با برنگ
جاپتری چهر چهریله هر همه را یکجا باریک آس کرده
بیندازد نوعی دیگر ترتیب پولانی تمر هندی

الاچی قرنفل جایتری نبات مشك كافور اندكی كلاب

بینداز و روغن خوشبوی بینداز نوعی دیگر

ترتیب بغرا آرد خشک که بغرا بریده در آب

بجوشاند بغرا بیرون کشد و آب آن بگیرد و

در آن آب سرکه بینداز بادام آس کرده

جلغوزه سیر نمك آنچنان بینداز که لذیذ شود

بعده قیمه در روغن خوشبوی پخته در آن انداز

و اندك نبات بینداز شربت کند و در میان آن

اینها همه بینداز نوع دیگر شربت آب میوها

هر جنسی بگیرد نبات اندك بینداز در بعضی

کافور

بیندازد و در بعضی ادرك پیاز فلفل اندازد آن مقدار
جنس شود و بخور هر جنسی بدهد و بهمین ترتیب دوغ
راست کند و بهمین ترتیب رایبی راست کند
و بهمین ترتیب آب راست کند و بهمین ترتیب هرچه خواهد
ب راست کند نوعی دیگر ترتیب نان
آن مقدار که حبوب هست آن قدر جنس نان
ببرد در بعضی نبات اندازد و در بعضی ترشیهاء میوه
بیندازد در بعضی میوها اندازد پس این قدر جنس را
نان شود و در بعضی آردها ترشی غوره انداخته نان
ببرد در بعضی آب میوهاء ترش اندازد نوعی دیگر

بهات بهات پختند را چهار رتی عنبر اشهب و یک رتی
کافور در گلاب حل کرده بمالند و روغن که
در آن گوشت برشته باشند قدری از آن روغن
درین بهات اندازد دیگر برنج را و کهچری را
و تهولی را و کهندیی را و شربت را و سرد را
و دوغ را هر کدام را که خواهند معطر کنند بهمین
نوع معطر سازند نوعی دیگر ترتیب معطر کردن
طعامها چهار رتی گلاب ده رتی گل سیوتی
بیست رتی الاچی یک رتی قرنفل چهار رتی جایتری
هر همه را آس کرده در طعامی که خواهند

بیندازد

بیندازد نوعی دیگر تعطیر طعامها شیرهٔ انبه ربع
سیر کافور دو ماسه زعفران سه درم آش کرده
در طعام هر جنس بیندازند عجایب شود نوعی دیگر
تعطیر طعامها بنهٔ برگ تنبول که آنرا دینت
گویند و کافور و الایچی و قرنفل آش کرده
در طعامها اندازند عجایب شود نوعی دیگر
تعطیر طعام برگ تلسی و کافور آش کرده
در هر طعام که بیندازند خوب شود نوعی
دیگر پودنه و سیر که آش کرده در
طعامها اندازند خوب شود نوعی دیگر

چو و نبات در همه طعامها که میشوند و در برگ

تنبول و مکهه باس بیندازند خوب شود نوعی

دیگر تعطیر هنگ بسیار در تیل برشته کند

و آس کرده در طعامها اندازد و آن تیل را بهر

طعام خواه ساگ یا کرهی یا دوغ یا متهه که

چاشنی دهد خوب شود نوعی دیگر تعطیر

سیب و گلاب یکجا کرده بخور دهد بخور

عنبر اشهب نیز بدهند و اندک مشک بر آن پاشند

و پوست نیشکر را بهر طعام که خواهند بخورد دهند

خوب شود نوعی دیگر بخورات هر جنسی بخور

شکوتری

شکر تری و بخور نبات و بخور شکر
و بخور لاکهه و بخور مصطکی و بخور غالیه
و بخور تیل چنپه و بخور تیل موکره و بخور
تیل چنبیلی و بخور صندل و بخور رال و بخور
آب کافور و بخور صمغ ابنه و بخور کهربا
و بخور زعفران و بخور کنجد دانه و میتهی
و نخود و زیره و سونف و کشنیز و برگ
ترنج را تعطیر و برگ لیمو تعطیر را و بخور برگ هلد
این همه بخورها جدا جدا اند هر طعام را که خواهند
یا هر شربت یا هر دوغ یا آب یا هر گوشت یا هر سبزی

راکه خواهند بخورد دهند و معطّر کنند نوعی

دیگر رابری دوغ خام شالِ برِشته زرّت

برِشته نخود برِشته عدس برِشته تور برِشته کنندم

جو منک بتله اینها همه رابرِشته و آس کرده

جدا جدا در دوغ بیندازد و نیک معطّر کند

در بعضی نمک بیندازد و بعضی بی نمک بدارد

نوعی دیگر دوغ اَستهٔ جامن استهٔ انبه استهٔ

کتهل بریاز کند و آس کرده در دوغ

بیندازد و بهمین اشتها بخورد دهد نوعی دیگر

ترتیب کوشت کوشت رانیک بجوشاند بیرون

آ

آرد و خشک کند و بسیخ چوب بزند زعفران
عنبر اشهب گلاب یکجا آمیخته بر گوشت مالد
در دیگ کند و برنج بپیندازد ادرک پیاز نمک
انداخته بپزد و با شوربا خوب فرو آرد نوعی دیگر
گوشت گوشت بریده بغیر هلد با نمک و ادرک
و پیاز و دوغ انداخته بپزد و هنگ انداخته در
روغن بکهارد هلد الاچی قرنفل لیمو فلفل
انداخته فرو آرد نوعی دیگر گوشت پهلوها
گوسپند استخوانهای سر سینه و چربی و
استخوان شانه با همه حوائجها انداخته بیامیزد هلد

وآرد برنج انداخته زرد رنگ بسازد شیره انبه آنچنان شوربا

کند و حوائجات همه بیندازد نوعی دیگر

ترتیب نان مرصع مروارید از منگ راست کند

و بجوشانند و در قیمه گوشت انداخته کوفته

کوچک کوچک راست کند و بپزد مویز

کشمش بادام جلغوزه پسته چارولی مقشر

نارگیل مقشر کافور مشک گلاب عنبر اشهب

انداخته بپزد و در روغن آنرا برشته کند الاچی

قرنفل بیندازد نوعی دیگر ترتیب تخم خربزه بزرگ

تخم خربزه با تخم خیار مقشر کرده آس کند و در

میانِ آن قدری آرد بیندازد و در میانِ روغن بری کرده

بریان کند و بالای آن نبات کافور کلاب

بیندازد نوعی دیگر ترتیب کرهی انبه کیری

و دوغ و نمک و فلفل

زیره میتهی

هنک

الاتچی

قرنفل

هر همه را یکجا کرده بپزد و بخور هنک بدهد

و بهمین ترتیب از کیتهه کند و بهمین ترتیب

از هرچه خواهد کرهی راست کند نوعی دیکر

کرهی شکرتری انداخته کرهی بپزد

و بخور هنك بدهد نوعی دیکر ترتیب بهت

منك را در روغن برشته کند بعده نمك و آب

و هنك و آب ادرك آب لیمو آب پیاز انداخته

فرو آرد چون پخته باشد و بخور خوب بدهد نوعی

دیکر ترتیب کهچری کهچری را در روغن

برشته کند یا در روغن بادام بریان کند یا

در مسکه برشته کند و آب انداخته

و نمك بپزد و هنك بریان کرده بسیار اندازد

بعد

52

بعده هر جنسی آچال و یا پرکرد برکرد صحن نهد
وادرك پیاز بریده بنهد نوعی دیگر کهچریی
کهچری را در دوغ یا در کانجی یا در آب لیمو یا
در آب تمر هندی یا در آب ترنج یا در آب خوشبویی
یا در آب پودنه یا در آب والا یا در آب دنکره
یا در آب کتهل یا در آب بدهل یا در آب
کافور یا در آب مشك ازین آبها هر کدام که
خواهد بریخ و منك درو ترکند بعده در روغن
برشته کند کهچری بپزد آچال یا پرکرد
برکرد صحن بنهد نوعی دیگر تهولی

در دوغ تهولی بیندازد و نمک و وصلهای پیاز اندازد

زیره انداخته بپزد و در کرهی نیز تهولی انداخته

بپزد و همچنین در شوربا تهولی انداخته بپزد و در کانجی

نیز زیره انداخته و تهولی و نمک انداخته بپزد نوعی

دیگر ترتیب پچهه پچهه را در دیگ اندازد

و قدری تلسی و ریحان و برگ تازه ترنج و لیمو دسته بسته

در و اندازد فرو آرد نوعی دیگر ترتیب هریسه ب

هریسه را طریق پچهه نرم اندام بپزد چنانکه

بکفچه توان خورد یا از گوشت تیتر یا

از گوشت بتیر یا از گوشت حلواز بپزد نوعی دیگر

ترتیب روده رودهٔ کوسپند پاك بشویند و در میان
آن حوایج هر جنسی در قیمه انداخته پر کنند و در
دتهاره بجوشانند و در روغن بریان کنند نوعی
دیکر ترتیب سیخ کوشت را نمك و پیاز و هلد
آمیخته با تمام حوایج بجوشانند بعده قطعه قطعه ببرد
و پاك کند بعده یك قطعه کوشت و یك وصله
پیاز در سیخ کشند و روغن و آزموده و آب لیمو
عنبر اشهب کلاب نمك بالای آن تمالند و سیك بریان
کنند چون نرم پخته باشد در نان تنك پیچند
و پیش آرند نوعی دیکر نان زردت نان زردت

بپزند و سرد کرده ریزه کنند و گلاب بزنند

بعده شهد و روغن خوشبوی یا روغنی که در آن

گوشت برشته باشند در آن بیندازند نوعی

دیگر تهومرهٔ زرت تهومرهٔ زرت بپزد

و در روغن بریان کنند بعده شهد و الاچی

کافور در آن انداخته پیش برند نوعی دیگر

کهیچرهٔ گندم نیز بهمان طریق بپزد

و بهات برنج نیز بهمین طریق بپزد نوعی دیگر

ترتیب کهیر از کنگنین کهیر کنگنین

بپزد و بالای آن خشخاش بسیار اندازد بعده شهد

و روغن

۵۹

۵۴

پنجاه و نه

و روغن خوشبوی بر آن ریزد شهد بیشتر انداز د روغن

کمتر انداز د نوعی دیگر ترتیب مهیری

در میان دوغ مهیری بپزد بعده در روغن بریان کند

و اگر خواهد

تیز کند

و اگر

خواهد

ترش کند

و اگر خواهند شیرین کند هر نوع که خوش

آید همان کند نوعی دیگر ترتیب سهالی

در خمیر مایه کاك تج پتح الاتجی کافور
عنبر اشهب پیاز یکجا آمیخته سهالی برشته کند
نوعی دیگر ترتیب دیك باغی آن سفید اکر سبزی
هست و بادنجان و کندوری و مجدبه و چچینده
و حبحب و سوا و کجری و کدو و توری همه
را یکجا کرده ببرد و بخور روغن بدهد و هینك
در تیل برشته آس کرده بینداز و نمك انداز
نوعی دیگر ترتیب شربت یك کاسه آب دو درم
شکر یکجا کند و این شربت را در آب هر
میوه که بیندازند آن قدر شربت شوند نوعی

دیگر ترتیب کرهی در میان کرهی برگ
کیوره بسیار بیندازد چون خوب معطر شده باشد
پس عود تیلیه و تکری و ملاگرا و گلاب
بیامیزد و بخور عود بدهد و خارهای کیوره دور کند
نوعی دیگر کرهی گلهای هر جنسی
در میان کرهی انداخته بجوشانند کافور الاچی
مشک قرنفل در آن قدری اندازد نوعی دیگر
نان زرت تنک نرم بالای آن پلیتهن بمالند و زیر آن
نیز بمالند و بپزند چنانچه سخت نشود بلکه شکنده
باشد بعده آنرا با شهد و روغن بخورند نوعی دیگر

ترتیب پهت تور و نخود یکجا کرده بپزند شوربا کرده
نرم با حوایج و خوشبویی بعده این پورز را در نان دو
پری یعنی دو تو از آرد گندم سونفا انداخته
بپزند و در آن نان این پورز را بیندازند و خواه در روغن
برشته کنند یا بر کریله بپزند و با روغن که
در آن تخنی برشته باشند آن نان بخورند نوعی دیگر
نان زره سفید صاف بپزند و مهرهاء مشک بر او بزنند
نوعی دیگر نان تنک پهن کرده کنجد دانه
بر او افشانند یا خشخاش یا سیاه دانه یا مویز یا کردکان
یا بادام بجای بالوان آرد این میوه‌ها را بر آن نان مالند

و بزم

ونزم یا آرد چاولی یا آرد نخود برشته مالیده نان بپزند
نوعی دیگر کرهی مغز کاک در دوغ بیندازد
بجوشانند بعده ماست شهد روغن بیندازد خوب شود
نوعی دیگر شربت آب پیاز آب ادرک بیامیزد
وآنرا بهنك بریان کرده بخورد دهد نوعی دیگر
شربت جلغوزه یا کردگانرا آس کرده شیره
بستانند وبا تهولی ساده ویا بهات ساده بخورند نوعی
دیگر شوربا هلد خام در روغن برشته کند
وبرنج شال برشته را آرد بستانند در آب وهلد بیامیزد
زعفران فلفل آس کرده بیندازد اگر خواهد

شیرین کند واکر خواهد تیز کند و بابهات

ساده نخورد نوعی دیکر ترتیب پورن دال

نخود تر کرده بجوشاند و جلغوزه خشك و

کرد کاز و فلفل و آب پیاز لیمو یکجا آش کرده

بیامیزد این را غیاثشاهی پورن کویند نوعی

دیکر شربت سرکه عسل بیامیزد چون

مزه خوب پیدا کند بعد از آن وصلهای کاك

در آن کند نوعی دیکر اوانه آچار کیری

را بارایی و نمك آمیخته تو بر تو نهاده دوازده روز در

آفتاب بدارد بعده در تیل سرسون بالاء آن بیندازد خوب شود

نوعی دیکر نان

بیندازد گوشت را با نمک و گشنیز و سالک
میتهی آس کند برک تنبول نیز آس کند
قرنفل الایچی آس کرده با هم بیامیزد نوعی
دیگر کرهی همراه بهات و برنج اگر
خواهد که بپزد این نوع بپزد و در میان آن
قطعهای ماست و قیماغ ماست یعنی ملایی و تهومره
زرت و بهات را بسهوک هر همه را بالا بیندازد نوعی
دیگر شربت شیره انبه آب کیری شکر تری
الایچی قرنفل مشک آس کرده یکجا بیامیزد
نوعی دیگر دوغ کیری را در دوغ

آش کرده شکر تری بالای آن بیندازد یا نمک اندازد
نوعی دیگر شربت کیری را با شکر یکجا
[یچی]
کرده آش کنند و آب آن بستانند بعده الا
کافور قرنفل در آن اندازد نوعی دیگر
شربت ادرک شکر آش کرده آب آن
صاف کرده بگیرد الایچی قرنفل در آن اندازد و آب
مولی و آب ادرک صاف کرده بگیرد و آن
الایچی و قرنفل و اندکی نمک در آن اندازد
نوعی دیگر ترتیب نان مسکه روغن نمک
آرد سونف یکجا آمیخته نان بپزد نوعی دیگر

٦٤
شصت چهار
58

دوغ لیموء نمکی در دوغ انداخته آش کند صاف
کرده بگیرد یا وصلهٔ لیمو اندازد نمک بیندازد
و بخور هنك و زیره بدهد نوعی دیگر کهچری
کهچری در روغن اندازد نمك اندازد و بخور هنك و
زیره بدهد و برشته کند کهچری بپزد و آب لیمو
نمکی و آب آچار ادرك و آب آچار بسنوته اینها همه
بالای کهچری بیندازد و بالای بهات دوغ و وصلهای
پیاز و نمك بیندازد نوعی دیگر کوشت کوشت
رانیك بپزد شوربا از آب جدا شود و کوشت علاحده
شود و روغن علاحده شود اینچنین بپزد بادنجان و کدو

انداخته بپزد نوعی دیگر ترتیب بهرت پیاز بسیار را
نخود بسیار دهد و نان آنکاکر را بروغن چرب کند
یا گوشت تنک چکتله را بروغن چرب کند
نوعی دیگر بهت منک بسیار در گوشت و دال
نخود انداخته و پیاز بینداز د بپزد نوعی دیگر
ترتیب نان نانرا با روغن خوشبوی با روغن که در
گوشت برشته باشند چرب کند نوعی دیگر
ترتیب گله کلهٔ گوسپند طریق خراسان بپزد
بعده منک را بپزد طریق کراس و پاچهٔ گوسپند بپزد
در برنج انداخته خوب شود نوعی دیگر خمیر مایه

یا بالای کریله بخنه د تهاره دهد نوعی دیگر
نان روه سفید گلاب نمک اندک چاشنی کافور دهد
نان بپزد صاف غیاثشاهی نان کافوری شود نوعی
دیگر کرهی آرد برنج دوغ نمک هلد زعفران
انداخته کرهی بپزد کافور بیندازد زرین کرهی
غیاثشاهی شود نوعی دیگر کهچری مشک و گلاب
در کهچری بیندازند نوعی دیگر کرهی عنبر اشهب
و گلاب انداخته کرهی بپزد این را کرهی
عنبری گویند نوعی دیگر ترتیب سیخ ایسیخ خوب
بپزد بعده در میان روغن برشته کنند و نمک و اجواین

انداخته بپزد وسرکه وشکرتری وشوربا بیندازد

وبالای آن چکتله لنواش اندازد وربع سیر

بادام آس کرده وکردکان وجلغوزه

وپسته مویز اینها همه پور رز کنند واندك

شکرتری اندازد ونازد وپری بپزد بالای

کریله وآنرا نیز کلاب بزنند نوعی دیکر

ترتیب آب وصلهای خزف نو بسیار در آتش کرم کنند

ودر آب اندازد چون آب خوشبو شود پس کلاب

وشکرتری در آن بیندازد واکر جنس دیکر خواهد

پس هنك ونمك بیندازد پس آب جنس دیکر شود

تهولی یا

تهولی یا بهات و دال یا زردت پیاز بسیار انداخته در روغن
برشته کند بعده آب و نمک انداخته بپزد و نخود
تیل بدهد و هفت برگ تنبول شش درم الاچی یک درم
قرنفل هلد زعفران گوشت را مالیده پیاز انداخته
بگهار دهد آب و برنج انداخته روغن دال نخود
باشوربا فرو آرد نوعی دیگر گوشت سیر سه درم
پیاز نیم سیر گوشت یک دیگ موازنه یک درم هنگ
ربع سیر ادرک نیم سیر دال نخود در روغن بگهار دهد
آب انداخته بپزد نوعی دیگر گوشت گوشت را
هنگ و دوغ بمالد پیاز ادرک انداخته در تیل بگهار دهد

آب انداخته شوربا کند یا لنواس بدارد نمک و

آب لیمو فلفل بیندازد نوعی دیگر گوشت

گوشت را ادرک پیاز سیر انبه بادنجان آرد برنج

میتهی نمک آمیخته در تیل سرسوز بپزد شوربا کند یا

لنواس بدارد نوعی دیگر برنج در روغن بادام

زعفران آمیخته برنج بریان کند آب انداخته

برنج بپزد نمک فلفل قرنفل اندازد نوعی دیگر

برنج ربع سیر بادام ربع سیر مویز کردگان

جلغوزه از هر یک ربع سیر برنج پنج سیر هلد نمک

ربع سیر قرنفل دو درم فلفل دو درم سندهی سه درم

با شوربا بیامیزد تج و روغن بسیار درو اندازد نوعی دیگر

شربت آب لیمو پنج درم هفت درم نبات دو سیر آب گلاب

برو بزنند نوعی دیگر شربت الایچی یکدرم

قرنفل یکدرم نبات پنج درم دو سیر آب

نوعی دیگر دوغ آب دوغ ترش بگیرد

نمک و هنگ بیندازد بخورد تیل یا هنگ بدهد نوعی

دیگر بهات در شربت گلشکر بهات

را ترسازد و گلاب برو افشانند نوعی دیگر بهات

انجیر جنگلی یعنی کولر را آس کرده شربت

کنند دو درم شکر تری درو انداخته بهات را

با او بیامیزد نوعی دیگر گوشت پوست نارنگی

برگ تنبول آش کرده در گوشت مالد نوعی

دیگر گوشت اجوائن را آش کرده در

پرکالهای گوشت بمالد نوعی دیگر بهات

چکتلهٔ موز تخته برابر دو شکره زر ببرّد

موز ده عدد مویز دو سیر در آب آش کند

بعده این شربت در بهات بیامیزد نوعی دیگر

کرهی آرد برنج خشخاش بادام مویز آش کرده

در آب بجوشاند قدری روغن در آن انداز د

الایچی قرنفل انداخته فرو آرد نوعی دیگر بهات

بیرون

بیرچون یعنی کنار خشک را در آب انداخته

در بهات بیامیزد گلاب بیندازد نوعی دیگر بهات

نخود برشته کنجد دانهٔ برشته آس کرده در بهات

بیامیزد نوعی دیگر گندم جوشانیده یعنی

کهون گهنین چاولی یکسیر گندم یکسیر

برنج یکسیر قرنفل ربع سیر الاچی ربع سیر سوندهی

دو درم مویز ربع سیر در آب انداخته بپزد سه درم نبات

انداخته کهونکنین بپزد دوره روغن بدهد نوعی

دیگر نان نان را در گلشکر و روغن

مالیده بدارند بسیار روغن بیندازد نان بپزد کوبخهی

از پودنه ببرد سهالی در تیل رایی ببرد نوعی دیگر
سهالی سهالی در تیل سی سوز برشته کنند سیر پیاز
آس کرده آب آن بستانند و بالای سهالی بپاشد
نوعی دیگر سهالی در روغن برشته کنند گلاب
بر و بزنند و شربت از گولر و شهد راست کنند و با
سهالی بخورد نوعی دیگر شربت آب دنگره
و شیره انبه شربت کنند گلاب کافور بزنند نوعی
دیگر شربت آب دنگره و شهد را شربت کنند
کافور گلاب بیندازد نوعی دیگر
گرهی آب کل سیوتی بگیرد آرد برنج

آمیخته

آمیخته

اگر بیندازد پس جنسی علاحده شود و اگر نمک و

فلفل بیندازد پس جنسی دیگر شود و اگر ترشی اندازد

جنسی دیگر شود و تج پترج الایچی قرنفل اگر بیندازد

پس جنسی دیگر شود نوعی دیگر ترتیب

جهکله جهکلی از زرت یا از برنج بپزند اگر شیر

در آن اندازند جنسی دیگر شود و اگر ترشی

انداخته بپزد جنسی دیگر شود و اگر نمک و

فلفل بیندازد جنسی شود و اگر خوشبویی

انداخته بپزد جنسی شود نوعی دیگر در زره

شیر و آرد برنج شکر تری آمیخته با کافور قدری

بپزند شکرتری اندک بینداز زند نوعی دیگر

ترتیب تهولی تهولی را جهکلی شیر کنند قرنفل ب

بینداز زند شیرینی اندک بکنند نوعی دیگر ب

دبره بهات را با ملائی آس کنند و در شیر بجوشانند

شکرتری اندک بینداز زند و اگر آرد یا

آرد نخود برشته یا آرد سنگهاره یا آرد بادام دبره

خواهند بهمین ترتیب بپزند نوعی دیگر دبره

جلغوزه در میان آب آس کنند و در آب بهات

بپزند چارولی کردکان بادام ارکیل سنگهاره

کهری بهر نوعی که خواهند بپزند آن قدر

جلنس شود نوعی دیگر دررە دررە بپزند در آب
هر میوهٔ ترش که خواهند بپزند پس آن مقدار جلنسها
شود نوعی دیگر شربت آب میوها و آب جامن
آمیخته چاشنی کافور دهد بعده شربت را در
کاسهٔ چینی لاجوردی فغفوری کنند
و بهمین نوع اگر خواهد شربت کیری و از ان کروندە
و از پهالسه و از دنکره و از سدا پهل و از
کتهل و از بدهل بهر نوع که خواهد شربت
کند و شکرتری بیندازد و در بعضی کافور
تج پترج الاچی بیندازد نوعی دیگر نواله

در سپیدی تخم مرغ قدری آرد انداخته بمالد و در زردی
جدا انداخته بمالد بعده نجامهٔ تر کرده بالای کریله
گرم پوتی دهد نان پولی تنک ببرد بادام الاچی
نبات قرنفل گلاب انداخته پورن کند این
پورن را در نان تخم مرغ بپیچد و در روغن برشته سازد
و بالای آن گلاب بزند و بهمین طریق از کردگان
و از جلغوزه و از پسته نیز نواله راست کند نواله غیاثشاهی
بهمین ترتیب هر جنسی از آنچه بعد ازین یاد خواهیم کرد
در نان پولی بپیچیده نواله کند و شکر تری اندک
بیندازد و وصلهای دیگر کره و نبات گلاب الاچی

قرنفل

قرنفل انداخته در نار پوله پیچد کافور تر کند و
روغن برشته کند و در میان آن شیرینی و سوندهی
بیندازد پس این قدر جنس شود دیگر گل نیلوفر
گل سیوتی برگ پوئی برگ پندالوا برگ پهلک
برگ تورئی برگ چینج برگ مجدبه شاخ تازهٔ ترنج
شاخ نورستهٔ لیمو شاخ نورستهٔ تمر هندی شاخ نورسته
بر شاخ نورستهٔ پیپل شاخ نورستهٔ انبه شاخ نورستهٔ
جامن اینها را آرد نخود و آرد برنج مالیده در روغن
برشته کند و حونج بمالد و بالای آن گلاب و
کافور و الاچی بزنند اگر شیرینی اندازد

١

پس جنسی دیگر شود واگر نمک و ترسی
و فلفل اندازد پس جنسی دیگر شود واگر در نخود
روغن و تیل کاک بپزند یا در نخود زیره و میتهی نان
پولی بپزد یا قرصک کوچک بپزد آنرا بدهد نوعی
دیگر برنج از برنج خرجی برنج بپزند و با متهد
زیره بخورند نوعی دیگر سرد انه شیر را ب
جوشانیده سرد کند و در میانهٔ آن شیرهٔ انبه بیندازد
و خوشبویی نیز بیندازد نوعی دیگر روغن
موز را در روغن بیندازد یا خرما بیندازد بعده این
روغن را بجوشانند و صاف کرده بگیرد و اندک

سوندیهی

۷۳

سوندهی کند بعده این روغن را با طعام نخورند وآن
موز وخرما که در روغن بود آنرا بیرون آرد
ودر میان آن شکر تری انداخته شربت کند
نوعی دیگر
شربت نارکیل
را کوفته
در آب
شیرهٔ او
مانند شیر سفید صاف کرده بستانند ودر میان
آن شکر خواهند شیرینی بیندازد واگر خواهند

نیز اندا بیندازد بعده با بهات بخورند نوعی دیگر ترتیب

روغن در میان روغن سوندهی و کتهل اندا زد

بجوشاند و آنرا با طعامها بخورد نوعی دیگر شوربا

قیمه گوشت راست کند و در میان آن دال نخود

اندا خته شوربا بپزد سیر بسیار در وافکند ادرک

پیاز آب لیمو الاچی قرنفل فلفل زیره میتهی در آن اندازد

و بخور هنک بدهد نوعی دیگر سیخ سیخ خوب

برشته کند بعده ترب و پیاز باریک ببرد آب لیمو

آب ادرک نمک هنک زیره میتهی آزموده روغن همه را

یکجا کرده در سیخ مالد و بالای آتش بکردانند

چون

چون برشته شود در نان تنک کرم بپیچد و پیش آرد

نوعی دیگر تخنی مغز موز بجوشانند بعده باریک

ببرد و ادرک و پیاز و آب لیمو نمک زیره میتهی هنک بسیار

بخور بدهد تخنی کند نوعی دیگر آچار

در شیرهٔ لیمو پودنه و نمک بیندازد نوعی دیگر

شربت در شیرهٔ شکر تری آب لیمو بیندازد چاشنی

کافور بدهد نوعی دیگر شربت سرکه

پیاز پودنه یکجا آس کند الایچی کافور

بیندازد نوعی دیگر هی دوغ با آرد برنج آمیخته

بجوشانند فلفل نمک بیندازد و بالای خرف هنک

تیل انداخته بخور دهد نوعی دیگر پلیو گوشت

بستیر آش کرده در دوغ بپزند و در خزف هنک و تیل

انداخته بخور دهد پلیو بستیر باشد نوعی دیگر پلیو

کان کر را جوشانیده استه او دور کند و نیک

بشورد و با دوغ آش کند و دوغ را صاف کرده بستاند

بجوشاند پلیو کند و در بالای خزف هنک و تیل

بخور بدهد نوعی دیگر آچار بر بسیار کولر

پهیپهر جامن کرونده آمله خام کنار نخود

سبز نخود برشته خیار کوچک در میان زاینها ترشی

و تیزی و نمک انداخته آچار کند پس چندین

بادام ربع سیر نارکیل ربع سیر در آن اندازد نوعی

دیگر برنج برنج نیک بپزد در میان آن برگ

ترنج برگ لیمو برگ گرنه تلسی ریحان همه را

در برنج اندازد بپزد یا در کهچره انداخته بپزد

بعده برگها را بیرون آرد دور کند

والاچی قرنفل بیندازد نوعی دیگر متهه

در میان متهه شکر تری و سرکه و قرنفل والاچی

کافور مشک بیندازد و نارنگ پولی اشکسته

بیندازد و گوشت بیندازد بغراء هندی

باشد نوعی دیگر پورن آرد تخم نیلوفر

قرنفل کافور شکر تری آمیخته در روغن

برشته کند نوعی دیگر پالوده کوکو ب

پالوده از آرد نیلوفر راست کند الاچی و شکر تری

را شربت کند و در پالوده شربت اندازد نوعی

دیگر گوشت کوکو دانه کتهل ب

افشرده در گوشت اندازد کسوندی اندازد الاچی

قرنفل اندازد نوعی دیگر برنج بالای ترنج قرنفل ٤

فرو برد و در اندرون او نیز خالی کرده قرنفل

الاچی مشک کافور زعفران گلاب پر سازند

بعده این ترنج را در برنج انداخته بپزند نوعی دیگر ٤

بعضشان هفت
ب

ترتیب بره از کودیی بره کند واز موتهه بره کند

وهمچنین بره از تهولی واز ماش واز منک واز

کنکنین واز مقدار که حبوب هست از هر

جنس بره کند واز بتله واز نخود واز زرت این همه

جنسها را بره راست کرده در میان آرد مسکه

انداخته بره بپزند ودر بعضی ترشی بیندازد ودر بعضی

خوشبویی اندازد در بعضی شیرینی اندازد در بعضی

خشک
خوانچهای هر جنسی بیندازد بعضی ساده بدارد

بعضی را ترکند نوعی دیگر کهیچره کند

کهیچره کندم بسیار بکوبد وسپید کرده بستاند

ودر آب صاف بپزد چون خوب پخته باشد فرو آرد بسیار

سرد کند بعده ماست جامه بیز کرده غلیظ

در کهیچره بیامیزد نمک رایی بیندازد چنانچه در رایته

می اندازند و روز دوم بخورد باسی شده نوعی دیگر

شربت در آب شش درم الایچی سه درم قرنفل نبات

آن قدر که مزه آید بیندازد شربت کند

نوعی دیگر دوغ در میان دوغ لیمو و قرنفل

بیندازد دیگر دوغ میان آن نمک و هنگ

بیندازد دیگر دوغ برگ تنبول الایچی قرنفل

کافور باریک آس کرده در دوغ اندازد نوعی دیگر

شربت

شربت خرماء سلیمانی دو عدد در روغن برشته آش کند
در میان آب حل کرده شربت کند نوعی دیگر بره در
میان انبلوانی بره منک بیندازد نوعی دیگر شربت
بدهل آش کرده در آب بیامیزد شکر تری
بیندازد یا نمک و رای بیندازد بعده گزر بریان کند
و در آب آش کند و شکر تری و خوشبویی اندازد
شربت کند نوعی دیگر گوشت در میان گوشت
انبوته و چوکه بیندازد یا در گوشت سبزی اندازد
نوعی دیگر شربت سرکه شهد آب شربت کند
دیگر بات دادو بری ماست را بریان کند بیندازد

بعده گوشت را النواس کند و در میان آن بریی

مذکور انداخته بپزد نوعی دیگر گوشت

وقتی که پخته باشد وقت فرو آوردن میتهی خشک

آس کرده بیندازد نوعی دیگر ترتیب

آش شام دو نیم سیر کهیچره دو نیم سیر گوشت

یکجا کرده بپزند روغن بسیار اندازند تا آن زمان

بپزند که گوشت و گندم مهرا شود و بگهار پیاز

بدهند نمک زیره میتهی هنگ بیندازد نوعی دیگر

گوشت را چوکدا انداخته یا شبت انداخته

بپزد نوعی دیگر نخود آب گوشت را بگهار هنگ

داده

داده بپزند و دال نخود بیندازد زیره میتهی هنک نمک هلد
فلفل آب لیمو سیر انداخته خوب نرم کرده بپزند
نوعی دیگر ساک ساک پویی را بگهار هنک داده
بپزند برنج و نمک بیندازد پخته باشد فرو آرد نوعی دیگر
تخفتن تیتر تیتر را خوب مهرا کرده بپزند بگهار
هنک بدهند و دال نخود بیندازد نمک زیره میتهی هلد
بیندازد نوعی دیگر مرغ مرغ را چنانچه در تیتر
گفته ایم همان طریق مهرا کرده بپزند
نوعی دیگر ترتیب چچیرک قیمه را باریک
ببرند و از آرد میده تکری کوچک راست کنند

وَيَكِي دَرْ زِيرَ وَيَكِي بَالَا وَمِيَانْ آنْ قِيمَهْ

پُرْ كُنَنْدَ وَكَارَهَا مُحْكَمْ كُنَدْ وَدَرْ مِيَانْ

گُوشْتِ دِيگَرْ بُرُدْ زِيرَهْ مِيتْهِي هِنْكْ نَمَكْ هَلَدْ

فِلْفِلْ آبْ لِيمُو اَدْرَكْ

پِيَازْ

بُرِيدَهْ

آسْ

كَرْدَهْ

بِيَنْدَازَدْ سُونْفْ نِيزْ اَنْدَازَدْ وَاَزْ هَمَانْ قِيمَهْ شَكْلْ كُنْدُونَكْ

وَشَكْلِ سِنْگَمَارَهْ رَاسْتْ كُنَدْ وَخُوبْ حَوِيجْ

انداخته فرو آرد نوعی دیگر ترتیب بری دال ماش
بشورد آس کرده بدارد یک شب و یک وصله نمک
در میان آن بنهد و زد دیگر هنک را موازنه
آن بیندازد زیره فلفل پیاز ادرک میتهی بریان کرده
نمک آس کرده بیامیزد بعده بریها بشکند
و بهمین طریق بری از منک نیز راست کند
نوعی دیگر بری آمله در میتهی ماش آمله
آس کرده بیندازد و حوایج انداخته بریهای
بزرک بزرک بشکند نوعی دیگر بری مجدبه
مجدبه را بجز اشد و مغز انده و زوی بستانند و دال ماش

بیندازد هنك زیره میتهی بریان کرده کشنیز ادرك
بیامیزد دیگر و زبیتهی آس کرده بدارد روز
دوم بری پیش کند نوعی دیگر سکبا در
میان شوربای گوشت سرکه اندازد تج پترج
الایچی و خوشبوئی و تمام حوتج بیندازد نوعی دیگر
ترید در میان شوربا روغن و پرکالهاء کاك
بیندازد شربت در میان شربت قطعهای کاك بیندازد
نوعی دیگر در میان دوغ وصلهای کاك
بیندازد و پیاز سیر نمك بیندازد و بخور هنك بدهد
نوعی دیگر دوغ دوغ را بخور بسیار بدهد نمك

زیره

۸۱

زیره میتهی بیندازد نوعی دیکر کوشت در شوربا
کوشت زیره و انار دانه و تمام حوایج بیندازد
نوعی دیکر دوغ در میان دوغ شکر تری
لیمو هنک آش کرده بیندازد نوعی دیکر
دوغبا در میان دوغ کوشت انداخته بپزد نوعی
دیکر قیمه آن مقدار که قیمه کوشت
باشد قیمه پیاز همان مقدار راست کند و از برک
پیاز نیز قیمه کند و نیمه آن قیمه برک ترب
و ثلث آن قیمه ادرک و دو کره سیر آب لیمو
زعفران قدری انداخته یخنی بپزد و با نان تنک کرم

بخورد نوعی دیگر قیمه دال نخود سیر قیمه یکجا کرده

بپزد آب لیمو فلفل بیندازد ترب ادرک پیاز بریده بیندازد

نوعی دیگر قیمه درمیان قیمه دوغ سیر و شیره

انگور و سرکه انداخته بپزد نوعی دیگر

قیمه درمیان قیمه دال نخود و شیره سونف و ترب

انداخته لنواس کند ادرک پیاز آب لیمو بیندازد

بخورد تیل بدهد هنگ نیز بیندازد با نان گرم بخورند

نوعی دیگر قیمه درمیان قیمه دنکره

انداخته بپزد تج پترج الاچی بیندازد خوب بپزد

نوعی دیگر کوفته زیره زنجبیل زیره ترب

زیره

۸۲

هشتاد دو

زیرهٔ هنك زیرهٔ پیاز زیرهٔ سیر اینها همه انداخته یك

کوفته راست کند بعده با شوربا بپزد بعده

آب لیمو و فلفل و حوایج انداخته فرو آرد نوعی دیگر

کوفته درمیان کوفته هفت زیره و

زعفران مقدار رایی مشك مقدار رایی کافور

همین مقدار عنبر اشهب اینها همه باهم آمیخته کوفته

سازد بعده شوربا پلیو کرده بپزد فلفل آب لیمو

حوایج انداخته بپزد برك کسوندی پودنه تلسی و همه حوایج

بیندازد نوعی دیگر ساك چوکه در قیمه ساك چوکه

را جوشانیده در قیمه بیامیزد بعده کوفته ببندد

بعده بپزد فلفل و ترشی بیندازد نوعی دیگر کوفته

کنهل در قیمه انداخته کوفته راست کند یا

دنکره انداخته یا بدهل انداخته یا شیرهٔ انبه انداخته

یا کیری یا شاخ نورستهٔ انبه انداخته یا از ترشی

ترنج یا از شاخ نورستهٔ ترنج این همه جنسها که گفته شد

در قیمه انداخته کوفته راست کند نوعی دیگر

شربت بر پیپل بهالسه خرما پهیپهر اینها را یکجا ب

آش کند با آب و شربت کند و خوشبویی بیندازد

و شیرینی موازنه اندازد نوعی دیگر کوفته چوکه

پوده سووا انبوتی در بخار تخته در آب ضمغ کوفته سازد

بعده د

بعده در روغن برشته کند و بالای آن شیرینی و گلاب
و کافور انداخته فرو آرد نوعی دیگر کوفته
کلاسیلو فراش کرده در قیمه اندازد و کوفته راست
کرده در روغن برشته نماید بعده بالای آن
چاشنی گلاب و کافور بدهد نوعی دیگر
کوفته گوشت را بکوبد و کشنیز زیره پیاز نمک
سونف زعفران کافور مشک یکجا آمیخته غلوله
بندد و در برگ لیمو بپیچد و شوربا پلیو دار کند
و اگر در برگ ترنج یا در برگ تنبول بپیچد جنس دیگر
شود نوعی دیگر هندوی نمک تمام حوج انداخته

کهند وی راست کند بعده آرد برنج و دوغ

انداخته کرهی کند و در آن کهند وی بیندازد

و اگر در کاچی بیندازد جنسی دیگر شود

و اگر در شوربا بیندازد پس جنسی دیگر شود و اگر

در آب میوهای ترش اندازد جنسی دیگر شود و اگر

در کرهی اندازد و بالای دده هنك بیندازد پس

جنسی دیگر شود و اگر در روغن برشته کند

و بالای آن زیر بنج و خوشبویی اندازد پس جنسی دیگر

شود و اگر در آبرای اندازد جنسی دیگر

شود

شود و اگر در شربت شیرین بیندازد پس جنسی دیگر

و اگر

واگر در آن بلوانی اندازد جنس دیگر شود

نوعی دیگر ترتیب شربت شکر پنج درم دو درم

ادرك قرنفل دو درم الایچی دو درم هر همه را آس کرده

یکجا و صاف کرده شربت

کند

و بالا

کافور

اندازد

نوعی دیگر حریره آرد خشخاش کشنیز زیره

آس کرده سونف سونده قرنفل الایچی همه را

در آب انداخته بجوشانند و اندک شکر تری و
روغن بیندازد نوعی دیگر حریرهٔ ترنجی ترشی
ترنج انداخته حریره راست کند و همه میوها آش کرده
در آن اندازد و سوندهی بیندازد و شیرینی اندازد حریره
ترنجی شود نوع دیگر حریره تخم خربزه با شکر تر
و سوندهی انداخته حریره کند و بالای آن لابجی و
قرنفل بیندازد نوعی دیگر آش شام کهیچره کندم
با گوشت انداخته بپزد تا مهرا شود طریق مسکه
و فلفل و برنج بیندازد و اگر آش شام منک کند پس
جنسی دیگر شود و اگر از زرت یا از برنج

آش شام

آش شام کند پس جنسهاء دیگر باشند
دیگر ترتیب آش شام زردک آش شام زردک کند
وآزموده در آن بیندازد وآن مقدار حبوب که هستند
اگر از هر یك آش شام کند پس آن قدر جنسها
آش شام شود نوعی دیگر شربت شکر تری الاچی
قرنفل آن کرده شربت کند واگر در میان آن
بهات بیندازد پس پان بهت شود نوعی دیگر ترتیب
کهندوی کیری شکر تری آرد الاچی
قرنفل انداخته بجوشاند رابری کند بعده کهندوی
راست کند ده درم عسل بیست درم روغن مغز کاك شیره

ادرك بیندازند پس جنسی شود و در بعضی اگر

ترشی ترنج اندازد پس جنسی دیگر شود و اگر آب

بهاجی نخود و آب ادرك و فلفل و نمك بیندازد پس جنسی

دیگر شود نوعی دیگر گوشت کباب بچه

تنك ببرد و چکتله پیاز و ادرك و الاچی و

قرنفل و آرد برنج انداخته در روغن بگهار دهد

و تمام حوتجها در آن اندازد و بالای آن آزموده بریان

کرده اندازد نوعی دیگر گوشت بستانند

از گوشت یك وصله و از پیاز یك وصله و الاچی قرنفل

زعفران بالای وصله اندازد و بالای آن وصله پیاز

نهد

نهد و بریسمان بپیچد بعده تمام حوتجها انداخته در
روغن بگهار دهد و آب لیمو و آب ادرك بیندازد
چون پخته شود فرود آرد و ریسمان دور کند نوعی
دیگر شوربا آب ادرك را و آب پیاز را اندك
چاشنی سیر بدهد و شورباء گوشت بپزد کشنیز
زیره میتهی آب لیمو و هنك بیندازد خوب شوربا شود
نوعی دیگر شوربا وصلهای گوشت در آب صاف
و آب ادرك و لیمو و زیره و میتهی و کشنیز و سونف
انداخته گوشت بجوشاند بعده آب صاف آن بگیرد بعده
تمام حوایج را در کره جامه بسته در آن اندازد ترشی

وقلفل در آن انداخته فرو آرد تعطیر چهر چهریله

موتهه کجری کیهو نله تج پترج الایچی قرنفل

اینها همه در آب انداخته بجوشانند و آز آب را صاف

کرده بستانند کافور و مشک بیندازد و در آن

آب بهات بپزد و هرچه خواهد بپزد نوعی دیگر

گوشت را خوب بجوشانند بعده سرکه

و پودنه انداخته فرو آرد نوعی دیگر تعطیر طعام

و پان و آب صندل دو درم مشک یکدرم عنبر اشهب نیم درم

گلاب هرچیز را که خواهند معطر سازند نوعی

دیگر تعطیر عود تلیه نبات انداخته در شیشه

چووه

چوزه بچکانند و در چوزه کافور و مشک و گلاب

بیندازد هرچه را معطر خواهند بسازند نوعی دیگر

تعطیر زعفران گلاب مشک کافور هرچه خواهند

با این معطر سازند نوعی دیگر گوشت گوشت

و چهار بادنجان معطر کرده نرم مهرا کرده بپزد

ترشی و تیز کرده تمام حوتج انداخته بپزد هنگ

در تیل برشته یا در روغن برشته آش کند و در دیگ

اندازد نوعی دیگر طعام غریب ساک را در آب

بجوشاند و در آب تور بجوشاند و نان زرت بپزد بعده

دتهاره دهد ساک چو که این همه طعامها را در تیل

وهنك بكهار دهد وبالاي آن ادرك پياز فلفل

بيندازد اينهارا همه يكجا كرده بپزد تيار هنك

بيندازد نوعي ديكر ساك كلنجره را

درميان

دوغ و

آب

بجوشاند

بعده

بيرون آرد وخوب بيفشارد وازهم بكشايد

وباد دهد بعده زيره نمك وكنجد دانه برشته آس كرده

۸۸

80

آب لیمو اجوابن برشته ادرک لنواسِ ساک قرنفل روغن تخته

کنجد شیرین مسکه گاو سیاه دانه عنبر اشهب

تمر هندی دیگر راسته هر جنسی تُرش و شیرین

و تیز و مولّه از خوشبوئی و بیخ و شاخ از هر چه خواهند

راست کنند و ماست و رائی بیندازد راسته شود

و اگر بخور خوشبوئی دهد پس جنسی دیگر شود

شکوفه سبستان شکوفه تمرهندی شکوفه سنهجنه

سرسون تنتریکهه سوندهی روغن قرنفل هنک

شاخ نو درخت پیپل خیار بالنک بخور تیل خیار بزرک

ادرک کبابه چینی سالِ چوکه کندوری

لیمو بادنجان خولنجان هلد رازیانج فلفل دراز

دوغ خیار کوچک توربی سیب نخود سبز حبحب

کدو ماست الایچی پترج اجواین فلفل عنبر اشهب

١ دیگر ترتیب پختن ماهی و اگر ماهی نباشد پس

گوشت را طریق ماهی بپزند آرد برنج ماهی در آن

که طریق مار میباشد چون پخته باشد آنرا نخورند

باقی همه جنس ماهی بخورند دیگر شیر و ماهی بادنجان

و ماهی ماست و ماهی یکجا نخورند نمک ترنج آرد برنج

تنتریکه عدس برشته زنجبیل خشک کنجد دانه برشته

قرنفل نخود زیره گشنیز سیر آرد منک برشته

زیره، تمرهندی، میتهی، هلد، کیری، فلفل، الاچی

آرد نخود برشته، کشنیز سبز، کانجی، کرنه، روغن بادام

روغن زنجبیل تر، تیل دار فلفل، تیل سسون، پیان تیل رایی

نخود سونف، سنکهاره برشته، بین چون، دیگر یک نوع ماهی

که بهندی ترکنتک گویند این راسه خار است

و در خار او زهر است خار او دور کنند گوشت او

خوب است بپزند بخورند، دیگر ماهی که

آنرا اوپت لکهمه مچهه گویند در زهره این ماهی یا در

جربی او زهر میباشد اگر آدمی بخورد بمیرد

دیگر نختن نان پولی و کاک و چپاتی و نان تنوری

١

و حوتجهای ملایم آن نان پولی و آرد نخود برشته و آرد کنجد

دانه مالیده پولی بپزد بعده با روغن چرب کند و در

جامه تر کرده بدارد دیگر نان نهاء هر حبوب

که بپزد باید که بالوان او از آرد حبوب دیگر

یعنی پلیتهن

باشد بر نان مالیده بپزند بتله رالله نخود سبز کنگنی

تهولی گندم نمک تهولی چارولی آرد بادام

کنجد دانه سونف آرد کردگان هنک

تیوره نخود هر جنسی جو اجواین زرت تور

کشنیز منک آرد میده کودیی روه کلونجی

نخود گندم خشکه کتکی دیگر

پکوره

کپور کسوندی کاک گلاب نمک دال نخود

مشک آمله کرنه چغندر ساک شبت ادرک

ریحان چوک ساک میتهی آل کونکلو انار دانه قرنفل

برگ لیمو الاچی آب کرم پخته تج آب لیمو بترج پیاز

دوغ هلد اجواین ترب عنبر اشهب رایی روغن

نخود تیل سونف کشنیز برگ ترنج برنج فلفل کرد

دیگر جوشانیدن شیر شیر را صاف کرده باشند

و آب آن مانده باشد آب آن شیر را با ماهی نخورند و شیر

با ماهی نخورند و شیر با ماهی و ترب و منک و ارد و موتهه

و عدس و کلتهه و کنکنی سبز و با

جملهٔ سبزیها و میوهاء ترش با این جمله شیر نخورند
و با نمك نیز نخورند و شیر که خراب و تباه شود نشاید
خورد و شیر و گوشت یکجا نخورند شهد بادام
داکهه نارکیل اونی گندم آب شیر
کهجور خرما آمله شهد تخم مجدبه نارنك آز آمله خشك
موز سیاه پوهیه برنج کردگان چارولی پسته
جلغوزه سنکهاره کسیرو کرهری نیلوفر
کافور مشك الاچی تج پترج سوند هی
فلفل کرد دار فلفل پلپل مول روغن شکر تری
لدو سهالی نبات تلسکلی پکهاجه پهینی

هراه بهات

نوذیکه

همراه بهات شیر و دهوند هن و تهولی و کتکی

و کودیی با این همه شیر بخورند دیگر

پختن بره از همه جنسها بره راست کنند و در روغن

یا در کنجد شیرین یا در روغن بادام یا در تیل

سرسون بره را برشته کنند و زهنک سوخته

روغن در میان آن مستهی زیره سونف انداخته درین

چیزها برشته کنند و کپ هندویی بزرک بزرک

نیز برشته سازد فلفل گرد ماش منک پیاز ادرک

شهد شکرتری راب شیره نیشکر خوشبویی

چولایی و آرد برنج برک رز و آرد برنج پهاتک و آرد برنج

جیسنج و آرد برنج پندالو و آرد برنج تیل راییی آرد چارولی

آرد نخود و چارولی منک و آرد بادام خرما و آرد برنج تمر

هندی و شکر تری و برنج پوییی و آرد برنج سونف

و آرد برنج

کشنیز

قرنفل

مشک

پترج

تج سونف سوخته در تیل تیل در میتهی سوخته تیل زیره

تیل در هنک سوخته الایچی روغن کردگان و برنج

تهولی وسن کهاره نازو ماست کافور سونف برگ
زردت و جلغوزه آرد تخم نیلوفر دار فلفل بتله و آرد برنج
روغن برگ تنبول عدس برنج کلتهه موتهه
سیاه دانه هنک سوندهی آزموده سونف نمک
کلاب میتهی بره از مجدبه تمر هندی کودیی
بتله زیره دال نخود تیل سرسون در شهد و شکرتری
و راب و شیره نیشکر کافور مشک کلاب
و خوشبویی در تمام حوایج انداخته و آب رانخور داده
یا دوغ یا متهه یا کرهی یا شربت یا کانجی یا آب لیمو
یا آب ترنج یا آب غوره یا آب زرشک یا شیره انبه یا شیره

آمله و سبات در میان اینها بره برشته بیندازد دیگر

در ذکر ادویه که طعام هضم کند و خوشی

آرد این ادویه را سلطان فیروز میخورد اجمود پنج درم
جاپتری پنج درم قرنفل پنج درم خشخاش پنج درم تخم
مکهاره پنج درم زعفران پنج درم مجموع ادویه را کوفته
بیخته در عسل بسرشند و موازنه کهرولی کلوله
بندند روزینه یک کلوله بخورند منی بیفزاید رای
کهونکهنیز زرنت الایچی شکر کافور
بیر چون کتهل مشک کهرنی نیلوفر صندل
کرونده کنکیرو دهامن سنکهاره بهات نبات

نمرك

کمرک کلن کلاب بدهل آمله کسیر و کتهه
کازر تیوره عود تیلیه انباره کهجور قرنفل تیند و شهد
بهالسه دیکر در ذکر داروهایی که باه را قوت
دهد و منی بیفزاید دار فلفل الایچی چارولی مسکه
کاو روغن کاو شیر کوسپند خشخاش قرنفل
سوندهی جلغوزه ادرک خشک شیر خرما شکر
نخود برشته چارولی بادام بن آمله شیر ماده کاو عاقرقرحا
و موین شهد برابر یکجا بیامیزد و بر قضیب مالد مباشرت
کند لذتی عظیم و خوشی آرد دیکر در
قوت باه و زیادتی منی کوشت کوساله کوشت کوسپند

مغز کنجشک خانگی کبوتر روغن شیر بادهٔ گاو

الایچی عاقرقرحا بسباسه کنجشک نر خانگی ده عدد

در میانه روغن برشته بخورند قوت شود شکر تری نخود

برشته مویز موصلی سفید بیخ کنکیر و شهد

اجمود قرنفل تخم کوچه آرد میده آس کهکی

شیر کیپا کوکهرو نمک سپند هاچارولی کوشت

کنجشک خانگی خشخاش خرما تخم مکهاره جلغوزه زرده

تخم مرغ نان کنده دیگر راست کردن

آچار تازه از چیزهای خام چون بیخها و برگها و کلها

و شکوفها یکجا ریزه کرده بیامیزند و حوائجات هر جنسی

اچار این در آن

86

۹۶ 86

نود و شش

اجواین تج ترنج مجدبه زرشک پترج هنک
میتهی شکوفه تمر هندی در ذکر خاصیت
این ادویه آنست که صفرا و بلغم دفع کند
و خون را صاف گرداند و بسیاری خوی دفع کند
و ترخر و اسهال ببندد و اگر بر پوست مالند
رنگ پوست و بشره صاف گرداند ادویه اینست
هلیله بلیله کل سیوتی آمله تر پوست بیه کولر
گات کلنبر بر پهیپهر استه جامن پوست کلنبر
پوست تینتو شهد کانتا سلیا کنول کند فوفل تازه
بهوج پتر مرجان کشته موتهه پوست درخت انبه

بنه کیته خام غوره خرما پوست کهو تلیه

اجمود کاپهل لود پوست مهو پرینک هوس موچرس

روهس انار دانه پوست انار کل دهاوه بندها را

کیرو روهرا دیکر ادویه قوت باه

خاصیت این ادویه آنست که منی بیفزاید و

پشت را قوت دهد پیرانرا و کودکانرا و جوانانرا نافع باشد

و ذهن تیز کند و چشم را روشن کند

و بشره را صافی کند و قوت شنوایی را و حس

سمع را یاری دهد و دهان و زبانرا مفید باشد

هد ساکر زنجبیل خشک دار فلفل شهد

کتهل

کتهل بادام مهامید داکهه کهرنی کوکهرو
سیوتی کالعل خرما پکهارک کسیرو مید چولائی
مجدبه کهیا توریی کندوری دودی مهو
تخم نیلوفر شیر رده برده انار دانه تج سیند هو آمله
سیر شیره نیشکر جیتی مد بلبج تخم کوچه
موصلی اسنده بر کهیرکنکولی کنجد دانه چارولی
جلغوزه پسته اکهروت نارکیل روغن نبات
موز کانکولی طبق زر ایزاد و یها مذکوره
بدن فربه کند و لاغر را و ضعیف را سود دهد و استخوان
شکسته را درست کرداند و باد و صفرا بشکند و زهر دفع

کند و عمر دراز گرداند و خوشی بیفزاید

دیگر جهت دفع تب این ادویه را کاڑهه کرده

طعام نپزند نخورند تب بلغمی و صفراوی و خونی و

بادی دفع شود ادویه اینست گز پیپل کندوری

بناب کلوی کپوری کانتا سیلوا بیخ ارند پتول برنگ

چرایته منکوانی پوست کره اندرجو بیخ بل کالی زیری

دار فلفل مهامیل پیپل مول نسوت کو پکهرو

مدهوری بالا ردهه جیتهی مدّ ماکهه ونا سدهه

بکاین سالونی دودهی ایستاده میان کندم

رونکهه بکهه سیون ورده ریکنین کوچک کای پهل

رینکینی بزرگ

رینگنین بزرک نارنگی بانسه پهکرمول

دارهلد راشنی جیوک کاکراسنک هلد پاده روهس

دیودار جواسه پت پاپره برن موتهه پادل کتکی

پتاس موربا مجیتهه تینتو کهیر کنکولی الاتچی

پته بنی سوندهی اجواین رت آنجن صندل کوته

ایلیا پدمك مایی

این دارو ها اکارهه کرده طعام ببرد یا پهلی

کرده در طعام اندا زد ادویه الست نیخ ارند

ناك کیسر بهیین کوسله تج برنا جیتهی مد

چوك نیخ سهجنه نیخ بلبیج داب نبات کهیره هلیله

را بهوك ككري تينتو كلت پاكهان بهيد شكر

روغن كنكيرو كالا بالا كپوري پيپل

كج لون نخ كانس دهماهه كوكهرو بانسه

شيره نيشكر آمله بيخ نيشكر دوب بيخ سالي مشك

كرماله

الايچي

داكهه

الايچي

بزرك

بهپهلي اسير ديگر جهت روشنايي چشم

اين اعم

این ادویه روشنایی چشم زیادت کنند اگر در میان
طعام یا در گوشت یا در ساک و سبزی انداخته بپزند
بخورند و اگر در میان کارهه جوشانیده آب آن دارو ها
بستانند و چشم را بشویند یا یکجا سرشته بر چشم بندند روشنی
چشم زیادت شود و علتهاء چشم تمام دفع کند
ادویه اینست پنج مول ماك وني پهلی الکهتیه کل بیله
کلاکهیته مجیتهه سیندهو سنهجنه زر کشته
جیتهی مد داکهه ذوذی زیره شبت اجمود هلیله
لود کافور دارهلد شهد سوزماکهی کشته آمله
شاخ تازه ستاور بهیره سنبهالی قرنفل مشك نیلوفر

رؤهس صندل رکت چندن مشک آنه تخم نیب

برک نیب مونک ونی سوپلی کتک پهل دیگر

ادویه دفع خارش اندام اینست مروه کبریت خاصه

عدس تور منک سیندهو زعفران سوندهی فلفل

پچی

آب لیمو سبزی پنوار برمهی اسنده کانتاسیلو الا

سنبهالی دیودار باپهی دارهلد هلد سانکر

پتول ناکبیل الایچی بزرک سلارس دارفلفل

دونه روهس لیمو ریسوک کهیر کرپته کتکی

تج دیگر نهال نبات ساختن و قرص و کوشک

از نبات ساختن و دن کره نبات رنک رنک سا ختن

بدم

بدم دمیده و مرغ مسمن قیمه پخته و پیاز ادرک و تمام
حوائج انداخته در شکم مرغ یا کبوتر یا هر جانور
که خواهند در شکم او پر کنند الائچی
قرنفل عنبر اشهب گلاب کافور مشک زعفران نمک
یکجا کرده و بالای جانور مالیده در روغن بگهار
دهد بعده برشته سازد و پیاز تازه را اندک کوک بکند
و آب لیمو پر کنند و بالا خوشبوی بمالد و در میان
قیمه بگیرد و در روغن بگهار دهد و تمام حوائج
بیندازد دیگر پوست لیمو خام را پر زهای
اندرون آن چنان دور کند که پوست امانت

بماند و ترشی و زیرهٔ او بیرون شود بعده قیمه را در میان
آن پر کند خوشبوی آمیخته و بریسمان بپیچد
بعده بکهار دهد خوب پخته باشد فرو آرد و بهمین طریق
از کرنه و از نارنکی و از ترنج راست کند بپزد دیکر
کل سیلو فرا بیارند و در میان آن بهات پر کنند و
بریسمان بپیچد بعده در دتهاره نهد چون پخته باشد
فرو آرد دیکر از بزرک ترنج دونه کند و بهات
بیندازد و بریسمان بپیچد بپزد چون بخار پر شده باشد
فرو آرد و با دونه پیش برد بسیار جنسها بپزد اینچنین
بسیار جنس کرهی نیز میشود و با پر کند

صدیکو

وازین شربت نیز بکند در دوغ و در ماست

پهلی کرده این ادویها بیندازد ادویه اینست

سنك شسته سوندهی شوربا لوه ترنج پاپر شاخ کرنه

شوربا بیتر کهری شیرنار کیله ایخ حلوان

کلش کر بیپل شهد نمکی سرکه کرهی

عنبر اشهب گندم زرد برنج بیرچون الاتچی دال نخود

ناك کیسر فلفل آس کرده زرت نبات کیلی

شکر تری قرنفل آس کرده دوغ گلاب برمی

کافور لیمو روغن دیگر طعامها

که بعد از مباشرت بخورند منی بیفزاید این همه

۱۲

چیزها را خوردن و استعمال کردن خوشی پیدا شود

و بلغم از اندام دفع شود و سستی برود و خوی آمدن

باز دارد و دل را فرح بخشد و نعوظ آرد و منی بیفزاید

اینست در جایهاء فراخ خواب کند

بادهای

سرد کناند

اندام بشوید

خوشبویی

بمالد گلهای خوشبوی ببوید با شیرین سخنان

حکایت کند سرودهای خوش بگویاند سپیدهی

که مست نباشد بخورند موز بادام کردگان پسته

جلغوزه چارولی کندم جو لاپسی لادو سور

برنج کنجد دانه شهد نبات نیشکر طعامهای خوب

کهیور بره ماش شیر آب شوربا رساله کهیر

دیگر کهیس و رابری تختن اگر این چیزها

را با دوغ خام بیامیزند پس شربت شود شود اینست

آرد سنکهاره آرد بادام آرد کنکنی شکر

شهد آرد کردکان آرد نیلوفر آرد تهولی آرد کودیی

دوغ آرد برنج نبات بخورتیل ادرک پیاز سیاه دانه

آرد جلغوزه آرد منک آب دوغ هنک در روغن سوخته

لیمو نخود آرد زرت گلشکر تیل هنک سوخته

میتهی اجوائن انبلی هنک شالی برشته نخود برشته

نمک دیگر جمع کردن اسباب ماست با که آنرا

کتهله گویند اینست شاخ تازه ترنج شاخ تازه لیمو

هنک زیره برشته مشک سرکه دوغ کانجی انباره

شاخ رز لوبیا برک پیاز شاخ تازه ادرک ببوته پهانک

میتهی برشته آب دوغ بتهله آب ماست پودینه آب لیمو

اجوائن برشته رائی برشته چولائی ساک سرخ برنج بریان

کرده کنجد دانه برشته نمک سیر بهاجی نخود دیگر

لیموء شیرین بیجانکری در میان حوتجها بیندازد دیگر

این همه برگها که نوشته میشود با ایشان برگهاء
تنبول را بیفشانند و طلا کنند و تنبول را بپرورند
اینست شاخ تازهء انبه با برگهاء کوچک او
و برگ ترنج برگ کرنه برگ نارنگی برگ جامن
برگ لیمو تلسی کیوره و تمام گلها و خوشبویها
هر جنسی برگهای ایشانرا گرفته برگ تنبول را
و فوفل را معطر سازند و بوی هر گلی که خوشبو باشد
و زودتر در چیزی دیگر تعطیر آرد تعطیر آن
کل برگ تنبول را بدهد دیگر عود تیلیه
و صندل و لبان و سلاکپهل و سلارس و چاند

و عود مرهته بخور اینها را به پان و فوفل و کات و چونه
بدهد و از پوست ترنج و از پوست کرنه و پوست لیمو
و پوست نارنکی نیز تعطیر دهد دیکر بیره
غیاثشاهی بالای برک تنبول از کافور و کلاب
طلا کند و از یازده برک یک بیره سازد و چونه
زعفرانی کند و در آب عود تلیه فوفل
چیکنه بجوشاند بعده در بو کند مشک و عنبر
اشهب و کلاب آن فوفل را بمالد و کهر ولی از کل لعل
کند نوعی دیکر سپاری چیکنی را
در آب صندل بجوشاند و با کافور بمالد و دیکر

صندل

صندل بمالد و گلاب بر و بیفشاند و بیره از
بیست و پنج برگ کند و کهرولی از مشک و
چونه از زعفران و گلاب سازد این هر دو
جنس را تنبول بکند دیگر تنبول غیاثشاهی
از پنجاه
برگ
بیره
سازد
و اندک
سپاری چیکنی و اندک سپاری دیگر و از

مشک بسیار انداخته کهروای راست کند و در
میان تنبول انداخته بکوبند نه بسیار مهین باشد و نه
بسیار کنده موازنه بکوبند بعده یک توله
الایچی نیم توله مشک دو توله کافور
نیم توله صندل موکره بیندازد بعده گلاب
بیفشانند و یک ماسه عنبر اشهب بیندازد بعده با
باد بیزن و الا باد کنند تا خوب سرد شود بعده
بخورند خاصیت این تنبول آنست که صفرا بشکند
و قی باز دارد و مضرت باد گرم و حرارت
و بسیاری خون که از گرمی باشد و سوختن

حلق و حنجره را نافع باشد دیگر تنبول
غیاثشاهی فوفل روپها را با گلاب آس کنند غلیظ
طریق صندل و برگ را بالای سنگ باریک آس کنند
و کمرولی مشک آس کرده بیندازند و کافور
پخته اینها همه یکجا کرده بخورند خاصیت
این آنست که درد دندان ساکن کند و زبان
نرم دارد و دهان را خوشبوی کند دیگر تنبول
غیاثشاهی از فوفل برشته بالاوسل آرد کنند بعده پان
و چونه و کپه هرولی با آن آمیخته در میان برگ
نرم و سست بپیچد و بیری کرده بخورانند

دیگر تنبول پان کهرولی و سپاری یکجا

باریك بکوبد بعده ست الایچی و ست قرنفل طریق نشاشته

بگیرد بکوبد دیگر تنبول کتهل

یا کولر یا دن کرده در آب اینها سپاری تر کند

و این سپاری را و پان و کهرولی و چونه و

سوندهی و خولنجان آن مقدار بیندازد که بسیار تیز

نشود اینها را همه در میان برگ انداخته تنبول

بکوبد دیگر تنبول چیول چرب و فوفل

بریان کرده و پان و کهرولی مشك و چونه هر همه

یکجا کرده بکوبد بعده ست گل چنپه و کافور و تیلیه

ومشك وزعفران درآن بيندازد بكوبد بعد عرق
بهار نارنج بروبرزند آن قدر كه تر شود ودرميان تنبول كيهونلد
يك يا دو انداخته بخورد وصله نارگيل مقدار يك درم
انداخته بخورد كبابه استه خرما استه تمرهندي
استه تيند وسينبل سپاري چيول برگ مروه پدمك
گل لعل سيوتي گل بولسري اينها را باش بدهد
ودرميان تنبول نيز اگر خواهد بخورد از خوردن
اينها زيان نيست وليكن تلخ ميشود اگر نخورد
بهتر باشد بنس لوچنه نخورند نبات اندك بخورد و نخورد
نبات نيز سپاري را بدهد ناك كيسر تج اين همه چيزها

که نوشته شده است آنها را یکیک در میان تنبول بیندازد
دیگر سنگهاره بادام نیلوفر کرهری شیره انبه
خشک کرده پاره کهرهری از میوه ناتر این چیزها
را یکیک میان تنبول انداخته بخورد دیگر
پنجه پان فوفل بریان کرده آس کرده
کات بهکوره کافور بادام مشک سپاری پان
نانک کیسر زعفران یکجا بکوبد و به بادبیز باد کند و
گلاب بیندازد بخورد دیگر پان سپاری
کات بینس بخور تیلیه مشک گلاب بیندازد به بادبیزن
باد کند صندل بینس مشک گلاب بخور عود پان

سپاری چونه کات الاچی عود تیلیه آس کرده
زعفران گلاب کافور دیگر سپاری کات
چونه پان کافور تخته گلاب زعفران دیگر
پان کات سپاری چونه کافور خاصیت کات
لاکهه تلخ و زمخت گرم چرب خون صفرا گرم
بلغم برن تب با فراط اینها را همه دفع کند زور آورد
روشنایی بیفزاید و برص و جذام و پیستی و بسرپ را
و سرفه را و زهر را دفع کند استخوان شکسته را
درست کند و همین خاصیتها در التایغی مها و رمیبا شد
دیگر تنبول کات پان سپاری چونه الاچی

نیز نولچه کافور یک ماسه گلاب در میان صحن

کلی نو تنک بنهد تا سرد شود بعده بخورانند یا زرد

کاسه کلی باشد یا وصله خزف باشد در میان آن بیندا

دیگر تنبول کرم غیاثشاهی تنبول کوفته کند

و فوفل مهین بکوبد آنچنانکه ریزهای او نرم

شود پنج عدد قرنفل آس کرده بیندازد یا ده عدد

قرنفل درست بیندازد و از دار فلفل چهارم حصه

یا فلفل کرد دو حصه یا یک فلفل برابر سوند

یا دو فلفل برابر خولنجان و غلوله چنبیلی و برگهای او

یا وصله هلیله جایی که دندا زرد کند بنهد

١٥١

98

وهر وقتي كه دندان درد كند وخواهد كه اين عمل

كند پس آن زمان بيارد دو عدد سروله وگرم كند ودر

ميان آن تنبول بيندازد وسروله را بپوشاند چون گرم شود

بخوراند

يا قدح

باشد يا

كاسهٔ

كوچك

باشد دريكي ازينها بيندازد يا وصلهٔ خزف گرم كرده باشد

درميان تنبول اندازد پس آن زمان تنبول حبشي شود مشك

وتر نفل بیندازد دیگر تنبول معتدل غیاثشاهی

تنبول کوفته صندل تیلیه کافور مشک نبات سوندهی

این همه بیندازد دیگر نرم تنبول غیاثشاهی

سپاری چرب توکهیر کافور پان نوتی باشد یا اپاکر

باشد یا کیور بیل درمیان آن انداخته بکوبند

دیگر تنبول پهرهره سپاری چیول برک کهنه

استه خرما استه تیند واسته جامن استه انبه مشک

گلاب کافور بیندازد دیگر تنبول

پهرهره صاف وخوشبوی سپاری چیول پان تا هلی

کهر ولی مشک آمله جنگلی بنس لوچنه کافور

مشک

مشك كولي مكهه باس غياثشاهي اگر خواهد كه
في الحال تنبول خورد پس اين كولي بخورد مشك
عنبر اشهب گلاب اين همه يكجا كرده غلوله بندد
نوعي ديگر كولي مكهه باس غياثشاهي
كافور تخته تبكهير صندل موكره الايچي
زعفران اينها همه يكجا آميخته همچنان بدارد كولي بندد
و پايك فوفل چهار برگ بخورد و چونه اندك بخورد
و كات موازنه بخورد اگر چونه
موازنه ميباشد پس رنگ خوب ميشود فوفل اگر
موازنه باشد رنگ خوب شود و اگر زيادت

... ان باشد رنگ خوب نشود باز اگر بسیار باشد

رنگ خوب شود دیگر تنبول تلخ علتهای حلق

و حنجره و درد دوره و پیستی و بدهضمی و خشکی دهن

دفع کند و تنبول تیز خوردن بدهضمی تازه

دفع کند کرم پیام جرم مربا داه صفرا این همه

را دفع کند تنبول را اگر غیر موافق

گوفته باشد و با همدیگر موافق جمع نشده باشد

پس خاطر خوردن آن نخواهد تنبول گرم خوردن

بهرمرا و تشنگی و کلانسبید و داه اینها را

دفع کند طعام هضم کند باد و بلغم دور کند

و بلغم صح

حلق را

حلق را صاف کند عمر دراز کند دل را قوت بخشد

دهد صفرا باد زهر را دفع کند دیگر راست

کردن تنبول این اسبابها را اندک اندک دو

یا یک همچنانکه کات می اندازند از مقدار

بیندازند در تنبول خاصیت آن دندانرا محکم

دارد و علتهاء زبانرا و علتهاء لب را و علتهاء حلق

و حنجره را و سوزش سینه این همه علتها را دفع

کند عقل بیفزاید چشم روشن کند

قوت شنوایی نیکو کرداند بینی را صاف

کرداند بوی دهن دفع کند و همه علتها را

نَغ كُند روشنايي آرد موي را دراز كند

وقوّت دهد استخوان شكسته را وصل

كند وطعام كه در شكم بسته

مانده باشد كه از

كند

وقوّة

هضم

را يار

دهد بلغم دفع كند وشكم

نرم دارد اشتهاء طعام آورد سوهن گرم وستي دن

كرم كند

کرم کند بادهای غلیظ که در شکم باشد

تحلیل دهد زحمت است صفرا و خون زیادت نقصان کند

بلغم نیز دفع کند خون را صاف کرداند خوی آمدن

باز دارد تن حزرا نافع باشد و قبض شکم کند و اکر

بالای پوست اندام بمالند چرکها دور کند و رنک پوست

صاف کرداند بخر دفع کند و زیور دهن است

دهن را صاف کرداند حرارت منی بیفزاید اینست

کل سیوتی ۰ پوست کهو ۰ چوب کهیر ۰ تن تری کهه

کل چنبیلی ۰ کنجد دانه ۰ خار سینبل ۰

کل کیسر ۰ کل پادل ۰ جهن ۰ الایچی بزرک ۰ بدمک

روغن تخم نیلوفر هوس تلسی تیز تنبر استه خرما
پترج استه تیندو کرد کان پان کپوری
ناك کیسی پتکله پان دساوری برنی
کپور کانتهه سیندهو پپل مول پان کهلره
موتهه کل بولسری روهس کل لعل بسباسه دار فلفل
فلفل لاکهه کیهونله نارکیل بادام بنسلوچنه
تخم هلیله سوندهی کبابه تیلیه الایچی کافور
تج سپاری پان کات چونه مشك عنبر اشهب
قرنفل دیگر درین چند محل تنبول نشاید خورد
یکی آنکه از سینه خون آید براه دهن و دیگر آنکه

رکت پت باشد یعنی شری داشته باشد و طعامهای
بی روغن خورد دیگر درد چشم دیگر اگر
بس خورده باشد دیگر بالای شراب نخورد
دیگر سرفه و سل داشته باشد نخورد دیگر
علت مور باد اشته باشد نخورد این علتها را تنبول
نزدیک نکنند دیگر در آنچه تنبول خوردن
نفع کند اینست یکی آنکه از خواب بیدار شود دیگر
بالای طعام دیگر بعد سر شستن دیگر بعد از
قی کردن درین چند جای تنبول نخورد
دیگر تنبول پان ناک بیل کات سپاری

شاخ تازه انبه دیگر تنبول ابهم اثر غیاثشاهی

بدین آب برگ بشوید و در میان برگ که بیندازد

و در خوشبویی بیندازد در آب خوردنی بیندازد

در آب سر شستن نیز بیندازد گات را هم در و تر کند

و سپاری را نیز در و تر کند اینست

آب دومن برگ ترنج برگ کرنه برگ کیتهه کالا با

بالا سفید موتهه چهر چهریله پترج پناک

ناک کیسر کیهونله قرنفل الایچی تیلیه

صندل کچور اینها را همه در میان آب انداخته بجوشانند

چون خوب بوی گرفته باشد پس آب را صاف

کرده

کرده بستاند وآن برگها را ریزه کند و در
خوشبوی اندازد و در صندل اندازد و چهار تولچه
زعفران تازه آس کرده جوشانیده بیندازد
دو تولچه مشک یک تولچه کافور دو ماسه عنبر اشهب
آس کرده در آب بیامیزد و شیشه پر کند و هر
جا که خواهد بکار برد یک قمقمه از گلاب بیندازد
و اگر خواهد که گلاب از و بچکاند پس
گلاب بچکاند و ثفل آنرا بگه سازد و در صندل
اندازد و گلوله راست کند دیگر بینس و
صندل سوکره برابر و فرو دستی تیلیه را بخور عجائب

میشود آن اگر کند و در میان آن بیندازد یک تولچه
مشک نیم تولچه کافور نیم تولچه زعفران یک ماسه عنبر
اشهب آس کرده بیامیزد و در شیشه نگاهدارد
وقت حاجت بکار برد
و بالا جامه
بیفشاند
و در میان
کهول
بیندازد دیگر بوی دادن پان یکصد پان را
زعفران یک درم مشک دو درم کافور یک درم الاتجی

سه درم عنبر سیاه نیم درم صندل ساویده سه درم کبابه

دو درم هر همه را با صندل آس کنند و گلاب

بیندازد و به آب آمیخته نماید و هر دو طرف پان را

این آب نمالد بعده پانها را در میان صحن نهد و بوی

عود تیلیه بدهد پان را گرد بر گرد صحن نهد و در

میان اخگر بنهد و بالاپوش شد تا خون بیرون

نرود و اگر داند که گلاب بسیار میرود پس بوی

آب بدهد باین ترتیب در میان آب گل چنبه گل موگره

کیتکی سیوتی چنبیلی گل لعل این گلها را

در میان آب اندازد و یکساعت بدارد بعده بیرون آرد

دور کند آب را ... بوی گرفته باشد این

آب صندل ... بی اندازد و پازرا بمالد

دیگر بوی دار آب کافور پنهس یک تو

دور کره جامه بسته بریسمان در میان آب بیندازد

و دست باب نرساند ریسمان در دست گرفته کره بیندازد

و همان ریسمان گرفته بیرون آرد دیگر

سرد کردن آب که بسیار سرد شود پنج سبو آب را

نیم درم کافور یکدرم الایچی موتهه نیم درم

کپور کچری ربع درم اسین نیم درهم کل پادله سه درهم کل سیو

دو درم برمی ربع درم صندل ساویده ربع درهم مجموع

دیوبدرا

105 114 185

صد پانزده

ادویه را آس کرده در میان جامه بسته

آب بیندازند نوعی دیگر بخور و بوی آب از آب

موازنه چهار سبو مشک نیم تولچه برگ ترنج دو درم

پوست نارنگی یک درم دونه یک درم برگ بیل سه درم سونف

بزرک یک درم هر همه را آس کرده در

چهار سبو آب بیندازند بوی خوب بگیرد دیگر

آمیختن ادویه عود مرهتی عنبر لادن نه درم لبان

نه درم صندل ربع سیر هوبیر نه درم بالای سفید

نه درم تکری نه درم چهر نه درم سلاکهل

سه درم کیهونله شش درم کوتهه نه درم برمی

نه درم تیلیه سی و دو درم کافور نیم تولچه زعفران
شش درم سلارس هژده درم شهد سی و شش درم ناخن بویا
بریان کرده نه درم چهریله نه درم مجموع را یکجا بیامیزد
عود اول تیلیه نیم سیر مشک یک نیم تولچه کافور ربع درم
عنبر سیاه سه ماسه هر همه را یکجا کرده در میان
آب گلاب اندک تر کنند و غلیظ کنند
نوعی دیگر مکهه باس ترنج نارنگی سدا پهل
بید کرنه پوست دیگره کتهل میان او پاک کرده
دور کنند کیوره سون کیتکی هر یک
تر کرده در کیسه جامه بیندازد و در یک کیسه خوشبو

اندازد

اندازد و در خمیرِ آرد گیرد و بپزد و گلِ موگره و باج
و سوسن زرد و سیوتی گلِ بولسری جاهی جوهی
سیوتی چنگالی چنبیلی گلِ نیلوفر در میانِ چندین
گلها خوشبویی را در میانِ کرهی
بسته بدارد و آن کره را با آن گلهای مذکور
در کیسه اندازد و در خمیرِ آرد بگیرد و بالای آن
بگل بگیرد و مکهنه باس بپزد نوعی دیگر
ترتیبِ پت پاک و دیگر ترتیبِ پختنِ مکهنه باس
مذکور میشود در میانِ چندین ادویه دو یا سه
جمع کند مکهنه باس بپزد و اگر خواهد که همه را یکجا

بپزد پس همه را جمع کرده مکهند باش بپزد از اینها اگر خواهند
کهول کنند واگر خواهند آب را معطر سازد و طعام
را بوی دهد و میوه را بوی دهد و مکهند باش راست کنند
اینست کالا بالا الایچی کوچک روهس سپاری
کچور جاپتری کبابه عنبر اشهب بالا سفید
بهپهلی موتهه تیز تنبر کیهونله کچری ناککیسر
زعفران بینس پترج تج کلاب کالعل کرسیوتی
چهریله چهر تیلیه الایچی کافور مشک نوعی دیگر
تختن مکهند باش دو سه چیز را ازین جمله که
مذکور میشود یکجا آمیخته بپزند بعده این مکهند باش را

بوی کلهای

بوی گلهای هر جنسی بدهد ادویه اینست

گلاب همه گلها جایتری بالا سفید گالا بالا سونف

چهر قرنفل ناک کیسر گلاب کافور کبابه چینی

کچری مشک دانه بینس تج چهریله موتهه

سوندهی تیز تنبل فوفل بابرنگ عود پترج سلارس

مشک کلت صندل نوعی دیگر ساختن

مکهنه باس سرد و در همه جای دیگر بکار

می آید اینست گل لعل کیهونله چهر برینک پاج

بالا سفید سپاری تخم آمله مروه مرواری پناک

ناک کیسر کهیر سار تبکهیر گل سیوتی پدمک

صندل تازه ملاکره عود عنبر اشهب کافور الایچی

کپور ایلیا اسیر کول کیس نوعی دیگر

مکهه باس وبخور جامه وبخور طعام وبخور آب و بخور

پان وبخور سپاری وبخور سر شستن وبخور موی سر

اینست سلارس مشک بینس کافور پوست نارنکی کافور

کلاب عنبر اشهب تکوی کل لعل بالا سفید کچور

پترج برهمی چنیا وتی تج باریک بهدر موتهه زعفران

تیلیه فرودستی صندل الایچی قرنفل کافور تخته

نوعی

دیکر ساختن وچکانیدن چوه خوشبویی درمیان آب

انداخته وکلاب انداخته بشورند اینست سلاکهل سلارس

لبان چاند دونه گلاب چهر چهریله بوی کلها

با گلاب شستن لاکهه رال روغن دهنا سری ملا کره

کنکوریه موم مشک کافور بهیندی صندل

موتهه بالا پترج برمهی سارسالی زعفران تیلیه نبات

شکر پربت کافور دهن عنبر اشهب عنبر سیاه

گل لعل کافور تخنه غالیه تیل شیرین نوعی دیگر

راست کردن کهول بوی تمام کلها بدهد

ادویه اینست دنکره الایچی گل بولسری

گل کیوره دوب جنیه سوندهی گل سیوتی چهر

بوی گل موکره چهریله کوتهه تکری سرکه دیودار موز

کل نیلوفر نغزک کنهل کپور کچری باونا چندن

صندل تخته مشک زعفران تیلیه فرودستی کنکوریه

بیخ کولر پوست کولر برهمی بینس پوست نارنکی کلاب

عنبر سیاه لیمو کمرک لیمسار کهیرسار هلد بیتج

ملاکره سلارس چاند غالیه کیهونله موتهه

کافور بالا اسپن کچور عنبر اشهب نیلوترا صندل

دیکر ترتیب کرنبه ماست جامه بین کافور نمک

ماست شیرین قیمه برک پیان ماست شیرین مولا نوعی دیکر

شیره انکور آب صاف قرنفل شکر تری الایچی

ملایی ماست کافور دیکر نوع بهات رایبهوک

آب ماست

آب ماست متهٔ ملائی ماست کهچرهٔ کندم بهات زرت

بهات کودیی بهات کنکنی متهٔ ماست جامه بخته

کافور مشك قرنفل زیرهٔ بریان کرده آن قدر اندا زند

کد سیاه رنك شود سوندهی شهد شکرتری کلشکر شکر

نبات سوین رایی نمك کبابه موتهه بترج

ترج ادرك شیرهٔ انکور آب صاف دیکر نخور دهنکار

روغن بخور هنك سین دوغ ترنج سیاه دانهٔ برشته

لیمو قیمهٔ برك پیاز دیکر کشنیز آب نمك زیره

سونف کافور قرنفل الاچی متهه دیکر

شکر نبات شکرتری تمرهندی ماست بیرچون

روغن بهات نوعی دیگر راست کردن تورانیت

آرد برنج برگ بادنجان بریده برگ چچینده برگ توریی

برگ پهانک برگ پندالو آرد نخود قیمه کندوری

برگ مجدبه برگ رز برگ تنبول برگ کندوری بریده

برگ خیار بریده برگ کندوری سیاه تمر هندی

برگ پوپی سوندهی آرد منگ نیمب قرنفل پیپل زیره

گل نیلوفر هنگ سونف نمک میتهی ادرک تیل

روغن تج الاتچی فلفل نوعی دیگر راست کردن

بورانی بادنجان تمر هندی کرنه تنتریکهه انار دانه

زرشک نخود تیل تعطیر بوی هر جنسی نخورات هر جنسی

سرکه آب لیمو زیره میتهی الایچی لوبیاء تخته نخود [illegible]

داده کندوری چینده قرنفل سوندهی نمک

ادرک پیپل تور زرد منک مجدبه دوغ رایی سیر

متهه کانجی فلفل کدو نوعی دیگر

راست کردن پاپر بهت شیره نبات راست کنند و چاشنی

کافور و الایچی او را بدهند و شربت کنند نمک سینده ها

زیره سوندهی شربت خرما فرد شربت کمرک

شربت مویز شربت انار شیرین شربت نبات شربت شهد

شربت شکرتری شربت میوهاء خراسانی شربت رب

میوهاء تین بهات از حبوب هرجنسی شربت شکر شیره

نانکر · شربت خربزه · شربت فقاع · شربت پیندو

شربت کهجور · شربت کلشکر · شربت کسیرو ·

شربت کولر · کشنیز · سونف · شربت بر · شربت کرونده ·

شربت پیپل · شربت آلو · شربت جامن · کافور · زعفران ·

پده تیل · پده روغن · شربت بدهل · شربت تمرهندی

شربت کتهل · موتهه · هنک · پیاز · دیگر خوشبو

کردن آب · در میان آب صاف میوها تر کرده

بدارند تا بوی ایشان آب بگیرد و اندک شیرینی بیندازد

آن آب بخورند یا در پان بهت بیندازند · بوی کتهل

آب خوشبوی · آب سرد · آب صاف · کافور · مشک · زعفران

بوی عنبر اشهب

۱۲۱

صدبیست یک

بوی عنبر اشهب بوی بالا سیاه کل هفت پره

بوی کیهونله بوی شکر بوی شهد بوی نبات

ترنج

کل سرپن بوی ریحان بوی ناکیسر بوی

بوی موز بوی لیموا بوی کیتکی بوی کیری انبه

بوی کرونده بوی انباره بوی شکوفه جامن بوی

شکوفه انبه بوی تلسی بوی کل نیلوفر بوی جامن

کل لیمو بوی سداپهل بوی موتهه برک کرنه

کرنه

کل کیوره بوی برک انبه آب خیار کل بت موکره بوی

الاچی بوی میتهی بوی هنک بریاز کرده کل موکره

بادل بوی روهس کل سیوتی کل بولسری کل کرنه بوی آمله

بوی کیوره بوی کچری گل چنبیلی بوی برگ ترنج

بوی تیلیه عنبر اشهب گل چنپه بوی گل جایی جوهی

بوی برگ لیمو بوی بدهل بوی پوست کرنه سلارس

بوی بالا

قرنفل

بوی

موز

گل ترنج

بوی صندل دیگر انواع دتهاره دتهاره روهس

دتهاره اسیر دتهاره بالا دتهاره تلسی واز برگ ریحان

و از برگ

وازبرك ترنج وازبرك ليموا وازبرك انبه وازبرك كرنه

وازبرك سداپهل وازبرك چنپه دتهاره الاچي قرنفل

زعفران از آب اينها قدري بيفشانند وازبرك كل نيلوفر

واز كل كيوره وكيتكي واز كل لعل وازبرك

پودنه دتهاره بدهند وبالاي اين دتهارها كوشت و

نان وكهونكني هرچه خواهند بپزند نيك خوشبوي

وخوش طعم شوند شاخ رز شاخ انباره چوكه

شاخ تمرهندي كل كرونده انبوتي جوشانيده

در روغن بكهار دهد وپياز بسيار اندازد

هنك بريان كرده نمك ادرك بيندازد نخود

اگر خواهد نیز اینهارا زد ابیندا فلفل و لیمو آب بدهد نمك

بهرت دیگر نوعی بپزد نیز ساك جدا جدا

سازند بهرت کرده بریان کرم کستر خا در

اجواین کرده بریان میتهی کرده بریان زیره

بکهه تنتری کرده بریان کلونجی اناردانه ساك ساق

تیندس برشته دانه کنجد حبحب توریی کهیا

تمرهندی کهری بادنجان کندوری جنکلی آمله

کگوره توریی کتهه بدهل کیتهه نمك الاچی قرنفل

لیمو پیاز کزر میکی فربه کرونده انباره سورن

انواع ساختن دیگر المسن تج بودنه رتالو هنك

آچار نو در دیگ سفالین نو سورن انداخته بجوشانند بعده
آچارها پوست دور کرده بیندازد آچار هلیله تیتر
کل سالی کانکر جامن تخته نمک در سفال برشته
تیل هنک سوخته آمله جنکالی جوشانیده انبه سهر
سنکهاره تازه کل کنوار بهنور چهال قرنفل
آب کرم تیل سی سون تیل رایی زعفران تخم نیلوفر تازه
سورن بتیر ماهی مینکی هلد زیره برشته میتهی برشته
لیمو الایچی پهالسه دهامن انباره نغزک تخته رایی
توت ماهی دوغ چنول بیلیه نیبهویی چهال کهلی
نوعی دیگ کرده علتهای سینه دفع کند

چون تشنگی بسیار غلبه کند آچار کند و در
طعام انداخته بخورد اینست انگور تازه انبارهٔ خام
نارنگی کانکره برک تمر هندی انبوتی لیموی ترش
کنار چوکه شاخ رز جنگلی ناز بیدپهمی
کرهی کهندوی کرند کانجی جامن پخته آمل بیتس
ترنج جنگلی کیتهه متهه ترنج ماست بی جز
انبه آمله تمر هندی چار تنتریکهه کرونده کمرک
انار انباره جنبهیری سرکه دوغ هلیله
کتهل خاصیت ادویهٔ مذکوره آنکه اشتهاء
و گرسنگی زیادت کند علت تهاء سینه دفع کند

طعام

۱۲۴

114

صد و بیست چهار

طعام هضم کند چون بخورند اندام گرم دارد

و طعام که در شکم هضم نشده باشد آن را نرم

کند و تحلیل دهد سبک شود نوعی دیگر

تفصیل ادویه چند که بلغم را دفع کند این است

بتهله سرخ . قرنفل . برگ تنبول . پاپل . هلد . تیلیه .

صندل . پتول . پهلی کره . بیلی تازه . روهس .

کموپی کنتهار . برگ سنهجنه . سرسون .

بتهله . شبت سبز . سورن . شهد خرما . تیز تنبر .

موتهه . کیر . پیپلو . لیمو . بادنجان . هنگ . سیر . ترب .

پیپل . سوندهی . فلفل . چب . بهپهلی . چترک . رائی .

[illegible] ادویهٔ مذکوره آنست که علتهای حلق دفع کند

بلغم دور کند دانه را و پیسی را بدهضمی را آماس را

دنبل را خوی را دفع کند گرسنگی آرد طعام

هضم کند شکم را رودها را پاک گرداند نوعی دیگر

ساختن مالیده و چونکه کلشکر شکر

کنجد دانه برشته قرنفل شکرتری شهد

تیل سرسون کنجد شیرین روغن بادام راب نان تهوالی

کافور مشک ابلوچ نان اخگر نان دوپیری

روغن چارولی تیل نارگیل مسکه موین نان خشکه

نان تمام حبوب قرصک کاک پیازکی کری

نان تنک

نان تنک تنوری انکاکی نان پوری الاتچی روغن

عسل بادام چارولی مغز خربزه سوندهی خولنجان

سیر سونف خشخاش نوعی دیگر ترتیب

ساختن حلوا باید که برابر انار شیرینی انداز زرد

یا کمتر بیندازد اینت در روغن تهولی

برشته کند خشکه در میان روغن برشته آرد منک

در روغن برشته آرد برنج شسته در روغن برشته

آرد کودهی در روغن برشته آرد لوبیا در روغن برشته

آرد نخود برشته در روغن بریان کرده آرد برنج

برشته در روغن بریان کرده آرد بادام آرد

جلغوزه آرد چارولی بوی عود هر جنسی بوی گلهای

جنسی فلفل قرنفل خرماء فرد مویز شکر تری

نبات کافور گلاب شهد سونف مشک

زعفران خولنجان تخ الاچی سوندهی نوعی

دیگر ساختن پالوده اینها را جدا جدا

طریق پالوده بپزد چارولی بادام بیندازد الاچی

نشاسته

نشاسته بادام نشاسته تهولی نشاسته سنکهاره نشاسته

برنج نشاسته کلت نشاسته تخم نیلوفر نشاسته کچور

نشاسته روه شربت داکهه تهولی زرت نشاسته زرت

نشاسته آرد عدس مشک شکر قرنفل تمر هندی

شربت آلو شربت خرما نبات کافور انار دانه گلاب

بشرح تخ نوعی دیگر بهوجی کدو یا حجب

یا محدبه هر کدام را که خواهند ازان راست

کند و مهین برند نمک زده بدست بمالند و آب

آن فشرده دور کنند بعده بکهار دهد اینست

کرلی تیندس بهلی بنبول کجری آمله کنهی سنهجنه

کیر استهٔ خرماء خام پیاز تخم سیم استهٔ جامن

مونک استهٔ نغزک کاندل پیپل بادنجان کندوری

جنبجب کهتا کر نبکی کرلی زیره بریان کرده کتهل

چچینده فلفل تمر هندی شکوفهٔ تمر هندی زیره خام

تیل هنک دره سوخته تیل سرسون سرکه آب لیمو

کاندل ترب روغن متهی سوخته هنک دوغ

توریی سینکره کنجد دانه برشته بیچهه کدو

نمک رایی کانجی متهه نوعی دیگر جوشانیدن ب

روغن مسکه بعد نافته شدن روغن کافور

و بالا بیندازند ایست برک تنبول آب نبات کافور

بالا

بالا روغن صندل تیلیه سیوتی کل لعل کولی بابت

خوردن زعفران مشک تلسی کلاب با روغن بن همه ز

عنبر اشهب پوست نارنکی پوست ترنج کل خوشبوی

کرم کرده بیندازند وصله سفال کرم کرده در

روغن اندازد زیره کشنیز کندم سیر پیاز

پودنه میتهی شاخ کرنده تازه کولی موتهه کولی کیرو

الاتچی پترج نخود برشته سونف سوندهی هنک

تنبول نامه و عطر نامه غیاثشاهی پازتا هلی شادیابا

کپور کانت کهرله نجلایی کهاکهره کپور بیلی نو

وقت چترا پت کتره پان لاتچی اداکر انباره پان پتکوله

این برگها را بشویند و پاک کنند و همچنان شاخهای

این پان را و بن پان را نیز بشویند و پاک کنند

سپاری چیول چیکنی سپاری پند و نادره سپاری کنزی

چیکنی سپاری کتله سپاری کپور کهندی

سپاری اتسار سپاری تازه سپیدی میاز سپاری سپاری

چیکنی سخت سپید کات کهیرسار کاتهه بهکوره

کاتهه پپری کاتهه کیتکی کلاب کاتهه

کاتهه چنپه کاتهه سیوتی کاتهه کرنه طلاء صندل

پان را طلاء کافور طلاء مشک درمیان چولی پن کرده

باز بدارد بعده کافور درمیاز آب کرده بالای پان

بیفشان

بیفشانند چندانکه سطبر شود بعده پانرا با سپاری ساده
بخورند کافور الایچی قرنفل طلا کنند طلاء برمهی
طلاء کیهونله طلاء کپور طلاء تج طلاء ناک کیسر
طلاء بهپهلی طلاء کیتهه طلاء بالا طلاء کچور
طلاء تیلیه نبات و تیلیه را چوه کنند و طلاء آن نیز
کنند طلاء عنبر اشهب طلاء ست عنبر اشهب
طلاء لبان طلاء ست لبان طلاء سلارس طلاء ست
سلارس طلاء ست تیلیه طلاء ست عود مرهته طلاء
ست کافور پان را با چندین جنس آبها بیفشانند
و بپرورند و طلا نیز کنند و باین آبها باس و بوی نیز بدهند

ان نا و سپاری رانیز باسربد هند و کات رانیز باسربد هند

رانیز باسربد هند و چونه راهم باسربد هند

و تنبول راهم باسربد هند دیگر فایده منقول

از کتاب

هارت

ساستر

در فایده

تنبول

و خواص آن کافور چاپتري کیهونله قرنفل

کبابه الاچي کاتهه چونه سپاري یا زایبهارا

برگ خوردن

تنبول

تنبول خوب میشود خاصیت پان دهن را صاف کند

کند اندک تلخ است باد دفع کند خاصیت

سارک شود کلو کیرست صفرا زیادت کند و اشتهاء طعام آرد

خاصیت چونه بلغم شور و شیرین را دور کند

خاصیت تنبول باد و صفرا و بلغم را دفع کند و فرح

و خوشی آرد و بوی دهن دفع کند و دهن را صاف کند

و روشنایی آرد و سخن کفتن را و طعام خوردن را

هشیار کند و زبان را سبک کرداند و دندان را و حلق را صاف

کرداند و منش کشتن آب اندر دهن آمدن

باز دارد و علتهای سینه دفع کند و علتهاء حلق را دور کند

سکر را و تشنگی را کف را باد را دور کند
باه را قوت دهد بیدار کند و نعوظ آورد و دل را قوی کند
بانی را قوت دهد پاک کند سپاری یک پاو دو چونه
کات کهیر از کولی چونه زیادت نخورد و اگر چونه سپاری
زیادت بخورد و از سپاری پان زیادت نخورد پان تیز تیب
پان تنبول خوش مزه آید پان سپاری چونه کاتهه اگر با هم
موافق و به اندازه باشد رنگ خوب شود شیرین و خوشبوی
و ملایم باشد و اگر سپاری زیاد باشد پس رنگ
قرو آید شیرین نباشد و اگر چونه زیادت باشد
دهن را آبله شود و جراحت کند و بوی بد آید و اگر پان

بسیار

بسیار باشد رنگ زیادت شود و خوشبوی باشد بعضی گویند
وقت فجر سپاری بیشتر باید خورد و وقت پیشین چون
زیادت تر از دیگر وقتها بخورد علتهای دهن را
جمله دفع کند گرسنگی آرد و چکیدن پیش آب دفع
کند هر روز چون از خواب بیدار شوند تنبول
بخورند و بالای طعام نیز و بعد سرشستن نیز بخورند
و بعد قی کردن نیز بخورند و چون کاهلی آید
بخورند کاهلی دفع کند و علتهای کام و علتهای
بات و کهار بند را دور کند و تمام علتها را و باد را دفع کند
دیگر چند کس را از خوردن تنبول منع کرده اند

دکسیرا که صفرا غلبه کرده باشد وکسی که

نفث دم داشته باشد وضعیف را وکسیرا که طعامهای

بزهین خورد وکسی که درد چشم داشته باشد

وکسیرا که زهر داده باشند وکسیرا که سی کرده وچشم

تاریکی کند وکسی که تب دایمی داشته

باشد وکسیرا که دق وسل باشد اینها را تنبول ندهند

وآب که اول در دهن آید فرو نبرند زیرا که بسیار علت

پیدا میکند وبار دوم را که جمع شود نیز نخورند

زیرا که شکم نرم کند وتب آرد وبار سیوم را

آب دهن که جمع شود فرو برند بسیار نفع کند

برای

برابر آب حیات نهاده اند باید که پان را باین ترتیب
بخورند و از خوردن بن پان که دینت گویند
نصرت برود و فقر آرد و زحمتها بیارد و رگ میانی پان
نشاید خورد در دولت نقصان کند و سر پان خورد
که عمر کم کند و رگ پان عقل را دور کند
و پانی که از آن چونه باشد اگر بخورند بی دولت
کند بسیار پان اگر دایم خورد چندین زحمتها
و بی خاصیتی آرد فقر آرد و رنگ روی زرد کرداند
و تاریکی چشم آرد و علتهای دهن آرد دیگر اگر
معطر کند به کل و خوشبویی مالند خاصیت از آنست که

منی بیفزاید دولت ترقی کند و بدن را خوشی آرد

و بد نظر دفع کند و حرارت و تیزی و نعوظ

افزاید نوعی دیگر ساختن بهجاوز در میان

هر جنسی تیل انداخته بپزند بعده

آش کرده

بیامیزند

در میان

آرد حبوب

برشته هر جنسی پس ابتنه خوب شود ادویه اینست

غالیه بینس پوست سیب پوست نارنگی گلاب

لبان سلارس لاکهه سلاکهل بالا هر دو جنس سیاه و سفید

هوس پترج چهر چهریله دیودار برهمی چپاوتی

کبابه چینی کلهای هر جنسی موم موز کیوره موتهه

الایچی خرد و بزرک کپور ایلا قرنفل بزرک چوب قرنفل

قرنفل تج چینی کپور توچه کپور کچری کافور تخته

کپور هر دو فرودستی تیلیه زعفران شکر

تیلیه هر جنسی صندل هر جنسی کل لعل مشک کافور

عنبر اشهب نوعی دیکر راست کردن ابتنه

ملد زعفران طبق زر زبره کل لعل چهر پسی

ناخن بریان کرده دیودار برک بر زرد شده

کواز نغزک شیرهٔ خوربزه برک هلد آب لیمو کمرک

کتهه جو سبوس کندم دار هلد

برنج عدس تخم پنوار کافور بادام سنکر موتهه

زیرهٔ کل نیلوفر زیرهٔ کل سیوتی نوعی

دیگر تعطیر نادره ادویه که مذکور میشود

جمع کرده آب گرم بر و بزنند بعده خشک کرده با ریک

آس کنند و بکلهای بسیار معطر سازند و بخورند

و در اندام بمالند و در طعام اندازند و پان را بویی

دهند و آب سر شستن را بویی دهند و در شربت

اندازند و جامه را بخور دهند و هرچیز را که خواهند

بوی

بوی بدهند و معطرها زند ترکیب اینست

مشک عنبر اشهب دونه لبان غالیه بیذس کلاب

پوست نارنگی پرینک تبکهیر کتهه کلکرنه ملاکره

نبلیه کافور ناککیس چپاوتی چاند کل لعل

زعفران قرنفل موتهه کیهونله پترج الاتچی

کجری سلارس برمهی کجور چهر چهریله تکری

بالاء سیاه بالاء سپید نوعی دیگر ساختن

تیلها این ادویه را با کنجد دانه بهم یکجا عصر

کنند یا در میان تیل اندازند و بجوشانند یا

بوی بدهند ادویه اینست نغزک چهر پری

عنبر لادن شکوفهٔ انبه گل کیتی گل بولسری

گل چنپه چنبیلی لیمو سرکه کمرک هلد

رکت چندن مجیتهه تون لبان پوست نارنگی

پوست ترنج کافور زعفران مروه حنا دونه

بالا کیهونله چووه سوله عنبر دن کره موته

مشک گل بیل بیل تخته پوست لیمو چووه گل کتهل

کتهل بیر نوعی دیگر ساختن کهرولی

ادویه اینست صندل تیلیه کچور کبابه تلسی موتهه

شاخ نو انبه پوست ترنج بینس نخود شکر گل سیوتی

زعفران ست چنپه شاخ نو رسته لیمو الاچی قرنفل

شاخ کهرنه نو

124

۱۳۴ 124

صد سی چهار

شاخ کرنه نو سلارس برمهی کل لسل کافور غالیه

نبات کل کرند کلاب شیره نغزک عنبر اشهب

کاتهه نوعی دیگر آمیختن عود و ادویه از هند

باید که بخور این بجامه و موی سر و آب و هر چه خوا

بدهند و معطر سازند ادویه اینست شهد نبات

لاکهه رال چنبیلی بالا راب پوست نیشکر سالی

کتهه چهریله چهر چووه چاند سلا کهل

عنبر سیوتی موم صندل کوکل ناخن مشک

شکر سلارس زعفران کافور کلاب

نوعی دیگر معطر کردن مکان و محل اگر

خواهند بخور کنند واگر خواهند بدیوارها

بمالند یا در آب انداخته بر دیوارها بیفشانند ادویه

اینست عبیر بسنت دلیله چووه بوکه کافور چینی

برگهای درخت

معطر

کرده

بیندازد

عنبر

لبان عود مرهتی بخور میده سیلا کهل آب

چوره عرق مرزنگوش کافور چینی بیفشانند آب

چھوپری

چهن پری جوشانیده گل بعود بوی داده بیننا زرد

بخور چهاند بخور شاخ بخور شیلیه عرق ریحان

عرق چنبه عرق دونه عرق برک هلد عرق تلسی

آب الایچی آب صندل نوع دیگر عبیر

محمود شاهی چهن چهار درم چهپلد چهار درم

موتهه چهار درم کچور دو درم کتهه چهار درم قرنفل

چهار درم صندل چهار درم برمهی چهار درم ملا کره

چهار درم بالا چهار درم پترج چهار درم برک هلد

چهار درم تکری چهار درم مروه دو درم تج

چهار درم بهپهلی یکدرم هوش چهار درم چپاوتی

چهار درم این همه داروها را کوفته و با آب گرم آمیخته

در آفتاب خشک کند بعده وقت آس کردن از این

مقدار ادویه دیگر بیندازند کیهونله چهار درم کچری

سه درم سینس سه درم نخ برشته چهار درم کنجد شیرین

نه درم درمیان تیل بیندازند ادویهٔ مذکور را و به

ناخن ریزه کند و بالای آس کند و نجامه ببیزند

بعده مشک شش درم کافور یک ماسه بعده سه بار

بوی گل بدهد دیگر سنت محمود شاهی

صندل آس کرده نه درم کچری یک درم کیهونله

یک درم پوست نارنگی یک درم ملاکره آس کرده سه درم

تبکه

126

١٣٦

126

صد و سی شش

تبت کهیر دو درم این همه را آس کرده و بیخته
یکجا بیامیزند و چهار کرت بوی گل موکره بدهند
بعده مشک نیم تولچه کافور دو رتی عنبر اشهب یکماسه
این همه کوفته بیخته بیامیزند دیگر دلیله محمود
شاهی صندل آس کرده نه درم ملاکره شش درم
زعفران سه درم کیهونله دو درم کپور کچری دو درم
تیلیه آس کرده سه درم هر همه را آس کرده در دیگ
سفالین لعل نو طلا کنند و در میان آن تیلیه دو درم
بخوبیاند و در شیشه بچکانند بعده صندل را خشک
کنند و در میان آن مشک یک تولچه عنبر اشهب یکماسه

کافور چهار رتی انداخته صلایه کنند

عبیر غیاثشاهی ملاکره ساویده چهار [illegible] و نیم

صندل آش کرده ربع سیر تگری نه درم

کپور کچری سه درم کیهونله دو درم کتهه شش درم

چهر شش درم چهریله شش درم پترج شش درم بالادو

قرنفل شش درم نخ سه درم هر همه را کوفته بیخته بدارند

و نخ را در ریگ گرم برشته کنند و چون سرخ شده باشد

از ریگ بیرون آرند بعده آن نخ را در میان ادویه مذکور

بیندازند بعده مشک سه تولچه کافور یکماسه آش کرده

بیندازند بعده سه کرت بوی گل معطر سازند نوعی

ساویده

127

۱۳۷

ساویده ربع سیر کپور کچری دو درم کیهونله دو درم تیلیه
ساویده نه درم ملا کره آش کرده شش درم هر همه را
یکجا کرده آش کنند و با گلاب آمیخته در
دیگ طلا کنند بعده شیشه بچکانند و در شیشه تیلیه
سه درم صندل یکدرم بالا یکدرم سلارس یکدرم
تیل موکره یکدرم انداخته بچکانند بعده زعفران
شش درم بیندازند و خشک کنند بعده مشک یکتولچه
عنبر اشهب یکماسه کافور نیم ماسه هر همه را آش کرده
بیامیزند دیگر مکهه با سرعیا نیانی ده هلی
نیم درم پوست ترنج یکدرم عنبر اشهب

[illegible] کافور سه ماسه هر همه را آس کرده یکجا

بخته باگلاب غلوله بندد مقدار ربع درم دیگر

مکهن باس غیاثشاهی پوست ترنج دو درم

پوست انبه دو درم کافور یکدرم مشک یکدرم و نیم

اشهب ربع درم چاند یکدرم باگلاب غلوله

بندد دیگر کهول غیاثشاهی نیلیه فرود ستی

چهار درم موازنه بسایند باگلاب و در میان آن مشک

سه ماسه کافور چهار رتی عنبر اشهب یکماسه در

میان کهول آتش کرده بیندازند دیگر

کهول غیاثشاهی صندل نه درم باگلاب صلایه کنند

و در میان

۱۳۸ 128

صد سی و هشت

و در میان آن مشک سه ماسه کافور یک ماسه کیهونله
چهار رتی کچری یکدرم در میان کهول اندازند و بعود
موهتی بخور دهند سه کرت دیگر کهول
غیاث شاهی ثلیثه فرودستی چهار درم صلایه کنند
مشک سه ماسه کافور چهار رتی عنبر اشهب
بیندازند کهول کنند نوعی دیگر
خوشبوی میاء عیش خانه طریق چووه بچکانند
بیامیزند و آب را خوشبو کنند یا بخور دهند
واگر خواهند بکد راست کنند ادویه اینست
مشک کافور چاند کتری صندل چووه شاخ صندل

گلاب · بخور مید خام · بخور شاخ بدهد · سلاکهل

سلارس · کپور کچری · ناگیسر · کیهونله · چووه مید

لبان · تیلیه · برنج برشته · مشک · آندی · شاخ کوفته

ناخن برشته · مید · شاخ · همه تیلها · شاخ · کنری · نافه

کوفته · آندی کوفته · زعفران نوعی دیگر

مالیدن خوشبویی عورتان در هر عضوی

خوشبویی علاحده بمالند · کهول خمیر کولی دست

بگلاب بشویند · آب پوست درخت نغزک · آب پوست

درخت بر و پیپل گرفته اندام بشویند · در بغلها

چووه ریکه و مشک بمالند · در بینی گلاب و مشک بمالند

بالای حلق

بالای حلق صندل بمالد در دهن کهرولی مشک نگاه دارد
در دهن بخور عود بالای روی چوه از تیلیه تنها
بمالد در پیشانی گلاب بمالد گل بشوید بالای
سر چهر پری انداز د روی را زعفران بمالد گل
لیه بسنت بخور هر جنسی دهد بوی نو شهی گل موگره
را عبیر بزند دو دندان پیش بمانجد رومال دست را
خوشبوی بمالد تمام اندام به گلاب بشوید
چادر سفید پوشیده بوی بهوکه بدهد اندام را شاخ
مالیده به آب سرد بشوید نوع دیگر سرد کردن
آب خود نی طبقه [illegible] سبوها [illegible] بنهد

و در زیر آن سوراخ کوچك کنند تا آب فرو آید در طغار

کلی آب پر کنند و در میان آن بیهره آب پر کرده بدارند

و بیهره باید که در فصل زمستان ساخته باشند که آن را

ماه ماس گویند

مشکها نیز

باید که در

فصل ماه

ماس

راست کرده باشند و در آن آب مکهنه باشهاء هر جنسی

بعضی را [illegible] کوزها و پیالها و قدحهای کلی تازه

آب نخورند

آب نخورند و بالای سبوها آب صندل طلا کشته کافور
بیندازد در ظرف زر آب بدارد دیگر سبوها آب پر کرده
در زیر آن بنهد و باد کند سبو را بالای شبکه
ریسمان بنهد و بیاویزد و بجنباند سبوها را در کوندله
بگیرد و باد بکند جامه پاک در میان آب اندازد
و باد بدهد بعده بیفشارد نخورانند کتک پهل در آب بیندازد
دسته بالا در آب بیندازد تخ در آب بیندازد مروارید
و کومیدک در آب بیندازد دیگر در یاد کردن
چیزهایی که در هوای تابستان مفید است اگر حرارت
غلبه کند و صفرا زیادت شود تا حرارت

بی[...]اشود از مشقت مانده شده باشد و از سواری شکار

[...] دوانیدن اسب در آفتاب گرمی آفتاب زده باشد رجوع

باین چیزها که مذکور میشود بکند و گلهای هر جنسی و میوهای

هر جنسی در بالین نهد و مردم ظریف ندیم پیش بنشاند

کهیره و خیار کولر بوی کند دولاب

آب پیش نظر بگردانند آب بر هوا اندازد کافور گلاب

بسوزانند برگ کهیره بالای اندام بنهد جامه بآب

تر کند و بالای اندام بنهد سبوهای آب پر کند

و سوراخ کند و جای بلند بدارد جامه خواب از پوست

[...] بدا[...]ند بر بالای آ[...]ند جامه کتان

کلاب

131

١٤١

صد چهل و یک

گلاب صندل کافور چادر در آب تر کرده

پهوئی بدهد بالای چشمها گلاب صندل کافور

جامه تر کرده بدارد چادر را بکافور و صندل و گلاب

تر کرده بالا بپوشند و بجنبانند بالای سر

مروارید شبکه کرده بنهد باتهال کانسه باد بکند

شبکه از مرواری بالای چشم و سینه بدارد چادر از

جامه چهونه در آب تر کنند و طرف باد بدارد چیزهاء

سرد بخورند خوشبوئیهاء هر جنسی باد بیزن را بمالد و

باد کنند گل چنبیلی و وصله بلور سرد کرده بالای

چشم بدارد گل [illegible] و چشم بدا[illegible]

بهای سفید پوشانیده و هار مرواری پوشانیده آب ١

بالای او بریزد عورتی که نزدیک نخسپانند اورا باب سرد

اندام بشورانند و مرواری بپوشانند بید و برگ نیلوفر

ودوب و برگ پیپل پیش بیندازند باب سرد و گلاب

غرغره بکنند و روی بشویند کولی الایچی و کافور

و گلاب در دهن بگیرد نوعی دیگر ٢

عمل آوردن خواب نام میوهاء هر جنسی بردن

عورتی شیرین سخن پیش بنشانند سرود گویند

گلهای هر جنس و میوها پیش نهند لبها بر هم زنند

و [illegible] را با پنج انگشت بزنند و سرود گویند

سرودها

الاچی کلاب کل لعل کل سیوتی مروه پا ملک بادیه
پهکرمول کاپهل روهس کافور بیخ کوچهه کهیر
پوست بیدس بیخ کولن بکاین لینب مهامید کسیس
پهتکری بیخ کهتونبر نوعی دیگر در ذکر ادویه
که منی بفزاید اینست نان کندم کوشت
نخود باکله کبوتر روغن کاو اکهروت
نبات چلغوزه بریان کنجشک سوندهی پرورده مویز
دارفلفل شهد پسته بادام خرما تخته کنجد دانه سپید
زعفران شیر جوشانیده با خرما عنبر اشهب نخود سپید
شقاقل پودنه نارکیل انکور تخته نان خشکه

مسلك لوبياء سرخ وسفيد بيضهٔ بط گوشت تخته گوشت

گوسفند كنند تا پياز تخم مرغ شكر تري

بط مرغ بريان ماهي تازه زيت نوعي ديگر

در ذكر طعامها كه مني بيفزايد وباه را قوت

دهد اينست پياز سپيد خراساني ده سير حلقه حلقه

ببرند ودر روغن گاو برشته سازند يا در

گنجد كبوتر بچه كه هنوز پر نكرده باشد برشته

در ميان روغن بياميزند بعده لوبياء سرخ ونخود سپيد

بكوبند وبياميزند وآب آن مقدار بيندازند كه مهرا

بعده بپزد وسر ديك مهر كنند [illegible] نرم كنند

تج یکدرم خولنجان نیم درم نان خشک چپاتی را
بری کرده در میان آن بیامیزد و طریق بغرا جوشانیده
چپاتی بیندازد یا چپاتی بالای کریله پخته در
میان شوربا انداخته بخورند نوعی دیگر
طعام گوشتهاء هر جنسی و تخم مرغ و کبوتر و مرغ
همه جنسی بپزد و پیاز و کبوتر بچه فربه را
قطعه قطعه پاره کند و در چربی بط برشته کند
نمک و نخود سپید نیم کوفته بیندازد و آب آن مقدار
کند که خوب بپزد و سر دیک مهر کند تا
آن زمان که [illegible] و نخود پخته شوند بعده یکدرم

133

تج در مر خولنجان بینداز د و ترشی کرنه بینداز د

این طعام خوردن منی بیفزاید و قوت زیادت

کند و کرده را قوی کند و قوت

زیادت شود نوعی دیگر

حلوان

فربه و

دو حصه

پیاز

سفیه در روغن کرد کاز برشته کند نمک

قرنفل الاچی دارچینی چون مهرا شده باشد

بینداز د

بیندازد بعده دیک کلی نو را بخور هنک و تیل سه چهار کرت

بدهد و ساک را در میان دیک اندازد و دیک را بجنباند و

سر دیک بپوشاند چون لذیذ شده باشد آب لیمو و تیل

و هنک بریان کرده بیندازد نوعی دیگر

بهرت بالای اخکر بادنجان برشته کند

بعده پیاز ادرک نمک فلفل ترشی بسیار بیندازد و نخود

بسیار دهد بعده سونف انداخته چپاتی ببزد و

و به آن بهرت بنوشند نوعی دیگر طعام از

میوهای هر جنسی آب بکشد بجوشاند بعده آرد را در

روغن برشته د [illegible] دران شیره اندازد و اندک

شکر تری بیندازد بعده الاچی کافور انداخته

فرو آرد نوعی دیگر ترتیب نان از حبوب هر جنسی

نان ببزد بعده نان را بسر انگشتان کاویده روغن

بیندازد نوعی دیگر ساک ساک نخود را باریک

ببرد و نمک و هینگ انداخته بجوشاند چون جوشیده

باشد فرو آرد و در روغن بگهار هینگ یا مشتهی

بدهد و ساک را در آن اندازد بعده کچه دانه بریان

کرده یا زیره بریان کرده نیم کوفته بیندازد

سه حصه ساك و یك حصه ادرك باریك بریده بیندازد

نوعی دیگر ترتیب بهات را سهوك را بهات

یک حصه

یکحصه و بهات جامز سه حصه یکجا بیامیزد نمک بیندازد

و بالاء آن کافور و مشک بیندازد و قدری گلاب

نوعی دیگر اگر داند که بدهضمی شده است

پس آنزمان طعامهاء سبک بخورد ترتیب بهات

و منک را بهت هنک و نمک ادرک الاچی قرنفل درمیان

بهت انداخته بپزد و از گوشت کردن گوسپند آش شام

بپزد برنج ادرک هلد فلفل هنک سونف کشنیز بیندازد

نوعی دیگر شوربا پلیو دار خوشبو قطعهای گوشت

و ادرک باریک بریده و آب زنجبیل و آب لیمو بیندازد بپزد

زنجبیل باریک [illegible] ان بخورد نوعی دیگر

تخمی نیمرو وخشک کباب روستایی وسیخ
خشک روستایی ادرک پیاز آزموده نمک هنک
همه حوتجها اندا خته راست کنند نوعی
دیگر کرهی دوغ ماده گاو وسیخ حلوان از
پنجگاه با تمام حوتجها ببرند ودر دوغ اندا زد
دیگر متهه بخورداده دیگر تهولی
پیاز ببرند دیگر کهچری از تهولی دیگر
کباب کوبیده این طعامها را با متهه بخورداده یا با
دوغ بخورند ودرمیان روغن سوندهی اندا خته
بجوشانند دیگر سالن چنیده وبستهله

وبهرت

و بهرت کندوری و بهرت مجدبه و گوشت با
بادنجان و گوشت باکدو و این طعامها را نیز بپزند
نوعی دیگر بیارند مجدبه و اندک از بالای
سر او بکارد ببرند و اندرون مجدبه بکاوند
و یک اخگر درو نهند و بالای آن هینگ
بیندازند و بعده ساک را با آرد بپیچد و دهن ببندد
و بالای اخگرها بریان کند بعده نمک
هینگ فلفل و آب لیمو انداخته بهرت کند و بخورند
و بهمین ترتیب بهرت بادنجان کند و بهمین ترتیب
بهرت د[illegible]کند و بهمین ترتیب بهرت کدو

136

ب

کند دیگر آب تور و پهت تور خوب

کرده بپزد و هر گاه که طعامهای سبک خواهند که

بپزند پس این طعامها بپزند اینست شورباء ساده دوغ

شورباء

گوشت

آمله

منک

وسوباس

هند از برنج برشته یعنی کهیل اینها همه را پچهه

بپزند و آچار هر جنسی و سرکه [illegible] جنسی و انکار

مابذه

137

مانده و کاک و نان تنک از خمیر مایه و نان تنک تنوری
و نان تهولی و تهولی جو و نان جوی و پست جو و آهری
و پورانی و کهچری و جهکلی و کهیس و رابری
از تهولی و کهاته از جو و مهیری جو و تهولی
ازروه و تخنی لوه و کباب لوه و شوربا لوه
و لوه بکهار داده پخته و سیخ جوزه و بهات
و پهت نخود و پهت منک و پهت تور و روغن
خوشبوی یا روغن در گوشت پخته و پاپر و آچار
لیمو و ادرک [illegible] انداخته پیش ببرد و متهه
زیره نیز با لیمو [illegible] ببرد دیگر زیره و

پرده نه و دارو کشنیز و نمک در شوربای گوشت

انداخته بپزد و گلاب بر و افشانند و سیخ نمک و جوغ

انداخته خوب نرم بپزد نوعی دیگر ترتیب

گوشت آغشتر که آنرا سوندنه گویند

گوشت نزار خوب بستانند و باریک ببرند بعده

هلد هنگ کشنیز نمک میان آن بیندازد و بیامیزد

و در دیگ انداخته بگهارد هد چون گوشت

آب خود گذاشته باشد پس آب گرم نیز بالای

آن بیندازد و بپزد چون نیم [illegible] اشده روغن بیندازد

و وقت فرو آوردن آب لیمو [illegible] ندازد نوعی

دیگر بپزد

۱۳۸ 138

صدچهل هشت ب

دیگر بهرت بادنجان درمیان بهرت مذکور

قیمهٔ گوشت قیمهٔ پیاز وصلهاء بادنجان که

در گوشت پخته باشد باهم بیامیزد بعده هنگ

آش کرده بیندازد و بخور هنگ بدهد و بالای

آن روغن پخته بیندازد بادنجان کند و ر[illegible]

توریی چینده سیم دنکره پویی ساک اینها راهمه یکجا

کرده در آب انداخته بپزد و روغن بیندازد

آب ادرک و لیمو وقت فرو آوردن بیندازد

دیگر قیمهٔ پخته درمیان قیمهٔ الاچی نفلی

زیره [illegible] کرده آش کند و بیندازد

بعده در دیگ روغن اندازد و بگهار هلد داده

قیمهٔ مذکور را برشته کند چون لنواس شده باشد

آب بیندازد و بچمچه بجنباند تا قیمه در آب آمیخته

و غلیظ گردد و چون شوربا دار و پخته شده

باشد وقت فرو آوردن زادرک پیاز آب لیمو انداخته

فرو آرد و در آن شوربا تهولی انداخته بخورد یا

بهات اندازد نوع دیگر ترتیب مهیری

مهیری را در دوغ بپزد بعده آزموده برشته میتهی

برشته هینگ برشته بیندازد و [illegible] برشته مهیری

بپزد نمک بیندازد و [illegible] روغن بدهد

نوع دیگر

نوعی دیگر

سر دیگ جامهٔ پاک ببندد و پورن مذکور را
بالای جامه نهد و ببخار بپزد بعده پیاز بیندازد
بعده هنک در تیل برشته یا در روغن برشته کند
و آش کرده در آن پورن اندازد و آن آرد را
که خمیر کرده داشته بود از آن آرد دو عدد نان
راست کند بالای یکی از آن دو نان قدری پورن
نهد و نان دوم را بالای آن نهد و کنارهای
هر دو نان استوار کند و در روغن برشته سازد
نوعی دیگر ... روه را در میان روغن
برشته کند بعده شکر تری و آب لیمو و آب

ادرک انداخته لاپسی ببرد و بالای آن الاچی قرنفل

بیندازد و اگر میوه بیندازد پس جنسی دیگر

شود نوعی دیگر لاپسی از شال برشته شال برشته

را بالای سنگ نیم کوفته کند بعده در روغن

برشته سازد و آب بیندازد و شیرینی و انار بیندازد

و بالای آن الاچی قرنفل گلاب کافور مشک

انداخته فرو آرد نوعی دیگر ترتیب مورکی

منک را در آب بخیساند بعده شسته آس کند و فلفل

ادرک کشنیز هنگ نمک انداخته برهم زنند

بعده در روغن برشته [illegible] ه همچنان بخورند

یا در

صد پنجاه

یا در شربت انداخته بخورند نوعی دیگر ترتیب

نان منک هنک و نمک بیندازد پودن اول منک را در آب

بخوسانند بعده دال را بشورد و اندک باد دهد بعده نیم کوفته

کند و در میان آن نمک و فلفل هنک و آب لیمو ادرک

باریک بریده و الاچی قرنفل هر همه را نیم کوفته کند و در

میان آنها بیامیزد بعده در میان برگ بر یا برگ موز بپیچد

و بالای آن خمیر آرد بپیچد بعده در خاکستر گرم بنهد

و وقت طعام خوردن بیرون آرد و آرد را از بالای

آن دور ک[illegible] را بیرون کند و

بخورد و [illegible] بر[illegible] راست کند و بهمین ترتیب

از مند وه راست کند و بهمین ترتیب از لوبیا راست
کند ولیکن اول لوبیا را نمک انداخته بجوشانند
بعده بیرون آرد و بدست بمالد بعده الاچی قرنفل
فلفل روغن آمیخته میان برک بپیچند و در خمیر کیرند
و در خاکستر کرم نهد و وقت طعام خوردن خمیر
از بالای آن دور کند بخورد این را طعام غریب کویند
و بهمین ترتیب از تور راست کند و بهمین ترتیب
از تخم سیم راست کند نوعی دیکر ترتیب نان غریب
روه خشکه را روغن بسیار [illegible] بریان کرده درست
و سونف بریان کرده د[illegible] بیندازد و اندک

آب در و

141

(۱۵)

صد سی و یک

آب در و بریزند موازنه تر کنند و نان سطبر کنده کنند

و فرو و بالای آن دو عدد نان دیگر از خمیر بنهد

و کنارهاء آن هر دو نان محکم کنند بعده آن

نان را بالای اخگرها بریان کنند تا آن زمان که

نیک برشته و پخته شود چون خوب پخته باشد بردارند

و نانهای فرو و بالای آن دور کنند و نان میانه را

بخورند نوعی دیگر طعام [illegible] از برنج را بشوک

بهات نرم بپزد و دال نخود سخت زرد پخته در کنار

صحن بهات بن[illegible] شکر نیز کنار بهات

بنهد و قیمهٔ اد[illegible] خوشبوی پر کاشه و پاین بالای

١

اخکر برشته ریزه کند و کرد بر کرد بهات بنهد

نوعی دیگر طعام غریب وصلهای گوشت را

روغن داده خوب بپزد چون پخته باشد پس وصلهای

گاك در آن بیندازد بعده گوشت را همیان زبرك

نهد بپیچد و خمیر کرد بر کرد بگیرد و در خاکستر

گرم بنهد تا بریان شود بعده وقت طعام خوردن

بیرون آرد و خمیر از آن دور کند بخورد نوعی

دیگر طعام غریب قیمهٔ گوشت را تمام حوج انداخته

بپزد بعده بالای خرف یعنی ت[illegible] ک[illegible] انداخته بریان

کند بخورد نوعی د[illegible] قیمه را همچنانکه

کباب

کباب در میان روغن برشته میکنند همچنان

قیمه را در میان روغن نیك برشته سازد نوعی دیگر

خاصیت بهات تشنگی دفع کند حرارت بنشاند اندام را

قوت دهد منی بیفزاید مویز خرما یکیك دو دو بیندازد

یا چهار چهار یا پنج پنج بیندازد موز یا کتهل یا بدهل

یا نارکیل یا بادام یا انار ترش یا نبات یا شهد یا روغن

یا متهه یا سوندهی یا فلفل الایچی تج پترج ناکیسر زعفران

کافور مشك در آب بخیسانند بعده با چوب ریی

بزنند و برهم زنند [illegible] از آبها آن قدر جنس بهات

بپزد چند [illegible] بود دیگر ادویه هرا

که زحمتهای مذکور را دور کند بسیاری
بلغم غلبهٔ باد غلبهٔ صفرا بسیاری تشنگی عدم اشتهای
طعام اندکی گرسنگی چندین زحمتها را دفع کند
و قوّت زیادت کند و منی بیفزاید اینست کانجی یا آب
گرم یا آب انار ترش را یی نمك آب انار شیرین
اینها را همه بیامیزد فلفل دار فلفل زنجبیل خشك الایچی
تج پترج زیره کشنیز زعفران مشك کافور عنبر اشهب
هر همه را یکجا آمیخته راست کند و آب صاف بشاترا بگیرد
از همه جنسها را که یا ... که در میان آن
سنگها ره برنج برشته نخود ... وفر گرم ...

بادام

بادام جلغوزه از میان این مذکور یک دو تارا آس کرده
بیندازد و انگشت پیچ راست کند چنانکه بانگشت
آنرا توان خورد آنرا لیهیه گویند و اگر تنک تر از آن کنند
که بکفچه توان خورد آنرا پیهیه گویند خاصیت
کهادو آنست که لیهیه سنگین میشود و پیهیه سبک
میباشد و هر جنس که ترکیب خواهد بکند آن قدر
جنسها ترکیب کند آچار [illegible] که طعام هضم
کند و کرسنگی آرد میوهای ترش و کرونده
انبه انباری [illegible] آچار کند چون هفت
آرد
روز بر آن کذ[illegible] [illegible]ل خوب شده باشد پس بیرون

وقطعه قطعه کند بعده رایی الاچی قرنفل

در آن بیندازد و در بعضی زیره و فلفل ادرک بیندازد

و در بعضی سیر بیندازد و در بعضی قطعهای پیاز بریده

بیندازد در هر طعام یا ساک یا گوشت که خواهد

در آن بیندازد نافع باشد گرسنگی آرد و بدن را

فربه کند و فرح و خوشی آرد نوعی دیگر

شاخ نو رسته بیلی در میان روغن بریان کند

بعده در حوتج بیندازد خوب خوشبو شود دیگر شاخ

نو رسته ترنج و اران لیمو و انار [illegible] شنیز تازه و برگ

زد

پیاز هر همه را در روغن بریا[illegible] و در حوتج بندا

و این

واین حوتج را در طعامها اندازد و در گوشت اندازد

و در ساک سبزی بیندازد نوعی دیگر آچار طعام هاضم

آمله مویز کیرو کوچهه تینتو

سیب کوندی کاکراسنک میندهاسنک رای آمله

کرلی توریی ادرک لیمو فلفل سپاری تازه انبه

و دیگر هر میوه که نازک باشد یا برکهای نازک باشد

یا بیخهای نازک باشد همه را بیارد و آچار کند بخورد

طعام هضم کند نوعی دیگر لابنی آرد خشکه را

در روغن بریش[illegible]ن بیندازد بجوشاند خوب

پخته باشد پ[illegible]ندازد و بامزه فرو آرد و مقدا

انار ترش شکر تري بيندازد بعده دوره روغن بدهد

وبهمين ترتيب از برنج راست کند وبهمين ترتيب

از نخود بکند وازهر جنسي که خواهد بپزد آن

قدر جنس شود

وسرکه

وشهد

بيا ميزد

آنچنانکه

ترش شيرين شود وبالاي آن ... لحي بيندازد ديگر

برنج در آب تر کند ... را بريان ميکند

برشته

۱۸۸ 145

برشته سازد بعده بکوبد و ترشی و تیزی بیامیزد یا شیرین کند

دیگر خوتجها کنجد دانهٔ بریان کرده یکدرم

مستهی بریان کرده نیم درم برنج بریان کرده دو

درم نخود برشته دو درم کهل بریان کرده نیم درم

هنك بریان کرده یکدرم سرکه چهار درم آب لیمو یك

مشك چهار رتی کافور چهار رتی بخور تیل بدهد

این خوتجها را در گوشت یا در طعام یا در شربت یا

در دوغ و در هرچه خواهد بیندازد دیگر [illegible]

هر جنسی [illegible] طعامها را بدهند ایست

بخور شد [illegible] ت نیشکر از کافور از مشك

از گلاب از صندل از عود تیلیه از تج از پترج از

الایچی از عنبر اشهب از سلارس از چاند از سلاکهل

از غالیه از والا از قرنفل از چهر از چهریله از موتهه

از تکری از زعفران از گل چنپه از گل جاتیی

از برگ هلد از گل موگره از گل سرخ از لوبان

از گیوره از گل بولسری از برگ موز از برگ سدل

از برگ ترنج از سیب از دونه از مروه از سیوتی از تلسی

از ریحان اینها را همه علاحده سوخته بخور دهد هر چه

را خواهد نوعی دیگر [illegible] آمله برنج برشته

در آن انداخته بجوشانند و ا[illegible]یند از نمک

نمک
فلفل

نمک فلفل انداخته فرو آرد بگهار هنک بدهد تج پترج بودنه
آب لیمو بیندازد و بالاء آن بخور هنک بسیار دهد و آب
ادرک بپزد و آن بیندازد نوعی دیگر بچهه آب نمک
تج پترج الاچی قرنفل بیندازد و بخور بدهد و اگر برنج برشته
انداخته بپزد پس جنسی دیگر شود و اگر برنج انداخته
بپزد پس جنسی دیگر شود ترتیب نان [illegible] در آرد
کندم سونف پیاز و روغن و نمک بیندازد بپزد
نان چپاتی از خمیر مایه چپاتی تنک بپزد طرح توچا شتی
جلغوزه جل [illegible] آ [illegible] کند بعده شهد یا
شکک [illegible] آن اندازد دیگر جا

نخود دیگر وچاشنی بادام وچاشنی برنج برشته
وچاشنی نخود برشته وچاشنی کردگان وچاشنی
چارولی وچاشنی خشخاش وچاشنی کنجد دانه برشته
وچاشنی پسته این همه جنسها را چاشنی راست کند چنانچه
چاشنی جلغوزه گفته آمده ایم همچنان چاشنی
اینها را نیز راست کند این چاشنی ها را چاشنی غیاث شاهی
گویند نوعی دیگر شوربای گوشت در شوربای گوشت
شتر یکمن انداخته شوربا کند نوعی دیگر
شوربا در شوربای گوشـ [illegible] ندازد نوعی
دیگر شوربای گوشـ [illegible] ت آمله انداخته

بپزد

۱۴۷

بپزد این ترتیب پختن کرهی است از دو ادویه یا
سه ادویه خوتج ازین جمله جمع کنند یک جنس
علاحده کرهی شود و ادویهاء مذکور اینست

دوغ نمک

آرد برنج

کودیی

جو

آرد نخود

قرنفل الاچی آ... انباره تمر هندی کانجی

آب لیمو آب... کرونده آمل بیتس مشک

تج کافور منك نخود درهت برنج بری منك

کهندوی زنجبیل خشك بری بزرك بزرك

فلفل تیل درهنك سوخته هنك در تیل برشته شکرتری

دنکره کیتهه آچال سیر چهارم حصه لیمو نمکی

زرت

تتماج بغراء بریده نان پولی نان کاك نان جواری

زرت [illegible] کر نبات کلشکر آب ماست

بالا دوغ زیره میتهی کلونجی سیاه دانه آزموده اجمود

دیگر [illegible] تعلق به شوربا گوشت دارند

شکرتری الایچی [illegible] رهنك بادام

نارکیل نیلوفر کهری [illegible] دانه برشته

نخود برشته

١٥٨

صد پنجاه هشت

148

نخود برشته نمک پودنه گل سرخ فلفل نخود مستهی مروه

نبات آمله شهد خرما مویز تلسی پیاز کردگان

نخود زیره بیرچون زنجبیل خشک آب ترنج کیری انبه

زعفران نخود عود تلیه تمر هندی کشنیز آمل بیتس

پسته بترج تنتریکهه آب لیمو زیره زرشک دیگر

حوتجات لیچار اینست نبات آلو شهد [illegible] هی

قمرک زعفران کولر تیندو تمر هندی انجیر

کتهل مویز گل سیوتی گل سرخ دنکره گرونده

شکر تری سو [illegible] که شاخ نورسته کرونده

شاخ نورسته [illegible] مله کافور شفتالو بر

١

پیپل بدهل انبوتی کنار انباره لیمو ادرک ترنج

دیکر ترتیب راست کردن جنسهاء آچار اکر یکجا

کرده بیامیزند پس ستو شود اینست الایچی

نخود سبز کزر بسونته سیر شاخ سوسن

شاخ ترب پیاز کل کیر کل سهجنه شاخ تازه لیمو

شاخ تازه ترنج جامن خام سونف سبز کتهل خام

شاخ تازه پیپل استه انبه ادرک نبات ترنج تیل شیرین

کنجد دانه برشته سرکه تیل رایی سیاه دانه قرنفل

پهلی اکتهیه شاخ تازه [illegible] ل رایی کشنیز

هنک انبه نخته دده هنک ا[illegible] جواین برشته

کشنیز

صد پنجاه نه

كشنيز برشته تيل سرسون زيره نمك سونف

برشته ليمو آب دوغ سرسون بريان كرده ميتهي بريان كرده

شاخ كل بيل خيار ميتهي كندوري بيج سنهجنه

پهلي چكنا نرم پهلي آسيترا نرم ديكر آميختن

طعامهاي سرد و ادويه سرد اينست بر مويز جامن

تيندو بدهل كسرني كتهل كولر الايچي شكر تري

زعفران كلاب كافور پيپل نبات آب ادرك سور

انار دانه آب دوغ تستريكهه كانجي برك تنبول آب ليمو

پهالسه آب [illegible] ادن كره متيره انار

شفتالو دها [illegible] رك پتنج نارنكي تج بير

مشك بهات عنبر اشهب زرشك ديگر پختن

شير برنجهاي هر جنسي اينست ارده كرده كان

ارده نارگيل ارده كرهي روغن خوشبوي

شيره انبه فلفل دراز اردهاي حبوب مويز آس كرده

بادام آس كرده پسته آس كرده جلغوزه

آس كرده نان تنك پهن كرده نان تنك سفيد

نان تنك تنوري گلاب خرماء سليماني ادرك

خشخاش تهولي كايك كنكنين شالي برشته

نا ... ولي زنجبيل خشك فا ... الايچي آب

حراء فرد ... شكر ترى ... نقل شير

بپنزارد

بیندازد فرو آرد بخورد قوت باه بسیار شود نوعی دیگر
وصلهای گوشت تنک تنک ببرد و آنرا حوبجهای
هر جنسی بمالد بعده خشتها را نیک گرم کند و بالای
آن خشتها گوشت مذکور بنهد تا خوب برشته شود و
بخورند نوعی دیگر طعام که منی بیفزاید
نخود سبز در روغن گاو برشته کند و دو برابر
آن جلغوزه و دو حصه کردگان در شکر تری بیامیزد
و بپزد و در ظرف نگاه دارد و پیش از طعام بخورد و
نماز شام نیز [illegible] دیگر کبوتر بچه
و مرغ یا کبک [illegible] بگیرد و خوب پاک کرده

حوبج تمالد بعده بچوب تیز سوزن زنند و بالای آن

خولنجان تخ نمک و آرد تمالد و بریان کند یا در شوربا

بپزد نوعی دیگر تخم ماهی را هر جنسی حوتج مالیده

در روغن برشته سازد یا در روغن کرده کاز برشته

کند و در میان آن پنج عدد تخم مرغ بیندازد

نوعی دیگر ماهی تازه و پیاز سپید در روغن

کرده کان بریان کند و نمک بیندازد بعده با نان

چپاتی بخورند خاصیت او آنست که قضیب استوار دارد

و نعوظ آورد بود در وقت مجامعت خرج شود

واین از سر ... ایشان اطبا ... این نمیکند

بسیار

بسیار نافعست طالیسفر آن مقدار که خواهند در آب
یکشب بدارد بعده آب دور کند و پوستِ وی
دور کند و در عسلِ صاف بیامیزد و بیست روز بدارد بعد
ناشتا مقدار ده درم بخورند آن مقدار که مجامعت کنند توا[نند]
و سست نشوند و قوّتِ مجامعت زیادت شود و هر کرا
منی بمشقّت بسیار بیرون آید او را از خوردنِ این دارو
در وقتِ انزالِ منی بلذّت تمام بیرون آید و بجهتِ
افزودنِ منی این دارو بغایت عجایبست ایستب
مغزِ پنبه دا[illegible] و تهه نیم درم کوفته و بیخته
در روغن[illegible] بیامیزد و لوقه[illegible] مالد در خود

[illegible] اورا بیند که هرکز ندیده باشد دیکر

طلا قضیب روغن بلسان روغن زیت مشک تبتی

اصلی یکدرم آس کرده در روغن مذکور بیامیزد

وبر سر قضیب مالند آن مقدار که خواهد مجامعت تواند

کرد و سیر نشود نوعی دیکر ازاربند که

منی بیفزاید ابریشم زعفرانی زرد کرده را نافع باشد و

کرم کند و محل منی را کرم دارد ∴ دیکر

ازاربند از پشم کنده راست کنند بسیار خوبست

واین کار را مفید بود و [illegible] سمور را به

پهناء چهار انکشت راست کنند [illegible] در هوای

زمستان

152

١٦٤

صد شصت چهار

دیگر در میان چوب خوشبویی ما آیده ودر

زمین بسوزانند وبعده چوب را بتکانند وپاك كنند

وزمین را بگلاب ترکنند وجامهٔ پاك انداخته

عورت بنشینند رطوبات که از رحم او آید خشك

کرد اند وخوشبو کند دیگر خوشبویی

ولایت حبشه از مجامعت حبشیه وزنگیه

درد کمن برود در هوای زمستان ودر

هوای تابستان مقابل سینه بپاشند دیگر

جلادادن عود سوخته شهد بیخ گانتا

سیلواسو تمالدی هلیله سوخته پی شت

نارکیل سوخته پوست بادام سوخته لیمو نمک سپیده ها

نارکیل سوخته زعفران عود سوخته جو سوخته

فوفل سوخته وصله سپید که بیاز سنگ مولی میباشد

آس کرده خشت آس کرده صندل سوخته

کاتهه عقیق آس کرده یکجا بیامیزند و بخوبسانند

در آب هر کدام که یافت شود و بر دندان زمالند

نوعی دیگر در رنگ کردن دندان پوست انار ب

مازو پهل بجیتهه آب پوست نارکیل که وقت سوختن

بیرون آید خبث الحدید یعنی ملیله آمله

لیمو با کسیس برد دندان را با الاچی

دندان

دندان نهند مهاور خوب بالای تخته آهنی بمالد وساعت

بساعت به آب کاهی بپاشد پهت کری و آب لیمو

غراره کنند بعده سیاری و بپند بالای دندان طلا کنند

دندان سرخ شود وسیاه نیز شود دیگر سوند هد

سکند هد جامه دو تو کرده مشک آلوده

در بغل بنهند در جیب مشک کرده بدورد در هر بند

وکتان چوره وصندل بمالد یک حمایل از والای سبز

بدورد و مشک پر کنند دیگر خوشبو شد

دم کل سیو [illegible] لی در دهن یک طرف بان و

یک طرف [illegible] ل هلد رال نغز از کل العل

153

کل مرکره عود مرهتی صندل کهربا پوست
نیشکر تیلینه نبات عود کافور بخور از راه
بینی بکیرد نوعی دیگر لازمه وقت باریدن
باران وهوای آن جریس بهرت اسیخ انکاکر مسکه
نان سونف انداخته
بریان
تلادبه
حیله
سنبوسه
بینی ... کو ... اری مالیده

چون

154

١٦٥
صد شصت و پنج

چونکهنه پوري سهالي روغني تخني باد[illegible] سرکه
نخود آب پیاز بورهٔ تخني مستهي لنواس اج[illegible]
ادرك ليمو ترب تخني مغلي تخني يزدايي نوعي
ديكر ملايم هواي زمستان كهچري مستهي
لنواس سوره ادرك شكر هاشمي تازه نان تنك تابه
ان خشكه نان تنك تنوري نان زرت و
روغن و شهد لنواس كسوندي كاك كرم خرما كرم
كهچري ماش كوشت وبادنجان كوشت وبرك مستهي
روغن [illegible] آچار رواسي كشنك بهت باچه
هرسه د[illegible] هواي تابستان كهيس

[illegible] کرده دره سرد از شیر کهیر سرد

آدر [illegible] ای کافور شیر کامیش بیرچون ساتو پازبهت

سکهرن انبلوانی دوغ شتر دوغ جهکلی شیره

رابری کرنبه ماست تازه سوندهی شربت پالوده

برساله کرنبه نوعی دیکر طعامهای

میهمانی لدو صد من بهینی دو دو کزی و سه سه

کزی [illegible] شاهی بریان ماده گاو درست

[illegible] دهن او ترب [illegible] نهد ریوری و مرچونی پنج

سیری کلیچهای بزرگ [illegible] هر جنس از نبات

ریختن بریان شتر درست [illegible] درست قدح

بجاهم

155

155

١٦٦

صد شصت شش

نجاهره از شکر تری خمهای بزرگ از شکر تری

سنبوسهٔ غیاثشاهی نهال از نبات قرص از نبات هاشمی

بزرگ صاف بالای بوریا برشته شاخهای سبز در زر و نقره

گرفته و معصفر و نقاشی کرده و بالای

پیندهاء حلوا و مالیده ترتیب سبز فرو برده در میان خربزه

تنکهای زر پر کنند هر که نخورد تنکها نیز بستانند

بالا گلها بیندا زند تنه سوزن و شاخهای تخته و برگهای

سبز نهال بی مخدومهٔ جهان را وضع است خوانچه

هفت رنگ ط[illegible] خوانچهٔ زر پر کرده بیارند

وهر جنس [illegible] عی صحن نقش کردن

۲

خوشبویی [illegible]یان زنجبیل مفرح غیاثشاهی سرد کیور

موتی [illegible]ر غیاثشاهی رب انار رب تمر هندی زمهریر

حلوای ادرک بهاسک رانجن مرهم هر جنسی رس

موتی ابلوچ و گلاب زده حلوای مجدبه بهوک لدو

کهچری از میوهای خراسانی هر جنسی کهول صندل زعفران

وقتی که ترکشبند تیغ بر سر دشمن میزند برهمند بخش کند

فوج دار حلقهای زر و نقره خمرهای عسل ریزه

تر لدو طغارهای زر و نقره پر شربت هماچله قمقمه گلاب

گلشکر کاسهای پر چووه [illegible]اهای شاخ خوشبویی

و تنبول و انعام قسمت کند [illegible] شما[illegible] کافور تر کرده

آمله عسل.

156

156

١٩٧

صد نود و هفت

آمله عسل رب کرونده حلوای رای آمله روغنهای

جراحت داروهای جراحت داروی هر جنس بجهت

دفع ماندگی و دفع خون بسته و کنجد دانه آس کرده

و آمله در اندام بمالد نوعی دیگر چیزهای

مناسب شکار بازی کردن آب برگ گلاب

کافور همراه بسیار بگیرند شکره و چیته مشک خراسانی

داغدار سیاه گوش بار [illegible] اندازان [illegible] زنان زورگر

سلاح پوشیده و آهن بسته همراه باشد مومیایی و

دیگر پازهر [illegible] و داروهای [illegible] خون هر جلیسی

و داروها [illegible] گراذویه همراه بگیرند و کرد

بر کوه [illegible] قلعه خواجه سرایان حلالخوار بدارند و
فیلها که مست نباشند همراه بگیرند برای شکار و
شکرانه بگزارند و بر اسپ مزاج دان سوار شوند
وقت سوار شدن بر اسپ دعا بخوانند شاخ مار و پوست
سی مار با کله مار در ترکش بدارند پازهر مسکین و
حلالخوار همراه بگیرند و طرفی که باد باشد
همان طرف بروند و بجهت [illegible] ختن باد رومال باریک
همراه بگیرند پهول پالکی و کنیزکان کهارنی
طعام توشه بالای اسپ تختن [illegible] و بی زعفران
و بادام بمالند [illegible] بالا [illegible] سرود گویان

همراه

همراه بگیرند در میان کفش کافور انداخته بدوزانند

محبوبان خوش شکل همراه بگیرد جامهای شکار بپوشند

عورتان خوش آمد گوی وندیمه همراه بگیرند پایها را

صندل وکافور مالیده در موزه کشند شکر انجایی

آرند وجایی که

دنبال

میگیرند

وقصد

میکنند

پوست بزکه ... انداختن زیرپا همراه بگیرند

بقیمت شناختن ساعت حلقهٔ اصطرلاب همراه بگیرند
و بر منازل [illegible] همراه بگیرند نوعی دیگر دایره
شکار رفتن مهرهای زر و نقره کوچک و بزرگ که چیزی
در زیر ترکش پر کنند یک اسپ جنگ همراه بگیرند
در دست آدمی زیرک بهاتری بسپارند پس پشت شیر و
کامیش نباید هشیار باشند نزدیک مور و نزدیک
پلاس از مار هشیار باشند [illegible] ده کوچک همراه بگیرند
[illegible] جا که خواهند بگرد [illegible] چتر کلاه سایه بان نمد تکیه
پوستین بگیرند [illegible] و تیز کش و تیر [illegible] دا و حمام روان
باید که آب گرم موجود باشد [illegible] اشی و سنگ

[illegible] همراه
شد صح

و چقماق

158

۱۶۹

صد شصت نه

[illegible]

وچقماق همراه بگیرند پلنگ مردن و نهالی و شیلک

همراه بگیرند خروس سپید همراه بگیرند یک اسپ شکار

همراه بگیرند شست ناک تهل بنسی چاره دام شلم نل

نل زمین تندکی دام بتیر همراه بگیرند چون قصد آهو

کنند دو آدمی حلالخوار پس پشت بدارند ناوک

همراه بگیرند شمشیر خنجر مسم جامه شهکلی ازان

پهوهی تفنگ چندزبان تیر دو کمان دوزه چراغ

کتاری خنجر جامه خواب سموز گارد بانه

دانه کرز حسکر سپر بزرگ که آدمی ایستاده

پس او پنهان [illegible] شکار رفتن

[illegible] دوا [illegible] زاسب دست تیر دراز بدارند و از خار مار

و [illegible] [illegible] فظت کنند محلّی که کوچه

و کژدم باریک باشد که آنرا پت بیچهو میگویند نایستند

جایی که عنکبوت بسیار باشد نروند سرسنگا

بهری دهوتی جرّا بار طبل بار کرم کوش لباچه

نیزه بیدر [illegible] کمته [illegible] کوپهن طناب پوست

بار و پوش جایی که [illegible] باشد اسپ ند و انند در آب

اسپ بد و انند کربه و [illegible] دیده اسپ پیشتر نرانند

چوکی و [illegible] آفه و چمانرون [illegible] نات و آمله همراه

بگیرند [illegible] مسا [illegible] ابرانام بما [illegible] انور بگریزد

کلاب و بکه

کلاب و بکه و تهنیتی پاز همراه بگیرند
نزدیک دیدکه خانهای کوچک باشد آنجا بازی کردن
نروند. تخت روان محمودشاهی و تخت غیاثشاهی
سکاسن. پالکی و سلهی نقره. جهجهی. بازوبند
پلنگ. نهالی ته کرده بر پشت بسته سوار شود
نوعی دیگر شکار. در جنگل شکار بازی
دکانها بنهند و سودا و معامله هرچیز بفرمایند و
خانهای ماست فروشان و محله ایشان و رفتن بخرید
شیرخانه ایشان. طعام خریدن. نیز بازیک بجهه
انداختن. طالی پر کاه کودیی کرده بدارند

بجهت شناب نهالی نهالیها کدو آب پر کرده بجهت

سرد کردن آب کواس پلنك از کدو با نوار ببندا زند

شمعها موم مشکها پر گاه کودیی پیال کرده بجهت شناب

در سوراخ و مغاکی

کرده دود

بیرون

آید

پیش آب

نزدیك آن [illegible] کنند بالای [illegible] کرك مار افتاده

باشد پیشاب نکنند هوایی [illegible] رند شهنا

طعامهای درکه خورلنجان کبابه سویدی
تج دار فلفل فلفل مشکهای آب پیتا وها جامه کتان
دمامه و نزغه و نفیری دار خوانچ هر جنسی و خمهای
روغن و تیل برنج و منک و سیخها هرجا بنهند و هر وقت
که خواهند فرود آیند طعام بپزند چهار گلی آب
پیش زین بیار و بپزد و بالای او سایه کنند نوعی
دیگر شکار شتر همرا بگیرند جامه پوستین
سوزن ریسمان ریسمان خام ستکه بجهت زدن
خرکوش دهتا [illegible] جات جهتری بجهت زدن ماهی
نشسته کتا [illegible] زدن آهو [illegible] بجهت زدن تیر

[illegible] بجهت پرانیدن بتین و تیتن بجهت گرفتن

[illegible] نور بجا نور هر جنسی زنده همراه بگیرند زهکین

و انگشتانه دام درخت جال بهنور جال کوندل
جال

پکسته شیر دهن هت کپری دم چیتل بربند

بنشانند در سیل برشته بدارند و بر کوهی باز بزنند بعده

دست بر ریش ننهند و در جدهٔ بر کوهی خارها مار

میباشد نزدیک کره نروند از دور بزنند نوعی

دیگر خوشبوی خام تیلیه کل هر جنسی

لوبان شکر ملیله [illegible] کنند کافور

مشک صندل زعفران [illegible] ایی یکدانه

برمهی

بن مهی چهن بله قرنفل تکوب مین اسن
مقدار دو برابی نوعی دیکر میوهای
خویسانیدن در آب شیرین بخویسانند و چون خوب
خویسیده باشد آب را دور کنند کافور مشک
کلاب بیندازند کلشکر ابلوج کولر تیندو
نکری سیب به عناب کنار نبات
مویز کشمش کلاب بادام بوی کلهای هر جنسی
بدهند در آب میوها بخویسانند زعفران مشک
کافور [illegible] سنکهاره خرما سلیمانی
شکر بادام [illegible] یلوفر مویز کهری شفتالو

خوربزهٔ خشک نوعی دیگر برشتن میوه‌ها بالای

اخگر برشته نماید گندم زرد کنجد دانه بتله

تور عدس کنگنی استهٔ انبه کودیی زرت منک

راله موتهه نخود سبز جو پسته شال تیوره

نیشکر نخود خام استهٔ تمر هندی سوندهی بادام

استهٔ جامن استهٔ کنهل بره در تیل برشته کند پوری

در روغن برشته بعده بالای اخگر برشته کند

تخم نیلوفر نارکیل خشک جلغوزه والله اعلم

بالصواب

١٧٣

162

صد هفتاد سه

بسم الله الرحمن الرحيم

الحمد لله الفاطر

وصلى الله على رسوله محمد

وآله الطيبين الطاهرين

وسلم

کتاب نعمت نامهٔ ناصر شاهی

وعطر نامه و ترکیب خوشبوییها و ترکیب چووه

و ترکیب تیلها [illegible] خوشبوی و ترکیب پختن کافور

و ترتیب [illegible] کلابها و ترتیب کرفتن ستهها

هر جنسی و ترکیب [illegible] ترکیب ترنج و مکهه

باسهها و ترکیب جمله نکهها و ترکیب شه بیشها اندرین

کتاب بیان [illegible] شود بترتیب

انشاء الله تعالی اکنون [illegible] ترتیب

پختن طعام مینابیم و ترتیب کوشتها و ترتیب بغراها

و ترتیب سیخها و ترتیب سنبوسها و ترتیب پختن ماهیها

و ترتیب تخنیها و ترتیب طعامهای سرد و ترتیب کهلیسها

و ترتیب برنجها و ترتیب کوشت درکه و ترتیب پختن

بره و ترتیب سکهرنها دیکر ترتیب

پکوانها نوشته میشود ماش پهتیها و لدوهاء

هر جنسی و تلسکلیها و پوریها و کپورنلیها

دیکر ترتیب [illegible] و ترتیب پان و سپاری

و ترتیب [illegible] ترتیب آچارها و ترتیب کباب کنواری

و ترتیب [illegible] ترتیب خوشبویها هر جنسی

ترتیب کهول نوشته میشود اینست صندل یکتولچه
کپری نیم تولچه کیهونله ربع تولچه برگ گل لعل یکتولچه
زعفران نیم تولچه کافور نیم تولچه مشک نیم تولچه
اینها را هر همه یکجا آمیخته آس کنند و بر اندام بمالند
نوعی دیگر کهول صندل یکتولچه کافور
یکتولچه مشک یکتولچه شاخ ربع تولچه باگلاب
آس کرده بر اندام بمالند و در سر نیز بیندازند
نوعی دیگر کهول صندل یکتولچه کافور یکتولچه
مشک یکتولچه شاخ ربع تولچه با [illegible] آس کنند
و بر سر و اندام بمالند نوعی دیگر کهول

بیفس یکتوله کافور نیم توله مشک نیم توله

زعفران ربع توله جمله را با گلاب بسایند و بر اندام

بمالند نوعی دیگر گهول تیلیه دو توله

در کاسه بیالاید و بخور تیلیه بدهد مشک ربع توله

کافور یکماسه بیندازد بعده با گلاب آس کرده

بر اندام بمالند نوعی دیگر گهول صندل

دو توله در کاسه بیالاید و [illegible] عود مرهتی بدهد

و بوی گلهاء هر جنسی بدهد مشک ربع توله کافور

دوماسه از [illegible] آس کنند و بر اندام بمالند

نوعی دیگر [illegible] بیفس یکتوله تیلیه یکتوله

آس کرده در کاسه بیالاید و بخور عود بدهد
و بر اندام بمالند نوعی دیگر کهول ناخن
بویا را با لای وصله خزف نو برشته کنند بعده مشک
یکدرم کافور نیم تولچه با گلاب آس کنند و بر
اندام و سر بمالند نوعی دیگر کهول صندل
یکتولچه [illegible]نبر [illegible] نا[illegible] راغ تولچه لچری یکتولچه کیهونله
یکتولچه زعفران نیم تولچه آس کرده یکجا
بر کاسه بیالاید کافور نیم [illegible] تولچه مشک نیم تولچه
هر همه را آس کرده [illegible] بمالند نوعی
دیگر کهول برک [illegible] صندل

میان

١٧٦ 165

صد هفتاد و شش

بیان گل موگره بوی داده یکتولچه مشک یکتولچه

عنبر اشهب یکدرم کافور نخنه یکماسه با گلاب بسایند

و بر سر و اندام بمالند نوعی دیگر کهگل

صندل بگل موگره بوی داده دو تولچه مشک خالص

یکتولچه عنبر اشهب ربع تولچه کافور یکماسه با گلاب

بسایند و بر سر و اندام بمالند [illegible] ترتیب چووه

نوشته میشود تیلیه خاص سه تولچه جو کوب کنند

نبات یکدرم بیندازند و با گلاب بسرشند و مید یکتولچه

درو بیندازند و [illegible] بوه بچکانند نوعی دیگر

چووه چو [illegible] یکتولچه در کاسه بمالد و آن

کاسه را زیر بدارد و در میان دیگ آب بیندازد

و بالا چوبه بخکاند تیلیه سه تولچه میدیک تولچه نبات

یکدرم با گلاب تر کند و شیشه را پر کند و آن کاسه را

که چوبه

خاصه

مالیده

داشته

بود او را

زیر چوبه بدارد و بالای او چوبه بخکاند بعده مشک

یکدرم کافور یکماسه انداخته بسا [illegible] ام بمالند

نوعی دیگر جو

نوعی دیگر چوره تیلیه سه تولچه نبات یکدرم

مشک یکماسه کافور نیم ماسه زعفران نیم ماسه میده

تولچه یکجا کرده بسایند بیامیزند و در شیشه پر کنند

بعده چوره نچکانند کافور نیم ماسه مشک نیم ماسه

انداخته با گلاب بسایند و بر اندام بمالند نوعی دیگر

چوره تیلیه دو تولچه چهر چریله تگری موتهه

دیودار از هر یک ده ماسه لبان سه ماسه نبات یکدرم

سلارس یکماسه مید دو تولچه هر همه را یکجا آش کرده

شیشه پر [illegible] چکانند و کافور یکماسه مشک

یکماسه [illegible] انداخته بسایند و بر اندام بمالند

نوعی دیگر چووه خاصه تیلیه سه توله نبات

یکدرم غالیه یکتوله با گلاب ترکرده و در شیشه انداخته

بجگانند کافور یکماسه مشک یکماسه انداخته در چووه

آس کنند و بر اندام بمالند نوعی دیگر

چووه تیلیه یکتوله نبات یکدرم و نیم پترج تج

تگری موتهه برگ ملد هلیله را ناگکیسر چهر

چهریله هوبیر نکهه یعنی ناخن بویا بالاء سپید

سلارس لبان صندل گچور از هریک یکماسه یکجا

جمع کنند کنجد شیرین یکتوله و نیم [illegible] توله انداخته

در شیشه پر کنند و چووه [illegible] کانند [illegible] مشک

یکدرم

صدهفتادوهشت

یکدرم با آن آمیخته بسایند و بر اندام بمالند. نوعی دیگر ب

خوره میدیکتو لخچه در کاسه بیالایند بالای اخگر عود

مرهتی انداخته بخور دهند چون بخور خوب گرفته باشد

پس بگیرد شاخ یکدرم کافور یکدرم مشک یکدرم در آن

بیندازد و قدری گلاب بیفشانند بعده باریک آس کنند

بعده بوی کار موکره بدهد بسیار عجایب و خوب

شود بر سر و اندام بمالند اکنون ترتیب عود هاء ب

هر جنسی نوشته میشود اینست تیلیه نیم سیر باریک

بکوبند [illegible] سیر آس کرده در و بیندازند

و در میان [illegible] ره نقره یا کتوره مس قلعی کرده

بِبندازند و کلاب درمیانِ آن ریزند آن مقدار که تیلیه

در آن فرو رود و کلاب بالای او بیاید و بالای

اخگر در بر نهند و بجنبانند تا آن زمان که کلاب تمام

خشك شود بعده فرو آرند و در میانِ آن مشك چهار

تولچه عنبر اشهب یك تولچه و نیم کافور ربع تولچه باریك

آن کرده در آن تلیه بیندازند و خوب بیامیزند

و غلولها بندند در سایه خشك کنند و هر وقتی که

خواهند یك غلوله بگیرند و بالای اخگر

نهند و بخور کنند [illegible] تلیله ربع

سیر [illegible] بکوبند [illegible] بات [illegible] نیم تولچه

مشك

۱۷۹ 168

صد هفتاد و نه

مشك يكتوله كافور يكدرم يكجا بيا ميزند در سايه خشك
كنند و چون خواهند كه بر اندام بمالند يا جامه
را خور كنند آن زمان بكار برند نوعي ديكر
تركيب عود مرهتي چهار چهار بله تكري موتهه
تج بالاء سپيد هو بير برمهي ناخن بويا را اديو دار
هليله كنهه كه جامه رنك ميكنند صندل از هر يك
ربع سير تليه دو سير لبان يكسير سلارس يكسير يكجا
كند بعده شهد چهار سير در ميان آن بمندا زند و در آفتاب
خشك كنند ... ميان جامه نهد تا بوي كيرد بعده در
ميان جامه ... كره بقيه از دبيله خوشبو ميشود

168

ربوی خوب میگیرد نوعی دیگر عود تیلیه سه سیر

لبان ربع سیر زعفران یکتولچه کافور یکتولچه مشک

یکتولچه نبات یکسیر اینهارا یکجا بیامیزد عود خوب شود

اکنون تیلهاء خوشبو نوشته میشود تیل موگره

یکتولیه کافور

یکماسه

مشک

دوماسه

شلخ

یکماسه [illegible] ابیا [illegible] وسن بمالند

نوعی دیگر تیل

نوعی دیگر تیل موکره یکتوله از پوست نارنگی

ربع توله کافور یک ماسه باریک آس کنند و

اندام بمالند نوعی دیگر تیل موکره و تیل

چنبیه و تیل چنبیلی و تیل کرنه یک درم مشک دو

درم کافور دو ماسه باریک آس کنند و بر اندام بمالند

نوعی دیگر تیل یک کرنه بوی داده یکتوله

مشک خالص یکتوله کافور نیم ماسه عنبر اشهب یک ماسه

هر همه را یکجا کرده آس کنند و بر اندام بمالند

نوعی دیگر تیل موکره دو توله کالعل

نیم توله [illegible] کافور [illegible] نیم ماسه یکجا کرده

بساید [illegible] و اندام بمالند نوعی دیگر تیل

نو کرده بوی داده چهار تولچه پوست ترنج تازه

تنک تنک بریده در تیل بیندازند و چون بوی ترنج خوب

گرفته باشد آنگاه پوست ترنج را از آن بیرون آرند مشک

یک تولچه کافور نیم ماسه انداخته باریک آس کنند و بر سر

و اندام بمالند نوعی دیگر تیل چهار تکه بی

بترنج موتهه کچور برمهی ترنفل پوست نارنگی خشک

پوست ترنج خشک سلارس کچری کیهونله الا[تچی]

از هر یکی یک [illegible] سخت باریک

مشک یک لیره کافور یک ماسه در [illegible] خوب بسایند

و بر اندام

وبر اندام بمالند نوعی دیگر ...

بخور بتلیه بدهند وچون بخور خوب کرد

مسک یک تولچه کافور ربع تولچه شاخ یکما

باریک آس کنند وبوی گل بدهند و

بمالند اکنون ترتیب پختن کافو

کافور مقدار ده وازده تولچه باریک آس کنند

ومشک یک تولچه آس کرده بپزند

آس کنند وبپزند زعفران نیم تولچه کر

سلارس نگ   ادویه را در کافور یکجا بیا

بعضی مسینه   ج تکری ریزه صندل با

كرده بينداز ند وبالاي آن تيليه نيم تولچه

داز ند وسيا ميز ند وبالاي آن كافور مذكور را

ته داشته است آن را يكجا برابر سيا ميز د وبالاي

شفال في بنهد بعده كل سپيد وصمغ يكجا كرده

از وباريك پاره كرده بر آن كل وصمغ تر كند

ر كند و ديكر جامه نيز كل وصمغ تر

لد مهر كند وديكر جامه بالاي او

بالاي او مهر كند بعده يكروز همچنان زند

ديكدان [illegible]

كند چون [illegible]

صد هشتاد و دو

بهتی کافور در بر نهد و چون بهتی خوب گرم شده باشد

پس جامه را در آب ترکند و ساعت بساعت بالای بهتی بما[لد]

دوازده تولچه کافور را در دوازده پاس بپزد و آتش از دو ...

زیادت نکند و هیزم باید که از چوب کهیر باشد و هیزم

در سطبری انگشت نر باشد بعده بهتی را فرو آرد و مهر

باز کند و طبقچه برگیرد بعده در دیک سر تنک

پر آب بیندازد و سر او را جامه ببندد و بالای اخگر

نهد چون آب گرم شده باشد آنگاه طبقچه را بالای

او نهد چ[illegible] گرم شود فرو آرد و چون [illegible] از بند و پهن

و تنک [illegible] بگیرد و به آن چوب طبقچه کافور را

171

از طبقچهٔ چینی بیرون آرد نوعی دیگر ترتیب

خشت کافور ریزهٔ صندل در میان بهتی کلاب بیندازد

و در و آب بیندازد و بالای او کافور آن قدر تولچه

که خواهد

آن مقدار

آش

کرده

و پخته

بیندازد بعد [illegible] بهتی را [illegible] سر کنند [illegible] کلاب

میچکد یک شیشه بدارد و بالای [illegible] ده بدارد

وچون اکرم

وچون گرم شود آن آب را دور کند و دیگر آب سرد
بینبارد تا کافور تخته شود آنگاه فرو آرد و بچوب
بنبو خراشیده بگیرد این کافور بسیار سود باشد اکنون
ترتیب چکانیدن گلابها نوشته میشود تلیه یکسیر
باریک بکوبند و جامه بین کرده در دو سیر آب بخیسانند
تمام شب بدارند روز دیگر در میان بهتی گلاب انداخته
بچکانند و محل چکیدن گلاب یک شیشه بدارد
وچون تمام گلاب چکیده باشد سر شیشه خوب مهر
کنند تا باد … و وقت حاجت استعمال کنند و بر اندام
بمالند … شانند و باز و بسیار بوی را بوی دهد بو

به خوب میشود و آن تیلیه که در میان بهتی مانده است

آن را برگیرد و خشک کند و هرچه خواهد ازان راست

کند و بخور کند و مکهه باش راست کند

دیگر عرق زعفران زعفران تازه ربع سیر آب

سه سیر زعفران را در آب بخوساند و یکشب بدارد روز

دیگر در میان بهتی گلاب انداخته بچکانند

و بر سر و اندام مالند و در طعام و آب بیندازند و پان

و سپاری را بوی دهند و در هرچه خواهد بیندازد

و زعفران که در بهتی مانده است [illegible] دارد و

خشک کند و هرجا که خواهد بیندازد [illegible] کر

عرق صندل

عرق صندل بگیرد صندل خوشبوی اعلی یکسیر و باریک
آس کنند و نجامه ببیزند و مقدار سه سیر آب بالا
آن بیندازند و تمام شب بدارد و روز دیگر در بهتی کرده
بچکانند عرق صندل باشد بخورند و بر اندام بمالند و بر
جامه بیفشانند و در طعام و آب کنند و هر جا که خواهند
بیندازند

دیگر عرق گل کرنه

گل کرنه را خوب خشک کنند بعده گل کرنه یکسیر بگیرد
و اندک بکوبند و در سه سیر آب بیندازد و تمام شب
بدارد و روز دیگر در بهتی گلاب انداخته بچکانند
این را عرق [illegible] گویند از همه عرقها بهتر است

در پیاله که خواهند بیندازند و بهرچه خواهند بمالند دیگر

گلاب گل موکره گل بت موکره را که از شاخ چیده

باشند و آب نرسیده باشد بستانند و خشک کنند بعد از ان

گل یکسیر بگیرند و آب دو سیر بیندازند و تمام شب پوشیده

بدارند تا بوی نرود آنچنان بپوشانند و روز دوم در بهتی

گلاب انداخته بچکانند بغایت گلاب خوب شود

و هر چند که در جامه خشک شود بیشتر بوی خوش آید

و بهمین ترتیب گلاب از هر گل که خواهند بچکانند

دیگر ترتیب گرفتن عرق الا[illegible] الایچی را

درشت بکوبند مقدار ربع سیر و آب [illegible] بیندازند

و تمام شب

و تمام شب بدارد روز دیگر در میان نهتی کلاب
انداخته بچکانند هرجا که خواهند بمالند و هرجا که خواهند
بیندازند و بهمین ترتیب عرق قرنفل بکنند و عرق
تج و عرق مروه و عرق دونه و هر جنسی که خواهد
بهمین ترتیب بچکانند اکنون ترتیب گرفتن ست
هر چیز نوشته میشود گل چینیه را در آفتاب خشک
کنند بعده ازان گل خشک ده سیر و آب دو من انداخته
بجوشانند تا آن زمان ببرد که آب مقدار پنج سیر بماند بعده
فرود آرد و آب صاف کرده بگیرد گل دور کند و آن آب را
در ظرف [illegible]ینه انداخته بجوشانند تا غلیظ شود آنگاه

آرد در هر خوشبویی که خواهند بیندازند

دیگ درست لبان قدح کلی را بالای اخگر

بنهند و محکم گرم کنند بعده با انبر بیرون

آرند و در میان آن ریزه

لبان

بندازد

و بالای

آن

کتوره نقره آب پر کرده بمانند و چون دانند که ست افتاده است

انگاه کتوره را بردارند فرو آرند و ... بنذو ترا شیده

بگیرند

بگیرند و در کاسه بدارند و بهمین ترتیب آن مقدار که خواهند
ست بکشند دیگر ترتیب لخلخهٔ ترنج بیارند ترنج
تازهٔ خوب و سر او را که طرف شاخ پیوسته است مقدار
یک حلقهٔ کوچک بریده بر دارد و ازان طرف میان ترنج
را خالی کند و دانه و ترشی و گوشت او بیرون آرد
و میان او این چیزها پر کند اینست الایچی دو تولچه
درشت بکوبد چهر چهریله تگری برهمی پوست
نارنگی خشک لچری قرنفل موتهه این ادویه را از هر یکی
نیم ماسه زعفران یک ماسه آش کرده و بجامه بیخته
در آن بیـ[illegible] مشک یک تولچه عنبر اشهب یک دهم کافور

[illegible] اینها را درشت آس کنند تیلیه یکتولچه

سخت باریک آس کرده و بجامه بیخته مجموع ادویه را

یکجا جمع کنند و با گلاب ترسا زند و صندل بمو کرده بوی

داده یکماسه آس کرده بیندا زند و در هم آمیخته

در میان ترنج بیندا زند و حلقه ترنج را که بریده داشته است

بالای ترنج بنهند و بالای ترنج را در خمیر گیرد و بالای

خمیر گل [illegible] بعده در میان اخگر یا آتش یا چلک

آن ترنج را انداخته بپزد بسیار از حد پختن ندهد

موازنه بپزد بعده از میان آتش بیرون آرد و گل و

آرد دور کنند و در جامه سپید بپیچند [illegible] وقتی که

خواهند

۱۸۷ 176

صد هشتاد و هفت

خواهند نخورند و اگر خواهند که بسیار روز

بدارند پس ادویه را از ترنج بیرون آرند و خشک کرده

بدارند و هر وقتی که خواهند خورند پس بگلاب

تر کرده نخورند و اگر ترنج یافت نشود پس از برک ترنج پاتیل

بدوزند و در میان آن ادویه مذکور انداخته بپزند

اندکی بسیار خوب شود روغنی دیگر مکهه باس

مشک یکتولچه کافور یکتولچه تیلیه یکتولچه کافور

و مشک را درشت بکوبند و تیلیه باریک آس کرده

جامه بیز کنند عنبر اشهب ربع تولچه آس کرده

بیندازند صندل موکره نیم تولچه یکجا کرده با گلاب

خمیر کرده بدارند بخورند دیگر مکهه باس الاچی
یک تولچه درشت خرد کنند کافور مشک نیم نیم تولچه اینها را
نیز درشت آس کنند و با گلاب آمیخته بخورند دیگر
مکهه باس گل لعل خشک دو تولچه مشک یک تولچه کافور
نیم تولچه آس کرده با گلاب بیامیزند و بخورند
دیگر مکهه باس ست چنبه نیم ماسه زعفران
یک درم الاچی یک تولچه درشت بسایند مشک نیم تولچه
کافور یک تولچه درشت آس کرده یکجا کرده و با گلاب
بخورند دیگر مکهه باس صندل بمو کرده بوی
داده نیم تولچه کافور تخته یک ماسه عنبر اشهب یک ماسه

آس کرد

آس کرده مکهه باس کنند و با گلاب آمیخته بخورند
تمام شد اکنون ترتیب شربتها نوشته میشود شراب
زعفران یکتولچه با آب بسایند بعده در شیرهٔ نبات
مقدار پنج سیر بگیرند و زعفران در آن شیره بیندازند
و با آتش آهسته نرم بقوام آ[illegible]ند کفچه بجنبانند و چون
غلیظ شده باشد گلاب بیندازند و عنبر اشهب یکماسه
کافور دو رتی مشک دو رتی آس کرده در و اندازند
و در ظرف بدارند و هر وقتی که خواهند بخورند
دیگر شربت لیمو شیرهٔ نبات چهار سیر بقوام آرند
و در کتوره [illegible] بیندازند بعده بستانند آب لیمو یکسیر

و در شیره اندازند و به آتش آهسته نرم بپزند چون
غلیظ شود این ادویه در آن بیندازند زعفران نیم تولچه
تج چینی بترنج چهر قرنفل تکری نیم ماسه
کوفته
و بیخته
درو
اندازد
مشک
کافور دو دو رتی عنبر اشهب یک ماسه باریک
آس کنند و وقت فرو آوردن بیندا[illegible] و در ظرف

سنگی نگاه دارند و هر وقت که خواهند بخورند دیگر

صفت شراب صندل نبات خوب چهار سیر آب صندل

بغایت خوشبوی دو سیر صندل را بآب بسایند و در جامه

صاف پاک انداخته آب او بگیرند و این آب را در شیره

مذکور بیندازند و بآتش [illegible] بپزند و چون غلیظ

شود فرو آرند و در ظرف نگاه دارند وقت حاجت بخورند

و بهمین نوع شراب ثلیه نیز بکنند نوعی دیگر

شربتها نوشته میشود شربت نبات پنج سیر سفید پاکیزه

بستانند و باریک آرد کنند و بجامه بپزند و آب

آن مقدار بیندازند که خوب شیرین شود بعده آب لیمو آن

که مزه خوب شود بیندازند فلفل قدری که مزه خوب

آید بیندازند همه را اینجا بیامیزند و از جامه بپیت صاف کنند

ولیکن نیفشارند و اول جامه بپیت یك لوصاف

کنند و بعد از آن جامه دو لوصاف کنند خوب صاف شود

بعد از آن بعود مزه [illegible] ابدهد وچون داند که سبوها

را خوب بخور گرفته است پس شربت در و اندازد و دهن

سبو را محکم کنند وچون داند که بوی عود

شربت را گرفته است آنگاه گل موکره را خارها دور کرده

در شربت بیندازد دیگر گل [illegible] تازه اگر

باشد نیز بیندازند وچون شربت خوب معطر شده باشد

وشود

یکصد بود

وسوده شده باشد پس قدری کافور و مشک و گلاب بیندازد

بعده بخورند دیگر شربت انگور انگور را پاک

کند و مغز اندرون او بستاند و بدست بمالد و در میان

آن نبات بیندازد و بعده صاف کرده بستاند و در سبو

آن شربت را بیندازد و سبو را بخور عود مرهتی بدهد

بعده شربت را درو اندازد و چون بوی عود در شربت

گرفته باشد آنگاه گلاب موکره بیندازد و گلا

و کافور و مشک نیز قدری بیندازد و بهمین نوع شربت

تمر هندی بکند و شربت هرچه خواهد بهمین نوع

بکند دیگر ترتیب پختن گوشت نوشته میشود

کوشت بیارند از کوسپند پر پیه فربه و از آن کباب بچه
بپزند و هلد و هنک و کشنیز سبز و پیاز و نمک انداخته
بجوشانند و چون خوب مهرا شده باشد بعده در روغن
خوشبوی بکهار هنک بدهد و آن کوشت را درو بیندازد
و چون خوب لنوا شده باشد آنگاه الاچی و قرنفل زیره زند
و میتهی بریان کرده آس کرده بیندازند و کشنیز بیندا
و ساعتی نختن دهد بعده کافور یک رتی مشک دو رتی
انداخته فرو آرد و آب لیمو علاحده در کاسه چینی کشیده
بدارد پیش ببرد و در کاسه دیگر سرکه بکند پیش ببرد هر کدام
که خوش آید در قلیه انداخته بخورند نوعی دیگر

کوشت

کوشت طغراز پریتی را در دیك انداز د و آب بوسنا او
ریزد و نمك و هنك و هلد و کشنیز سبز و پیاز بینداز د و نرم
بپزد بغایت چنانکه مهرا شود بعده الایچی و قرنفل میتهی
زیره فلفل آب لیمو بینداز د بعده طغراز را در صحن کشد
و بالای آن روغن خوشبوی انداز د و یك رتی کافور
و یك رتی مشك بینداز د انکاه آب لیمو و سرکه آن
مقدار که خواهند بالای او انداخته بخورند نوعی
دیکر کوشت نرم پیتی بکیرد فربه و کباب
نچه ببرد خوب بجوشاند بعده فرو آرد انکاه در روغن
بکهار ده نغزك بدهد و در میان آن کوشت بینداز د

بادیان زیره الایچی قرنفل میتهی آب لیمو وقدری

اجواین درست بیندازند پیاز بیندازند و بخورند نوعی

دیگر کوشت که آنرا اوکهر کویند کوشت

پربهتی راکه چربی

فربه

داشته

باشد

قطعه

قطعه ببرند و اندکی را زیره ببرند و همه را یکجا

کرده خوب بشویند و در دیک بیندازند بعده نمک و

کشنیز

کشنیز سبز بیاز ادرک هنک بیندازد و نیک بجوشانند
و در میان آن ساق ساک بیندازد و چون خوب مهرا
شده باشد بعده آب لیمو و فلفل انداخته فرو آرد هلد
نباید انداخت بعده دو وصله خزف گرم کنند
آنچنانکه سرخ همچو اخکر شوند و یک وصله خزف نو
سرد در دیک نهد و بالای او یک وصله خزف گرم نهد
و در میان آن خزف گرم زیره میتهی الاتچی قرنفل
هینک خال الرتیل کنجد یکجا کرده بیندازد و وصله خزف
دوم گرم کرده را بالای او بنهد و سر دیک مهر کنند
و بخور بدهد بعده بخورند نوعی دیگر گوشت

کته [illegible] خوب بشنانند و قیمه کنند بعد شستن بعده

هلد زیره میتهی کشنیز الایچی پیاز قرنفل انداخته بیامیزند

و در روغن بگهار رهنک بدهند و قیمه درو اندازد

و آب اندازد و چون مهرا شده باشد پس آب لیمو فلفل

انداخته فرو آرد و یکیک رتی کافور و مشک بیندازد

فرو آرد نوعی دیگر [illegible] نرم گوشت را

خرد ریزه کنند بعده بجوشانند بعد از آن روغن

خوشبو را بگهار رهنک بدهند و چون بگهار خوب

شده باشد آنگاه گوشت را بغیر هلد درو بیندا زند

سپید و در میان آن ماست بیندازند و الایچی و قرنفل

بیندازند

بیندازند کافور و مشک یکیک رتی بیندازند و نمک
بیندازند و فروآرند بخورند نوعی دیگر تیتر
و بتیر تیتر و بتیر نرم راست کنند و هلد و هنگ نمک
مالیده در میان دیگ دتهاره انداخته و آب انداخته
در بر نهند و چون آب [illegible] آید بعده بالای دتهاره
تیتر و بتیر بیندازد و سر دیگ مهر کنند و خوب مهرا
کرده بپزد بعده آن تیتر و بتیر را سیخ کنند و حوائج هر
بمالد و سیخ بریان کنند و در میان روغن قدری
کافور و مشک بیندازد و آن روغن را بر سیخ بمالد
بریان کنند و آن زمان که خواهند که سیخ بخورند

آنگاه در آب لیمو یا در سرکه انداخته بخورند و نیز
گوشت جوشانیده در دتهاره را قدری بدارد و میان آن
حوائج هر جنسی بیندازد و در تاوه روغن تازهٔ خوشبوی
بیندازد و چون گرم شده باشد آن گوشت را
بیندازد و بکفچه آهسته آ[illegible]ه روغن برگیرد و بالای
گوشت اندازد و نیک برشته کند بعده در صحن کشد
و کافور و مشک قدری و گلاب بیندا[illegible] وقت خوردن
در سرکه یا در آب لیمو فرو برده بخورد اکنون ترتیب پختن
نوشته میشود تیتر بتیر یا طغرا از برنج یا گوشت مرغ
یا گوشت آهو یا گوشت خرگوش یا گوشت گردن اینچنین گوشتها

باشد با

183

۱۹۴

صد و نود و چهار

باشد یا زبان خرگوش یا زبان گاو کیني یا زبان

گوسپند پر بتي در دتهاره انداخته بجوشانند چون خوب

جوشیده باشد انگاه فروآرد هلد نمک هنگ کشنیز

انداخته بجوشانند چون مهرا شده باشد فروآرد بعده

ب لیمو هلد زیره میته [illegible] ابیا میزد

وآن گوشت را [illegible] است این [illegible] بمالد

[illegible] کند و اگر سخت مهرا باشد پس

بریسمان بپیچد و بالای اخگر بریان کند بعده در

بیان [illegible] خوشبوی یکرتی کافور بیندازند و برسیخ

بمالند چون خوب بریان شده باشد پس فروآرد و وقت

خوردن در آب لیمو یا در سرکه فرو برد و بخورد ترتیب
پوری نوشته میشود گوشت پربتی یا گوشت آهو را نیک
قیمه کند و هلد و نمک بمالد و در روغن خوشبوی بگهار
هنک
بدهد
و قیمه
در رو
اندازد
و آب گرم آن قدر اندازد که در آن پخته شود و هیچ آب نماند
روغن نماند آنگاه زیره میتهی الاچی قرنفل کافور مشک

184

195 184

صد و نود و پنج

یکیک رتی یکجا بیامیزد بعده فلفل آب لیمو بیاز در دیگ
بیندازد فرو آرد بعده بالای نان تنک برگ کل العل یا کل سیوتی
بگسترد یا برگ پودنه بگسترد و بالای آن قیمه را بیندازد
پوره بندد و بریسمان بپیچد و بجامه سپید تنک باریک
ببندد و چون خواهند که بخورند در میان سرکه یا در آب
لیمو گوشت را در نان تنک پیچیده فرو برند و بخورند
و از همین گوشت قیمه بدارد و در میان برگ کیوره پر
سازد و بریسمان بپیچد و دیگر از همین قیمه قدری بدارد
و از برگ ترنج یا تلبد وزد و در میان آن قیمه پر کند
و بریسمان بپیچد و در میان دیگ انداخته بدارد

و چون خواهند که نخورند با سرکه یا آب لیمو نخورند دیگر
ترتیب بغرا سرکه یکسیر آب لیمو ربع سیر نمک یکتولچه
نبات یکسیر بادام پوست کنده آس کرده ربع سیر
بغرا بریده بپزد آب یکسیر سیر دو تولچه هر همه را
یکجا کرده بیامیزد و در میان [illegible] بغراء تخته را بیندازد
و بالای آن لنواس خوب از گوشت فربه تخته بیندازد
بغراء خوب شود نوعی دیگر بغرا برنج سپید
بپزد و قیمه را علاحده در دیگی دیگر خوب بپزد
و بغرا بریده جدا بپزد بعده هر همه را یکجا کرده بیامیزد
و یکتولچه سیر آس کرده بیندازد و نیم سیر سرکه

بیندازد

بیندازد بغراء خوب شود نوعی دیگر بغرا
را بریده ببرزد وآن آب یکسیر وسرکه نیم سیر آب لیمو ربع
سیر نمك یکتولچه آن مقدار که خوش مزه شود آن قدر
بیندازد ودر میان آن بغراء تخته بیندازد سیر یکتولچه
انداخته خوب باهم بیامیزد وبالای او لنواس خوب تخته
بیندازد بغراء خوب شود ترتیب سنبوسها کوشت نرم
بی پی یا کوشت آهو باریك قیمه کند ومیان آن هلد زیره
مستهی کشنیز الاتچی قرنفل انداخته بیامیزد ودر روغن
خوشبو ب[illegible]رهنك اصلی بدهد چون بکهار خوب
شده باشد قیمه را در او اندازد وبکدارد تا خوب تخته شود

بعده آب لیمو و فلفل بیندازد بعد ازان ادرك ربع سیر پیاز

یکسین بریده درو اندازد و فرو آرد بعده کافور یک رتی مشك

یک رتی بیندازند و اندك سنبوسه بزرك بزرك راست

کنند و اندکی کوچك کوچك مقدار یک نواله راست

کنند و قیمه درو پر کرده در روغن خوشبو برشته سازند

و وقت خوردن در سرکه یا آب لیمو فرو برده بخورند دیگر

ترتیب پختن بره از گوشت گوشت فربه خوب بستانند

باریك قیمه کنند و دیگر بالای سل نهاده باریك

بساید بعده در میان آن هلاد زیره میتهی الا قرنفل نمك

فلفل انداخته بیامیزد کافور مشك یکیك رتی بیندازد

ب

پیاز باریک

پیاز باریک بریده بیندازد بعده ادرک پیاز قدری سیر نمک
لیمو در آن بیامیزد الاتچی قدری و قرنفل بیندازد و
سونف درست بیندازند بعده ازان قیمه دو عدد تکری
کنند یعنی طریق نان کوچک پهن سازد و چنانچه
در پوری پوران می اندازند همچنان آن ادرک و پیاز را
که بریده داشته است در آن تکریهای گوشت بیندازد و
کنارها هر دو تکری را محکم کنند بعده تکری مذکور را
در دیگ نهاده دتهاره بدهد و بجوشاند بعده در میان دیگ
موازنه دو سیر روغن بیندازد و بگهار هنگ بدهد
بگهار [illegible] گرفته باشد آن بره گوشت را بعده درواندازد

الاچی قرنفل فلفل آب لیمو پیاز انداخته فرو آرد و وقت

خوردن در سرکه یا در آب لیمو فرو برده بخورند نوعی

دیگر قیمه باریک ببرند بعده بالای سل

آن کنند

و درمیان

آن هلد

قدری

هینگ زیره

ـتی الاچی قرنفل سونف درست بیندازد ادرک

پیاز سخت باریک بریده بیندازد آب لیمو نمک بیندازد

187

187

۱۹۸

صد و نود و هشت

بعده مقدار لیمو غلولها کند و در دیک آن مقدار آب کند که

خوب تخته کرده اول دیک را بالای دیگدان بنهد و آب

گرم کند چون خوب گرم شده باشد آن زمان آن غلولها در

زد

آب بیندازد و خوب بپزد انگاه فلفل آب لیمو نمک بینداز

یی

و فرو آرد و روغن خوشبوی در واندازد و قطعها

بزرگ بزرگ از پیاز بریده بیندازد و فرو آرد دیگر

ترتیب تخنی مغلی طعم از پر یتی هر دو بستانند یا

زد

از آن آهو بستانند و دیک بجوشانند بعده هینک بیندا

الاتچی قرنفل زیره میتهی فلفل بسیار ادرک نمک

آرد

بیندازد بالای او روغن خوشبوی بیندازد و فرو

و وقتي كه بخورند بكارد تيز تنك ببرند و در آب ليمو فرو

برند و بخورند نوعي ديكر بوره تخني تيتر هنك

نمك انداخته سپيد بجوشانند بعده بيرون آرد و طريق

بوره باريك تخني كنند بسيار قدري ادرك باريك بريده

در و اندازد و بكهار هنك بدهد بعده برك پلاس جهار

عدد زير نهد و جهار عدد بالا نهد و در ميان آن برك‌ها

تخني اندازد و بر كهار بسيار باريك از چوب بدوزد

وقتي

و بالاي آن خمير آرد بكيرد و در خاكستر كرم فرو برد و و

كه خواهند بيرون آرند از ميان برك‌ها و باسركه و آب ليمو

انداخته بخورند ديكر ترتيب جيم‌ماي سرد

بهات

بهات سرد آب لیمو نمك آنچنان بیامیزند که مزه خوب
شود بعده بخور عود مرهتی بدهند سبو را ده دوازده کرت
بعده سر سبو را بجامه بگیرند و آن آب لیمو که آمیخته
داشته است در میان سبو بیندازند و بهات را در میان سبو
آن مقدار کنند که در زیر آب لیمو فرو رود بعده بیرون
آورده هفت کرت بشویند بعده در میان آن آب بیندازند
بعده گلهای هر جنسی بیندازند و چون بوی گل خوب
گرفته باشد انگاه گلها را بیرون آرند و گلاب بیندازند و
پیش بیرند نوعی دیگر سرد انه تمر هندی خوب
خوب چیده بگیرند و در آب بخوسانند چون خوسیده باشد

تتو را دور کند و بجامه بپیت صاف کند و نمک بیندازد

بعده سبو را بخورهاء عود مرهتی بدهد چون بخورها خوب

کرفته باشد برسر سبو جامه بنهد و آب تمرهندی در آن

اندازد و کلهای موکره در سبو اندازد چون خوشبو شود

کلها را دور کند و اندکی کلاب انداخته بخورد

نوعی دیکر [illegible] برنج را بهوک خوب

کرده بشوید بهات مهر را ببرد بعده بهات را بدست بمالد

و بجامه کرباس صاف کند و آب برسر او بریزد و صاف کند

بعده نبات سپید اعلی آس کند باریک و شربت کند و بهات

مذکور را که صاف کرده داشته است در میان شربت بیندازد

همرا

همه را یکجا بیامیزد و آب بر سر او ریزد و تنک کند بعده دو
همچنان بکذارد بعده کلابت موکره در و انداز د چون بوی
کلا در و کرفته باشد آن زمان کلا دور کند و قدری کلاب
بینداز د و بنوشند ترتیب پختن کهیس آب دوغ ترش
بستانند آن مقدار که کهیس در و پخته شود و اندکی آب
لیمو در و بیندازد و بالای دیکدان نهد و چون ادهن بیاید
بعد [illegible] بر آید انکاه آرد برنج را با دوغ آمیخته بینداز د
و بکفچه نیک بجنبانند تا کره کره بسته نشود برنج را
خوب بشوید و در آب بخوسانند بعده بالای سل آتش کند
و بجامه [illegible] وی او بکیرد آن روه را با آب دوغ آمیخته

زد

دردیگ انداز د بعده ادرك یكتولچه باریك بریده بیندا

آب این یكدرم بیندازد نمك بیندازد چون خوب پخته

باشد فرو آرد و بخور تیل و هینگ بدهد بعده بخورند

نوعی دیگر

کهیتی برنج را خوب بشوید

و چون خوب خوسیده باشد انگاه آس کند بعده از تمر

هندی انبلوانی تنك بكند و ادهن دهد چون از هر

شده بر

شده باشد آن آرد برنج را که آس کرده داشته است
با آب آمیخته در دیک بیندازد و بکفچه بجنبانند تا کره
نیفتند و پخته شود بعده چون سرد شود ملایی از بالای
او دور کنند و بگلاب مو کره معطر کنند بعده با تشتها
و آبهای سرد که بالا گفته شد بخورند اکنون ترتیب
برنجها نوشته میشود برنج را خوب بشویند و زعفران
آن مقدار بیندازند که خوب زرد شود بعده در دیک دو سیر
موازنه روغن بیندازند و بهار زعفران بدهند بعده
برنج مذکور را در آن بیندازند و خوب برشته سازند انگاه
آب بر زبر ریزند آن مقدار که برنج خوب پخته شود و نمک بیندازند زرد

بعده گلاب بزنند و بخورند دیگر برنج زرد رانیك
بشویند و در آب تر کرده بدارند تا آن زمان که ادهن بیاید
انگاه در ادهن مقدار سه تولچه زعفران آس کرده بیندازد
و چون ادهن خوب شده باشد در میان برنج نیز مقدار
دو تولچه زعفران آس کرده بیامیزد و در ادهن
بیندازد و نمك آن مقدار اندازد که خوش مزه شود و چون
طریق بهات پخته باشد آب زیادتی بریزد بعده روغن
خوشبوی دو سیر بیندازد و آب لیمو موازنه یک سیر بیندازد
و دم پخت کند بعده فرو آرد و گلاب بزنند و بخورند
نوعی دیگر برنج سپید ادهن آب بدهند و در

میان آن

میان آن گوشت پی بی قطعه قطعه بکالها بیندازد و صلها

چربی فربه نیز بیندازد نمک و هنک بیندازد چون گوشت تخته

و چربی مهرا شده باشد آنگاه برنج بیندازد و چون برنج

شود آب زیادتی از و برگیرد آنگاه دو روغن خوشبوی

دو سیر بیندازد آب لیمو یکسیر و نمک بیندازد و دم تخت

کنند آنگاه فرود آرند و بخورند ترتیب بریان کردن در

زمین گودال در زمین بکنند آن مقدار که گوشت

موجود عنه شود و در میان آن گودال آتش بسوزانند تا

سخت گرم شود و سنگهاء خرد خرد گرد بر گرد گودال بنهند

و بالاء سنگها نیز آتش کنند تا گرم شوند بعده ظرف آن

کاورا خوب بشویند و هلد و نمک و زیره و میتهی الاتچی

قرنفل کشنیز اندک هنک هر همه را یکجا کند و آب لیمو بر و

ریزد و پیاز و ادرک بیندازد و حوتج را با روغن آمیخته بالای

کوشت بمالد بعده بالای کود المذکور برکهای موز

بکسترد و بالای برک موز کوشت را بنهد و دیکر برک موز

بالای کوشت بپوشاند انکاه سنکهاء کرم کرده بالای برک

موز بیندازد و باز بالای سنکها برک موز بکسترد و بالای

او کوشت نهد و دیکر برک موز بالای او بپوشاند و بالای برک

سنک ریزها اندازد و بهمین طریق آن مقدار که خواهند

بیندازند بعده برک موز بالای آن بیندازند و سنک کرم کرده

۲۵۳

دولت سه

بیندازند و دیگر بالای آن برگ مرزبید ازند و دهن

کودال بگیرند بگل و آب درهم سرشته چهار کرد تا هیچ بخار

بیرون نیاید و بالای او دو سه پشته هیزم بسوزانند و چون

وقت طعام خوردن باشد آتش را از بالای کودال دور کنند

و کودال وا کنند و گوشت بیرون آرد و با سرکه و یا آب لیمو

ورید
بخورند ترتیب پختن بره د الیاش بخوابانند و بعده بشو

عدد
دا باریک آس کند اگر بنج سه دال باشد پس کسیروده

باریک آس کرده در دال بیامیزد و نیم سیر مسکه

تازه بیندازد و بدست بزنند تا یکسان شود و اندک هلد

بیندازد نمک بیندازد بعده بره راست کند و در روغن

خوشبوی بپزد واز روغن بیرون آرد وقدری نبات
آس کرده وکافور ومشک بر وافشانند وبخورند نوعی
دیگر بره دال ماش خوب بشوید وباریک آس کند
وبدست
بزنند
وبمالند
وهنگ
بندازد
وکشنیز وفلفل درست بیندازد ودرهم بیامیزد
وبره راست کند ودر روغن برشته سازد یا در تیل برشته

نماید

193

۲۵۴

دویست چهار

193

نماید بعده از تمر هندی انبلوانی کنند و در و نبات

بیندازند و شیرین کنند و قدری کافور و مشک و گلاب

الاچی قرنفل بیندازند و خوب بیامیزند و در و بره بیندازند

نوعی دیگر بره از دال ماش بره خوب راست کنند

بعده دوغ ترش بگیرند و در و برنج نخود بسانند بعد از آن رکد

شسته باشند و نمک و هنک و کشنیز سبز بیندازند و بجوشانند

و چون خوب پخته باشد آنگاه زیره میتهی الاچی قرنفل

فلفل انداخته فرو آرند و آب را خوب گرم کرده در میان او

ه بیندازند بعده گرهی را نخور هنک بدهند و در میان آن

ة انداخته بخورند اکنون ترتیب سکهرز نوشته میشود

ماست خوب بستانند و میان آن نبات آس کرده بیندازند و

جامه بیز کنند و در میان آن کافور و مشک الایچی قرنفل

بیندازند و گلاب بیندازند و سوی گل معطر سازند چون بوی

گل در وی گرفته باشد گل را دور کنند بعده مغز موز را

قطعه قطعه ببرند و در آن بیندازند و در میان ماست پاره

مغز کهل بیندازند نوعی دیگر سکهرن خربزه ب

خربزه شیرین بیارند و مغز او قطعه قطعه ببرند و تخم او

دور کنند و بدست بمالند و نبات بیندازند و بجامه تنک بپالا

و بسوی گل معطر کنند چون بوی گل گرفته باشد گل را دور

کنند بعده قدری کافور و مشک بیندازند و گلاب

افشاتند

۱۹۴

۲۰۵

دو بیست

افشانند و نخورند ترتیب بکنه بهتی کچری کیپه و تله

زعفران صندل بکه تیلیه مقداری و همان مقدار بینس

باریک آس کنند و بجامه تنک ببیزند و قدری

گلاب بر و افشانند و از عود مرهتی بخور بدهند ترتیب

چوه شوله تیلیه کافور مشک زعفران در تیل موکره

تر کنند و در صحن آب بیندازند و بالای او

سپایه بدارند و شوله را گرم کنند میان اخگر

بعده بیرون آرند و بالای سپایه بدارند و ادویه کوزه

زردا که آمیخته داشته است بالای شوله بیندا

زد و پیاله چینی را با تیل موکره آلوده بدارد و بالای

شوله بپوشد و بجامه تر کرده بالای کاسه بمالد

بونی دهد و این چوره را بخور عود مرهی بدهد زعفران

آس کند بعده تیل موکره بیندازد بعده

سخت باریک بساید کافور مشک سلارس شاخ قدری

گلاب انداخته بمالند ترتیب پاپر آرد ماش

اگر یکمن باشد پس هنگ هشت تولچه نمک چهار سیر

آب سی سیر روه شش سیر آب کهاریک سیر و نیم

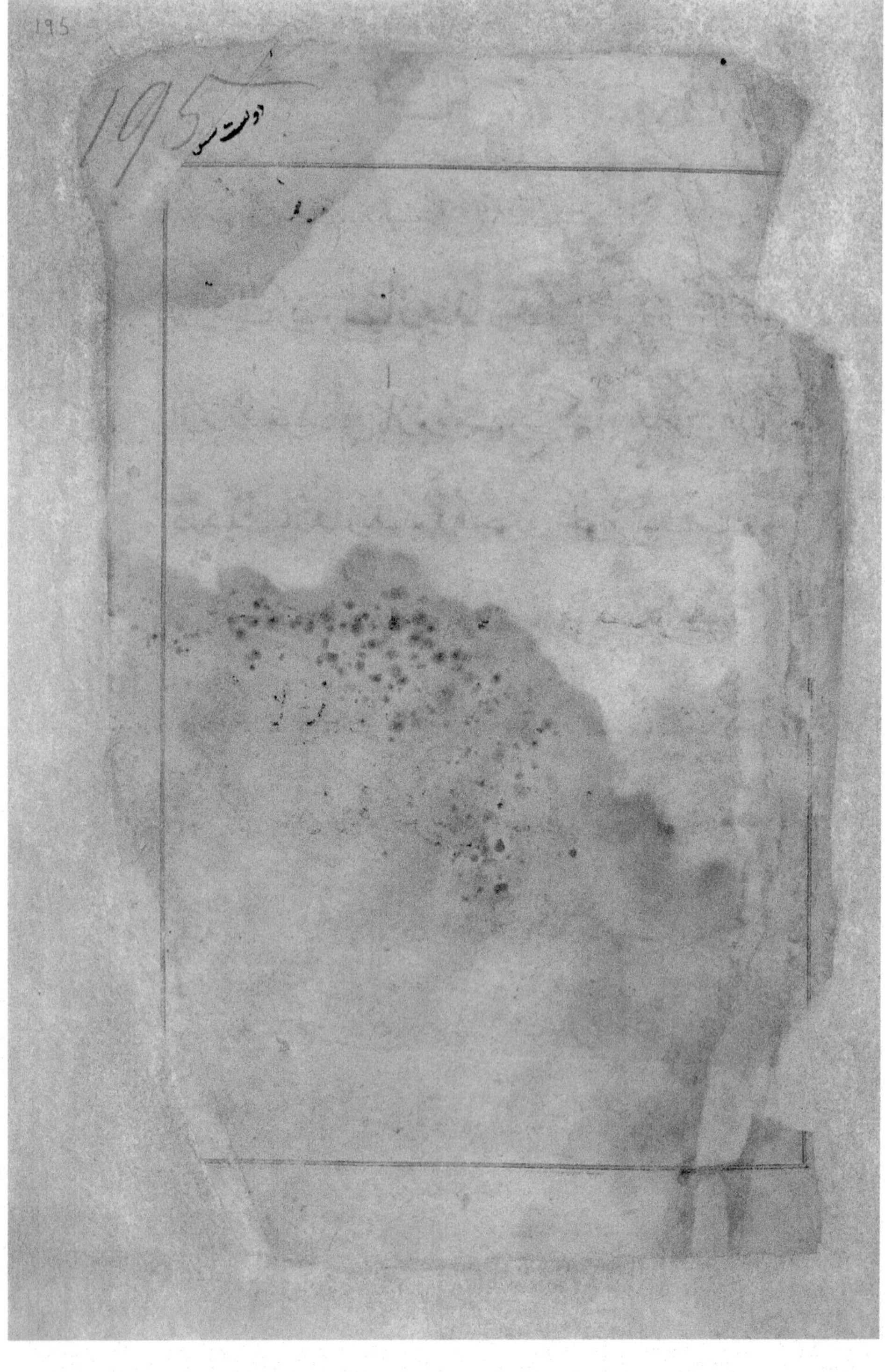

ترتیب برنج ناصرشاهی خلد الله ملکه وسلطانه

در دیگ روغن بسیار بیندازند وآب سبزی بستانند

از زیره خراسانی یا زیره مشهور بکهار بدهند وآب

در دیگ بیندازند بعده چون بجوش آید برنج سفید

بادام آکهروت سیر الایچی فلفل بیندازند دیگر

لبوب ناصرشاهی مد ظله برنج را خوب بشویند وباریک

آس کنند وبجامه تنک ببیزد ودر تاوه روغن

بیندازد بعده آرد را در او برشته سازد وآب ادرک وآب زرد

لیمو وآب سیر این هرسه آب را یکجا بیامیزد بعده در خمیر بیندا

بعده دیگ فرو آرد ووصلهای گوشت ببرد وپاک بشوی

ودر دیگ

۲۵۷

دویست هفت

ودر دیك بیندازد وچون دیك بجوش آید ودیك تخته

ونه آرد وآب او صاف کرده بگیرد ادرك پیاز

آب لیمو هر همه یکجا کند

یا کیبلج

در دیك بیندازد

این را کوشت

سپید

کویند

م

مجموع نعمت نامه
دویست هفت وارق

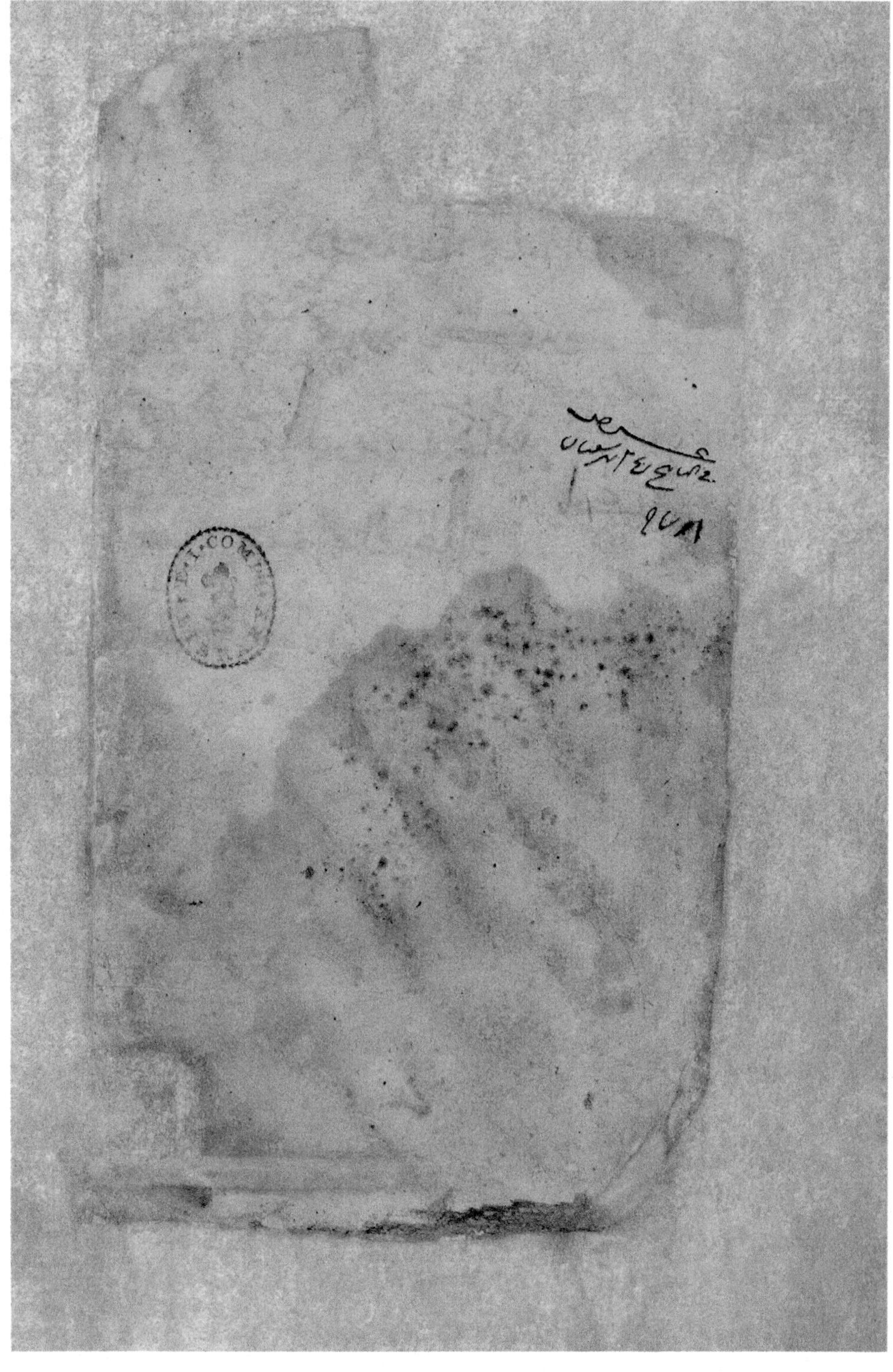

Plate 52 Ghiyath Shahi fishing (*f.192b*).

Plate 53 Ghiyath Shahi offered gold shoes (*Or. 3299, f.146b*).

Plate 50 Kūfta (minced-meat balls) being prepared (*f.186b*).

Plate 51 Khis (flummery) being prepared (*f.189b*).

Plate 48 Ghiyath Shahi feasting (*f.180b*).

Plate 49 Ghiyath Shahi in a garden (*f.183b*).

Plate 47 Ghiyath Shahi on horseback offered refreshment (*f.177b*).

Plate 45 Distillation of perfumes (*f.171b*).

Plate 46 Distillation of perfumes (*f.174b*).

Plate 43 Preparation of aromatic paste (*chūva*) (*f.165b*).

Plate 44 Ghiyath Shahi offered refreshment (*f.168b*).

Plate 41 Ghiyath Shahi on a hunting expedition (*f.157a*).

Plate 42 Ghiyath Shahi arriving at his camp (*f.159b*).

Plate 39 Musicians entertaining Ghiyath Shahi (*f.147a*).

Plate 40 Preparation of food for the monsoon season (*f.153b*).

Plate 37 Soft food being prepared (*f.136b*).

Plate 38 Preparation of pottage (*lāpasī*) (*f.144b*).

Plate 35 Water cooling (*f.129b*).

Plate 36 Preparation of aphrodisiac food (*f.133b*).

Plate 33 Aromatic paste (*abtāna*) being prepared (*f.121b*).

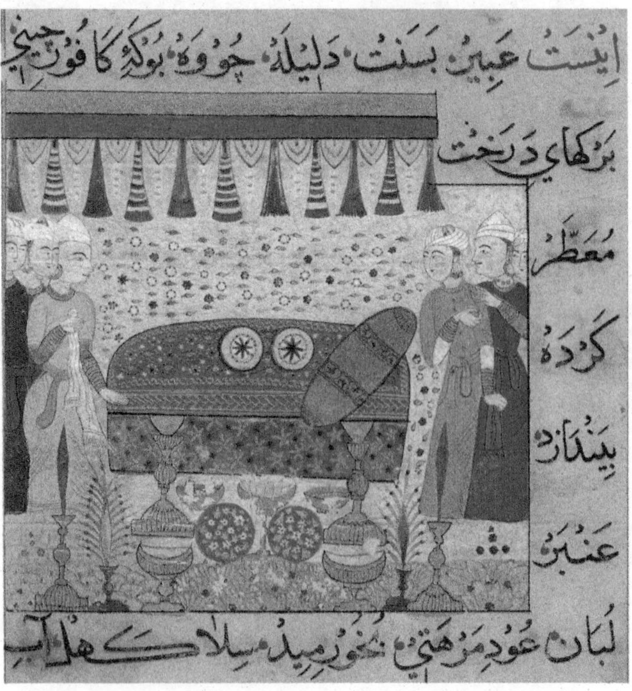

Plate 34 Advice on the domestic use of perfume (*f.124b*).

جلغوزه آرد چارولی بوی عود هر جنسی بوی کلها

هر جنسی فلفل قرنفل خرماء فرد مویز شکر تری

نبات کافور کلاب شهد سونف مشک

زعفران خولنجان تج الاچی سوندهی نوعی

دیگر ساختن پالوده اینها را جدا جدا

طریق پالوده بپزد چارولی بادام بیندازد الاچی

Plate 31 Preparation of halva (*f.115b*).

Plate 30 Distillation of perfumes and essences (*f.111b*).

Plate 32 Betel preparation (*f.118b*).

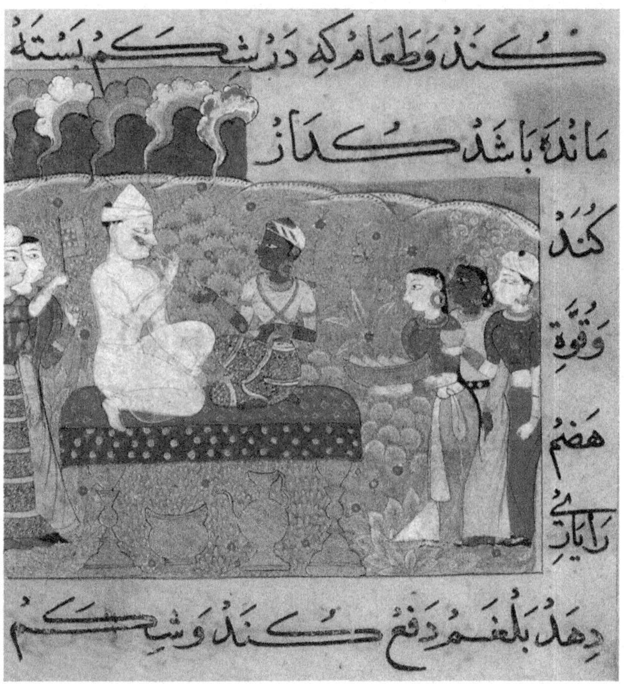

Plate 28 Enjoyment of betel (*f.100b*).

Plate 29 Preparation of flavouring for betel (*f.103b*).

Plate 26 Betel preparation (*f.94a*).

Plate 27 Betel preparation (*f.98a*).

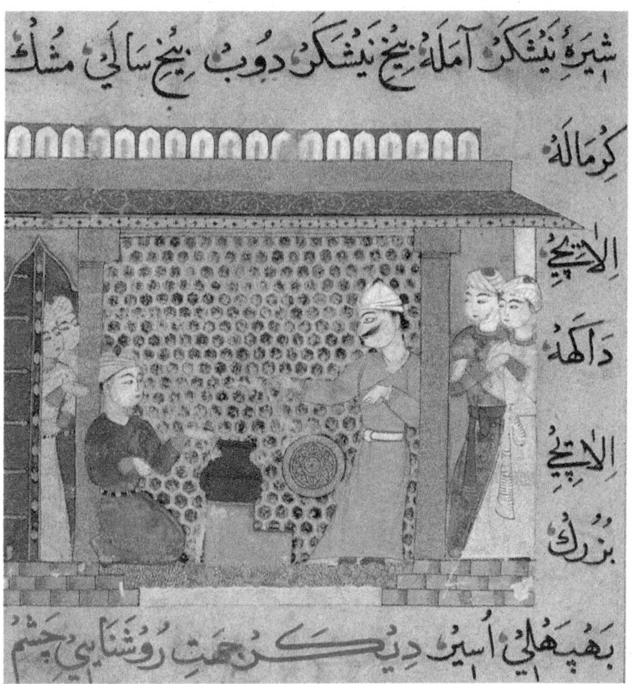

Plate 24 Preparation of medicinal food (*f.88b*).

Plate 25 Illustration to advice on a healthy life-style (*f.91b*).

چسینج و آرد برنج پندالو و آرد برنج تیل رایی آرد چارولی

آرد نخود و چارولی منک و آرد بادام خرما و آرد برنج تمر

هندی و شکر تری و برنج پویی و آرد برنج سونف

و آرد برنج

کشنیز

قرنفل

مشک

پترج

تج سونف سوخته در تیل تیل در میتهی سوخته تیل زیره

تیل در هنک سوخته الایچی روغن کردگان و برنج

Plate 23 Samosas being prepared (*f.83b*).

واگر در آنبلوانی اندازد جنس دیگر شود
نوعی دیگر ترتیب شربت شکر پنج درم دو درم
ادرک قرنفل دو درم الایچی دو درم هر همه را آس کرده
یکجا و صاف کرده شربت
کند
و بالا
کافور
اندازد
نوعی دیگر حریره آرد خشخاش کشنیز زیره
آس کرده سونف سونٹھ قرنفل الایچی همه را

Plate 21 Soft food and sherbet (*f.76a*).

Plate 20 Preparation of minced meat (*qīma*) (*f.71b*).

Plate 22 Greens and potherbs (*f.79b*).

Plate 18 Preparation of buttermilk (*f.54a*).

Plate 19 Preparation of sherbet (*f.66a*).

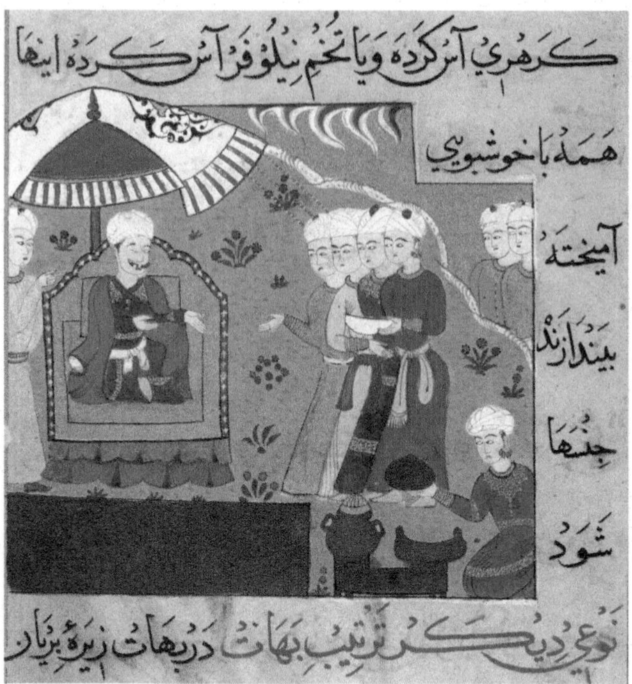

Plate 16 *Bhāt* being prepared (*f.44b*).

Plate 17 *Kaṛhī* being prepared (*f.51a*).

یکجا آمیخته کنند ودو بر کاله خزف گرم کنند
بالای یکی این حویج بنهد و دوم را بالای آن نهاده
دیگ را چهار بنج کرت بخور دهد بعده کانجی را
در دیگ اندا زد نوعی
دیگر
ترتیب
شد
آب
لیمو نبات فلفل یکجا آمیخته صاف کرده بستاند
و بخور عود بدهد و بوی گل معطر سازد و گلاب

Plate 15 Congee being prepared (*f.40b*).

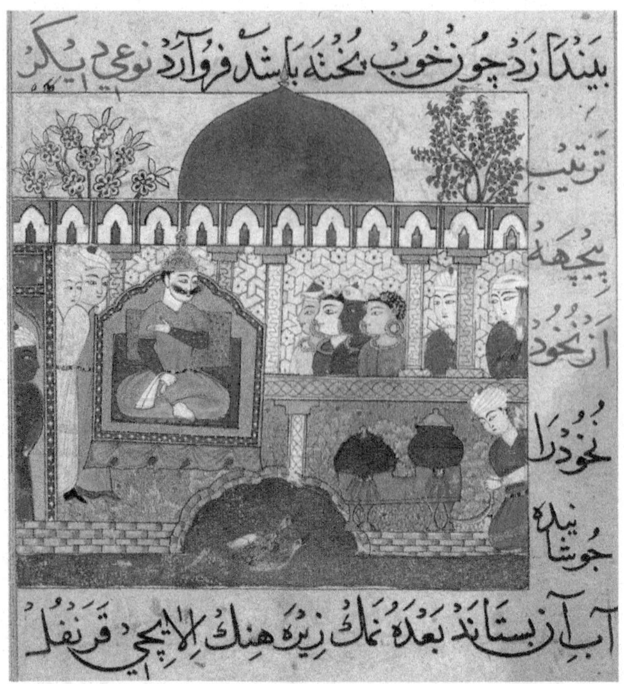

Plate 13 Preparing rice water (*pīchha*) (*f.32a*).

Plate 14 Soup being prepared (*f.35b*).

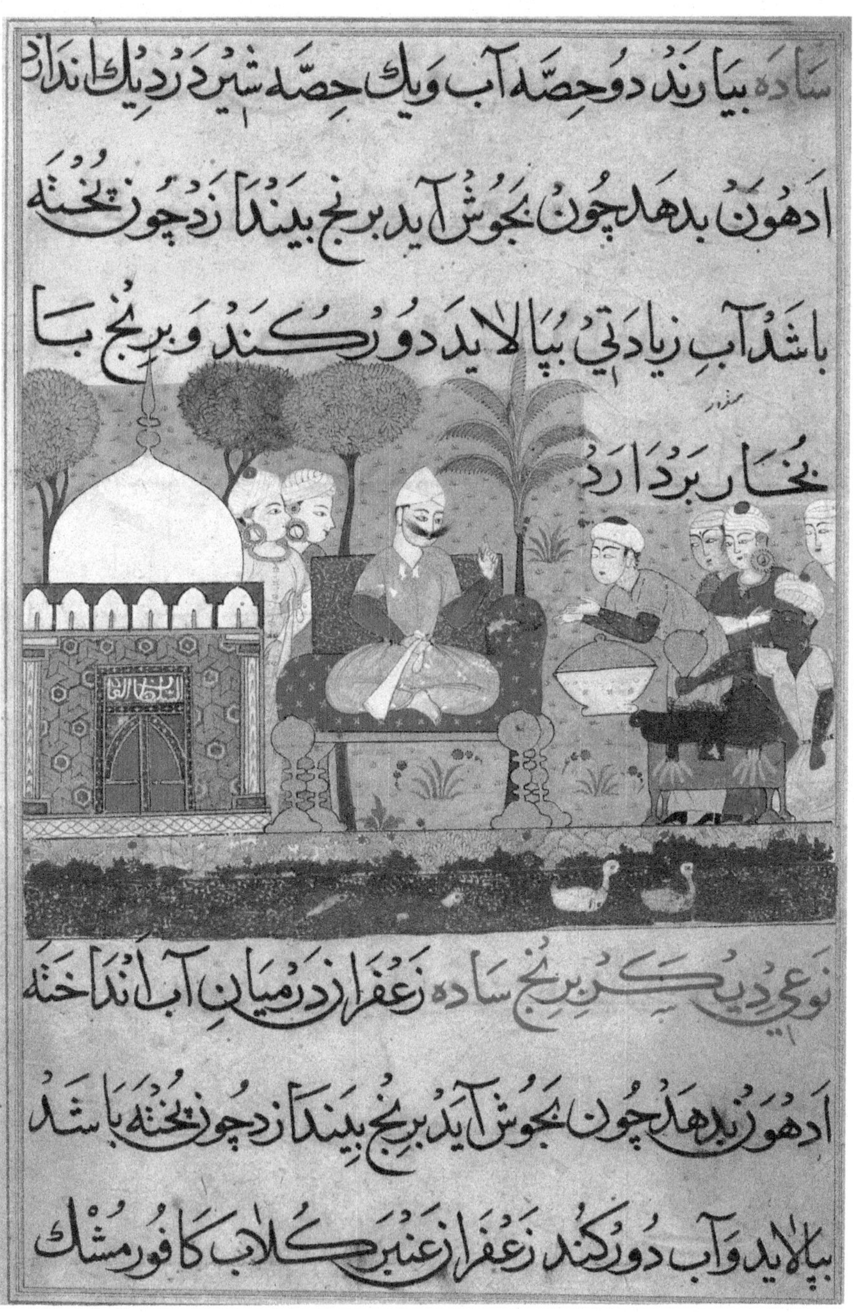

Plate 11 Rice being boiled (*f.25b*).

Plate 10 Soup and *lās* being cooked (*f.23a*).

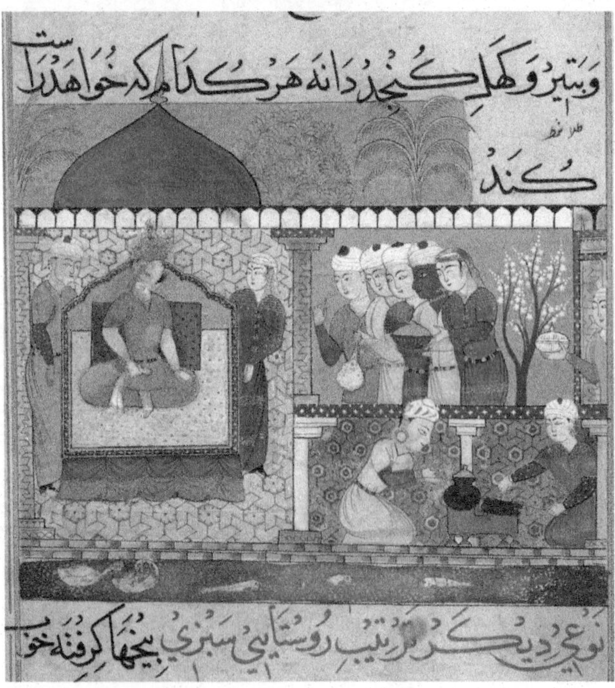

Plate 12 Preparing vegetarian food (*f.29a*).

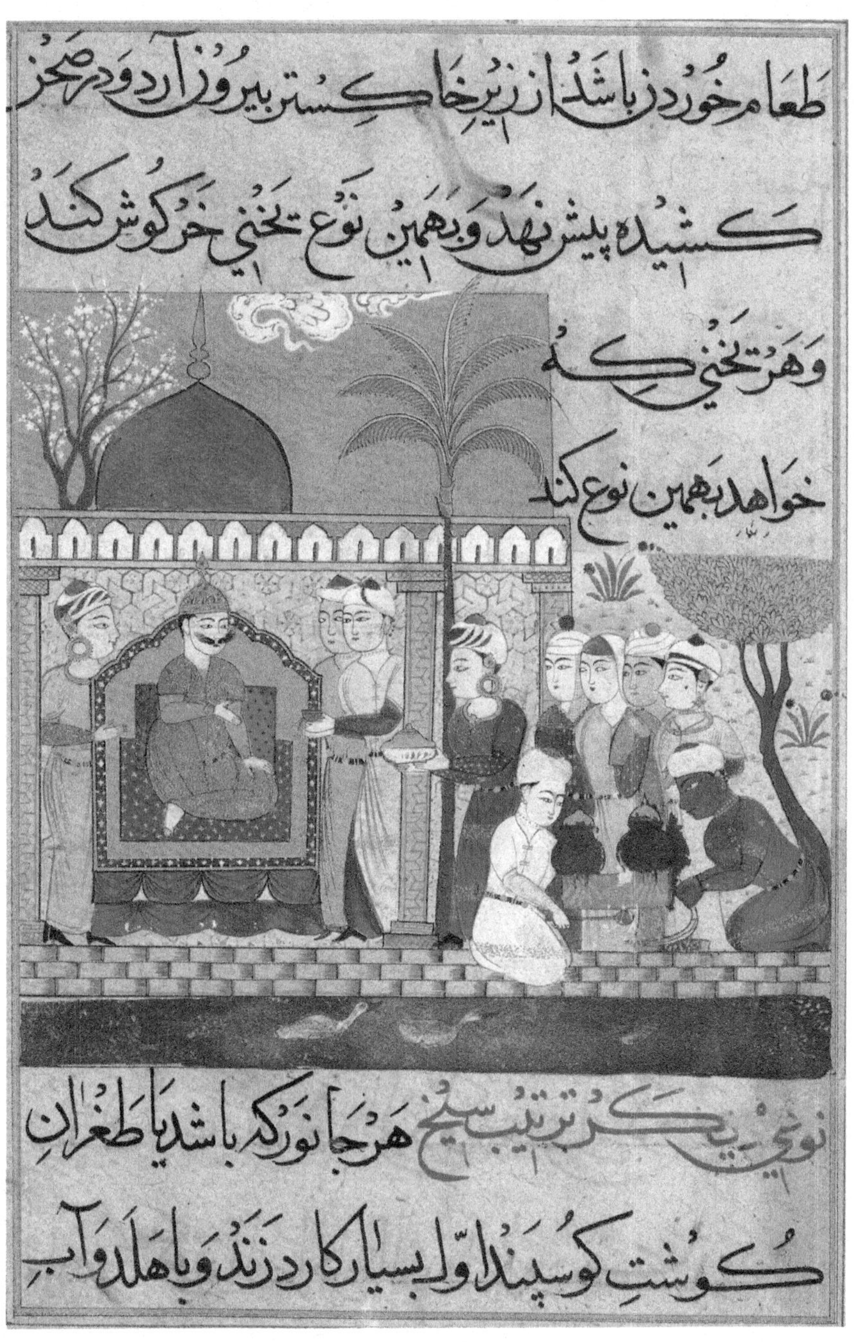

طعام خوردن باشد از زیر خاکستر بیرون آرد و در صحن
کشیده پیش نهد و بهمین نوع تخنی خرگوش کند
و هر تخنی که
خواهد بهمین نوع کند
نوعی دیگر ترتیب سیخ هر جانور که باشد یا طغران
گوشت گوسپند اول بسیار کارد زنند و باهلد و آب

Plate 9 Soup being prepared (*f.18a*).

بیندازند و چون زرد چوبه سرخ شود گوشت را در دیگ کنند
و چون گوشت خوب برشته شود آب بیندازند و سونف
و گشنیز و زیره و میتهی و ساگ را جوشانیده آب او
بیفشارد و دور کند و ساگ را در گوشت کنند و نمک بیندازد و چون
خوب پخته
شود و صلهای
بزرگ بزرگ
و آب نیبو
لیمو با اندک
نمک انداخته فرو آرند نوعی دیگر ترتیب پوری پوری

Plate 8 Cooking meat (*f.14a*).

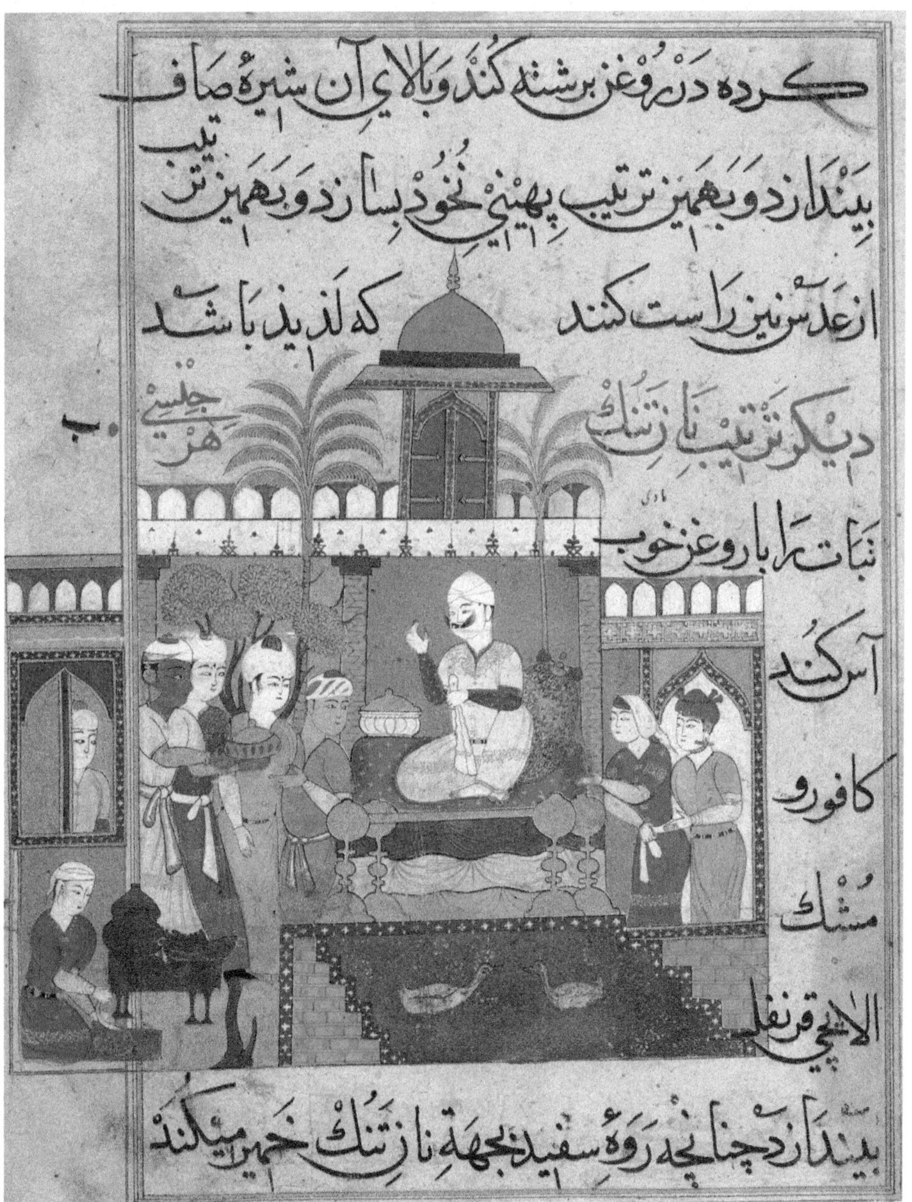

Plate 7 Food preparation (*f.11a*).

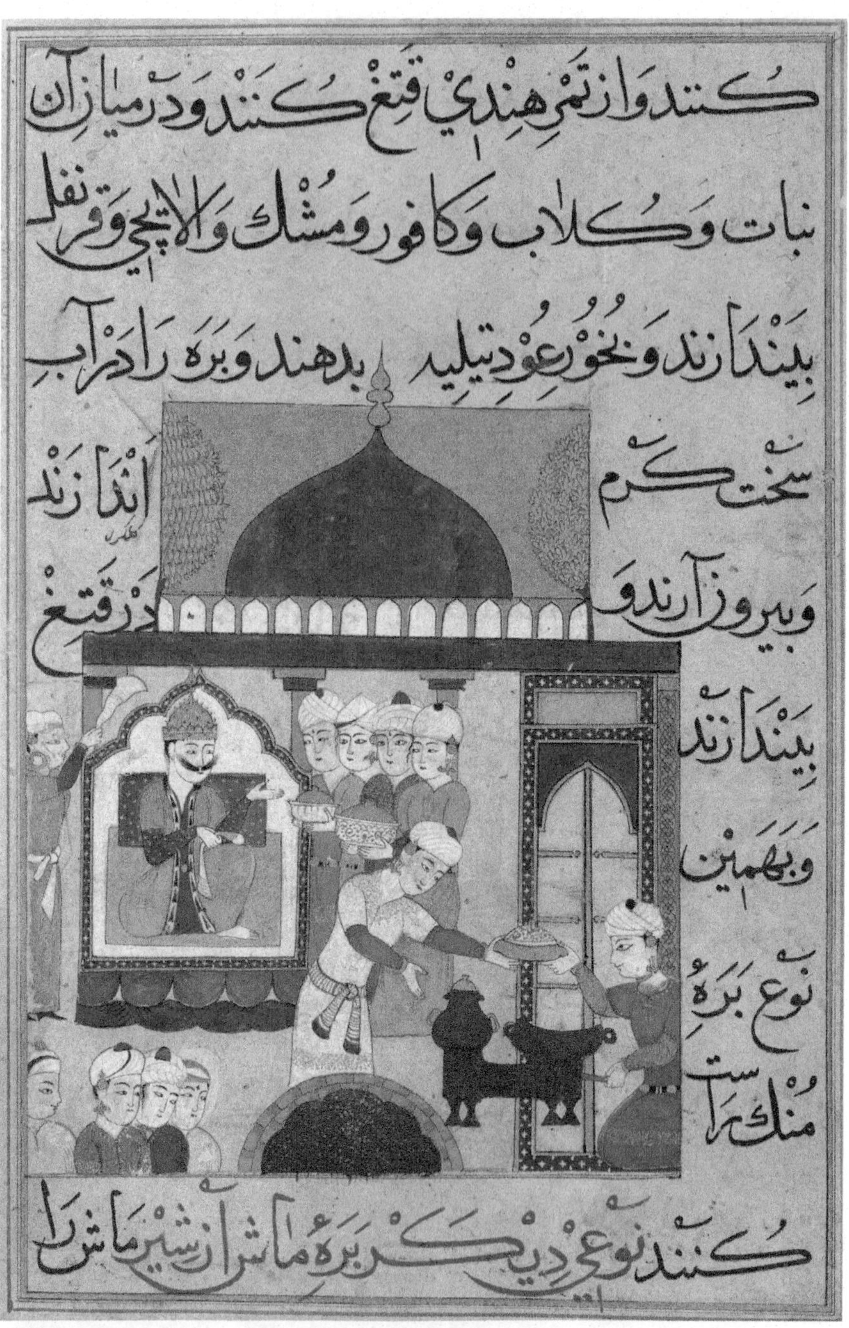

کنند و از تمر هندی قتغ کنند و در میان آن
نبات و گلاب و کافور و مشک و الاچی و قرنفل
بیندازند و بخور عود بدهند و بره را در آب
سخت گرم
اندازند
و بیرون آرند و
در قتغ
بیندازند
و بهمین
نوع بره
منک راست
کنند نوعی دیگر بره ماش از شیر ماش را

Plate 6 Ghiyath Shahi supervising his cooks (*f.8b*).

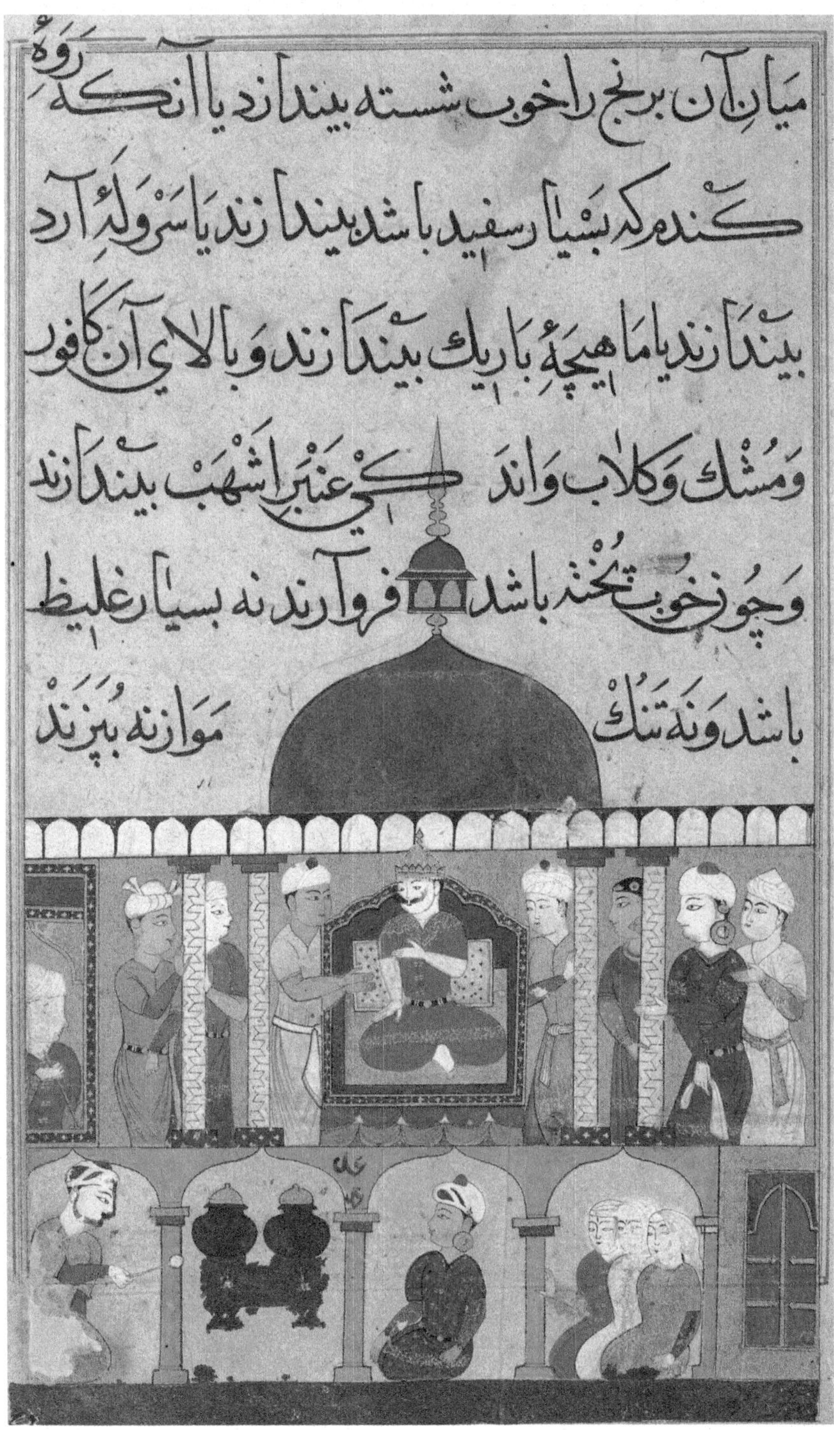
میان آن برنج را خوب شسته بیندازد یا آنکه
کندم که بسیار سفید باشد بیندازند یا سر ولهٔ آرد
بیندازند یا ماهیچهٔ باریک بیندازند و بالای آن کافور
و مشک و کلاب و اندکی عنبر اشهب بیندازند
و چون خوب تخته باشد فرو آرند نه بسیار غلیظ
باشد و نه تنک موازنه بپزند

Plate 5 Rice cooked with pulses or milk (*f.6b*).

Plate 3 Milking (*f.4b*).

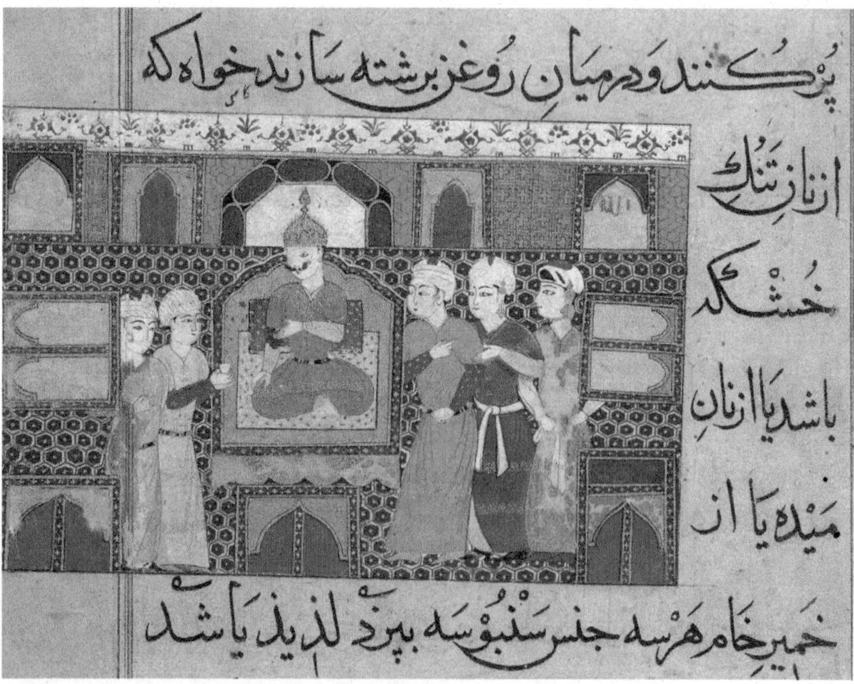

پر کنند و در میان روغن برشته سازند خواه که
از نان تنک
خشک
باشد یا از نان
میده یا از
خمیر خام هر سه جنس سنبوسه بپزد لذیذ باشد

Plate 4 Preparation of samosas and *lās* (*f.5a*).

Plate 1 Pavilion known as the Jahaz Mahall or 'Ship Palace', from the later Ghiyath Shahi period (1469–1500). Photo: Barbara Brend.

Plate 2 Courtyard with pool from the so-called 'Palace of Baz Bahadur', actually built by Nasir Shah in 914/1508–9. Photo: Barbara Brend.